W9-COS-385

Jobs for Disadvantaged Workers

Studies in Social Economics

TITLES PUBLISHED

STUDIES IN SOCIAL ECONOMICS

Robert H. Haveman and John L. Palmer
EDITORS

Jobs for Disadvantaged Workers: The Economics of Employment Subsidies

THE BROOKINGS INSTITUTION
Washington, D.C.

Soc
HD
5724
J68

Robert Manning Strozier Library

OCT 4 1982

Tallahassee, Florida

Copyright © 1982 by
THE BROOKINGS INSTITUTION
1775 Massachusetts Avenue, N.W., Washington, D.C. 20036

Library of Congress Cataloging in Publication data:

Main entry under title:
Jobs for disadvantaged workers.

(Studies in social economics)
Includes bibliographical references and
index.
1. Employment subsidies—United States.
I. Haveman, Robert H.   II. Palmer, John Logan.
III. Series.

HD5724.J68   362.8'5   81-38544
ISBN 0-8157-3506-5   AACR2
ISBN 0-8157-3505-7 (pbk.)

9 8 7 6 5 4 3 2 1

Board of Trustees

Robert V. Roosa
Chairman

Andrew Heiskell
Vice Chairman;
Chairman, Executive Committee

Louis W. Cabot
Vice Chairman

Vincent M. Barnett, Jr.

Barton M. Biggs

Frank T. Cary

A. W. Clausen

William T. Coleman, Jr.

Lloyd N. Cutler

Bruce B. Dayton

George M. Elsey

Hanna H. Gray

Huntington Harris

Roger W. Heyns

Bruce K. MacLaury

Robert S. McNamara

Arjay Miller

Herbert P. Patterson

Donald S. Perkins

J. Woodward Redmond

Charles W. Robinson

James D. Robinson III

Henry B. Schacht

Roger D. Semerad

Warren M. Shapleigh

Gerard C. Smith

Phyllis A. Wallace

Honorary Trustees

Eugene R. Black

Robert D. Calkins

Edward W. Carter

Douglas Dillon

John E. Lockwood

William McC. Martin, Jr.

H. Chapman Rose

Robert Brookings Smith

Sydney Stein, Jr.

THE BROOKINGS INSTITUTION is an independent organization devoted to nonpartisan research, education, and publication in economics, government, foreign policy, and the social sciences generally. Its principal purposes are to aid in the development of sound public policies and to promote public understanding of issues of national importance.

The Institution was founded on December 8, 1927, to merge the activities of the Institute for Government Research, founded in 1916, the Institute of Economics, founded in 1922, and the Robert Brookings Graduate School of Economics and Government, founded in 1924.

The Board of Trustees is responsible for the general administration of the Institution, while the immediate direction of the policies, program, and staff is vested in the President, assisted by an advisory committee of the officers and staff. The by-laws of the Institution state: "It is the function of the Trustees to make possible the conduct of scientific research, and publication, under the most favorable conditions, and to safeguard the independence of the research staff in the pursuit of their studies and in the publication of the results of such studies. It is not a part of their function to determine, control, or influence the conduct of particular investigations or the conclusions reached."

The President bears final responsibility for the decision to publish a manuscript as a Brookings book. In reaching his judgment on the competence, accuracy, and objectivity of each study, the President is advised by the director of the appropriate research program and weighs the views of a panel of expert outside readers who report to him in confidence on the quality of the work. Publication of a work signifies that it is deemed a competent treatment worthy of public consideration but does not imply endorsement of conclusions or recommendations.

The Institution maintains its position of neutrality on issues of public policy in order to safeguard the intellectual freedom of the staff. Hence interpretations or conclusions in Brookings publications should be understood to be solely those of the authors and should not be attributed to the Institution, to its trustees, officers, or other staff members, or to the organizations that support its research.

Foreword

The last decade has witnessed a dramatic growth in federal support for employment programs motivated by both countercyclical and structural concerns. Federal outlays for this purpose rose from less than $1 billion annually in the early 1970s to an annual average of about $7 billion in 1978–81. The vast bulk of these expenditures was for public service employment, primarily through grants to state and local governments under the Comprehensive Employment and Training Act (CETA). Much more modest efforts to subsidize private sector jobs were also funded under CETA and the work incentive program. They were augmented in the late 1970s by the now lapsed new jobs tax credit and the still extant targeted jobs tax credit. As a result of growing interest in job creation programs and the problems they are intended to address, various analyses of these activities have been undertaken by the research community. This volume contains the most current such effort by the Brookings Institution and follows closely upon two other recent Brookings publications on related topics, *Creating Jobs: Public Employment Programs and Wage Subsidies,* edited by John L. Palmer (1978), and *Public Service Employment: A Field Evaluation,* by Richard P. Nathan and others (1981).

This volume, the twentieth in the Brookings Studies in Social Economics series, focuses on subsidizing private sector job creation for workers with structural employment problems. Targeted employment subsidies were chosen for intensive analysis for several reasons. First, most research on employment programs to date has focused upon countercyclical concerns and public service employment. Structurally oriented private sector job creation has not received much analytic attention and information has been lacking on many important policy questions. Second, there appears to be a growing consensus that employment programs should be focused on the labor market problems faced by specific groups of unskilled or semiskilled workers afflicted by high unemployment, rather than on countercyclical concerns. Finally, both Congress and President Reagan are adopting budget and economic policies that place far greater emphasis on an overall expansion of private sector job opportunities relative both to regular public sector employment and particularly to public service employment (for which funding was eliminated in the 1982 CETA budget).

The authors of this volume deal with a wide range of concerns that should help inform federal policy decisions on whether the use of targeted private sector employment subsidies should be expanded—and, if so, under what conditions and in what form. The papers and formal discussion presented in this volume were delivered at a conference held at the Brookings Institution on April 3–4, 1980, and attended by the participants listed on pages 329–30. The first chapter summarizes the papers and conference proceedings. Subsequent chapters contain theoretical and empirical analyses of the effects of targeted employment subsidies on inflation and economic efficiency, on the distribution of employment, on firm behavior, and comparisons of the effects of worker wage subsidies with those of employer wage subsidies and family income–tested cash grants. The final chapters discuss administrative issues affecting program design and summarize European experience with employment subsidies and its implications for program evaluation.

Robert H. Haveman, professor of economics at the University of Wisconsin and a fellow of the Institute for Research on Poverty, and John L. Palmer, a senior fellow of the Urban Institute, edited the conference proceedings. Both worked on this project as members of the Brookings associated staff. The manuscript was edited by Caroline Lalire and checked for accuracy by Flor Cardemil and Penelope Harpold. The index was prepared by Florence Robinson.

Financial support was provided by the Ford Foundation and the Andrew W. Mellon Foundation.

The views expressed here are those of the authors and discussants and should not be ascribed to the funding organizations or to the trustees, officers, or other staff members of the Brookings Institution.

BRUCE K. MAC LAURY
President

October 1981
Washington, D.C.

Contents

Figures

Robert H. Haveman and John L. Palmer

Introduction and Summary

In the spring of 1977 the Brookings Institution and the Institute for Research on Poverty jointly sponsored a conference to examine the economic issues surrounding direct job creation efforts by the public sector. That conference was designed to remedy the serious lack of analytic information about the economic effects of public service employment programs and subsidies to private firms contingent on job creation. Before the papers for that conference were commissioned, little thought had been given to how this policy strategy would affect such basic concerns as employment, inflation, costs to public budgets, economic efficiency, or the distribution of employment and earnings. The papers presented at that conference addressed these issues and resulted in a 1978 Brookings volume, *Creating Jobs: Public Employment Programs and Wage Subsidies,* edited by John L. Palmer.

The principal findings of those papers, as discussed by Palmer and Irwin Garfinkel in their introductory essay, can be summarized as follows:

—Direct job creation programs (for example, public service employment) are likely to generate more employment than either general tax cuts or direct public expenditures with an equivalent fiscal impact.

—Under certain circumstances, however, displacement effects (for example, fiscal substitution by state and local governments receiving federal public service employment funds) may erode the job creation effects of these programs, so that their effect on employment is not much, if any, greater than more general stimulative measures.

—The employment stimulus from direct job creation programs is likely to produce less inflationary pressure than the stimulus from alternative fiscal measures of the same magnitude. This is especially true if the program is targeted on groups with substantial excess supply, so that increases in employment are accompanied by less upward wage pressure.

—Over the longer run, these direct employment programs will have

1

little effect on total unemployment if relative wages can adjust freely and depend primarily on excess supply conditions in labor markets.

—These programs could target job opportunities on geographic and demographic groups, thereby altering the distribution of employment opportunities and reducing disparities in the distribution of earnings.

—Nontargeted programs are likely to have a greater impact on total employment than those targeted on special hard-to-employ groups but are also likely to be more inflationary and less redistributive.

—Direct job creation programs may have difficulty meeting a strict economic efficiency test because of the relatively low value of the output, the low level of skills among participants (especially if the program is a targeted one), the input-biasing nature of the programs, and the small amount of job training participants receive.

These research findings, while they increased the understanding of the potentials and realities of certain public policies to create jobs, raised as many questions as they answered and made clear how much more needed to be learned about the mechanisms by which those policies could affect the economy. For example, though it was concluded at the conference that direct job creation programs could alter the unemployment-inflation trade-off, there was little empirical evidence on the extent to which such a shift might occur. Or, again, while it was expected that targeted, or categorical, employment subsidies would assist low-income families, the degree to which such income redistribution would occur was unknown. Because of the importance of this second round of questions to the formulation of effective policy, it was decided to hold a follow-up conference.

This second conference was planned largely in 1978 by a working group whose task was to determine the main issues on which additional work was required and to name people capable of undertaking the research.[1]

First, the group decided that the second conference should emphasize job creation in the private sector rather than public service employment. For one reason, the evidence from the first conference regarding efficiency, budget costs, and administrative arrangements suggested that private sector employment subsidies are likely to be preferred over public service employment, at least on those grounds. For another reason, Congress was showing increased interest in stimulating employment in the

1. The members of the working group were John H. Bishop, George J. Carcagno, Walter S. Corson, Larry Dildine, Robert J. Flanagan, Robert H. Haveman, Bryce Hool, George E. Johnson, Robert I. Lerman, and John L. Palmer.

private sector through an incentive or subsidy arrangement rather than continuing such heavy reliance on public service employment. Indeed, in 1977 the new jobs tax credit was instituted, and preliminary studies suggested it was having an effect on employment.[2]

Second, the working group decided that the conference should focus on the use of employment subsidies to achieve structural, as opposed to cyclical or macroeconomic, objectives. The country was already experimenting with a nontargeted employment subsidy (the new jobs tax credit), and at the time the most serious labor market problems were judged to be those faced by specific low-skill, high-unemployment groups—like minority youth and welfare recipients—not those caused by a lack of aggregate demand. In addition, Congress had before it several bills designed to offer financial incentives to private employers to provide low-skill, high-unemployment groups with jobs. As a result, topics most pertinent to understanding and evaluating the effects of targeted employment subsidies were examined by the working group.

Third, therefore, the group identified the economic issues relating to targeted employment subsidies on which information and insight were most needed—a difficult task because of the lack of work done in that area. Ultimately, the group specified the following questions, which were then addressed by the authors of the conference papers.

—If one adopts a theoretical perspective other than that of standard neoclassical economics (for example, disequilibrium analysis), does one gain any fresh insights into the economic effects of employment subsidies?

—What are the implications of alternative labor market models for defining target groups or for expecting employment and distributional effects from employment subsidies?

—What guidance can various macroeconomic and microeconomic models give to the evaluation of targeted employment subsidies, like the targeted jobs tax credit?

—Can evidence be found, or estimates be made, of the potential effect of targeted employment subsidies on the unemployment-inflation trade-off? Stated differently, to what extent can the noninflationary unemployment rate be reduced by targeted employment subsidies?

2. John Bishop and Robert H. Haveman, "Selective Employment Subsidies: Can Okun's Law Be Repealed?" *American Economic Review,* vol. 69 (May 1979, *Papers and Proceedings,* 1978), pp. 124–30; and Jeffrey M. Perloff and Michael L. Wachter, "The New Jobs Tax Credit: An Evaluation of the 1977–78 Wage Subsidy Program," ibid., pp. 173–79.

—Under what conditions can employee-based subsidies be more potent instruments for generating employment increases than employer-based subsidies?

—How effectively will employee-based subsidies (for example, wage rate subsidies) achieve antipoverty and income distribution objectives, and how will their effectiveness in so doing compare with that of more conventional income maintenance programs? And to what extent will the labor supply effects of employee-based subsidies differ from those of standard, income maintenance programs?

—Can targeted employment subsidy programs be designed to encourage efficient firm responses to the incentive, and how does the firm response to various program designs vary in cost effectiveness?

—What are the costs and benefits of various program design and administrative arrangements, and what principles can be evolved for achieving the most efficient administrative arrangements consistent with broader policy objectives?

—Are there lessons regarding program structure and effectiveness to be learned from the more extensive experience with employment subsidies in Western Europe? And what have the evaluations of these programs shown?

Theoretical Analysis

Up to now, most analyses of the effects of employment subsidies have relied on conventional economic theory. Given the characteristics of present-day economies—for example, high unemployment accompanied by high inflation and wide differences in unemployment rates among various population groups—many alternative methods of analysis could seemingly contribute to an understanding of the effects of employment subsidies. Several approaches are explored in part one of this volume.

In the first paper Kenneth Burdett and Bryce Hool use an explicitly "disequilibrium" model to investigate some macroeconomic effects of employment subsidies. This model is a short-run model in which sticky wages and prices are a normal part of the economic landscape. Because of this stickiness, excess supply or demand can exist in the short run in any of the labor or goods markets. The pattern of excess supplies and demands among markets depends on the institutional and legal considerations affecting market operations and on what phase of the business cycle the economy is in at any given time. Three labor groups are distinguished in the model: the target group, nontarget group labor, and workers not in the labor force. The net cost of the targeted employment subsidy, after allowing for the budgetary effects of induced employment and income changes, is assumed to be financed through a reduction in other public spending. Burdett and Hool describe alternative regimes in which excess supply in the target group's labor market coexists with various disequilibrium conditions in the other markets. For each regime, they analyze the impact of the subsidy on (1) unemployment, (2) the inflation-unemployment trade-off, and (3) the distribution of employment and income.

Several results emerge. First, the impact of the subsidy depends on the pattern of disequilibrium conditions in all markets, not just on the presence of unemployment in the target group. But in almost all circumstances, both the target group's employment and total employment are increased. Thus the subsidy generates employment more effectively than general government spending does. Second, the stimulus to employment will be greatest when there is no slack (excess supply) in the product market. It is then that firms should be most responsive to price signals and, in particular, to the lowering of the real wage paid. Third, except when all markets are slack, the subsidy will serve to reduce inflationary pressure. Finally, by associating the various regimes studied to phases of the business cycle, Burdett and Hool conclude that employment subsidies are especially potent tools for achieving employment, price level, and distributional goals during both the upswing and the downswing phases of the cycle, with aggregate demand policies being more effective at the trough and peak.

These results support the general conclusions of more conventional analyses about the efficacy of employment subsidies. They also provide insight into the economic conditions under which such subsidies may be most effective and into the optimal timing patterns for temporary subsidy programs.

In the second paper George E. Johnson also uses models in which standard neoclassical equilibrium is not permitted in labor markets for target group workers or in which unemployment of these workers is induced by income-conditioned transfer programs. These models serve to answer the question of how to define most effectively the eligible population for a targeted subsidy program.

Johnson finds that the effectiveness of a targeted employment subsidy is heavily dependent on the kind of unemployment the target group is experiencing. On the one hand, if the unemployment of the target group is structural—say, because of minimum wages that restrict the downward adjustment of target group wages—an effectively targeted employment subsidy may not have a strong impact on the target group's employment unless the subsidy covers most of the problem population. If coverage is not so comprehensive, covered target group workers will simply be substituted for those not covered.[3] On the other hand, if the unemployment of the target group is induced by the disincentive effects of income transfer programs, even partial coverage will be effective.

Johnson also estimates the cost effectiveness of targeted employment subsidies under various assumptions about the demand elasticity in the private sector for target group labor. If the structural unemployment model holds, the budget cost per job created is far less than the wage rate paid. Johnson then compares such subsidy programs with targeted public employment programs under various labor market conditions. He finds that the relative effectiveness of the two strategies again depends on the private sector demand elasticity for target group labor—that is, whether the programs in fact do reach the problem population. With perfect targeting in both cases, the subsidy approach is more effective than public employment if the unemployment is structural.

Since the employment-generating effectiveness of a targeted subsidy depends so much on the labor market conditions that gave rise to target group unemployment, Johnson attempts to evaluate the patterns of losers and gainers under various assumptions about labor market conditions and coverage. His most important conclusion is that *both* the target group *and* taxpayers can gain from a targeted subsidy that fully covers the problem group, whether target group unemployment is caused by structural factors or is induced by income transfer programs.

Both Burdett-Hool and Johnson, then, find the effectiveness of targeted employment subsidies to be heavily dependent on the macroeconomic and labor market conditions into which they are introduced. A general conclusion can be drawn from these two papers: during the upswing and downswing phases of the business cycle, targeted employment subsidies are likely to be effective in increasing employment and reducing inflationary pressure. The employment-generating effects will be particularly strong if the unemployment of the target group is caused by structural factors—for example, a minimum wage—and if the subsidy is targeted on the

3. Moreover, if there are multiple problem groups, a subsidy targeted at only one group may simply benefit it at the expense of other target groups.

entire problem group rather than on part of it. If so, both members of the target group and taxpayers can benefit from the subsidy. Unfortunately, the basic causes of the unemployment of problem groups are not at present well understood, nor can the phases of the business cycle (or, more generally, the conditions of disequilibrium in the economy) be clearly determined ex ante. As Johnson puts it, "No one has the detailed knowledge of the relevant labor market adjustment and demand parameters that are necessary to perform a reliable evaluation of what a particular [targeted employment] subsidy can do."

It is to this evaluation issue that Jeffrey M. Perloff turns in the third paper, again in the context of both standard and nonstandard economic models. He poses much the same questions as Burdett-Hool and Johnson. What are the effects of a targeted employment subsidy on target group and total employment? On the earnings and unemployment of the target group? On labor force participation rates and output? Perloff's main purpose, however, is to evaluate the effectiveness of the targeted jobs tax credit, and the models he discusses guide that evaluation.

The first model Perloff uses to analyze targeted employment subsidies is a fairly standard two-sector general equilibrium model. Prices and wages are assumed to be flexible and markets clear. In this case a targeted employment subsidy will probably increase the employment of the target group; if the labor supply is not totally inelastic, total employment will increase as well. In addition, Perloff explores the implications of the subsidy for output shifts and wage increases in the economy and the ability of a subsidy program to offset preexisting distortions in the economy and hence increase the efficiency of resource allocation.

It is by extending his analysis to a framework in which unemployment exists that Perloff's paper is able to deal with the employment effects of targeted subsidies. As was found in the first two theoretical papers, the effect of the employment subsidy on significant variables depends on the particular market conditions, behavioral relationships, and institutional distortions that one assumes. And again the problem is to frame a judgment about which set of assumptions most closely corresponds to real world conditions. Perloff does demonstrate that economic efficiency can be increased only if the subsidy corrects existing distortions or decreases the unemployment of the target group. As in the models developed by Burdett and Hool and by Johnson, the extent of the decrease depends on both the supply and demand elasticities in the market for this group of workers.

Empirical Evidence

Perhaps not surprisingly in an area as complex as labor market policy, theoretical explorations by themselves cannot provide reliable guidance for policy. This is particularly true when the explicit purpose of these explorations is to investigate the implications of various theoretical models or perspectives. One is left with a range of possible results (on, say, the employment effects of a subsidy) that follow from the underlying assumptions incorporated into the models. The task of empirical researchers and policymakers, then, is to determine which constellation of assumptions most closely corresponds to the real world and the magnitude of the responses that are incorporated in the relevant economic relationships.

Three papers in the second part of this volume contain empirical work designed to shed light on the magnitude of the effects of employment subsidies. In his paper Donald A. Nichols addresses the central issue in this area: to what extent can targeted employment subsidies lower the aggregate unemployment rate without stimulating additional inflationary pressure? The analysis of this question follows directly from Martin Neil Baily and James Tobin's paper, "Inflation-Unemployment Consequences of Job Creation Policies," in *Creating Jobs,* and Nichols undertakes his empirical analysis in a manner consistent with the theoretical framework set out in that paper.

Nichols begins by estimating an aggregate wage equation in which unemployment rates for two separate occupational groups (a high-skill and a low-skill group) are entered as explanatory variables. From this he obtains a set of occupational unemployment rates consistent with an aggregate unemployment rate that does not cause wage acceleration. The minimum such aggregate unemployment rate is estimated to be between one-half and two-thirds of a percentage point below that which can be obtained by stimulating or maintaining the economy through conventional macroeconomic policy means alone. And obtaining that rate requires considerably *less* unemployment for the low-skill group at the cost of some *additional* unemployment for the high-skill group. This result is consistent with that of Baily and Tobin, whose analysis suggests that tight labor markets for high-skill, high-wage workers contribute more to wage inflation than tight labor markets for low-skill, low-wage workers.

To secure this one-half to two-thirds point reduction in the aggregate unemployment rate, which is available by altering the structure of employment, Nichols posits a wage subsidy targeted on the low-skill group. He simulates the effect of the subsidy on the aggregate unemployment rate by using a standard production function for the economy, including a plausible range of values for its parameters. This simulation suggests that a reduction of one-half to two-thirds percentage point in the aggregate unemployment rate is possible with a targeted employment subsidy costing from $7.5 billion to $29 billion. Additional reductions in the unemployment rate (without increasing inflation) require much greater expenditure and impose changes in the employment structure that would most likely cause substantial losses of gross national product.

The results of this estimation are fairly optimistic. They indicate that about 500,000 jobs can be created with a targeted wage subsidy without generating increased inflation. They also suggest that these jobs can be created at a budget cost of from $10,000 to $25,000 per job—a cost that is far less than that required for job creation by expanding aggregate demand. These results complement those of the theoretical explorations, giving some substance to the general result that employment subsidies can induce employment increases without triggering additional inflation.

Robert I. Lerman undertakes a quite different kind of empirical exploration. As he points out, most of the literature on employment subsidies has focused on subsidies paid to employers. Those paid directly to workers—particularly wage rate subsidies—have been analyzed far less, and what has been done has usually emphasized their income maintenance rather than employment effects. Yet for several reasons such subsidies—operating primarily through the supply side of the labor market rather than the demand side—can probably have at least as powerful an employment stimulus as ones paid to employers.

Lerman uses both empirical evidence and theoretical inferences to compare the employment stimulus of employer- and employee-based subsidies. By considering such factors as labor market structures, institutional constraints, program design considerations, and the presence or absence of statistical discrimination in labor markets, he concludes that in many situations employee-based subsidies can generate larger increases in employment than employer-based ones.

For example, using micro data from the Current Population Survey, Lerman shows that the targeted jobs tax credit program—and targeted employer-based subsidy programs in general—failed to cover a large proportion of the relevant target group. Therefore, when unemployment is caused by downwardly rigid wages, such a program will shift jobs toward the target group but will not reduce overall unemployment, whereas a subsidy paid directly to target group workers would both decrease their unemployment and increase overall employment.

Lerman also demonstrates that a worker-based wage subsidy can increase the perceived market wage for low-skill workers, making employment appear more attractive than its alternatives (such as collecting income transfers). Again using Current Population Survey files, he shows that such a subsidy would primarily affect youths and women—groups whose labor supply is very sensitive to wage rates—and result in substantial employment increases for those groups. Furthermore, because women make up only a small part of the low-wage labor market—about 5 percent by Survey estimates—the increased labor supply would not tend to cause offsetting reductions in the subsidy-induced increase in wage rates.

Because of these and other examples incorporating plausible hypotheses of labor market characteristics, Lerman throws into doubt the previously held assumption that employer-based subsidies stimulate job creation more than employee-based subsidies do. This doubt is reinforced if one examines how the required categorical limitations on eligible workers affect employers' behavior. As Lerman points out, experience in the United States with categorical employer subsidies shows that only a small fraction of eligible employers has made use of them. One advantage of employee-based subsidies is that they do not require employers to change their recruitment practices or, indeed, even to be aware of the subsidy, for favorable employment effects to occur.

Besides stimulating employment with a minimal upward pressure on inflation, targeted employment subsidies are also expected to generate a redistribution of jobs and incomes toward low-wage, low-income target groups. This result, of course, is implicit in Nichols's paper and led him to expect that an employment subsidy would bring about a noninflationary reduction in unemployment at moderate cost.

In their paper David M. Betson and John H. Bishop directly address this question of redistributive effects. Moreover, they follow up Lerman's discussion by focusing on employee-based wage rate subsidies.

But unlike Lerman, Betson and Bishop are primarily concerned with the work disincentive, cost, and distributional effects of a wage rate subsidy, and in comparing them with those of a competitive income maintenance tool—family income–tested cash grants or a negative income tax. The main advantage of a wage rate subsidy is that, by providing assistance only to those who are employed, it may encourage rather than discourage additional work effort. Its main disadvantages are that it may not be as redistributive as a family income–tested cash grant and that in an overall income maintenance program it would have to be supplemented by other measures to ensure the availability of jobs for those expected to work and to provide cash assistance to those not expected to work.

Because wage rate subsidies are focused on low-wage workers, irrespective of family income, much of their outlays would go to lower-wage workers in relatively affluent families (for example, teenagers or wives) if eligibility were not further restricted. For this reason Betson and Bishop limit their analyses to subsidies provided only to primary earners in households with children. Using a comprehensive micro-data simulation model developed at the Department of Health, Education, and Welfare (now the Department of Health and Human Services), they evaluate two such kinds of wage rate subsidies—one with and one without a target wage conditioned by family size—and compare them with a program of family income–conditioned cash grants of equal cost. The model evaluates how families' benefits change in response to such a subsidy program, taking into account how recipients alter their work effort in response to the incentives of the program.

Betson and Bishop's primary findings are the following: (1) wage rate subsidies may reduce the net labor supply, but probably less than family income–conditioned cash grants would;[4] (2) about one-third of the budget cost of the employment subsidy is recouped by reductions in transfer payments and increased taxes; and (3) neither kind of wage rate subsidy is as effective as family income–conditioned cash grants in targeting income gains on the current-income poor, but when an alternative measure of economic well-being based on earnings capacity is used, a wage rate subsidy conditioned by family size is more redistributive than family income–conditioned cash grants. These results suggest that insofar as work disincentives are a major concern in the design of income maintenance programs, greater consideration should be given to wage rate subsidies as a way to assist the working poor.

4. The estimates of a labor supply response to family income–conditioned cash grants were quite stable across three different sets of assumptions used by the authors, but those of the wage rate subsidy varied dramatically from a disincentive effect comparable to that of the negative income tax to an incentive effect of equivalent magnitude.

Program Design and Evaluation

The three papers in the last part of the volume are concerned with the efficiency and cost implications of alternative designs for employment subsidies. One of the papers is theoretical; the two others are applied and practical.

In their paper John H. Bishop and Charles A. Wilson explore the potential incentives of various employment subsidies for inducing intertemporal employment substitutions. The issue, simply stated, is this: if an employment subsidy—for example, the new jobs tax credit—has a threshold (above which firm employment must grow to be eligible to be subsidized) designed to increase the employment impact per dollar of cost, a firm may be able to take actions in one year that will affect the subsidy it receives in another year. Such actions, if continued over time, may induce inefficiencies. The problem is to determine what kind of program design can minimize this distortionary behavior.

Bishop and Wilson calculate the cost effectiveness of three program designs: a fixed threshold, a yearly updated threshold, and a peak employment threshold. Under a fixed threshold program, relatively little distortion will occur if the firm is growing (it cannot be eligible if it is declining). Quite the opposite is true when the employment threshold is updated yearly. In this case, a growing or declining firm has a substantial incentive for cyclical behavior—that is, reducing output and employment in one period in order to maximize the subsidy by increasing output and employment more than otherwise in a later period. Under the peak employment program, the strength of the incentives for firms to adopt distortionary behavior over time is intermediate to the other two cases. Bishop and Wilson conclude that it is difficult to devise employer subsidy programs that are more cost effective than a simple marginal subsidy program with a fixed threshold. Although Bishop and Wilson's analysis is somewhat limited because it does not consider the many constraints that firms face in altering their output and employment levels, it does point up the importance of choosing an approximate employment threshold for achieving a cost-effective subsidy.

A more broad-brush approach to design and administrative issues is taken by George J. Carcagno and Walter S. Corson. In their paper they seek to identify and assess the administrative implications of alternative features of employment subsidy programs. They examine the alternative administrative models that could be used to operate a program, the administrative implications of the most commonly discussed program features, and the administration of the operating functions common to all employer-based subsidy programs—that is, the determination of both worker and firm eligibility and the mechanisms available for calculating and dispersing the subsidy, for enforcing program rules, and for outreach and publicity.

Carcagno and Corson find that many design options, including some that are often proposed for employment subsidies, confront serious administrative difficulties. In particular, they cite reservations about regional variations in the subsidy, about subsidies that are both incremental and narrowly targeted, and about eligibility determinations that include an assets test. They then present a general and simple administrative arrangement for targeted programs, which they prefer. For subsidy disbursement, they conclude that the tax system should be used, and if separate eligibility determinations need to be made, another administrative agency working closely with the tax system should be responsible for certification and administration of that part of the program. Finally, they suggest additional provisions for disbursement arrangements that would permit the credit to be taken against any of the employers' federal tax obligations.

In the last paper Peter Schwanse examines both the design and evaluation of employment subsidies in Western European countries. After reviewing the structure of several European employment subsidies, Schwanse appraises the evaluations of two of them and suggests ways in which evaluations could be improved. Most of the evaluations, Schwanse points out, emphasize the net employment effect and the net budget effect of the programs, with little effort being paid to the distribution of general employment effects or the impact of programs on inflation or the unemployment rate.

The primary issues of concern in Western Europe appear to be different from those in the United States. Because employment subsidies in Europe are designed not as separate programs but as part of overall labor market policy packages, they are accepted with far less criticism; analytic attention has been focused on improving elements of their design and administration rather than on evaluating their employment, efficiency, inflationary, and distributional effects.

Nevertheless, some evaluations of those economic consequences of European employment subsidies have been undertaken. For the most part

Schwanse finds them lacking. Among their major problems are inadequate evaluation designs (for example, lack of appropriate control groups), which make it difficult to separate employment changes due to the subsidy from employment changes due to other factors; reliance on employer questionnaires in which respondents have incentive to reply erroneously; the failure to use statistical methods to identify the net employment effects of the subsidy; and the failure to compare the estimated employment impact of the subsidy with that of an equivalent general fiscal stimulus. Schwanse concludes the paper with several suggestions designed to improve the reliability of evaluations of employment subsidy measures.

A Bottom Line?

What is learned from these papers about the macroeconomic and microeconomic effects, the efficiency and equity effects, and the design issues of targeted employment subsidies? While perhaps failing to do justice to the full range of issues addressed, the following conclusions represent the essential findings of the papers and the consensus of the conference participants:

—The positive employment and inflationary effects of employment subsidies predicted by standard economic theory are corroborated by nonstandard disequilibrium and job search models. When assumptions corresponding more closely to real world conditions are reflected in these models, the results usually indicate that targeted subsidies can serve an important policy role. Evidence exists to suggest that a targeted employment subsidy can achieve a one-half percentage point reduction in the unemployment rate without aggravating inflation, and can do so at a reasonable cost per job.

—The effectiveness of employment subsidies is most potent during the upswing and downswing phases of the business cycle, which suggests a role for temporary targeted subsidies if countercyclical as well as structural goals are to be pursued.

—The use of targeted employment subsidies seems particularly warranted when preexisting labor market distortions are present. The effect of minimum-wage legislation on low-wage labor markets is one such distortion that can be offset by an appropriately designed employment subsidy.

—The definition of the target group is of signal importance if a subsidy program is to have its desired impact. The definition must follow from a correct diagnosis of the relevant labor market problem. Also, the pool of eligible workers must be largely congruent with the problem group; otherwise the main effect of the subsidies will simply be to shift employment among members of the problem group—from those not in the eligible portion to those in the eligible portion—and not to achieve an overall increase in the problem group's employment.

—Under certain conditions, employee-based employment subsidies may provide an attractive alternative both to employer subsidies and to other kinds of income maintenance programs. Depending upon the specific causes of the target group unemployment, they may be more effective instruments for achieving employment increases for disadvantaged workers than demand-oriented, employer-based employment subsidies. And if they are limited to primary earners in families with children, they can be effective instruments for targeting income gains on households of low economic status, with less potential for adverse labor supply results than cash assistance grants conditioned on family income.

—Substantial design and administrative problems must be overcome if a targeted employment subsidy is to be an effective policy measure. One important design issue concerns how to define the threshold of employment above which subsidies will be paid. With an inappropriate definition, the subsidy program will probably induce firms to adopt undesirable behavior in order to maximize the subsidy received. Other issues involve the choice of the administering agency, the base on which the subsidy is to be paid (hours, wage rate, earnings), the method of determining eligibility, and the mechanisms for calculating and disbursing the subsidy and for enforcing program rules.

—Effective evaluations of employment subsidy programs are difficult to achieve, as witnessed by the inadequacies of the evaluations of European programs. More adequate data are required, as well as an experimental design for evaluation and statistical measures to distinguish the effects of the program on employment from other, nonprogram effects.

These conclusions represent a considerable advance in knowledge about the economic effects and preferred program design of targeted employment subsidies. Although they are sometimes less definitive than would be desired, we have been able to answer far more confidently than before the conference the major policy questions surrounding those subsidies.

Part One

Theoretical Analysis

Kenneth Burdett and Bryce Hool

Effects on the Inflation-Unemployment Trade-off

The economic experience of the last two decades has provided clear evidence that aggregate monetary and fiscal policies are not adequate for the task of ensuring full employment without unacceptably high rates of inflation. At this writing, when the overall unemployment rate is 5.7 percent, considered by some to be not far above the economy's "natural" rate, and when inflation is still being sustained at unprecedentedly high annual rates of between 10 and 14 percent, the first priority of domestic policy is to reduce the rate of inflation. But history leads one to suspect that in due time, as inflation-fighting policies meet with more success, the scales will tip and unemployment will become the dominant concern.[1]

Regardless of whether or not this happens, there is reason for concern about unemployment now. The aggregate unemployment rate hides a multitude of sins that may nevertheless indicate some potential for alleviating the inflation-unemployment trade-off. Unemployment and poverty are not uniformly distributed across the population but are concentrated in inordinately depressed geographic regions, inner cities, particular demographic groups, and so on. For example, while the unemployment rate for prime-age white males is only 3.3 percent, the rate for black teenagers is an alarming 36.9 percent. This structural imbalance in the incidence of unemployment adds a further dimension to the problem, one that has doubtless contributed to the inadequacy of conven-

Many persons provided valuable comments on drafts of this paper. We especially thank Robert H. Haveman and our official discussants, Karl-Gustaf Löfgren and Jeffrey M. Perloff; George E. Johnson; Hank McMillan; and Mary Kay Plantes.

1. This was written in mid-1979, when the preceding figures were current. Since then the rate of inflation has peaked and declined, and it is now, in the second quarter of 1981, holding below 10 percent. During the same period unemployment climbed more than 2 percentage points, and is now holding above 7 percent.

tional macroeconomic policies. It suggests the need for an additional, corresponding dimension in government policy: the ability to treat unemployment on a selective basis.

In response to this need for selectivity, many measures have been proposed in recent years. Some of them have been directed at manipulating disposable income through systems of taxes and transfers designed to preserve or promote work incentives. The negative income tax and other income maintenance programs like the earned income tax credit fall into this category. Others have taken the form of intervention in the labor market, to put more people to work or, if necessary, to induce a redistribution of employment in favor of the structurally disadvantaged. These labor market policies include reducing minimum wages; reducing the level of, or altering the structural incentives in, unemployment compensation; increasing job information and mobility; and creating jobs directly through public employment or wage subsidies. The efficacy of these various programs remains open to question. Practical experience with them has been limited and the results so far inconclusive. Likewise, relatively little analytical evaluation of the potential impacts has been done.[2] Our objective is to shed some light on the latter, with specific regard to one kind of categorical employment incentive: targeted employment subsidies. The framework we use can, however, provide the basis for an analysis of more general unemployment policy issues.

Objectives of the Analysis

The employment subsidy we analyze in this paper takes the form of a payment to employers that is proportional to incremental employment above a specified base level. It is therefore a marginal employment subsidy on the wage costs of workers hired beyond a given base. Furthermore, it applies only to the wage of a particular category of worker.[3] Though we refer to this in the formal analysis simply as a targeted employment subsidy, it should be distinguished from the several variants. In particular, a general, as opposed to a marginal, wage subsidy, whether

2. See Robert H. Haveman and Gregory B. Christainsen, "Public Employment and Wage Subsidies in Western Europe and the United States: What We're Doing and What We Know," in *European Labor Market Policies,* Special Report 27 (National Commission for Manpower Policy, September 1978), pp. 259–345.

3. The particular wage subsidy we analyze is subject to difficult design problems. See the paper by Carcagno and Corson in this volume.

targeted or not, applies to the entire wage bill and therefore subsidizes existing as well as incremental employment. This has intramarginal consequences not present with the marginal subsidy. An alternative form of marginal subsidy is a recruitment subsidy, a subsidy on wages paid to new hires. Since this subsidy attaches to a particular worker rather than to employment above some base level, it may induce employers to increase labor turnover and is consequently less attractive.

All the preceding wage subsidies are payable to eligible employers. They are usually administered through the tax system as credits to employers (the new jobs tax credit, for example) or directly through the firms involved. They are to be contrasted with wage subsidies, or earnings supplements, that are paid to the workers rather than to employers and have income support as their primary objective. For such subsidies, any labor market impacts are secondary and operate through labor supply rather than demand.

In our analysis we ask familiar questions, although the framework for answering them is less familiar. The main issues addressed are the following.

—*Bang for the buck.* What are the circumstances under which a targeted employment subsidy will be more effective in reducing unemployment than alternative programs (in particular, general government spending) with equivalent net budgetary impact?

—*Inflation-unemployment trade-off.* What are the inflationary consequences of a targeted employment subsidy? What are the circumstances under which such a program will improve the trade-off between unemployment and inflation, compared with alternative programs?

—*Distributional effects.* Under what circumstances and in what way will a targeted employment subsidy alter the composition of employment and unemployment and, consequently, the distribution of income?

—*Timing of stimulation.* What is the appropriate timing or phasing for a targeted employment subsidy, in terms of the business cycle?

We do not address such issues as (a) the social value of any net addition to output resulting from a targeted employment subsidy, (b) the circumstances under which such a program will help to alleviate balance-of-payments problems, (c) the conditions that must be met to make such a program economically efficient, and (d) the program's administrative advantages and disadvantages.

The analysis deals with macroeconomic effects, but our model contains more microeconomic structure than is usual. As a result, more explicit relationships are available for determining the short-run consequences for the key variables. (The short run is characterized here by wage and price stickiness.) In particular, and in contrast to some other models that have been used to analyze unemployment, unemployment in our model is an integral, logically consistent feature of the framework.

On the other hand, we make less definite statements about the long-run consequences than do other analysts. The long-run evolution is viewed here as a sequence of short runs in which the responses in each short run influence the environment for the next short run. Specifically, the short-run adjustments affect price and wage inflation by changing the excess demand or supply pressures in the product and labor markets. The analysis focuses on these changes, and the manner in which they vary through the business cycle, rather than postulates a uniform Phillips curve for the short or long run.

This approach clearly contrasts with the more aggregative model of Baily and Tobin, in which the key influences on inflation are incorporated in a Phillips curve relationship, without an explicit specification of the underlying market mechanism.[4] In their model, as also in the Johnson model,[5] the selection of ingredients for the aggregate functional relationships is crucial in determining the long-run consequences.

Our analysis of the short-run interrelationships and the details of inter-market responses should be regarded as a complement to the work of Baily and Tobin, whose primary concern is with the long-run trade-off. It provides further evidence that may help to clarify the mechanism producing the unemployment-inflation dilemma.

Methodology and Framework[6]

Since our topic is essentially unemployment that is both cyclical and structural, the framework we use for policy evaluation must be consistent

4. Martin Neil Baily and James Tobin, "Macroeconomic Effects of Selective Public Employment and Wage Subsidies," *Brookings Papers on Economic Activity, 2: 1977,* pp. 511–41; and Martin Neil Baily and James Tobin, "Inflation-Unemployment Consequences of Job Creation Policies," in John L. Palmer, ed., *Creating Jobs: Public Employment Programs and Wage Subsidies* (Brookings Institution, 1978), pp. 43–76.

5. George E. Johnson, "Structural Unemployment Consequences of Job Creation Policies," in Palmer, ed., *Creating Jobs,* pp. 123–44.

6. The conceptual framework is a short-run general equilibrium model of output and employment, based on the models of Barro and Grossman and, in particular, Malinvaud. See Robert J. Barro and Herschel I. Grossman, "A General Disequilibrium Model of Income and Employment," *American Economic Review,* vol. 61

with this phenomenon. Accordingly, we base our analysis on a model in which proximate causes of unemployment can be identified. No attempt is made, however, to provide within the model an explanation of these causes. (Short-run price and wage rigidities, for example, are taken as given. The question whether the inflexibility might be due to the existence of implicit contracts, adjustment costs, social or institutional factors, or incomplete information is not addressed.) The existence of nonfrictional unemployment is indisputable evidence that the labor market is not clearing in the traditional manner through the mechanism of price adjustment. It may be that the money wage itself is at the "correct" level (in the sense that general market-clearing equilibrium may be achieved at a vector of absolute prices that includes the prevailing money wage) and that the necessary price adjustment is in another sector. But in any event, once the existence of cyclical and structural unemployment is acknowledged, it does not take much to realize that unemployment is but one aspect of a more general description of the economic situation.

A given observation of employment and unemployment for a particular labor group can in fact be consistent with any of several different conditions in other markets. It is therefore appropriate to identify the corresponding regimes. As detailed in the next section, each regime involves unemployment of the target group in conjunction with either full or less-than-full employment of other labor groups and with either excess demand or excess supply in the market for output. The state (of excess supply or excess demand) of any given market is the primary determinant of inflationary pressure in that market. The regimes themselves have historical illustrations (the evidence being more apparent in retrospect) and can be associated in a natural way with phases of the business cycle. As one might suspect, the impact of any given policy or program varies across regimes; or, alternatively stated, the appropriate policy mix differs from one regime to another. The effect of a policy intervention on the economy (for example, on the level and distribution of employment) depends not only on conditions in the targeted market but also on conditions in other, related markets. In the course of the analysis it becomes evident that the various possible responses are quite plausible once the environment has been clearly identified. In particular, some commonly held views about the response to policy are seen to be justified in some contexts but not in

---

(March 1971), pp. 82–93; Edmond Malinvaud, *The Theory of Unemployment Reconsidered* (Wiley, 1977). A similar framework was used in Bryce Hool, "Monetary and Fiscal Policies in Short Run Equilibria with Rationing," *International Economic Review,* vol. 21 (June 1980), pp. 301–16.

others. Consequently, it becomes important to be able to recognize the various regimes in practice.

Labor Market

Because of our focus on the structural aspects of unemployment, we want to be able to establish, as an equilibrium phenomenon, the existence of different unemployment rates for different labor groups. The representation of the labor market is central in explaining these variations and in determining the predicted outcome of government policies or programs. When it comes to specifying the key features of the labor market, several aspects of the segmented labor market theories seem likely candidates.[7] Indeed, one reason for investigating the potential of targeted employment incentives—the inadequacy of conventional monetary and fiscal policies for the task of ensuring full employment without unacceptably high rates of inflation—was also a primary reason for developing a segmented labor market theory.

This theory emphasizes problems on the demand side of the labor market. It views labor requirements as being largely determined by technology but the wage structure as being largely determined by social and institutional factors. The rigidity of wages, and also of prices, is seen as promoting macro instability and a tendency to high levels of unemployment, which provides cause for rejecting the neoclassical models of the labor market. Accordingly, the selective policies that are advocated include public employment and wage subsidy programs along with expansionary macroeconomic policies for full employment.

In particular, the differences between unemployment rates of high-skill and low-skill workers are attributed to the fact that the former (a) have invested in them more on-the-job, firm-specific training than the latter, (b) are more complementary with fixed, physical-capital factors of production,[8] and (c) involve higher overhead costs of recruitment and lay-

7. For discussion of these theories, see Glen G. Cain, "The Challenge of Segmented Labor Market Theories to Orthodox Theory: A Survey," *Journal of Economic Literature,* vol. 14 (December 1976), pp. 1215–57.

8. See Jonathan R. Kesselman, Samuel H. Williamson, and Ernst R. Berndt, "Tax Credits for Employment Rather than Investment," *American Economic Review,* vol. 67 (June 1977), pp. 339–49; Sherwin Rosen, "Human Capital: A Survey of Empirical Research," in Ronald G. Ehrenberg, ed., *Research in Labor Economics,* vol. 1 (JAI Press, 1977), pp. 3–39; and Daniel S. Hamermesh and James Grant, "Econometric Studies of Labor-Labor Substitution and Their Implications for Policy," *Journal of Human Resources,* vol. 14 (Fall 1979), pp. 518–42.

off. Consequently, low-skill workers are the first to go when production experiences a downturn. The persistent rigidity of wages is seen as preventing them from competing with high-skill workers on a cost basis.

Since, for our present purposes, the labor market is to be modeled at the macro level and not to be confined to a high-skill, low-skill interpretation, these ideas must serve mostly to suggest the appropriate sort of representation. Formally, we treat the labor market simply as a segmented market for two types of labor that have a finite degree of substitutability in the productive process. However, in further development of this framework and in empirical investigation of the underlying elements, it should prove valuable to incorporate these institutional features more explicitly. The segmented labor market view also assists in relating our economic regimes to phases of the business cycle.

Household Sector

Our policy evaluation is based on the following model. The economy is divided into three aggregate sectors: production, household, and government. The household sector is subdivided into three groups according to the type of labor supplied. The analysis formally treats types of labor as types of jobs (high-skill, low-skill, and so forth) rather than as categories of individuals (prime-age white males, black teenagers, and so forth). But because of the observed broad associations between job classes and demographic groups, it does no violence to the argument to interpret labor types also as demographic groups. Group 1 is the one least afflicted with unemployment. It may be thought of as supplying high-skill or white-collar labor (or as comprising prime-age white males), for example. Group 2 is the target group, which experiences chronically higher rates of unemployment. It may be thought of as supplying low-skill or blue-collar labor (or as comprising teenagers or blacks), for example. Group 3 consists of potential workers who are not currently part of the labor force. We refer to group 3 as "discouraged" workers, but the real distinction between groups 2 and 3 is between the active and inactive unemployed. The latter category may include such people as housewives and school returners as well as the discouraged, long-term unemployed. No endogenous reasons are provided to explain why workers fall into group 3 rather than group 2. Although this may be an important issue, it is not central to the present analysis.

We assume that, in the short run, there is no mobility between groups

1 and 2,[9] and that each worker in these groups supplies a fixed amount of labor in each period of time. The assumption of inelastic individual labor supply is made on the basis of an institutionally fixed working week and the tendency of the average person to be prepared either to take a job (with its fixed hours) or not to work at all. We thus ignore the possible macroeconomic effects of part-time or overtime work.

For simplicity, we assume that each worker supplies one unit of labor per period. We can thus identify wage rate with wage income, and quantity of labor employed with number of workers employed. We also assume that if group 3 workers enter the labor force, they become members of group 2. Therefore, while group 1's aggregate labor supply is inelastic, group 2's aggregate labor supply is elastic to the extent that there is movement between group 2 and group 3. Groups 1 and 2 are each further divided according to whether a worker is employed or unemployed. Because of the preceding assumptions, changes in group 1 employment and unemployment are equal and opposite, whereas the change in group 2 employment will differ in magnitude from the change in group 2 unemployment by the change in the size of the labor force. The income components for each group are specified below.

Production Sector

The production sector is treated as an aggregate, profit-maximizing firm producing a single output and using variable quantities of the two types of labor, all other factors being fixed in the short run. Real investment (I) is treated as an exogenous accumulation of stocks or "capital," influenced primarily by expectations. Output (y) is positively related to each of the labor inputs (e_1 and e_2) according to a production function

$$(1) \qquad\qquad y = f(e_1, e_2)$$

that is continuously differentiable and strictly concave (which implies diminishing marginal product for each factor, diminishing marginal rates of substitution, and decreasing returns to scale). From available empirical evidence one cannot assume either that the two labor factors are tech-

---

9. The model could be extended to incorporate degrees of mobility in one or both directions.

nical complements or that they are substitutes for each other.[10] Therefore, in the analysis we consider the implications of both alternatives, taking first the case of complementarity (including independence) and then indicating what modifications follow from the assumption of substitutability.

Corresponding to this production structure are three markets: one for output and one for each type of labor. In the short run the price of output (p), the money wage of an employed group 1 worker (w_1), and the money wage received by an employed group 2 worker (w_2) are all fixed. At the margin, a wage subsidy at rate s lowers the price of group 2's labor to the firm to $(1 - s)w_2$. Usually supply and demand are not equal in any given market. If the demand for output exceeds the supply, some demanders will be rationed and will consequently save more than was desired. If the reverse is true, firms will be assumed to cut back production to the level of demand. Likewise, if the supply of either type of labor exceeds the demand, there will be unemployment of that labor. If the converse is true, the firm will be constrained in its production decision by the available quantity of that type of labor.

Government Sector

The government sector is essentially described by the policy parameters and their interrelationship in the government's budget. The government is assumed to choose the level of its direct real expenditure on goods (g), income tax rates (t_i for group i; $i = 1,2$), the rate of transfers to the unemployed (T for each group 1 or group 2 worker; 0 for group 3),[11] and the group 2 subsidy rate (s). The money stock and the size of the government budget deficit are held constant throughout the analysis. Changes

10. In their summary of econometric studies of labor-labor substitution, Hamermesh and Grant conclude that it seems possible that in many disaggregations of the labor force (in particular, production and nonproduction, middle-age and other age groups) the more highly skilled subaggregates are complements with capital and are jointly substitutable with capital for less-skilled labor. "Econometric Studies of Labor," p. 537.

11. The payment T is a payment for which only the unemployed who are actively searching for a job are eligible. The fact that group 2 gets T while group 3 gets 0 is of no significance for the conclusions. The reason for having group 3 is to keep in mind the potential expansion of the labor force and the distinction between the change in employment and the change in unemployment for group 2.

in tax receipts must therefore balance changes in total government expenditure on goods, transfers, and the wage subsidy program. We assume that tax and transfer *rates* are not changed in the short run. Consequently, the net change in the deficit resulting from endogenous changes in tax receipts, transfer payments, and subsidy program costs that are induced by the introduction or expansion of the targeted employment subsidy must be balanced by a change in government spending on goods.

In the subsequent analysis, therefore, the targeted employment subsidy is a policy alternative to government spending on goods, and the *net* cost of the subsidy program is the required reduction in direct government spending. As a result, the impact of the subsidy on unemployment and inflation measures directly the *comparative* impact ("bang for the buck") of the subsidy relative to expenditure on goods. But we also note the potential consequences of expansionary policy and such alternatives as "incomes" policy.

Inflationary Effects

The inflationary impact of the targeted employment subsidy is derived in the following way. In the short run there are three distinct rates of inflation, one in each market. Product price inflation is denoted by $\dot{p}$, group i wage inflation by $\dot{w}_i$ ($i = 1,2$). With a given exogenous environment, including skill levels, the two rates of wage inflation tend to be equalized in the long run (alternatively, on average over time), so that the relative wage is constant. Further, the rate of product price inflation is in the long run in a constant relation to these rates of wage inflation, with real wages growing with productivity. In the short run, however, these inflation rates vary according to the different pressures prevailing in the corresponding markets. Although there is some feedback from the pressure in one market to the inflation in another, we assume that the short-run *change* in the inflation rate in a particular market is in the direction of the change in excess demand in that market. We are thus postulating that the dominant short-run influence on an inflation rate is the pressure of own excess demand or supply. Denoting change by Δ, we have

(2) $$\Delta\dot{p} = f(\Delta D), f' > 0,$$

and

(3) $$\Delta\dot{w} = g_i(\Delta u_i), g_i' < 0, \qquad i = 1, 2,$$

where D = aggregate excess demand for goods, and u_i = unemployment (excess supply) of labor group i. If expected rates of inflation are taken as given, the main feedback effect not included in equations 2 and 3 is that of primary unemployment on secondary wage inflation. The latter will be smaller or greater than otherwise as the former is increased or decreased.[12]

Further Relationships

The after-tax wage income for an employed worker in group i $(i = 1,2)$ is $(1 - t_i)w_i$. It is assumed that each person within a given group i $(i = 1,2,3)$ has the same level of assets (different in general across groups). Since the short-run household consumption effects that concern us result from shifts between employment and unemployment categories, we need know only the corresponding changes in income from wages or transfer payments. The change in income resulting from a shift from unemployment to employment for a worker in group i $(i = 1,2)$ is $(1 - t_i)w_i - T$; that resulting from a shift from group 3 to group 2 unemployment is simply T. The corresponding per-worker changes in government receipts are $t_i w_i + T$ $(i = 1,2)$ and $-T$.

The consumption demand of an employed worker is x_i $(i = 1,2)$, and that of an unemployed worker (a nonparticipant in group 3) is $\tilde{x}_i$ $(i = 1,2,3)$. These depend, in particular, on the associated after-tax wage income or transfer payment. Total employment levels are, as mentioned before, e_1 and e_2, and N_i $(i = 1,2,3)$ is the number of workers (households) in group i. The aggregate private and public demand for goods is therefore

(4) $e_1 x_1 + (N_1 - e_1)\tilde{x}_1 + e_2 x_2 + (N_2 - e_2)\tilde{x}_2 + N_3 \tilde{x}_3 + g + I.$

In differential terms, with $dN_1 = 0$ and $dN_2 + dN_3 = 0$,

(5) $(x_1 - \tilde{x}_1)de_1 + (x_2 - \tilde{x}_2)de_2 + (\tilde{x}_2 - \tilde{x}_3)dN_2 + dg + dI$

is the change in aggregate demand.

12. Further development of the price and wage dynamics would require also a linkage between the price and wage adjustment equations. See Baily and Tobin, "Macroeconomic Effects," and "Inflation-Unemployment Consequences." Here our limited objective is to determine the immediate inflationary impact of the targeted employment subsidy.

The government's budget deficit is

(6) $pg + [(N_1 - e_1) + (N_2 - e_2)]T + sw_2(e_2 - e_2^0) - e_1 t_1 w_1 - e_2 t_2 w_2,$

where $e_2 - e_2^0$ indicates the number of workers (quantity of labor) whose wage is currently subsidized. Before the introduction of a subsidy, $e_2 - e_2^0$ and s would both be equal to zero. On the assumption that the government budget deficit is kept constant, the adjustment in government spending on goods required by the introduction (or expansion) of a targeted employment subsidy is

(7) $pdg = (t_1 w_1 + T)de_1 + (t_2 w_2 + T - sw_2)de_2 - TdN_2 - w_2(e_2 - e_2^0)ds.$

This compensation is readily interpreted as follows. If group 1 employment were to increase by one, the government would receive an additional $t_1 w_1$ in taxes and would also save the transfer payment T. A unit increase in group 2's employment would similarly increase the government's receipts by $t_2 w_2 + T$, but would also require a subsidy payment of sw_2. For each additional person attracted into the target group labor force, the government must make the transfer payment T. The final term represents the increase in payments to currently subsidized workers when the subsidy rate is increased (from s to $s + ds$). As noted above, this term will be zero if there is no preexisting coverage. From now on we shall assume this to be the case.

Then, combining the differential expressions to incorporate the induced change in government spending, we can rewrite the change in aggregate demand as

(8) $[x_1 - \tilde{x}_1 + \dfrac{1}{p}(t_1 w_1 + T)]de_1$

$+ [x_2 - \tilde{x}_2 + \dfrac{1}{p}(t_2 w_2 + T - sw_2)]de_2 + \left(\tilde{x}_2 - \tilde{x}_3 - \dfrac{1}{p}T\right)dN_2 + dI.$

We have already noted that the change in income resulting from a shift from unemployment to employment for a worker in group i $(i = 1,2)$ is $w_i - (t_i w_i + T)$. If the marginal propensity to consume of a group i household is less than unity, it follows that the change in the household's demand, $x_i - \tilde{x}_i$, will be less than $(1/p)[w_i - (t_i w_i + T)]$. The corresponding change in the government's real receipts (not counting the cost of the subsidy), and therefore in government demand, is $(1/p)(t_i w_i + T)$. The combined change in demand, $x_i - \tilde{x}_i + (1/p)(t_i w_i + T)$, is therefore less than w_i/p, the group i worker's real wage income. Similarly, $\tilde{x}_2 - \tilde{x}_3$ will be less than $(1/p)T$, the reduction in government real spending, so that each move from group 3 to group 2 unemployed will reduce aggregate demand.

On the supply side, any change in actual output must be technologically related to changes in employment according to

(9) $$dy = f_1(e_1, e_2)de_1 + f_2(e_1, e_2)de_2,$$

where

$$f_i(e_1, e_2) \equiv \frac{\partial f(e_1, e_2)}{\partial e_i} \qquad \text{for} \qquad i = 1, 2$$

is the marginal product of group i labor.

Combining the changes in both aggregate demand and aggregate supply, we have the net change in aggregate *excess* demand (D) due to the subsidy,

(10a) $$dD = a_1 de_1 + a_2 de_2 + a_3 dN_2 + dI,$$

where

$$a_1 \equiv x_1 - \tilde{x}_1 + \frac{1}{p}(t_1 w_1 + T) - f_1,$$

$$a_2 \equiv x_2 - \tilde{x}_2 + \frac{1}{p}(t_2 w_2 + T - s w_2) - f_2,$$

$$a_3 \equiv \tilde{x}_2 - \tilde{x}_3 - \frac{1}{p}T.$$

Corresponding to changes in employment levels for groups 1 and 2, respectively, the coefficients a_1 and a_2 reflect the net effect of the induced changes in private and government spending and the change in output. The net effect of expanded transfer payments for new entrants into the labor force is given by a_3. In view of the preceding observations on the magnitudes of the induced demand changes relative to real wages, we have

(10b) $$a_1 < \frac{w_1}{p} - f_1; \qquad a_2 < \frac{(1 - s)w_2}{p} - f_2; \qquad a_3 < 0.$$

The coefficients a_1 and a_2 will therefore both be negative if the real wages (paid by the firm) are at most equal to the respective marginal products of labor.

The inflationary impact of the targeted employment subsidy on the product price is, in the later analysis, derived through 10a in conjunction with 10b. For example, it follows from these equations that if (an increase in) the subsidy induces a general increase in employment, the endogenous net impact on aggregate excess demand will be negative and therefore deflationary. Aggregate excess demand declines because aggregate demand increases by *less* than the increase in aggregate income, the latter being equal to the sum of real wages paid to newly employed labor of both types, whereas aggregate supply increases by the marginal product of this labor, which for each type is *at least equal* to the real wage paid.

Policy Evaluation for Unemployment Regimes

It is possible to identify two aspects of the economic environment that separately or together provide immediate reason for the existence of unemployment. One is an inappropriate structure of relative prices and wages; the other is an insufficient level of aggregate effective demand for goods.

The presence of unemployment is often taken as an indication that labor's real wage is too high. It is argued that if the real wage could fall— if it were not prevented from so doing by downward rigidity due to minimum wage laws, union policy, or whatever—then firms would want to expand employment until the marginal product of labor is reduced to the lower level of the real wage. This view is appropriate so long as firms are indeed choosing employment levels to equate marginal products with real wages, which is the optimal thing for competitive, profit-maximizing firms to do if they are able to hire and fire workers without cost and to sell at the going price whatever level of output they choose. The latter presumption is reasonable if the product price is flexible enough to keep the product market always in a state of balance between supply and demand, or if the product price is fixed but the product market is in a state of excess demand. Since we are adopting an assumption of price and wage rigidity in the short run, it is therefore the excess demand state of the product market (with zero excess demand as a special case) that is pertinent here.

Given that state, unemployment of the target group may exist in conjunction with either unemployment or full employment of (more generally, excess demand for) the nontargeted group. The first set of circumstances—excess demand in the product market and unemployment in both labor markets—is referred to as regime A. In this context the unemployment of both groups could be remedied by an adjustment in real (and usually also relative) wages, were this feasible. The second set of circumstances—excess demand in the product and nontargeted labor markets together with unemployment in the target labor market—is labeled regime B. Here the real wage of the nontargeted group is too low, that of the target group too high.

A second approach to unemployment policy stems from the view, usually regarded as Keynesian, that the essential problem is an inadequate effective demand for goods. The case for government intervention is therefore based on the need for stimulation of aggregate expenditure, thence of output and employment. The main distinction between the economic contexts that are appropriate for this view, rather than the first, is that the product market is in a state of excess supply, not excess demand.

The economic environment in which all markets are slack—that is, with excess supply in the product market and unemployment of both labor groups—is called regime C. When unemployment of the target group occurs with excess supply in the product market but full employment of (excess demand for) the nontargeted group, the economy is said to be in regime D. The uneven incidence of unemployment, which is most evident in this last regime, is sustained by an inappropriate structure of relative wages.

For reference, we summarize the characteristics of these four regimes in which there is unemployment of the target group (labor 2 market):

Regime	Product market	Labor 1 market	Labor 2 market
A	Excess demand	Unemployment	Unemployment
B	Excess demand	Excess demand	Unemployment
C	Excess supply	Unemployment	Unemployment
D	Excess supply	Excess demand	Unemployment

We now take these unemployment regimes in turn and analyze the impact of a targeted employment subsidy on each one. We also consider the impacts of alternative, more traditional policies. Remember the assumption that net expenditure on the subsidy will be compensated for by an equal reduction in general government spending on goods. This assumption allows for a direct comparison of the relative efficacy of the two policies in attaining the goal of reducing unemployment without exacerbating inflationary pressures.

Regime A

Consider a state of the economy in which the product market is tight (that is, there is an excess demand for goods) and some degree of non-frictional unemployment exists among both labor groups. In this situation the levels of output and employment are being freely determined by firms through their profit-maximizing objective, since firms are on the short side of each market. The equilibrium is therefore characterized by the marginal conditions (marginal product equals effective real wage) for the firm's optimum,

$$(11) \qquad f_1(e_1, e_2) = \frac{w_1}{p} \qquad \text{and} \qquad f_2(e_1, e_2) = \frac{(1 - s)w_2}{p},$$

and by the technological relationship between employment levels and output,

$$(12) \qquad\qquad\qquad y = f(e_1, e_2).$$

What will be the impact, in this context, of increasing the targeted employment subsidy rate (above zero, in particular)? The target group's labor will become cheaper relative to that of the nontarget group, and in the manner of the traditional theory of the firm, a substitution of the former for the latter will occur. Employment of group 1 will increase or decline according to whether the two labor types are complements or substitutes. For the target group 2, the reduction in unemployment will fall short of the increase in employment to the extent that "discouraged" workers (group 3) are induced to enter the labor force. For the supply-inelastic group 1, the change in employment will be reflected in an equal and opposite change in unemployment.

All these output-employment reactions can be predicted from technology and wage-price data. But when it comes to predicting the price-inflationary effects of the subsidy, one must consider the variety of adjustments in the composition of aggregate demand. When the labor factors are complementary, a shift occurs within each group from unemployed to employed, as well as a shift from group 3 to group 2. Each of these shifts will bring an associated expansion of private consumption. (The reverse effect occurs for group 1 when the labor types are substitutes.) There will also be associated changes in the tax receipts and transfer payments of the government. The net increase in government receipts will offset to some degree the reduction in government spending on goods required to balance the government's spending on the subsidy program. The ultimate effect of the subsidy on excess demand for goods, and hence on price inflation, will then depend on the expansion of aggregate (private and public) demand relative to the predicted expansion of supply.

We have already derived, as equations 10a and 10b, general expressions for the change in the aggregate excess demand for goods in terms of the net impacts from the employment shifts just mentioned. It remains to specify these terms for regime A.

From the first-order conditions (equation 11) it is seen that (w_1/p) $- f_1 = 0$ and $(1 - s)w_2/p - f_2 = 0$, so that the coefficients a_1 and a_2 in equation 10a are both negative. The expansion of employment of either labor group thus leads to a net reduction in excess demand. (See again the remarks that follow equation 10b.) Also, from equations 10a and 10b, a negative (though presumably small) net effect results from an expansion of the group 2 labor force. Ignore for the moment the possible response in exogenous investment. If the labor types are complementary, therefore, the introduction of a targeted employment subsidy, with government spending elsewhere adjusted to preserve the budget deficit, brings about a reduction in the aggregate excess demand for goods by households and government. The subsidy will thus tend to reduce the inflationary pressure on prices. If the labor types are substitutes, the decline in group 1 employment will, by the same reasoning, contribute to an increase in excess demand. Whether aggregate excess demand will be increased or reduced depends on the sizes of the two groups' propensities to consume and on the precise form of the production function.

In the short run, then, with complementary labor, the impact of a targeted employment subsidy is beneficial in all respects except for the reduction in downward pressure on wages that accompanies the reduction in unemployment. There is obviously no way to avoid the latter when employment in general is stimulated. But the shift in favor of group 2 employment will help, insofar as secondary unemployment exerts a lesser restraint on wage inflation than does primary unemployment.[13] Also, the

13. See ibid. for further discussion.

tendency toward wage inflation will be mitigated by at least two factors: the alleviation of upward pressure on product price and the expansion of the group 2 labor force. The latter will make less impressive the reduction in the target group's unemployment rate (as opposed to employment level), but that cannot be regarded seriously as a negative effect.[14] The employment level is the relevant indicator of the unemployment effect, and any dampening effect on wage and price inflation is desirable. If groups 1 and 2 are substitutes in production, the employment and price-inflationary effects of the subsidy are less attractive. But the trade-off is a reduction in wage-inflationary pressure, directly for group 1 and indirectly for group 2.

It is not possible to say anything definite about the effects on or through investment. If the subsidy stimulates investment, the immediate reduction in inflationary pressure on prices will be diminished. In the longer run, however, the increased investment may further stimulate employment and reduce inflationary pressure by increasing the productivity of labor in general. In the short run, the *measured* productivity of labor will decline because of the subsidy's effect on the composition of employment.

Regime B

Consider now a state of the economy that differs qualitatively from the preceding only in that the primary labor market is tight: there is an excess demand for group 1 labor. This state is characterized by full employment of group 1 labor,

$$(13) \qquad\qquad\qquad e_1 = N_1,$$

by the marginal condition for the firm's optimal employment of group 2 labor (given the employment of group 1),

$$(14) \qquad\qquad\qquad f_2(N_1, e_2) = \frac{(1 - s)w_2}{p},$$

and by the output-employment relationship,

$$(15) \qquad\qquad\qquad y = f(N_1, e_2).$$

14. See John Bishop and Robert Haveman, "Selective Employment Subsidies: Can Okun's Law Be Repealed?" *American Economic Review*, vol. 69 (May 1979, *Papers and Proceedings, 1978*), pp. 124–30, for a discussion of the Okun's law effect.

Note that, in contrast to the first regime, there is not equality between group 1's marginal product and its real wage. Now

$$(16) \qquad\qquad f_1(N_1, e_2) > \frac{w_1}{p}.$$

The proximate cause of the target group's unemployment is too high a real wage, perhaps because of a minimum wage law. Introduction or expansion of a subsidy will lower the real wage paid by firms and will stimulate employment of the target group under the first-order condition for profit maximization. Output goes up correspondingly. In this regime, however, there can be no expansion of group 1's employment, which is already at the maximum.

The impact of the subsidy on product price inflation is negative; the aggregate excess demand for product is reduced for exactly the same reasons as in regime A. The only difference here is that no demand adjustment occurs within group 1. Other things equal, the absence of adjustment in primary employment will result in a smaller expansion of target group employment and hence a smaller reduction in excess demand for the product than in regime A.

Because the subsidy has no effect on group 1 employment, the employment and aggregate excess product demand changes do not depend on whether the labor types are complements or substitutes. But firms' demand (and hence the excess demand) for group 1 workers does depend on that factor. Accordingly, as the labor groups are complements or substitutes, the excess demand for group 1 will increase or diminish, as will the upward pressure on the group 1 wage.

In regime B, therefore, the targeted employment subsidy is beneficial in almost every respect, but particularly when the labor groups are technical substitutes. In that case the only negative aspect of the subsidy is the inevitable increase of inflationary pressure on the group 2 wage because of a net increase in employment. But wage inflation for group 1 will be reduced, without any reduction in actual employment, and this will in turn help to reduce the pressure on the wage for group 2 workers.

Regime C

We now consider a state of the economy in which a slack product market is accompanied by slack labor markets—that is, unemployment exists in both labor groups. Here unconstrained profit maximization is no longer the relevant objective for competitive firms. Aggregate demand for output is limiting the amount that can be sold; given this demand, the firm's objective is to supply it at minimum cost. The prevailing price and wages will determine the distribution of employment between the two labor groups, but the marginal productivity of each group will exceed the group's real wage (the subsidized real wage for group 2). Thus the employment levels will be optimally chosen by the firm when the marginal rate of substitution between labor types is equal to their relative wage,

$$(17) \qquad\qquad \frac{f_1(e_1, e_2)}{f_2(e_1, e_2)} = \frac{w_1}{(1 - s)w_2},$$

and also output $f(e_1, e_2)$ is equal to the aggregate demand by the private and public sectors. This aggregate comprises government and investment demands and the consumption demands of five household categories: employed and unemployed group 1 and group 2 households and the discouraged worker households.

Consider first the case in which the labor groups are complementary. The effect of a subsidy will come from two factors. On the one hand, the subsidy will affect the employment balance, tending to cause a substitution of subsidized group 2 for group 1 workers at the initial output level. On the other hand, a change in the composition of employment, together with the financing of the subsidy, will cause shifts in the composition of aggregate demand. If these shifts happen to leave the *level* of aggregate demand unaffected, then the subsidy will make the production of that level of output cheaper for firms but will not induce any change in the level of production. Firm owners and group 2 labor will become better off at the expense of group 1 labor. But if the change in composition causes the level of aggregate demand to be increased (reduced), production will be similarly increased (reduced), and with it the employment of both labor groups.

In qualitative terms, the demand shifts due to employment shifts are the same as those discussed for regime A. A drop in employment of group 1 is accompanied by a reduction in consumption demand (because of the lower income) and a reduction in government demand (because of lower income tax revenue and higher transfer payments). An increase in group 2 employment brings the reverse effects. There is, however, an offset to government demand equal to the cost of the subsidy. There is also a demand transfer from government to previously discouraged workers, with a negligible net effect. Added to these effects is the net change induced in investment demand, which is likely to take the same direction as the net change in aggregate household and government demand.

On the supply side, the rate at which group 2 labor will be substituted for group 1 labor at any given level of output, when the subsidy is introduced or increased, is determined by the effective wage rates and the characteristics of the production function. Complementarity of the labor groups will moderate the reduction and expansion for groups 1 and 2, respectively, that is dictated by the diminishing marginal productivity of each group.

So if no change occurs in investment demand and if the net cost of the subsidy replaces other government spending (as we have been assuming), the subsidy will unambiguously increase target group employment and decrease other employment. Whether GNP will rise or fall is ambiguous. If investment responds positively (negatively) to the subsidy, employment of both groups will be greater (less) than otherwise.

More important, however, this unemployment situation is one for which expansionary government policy (fiscal or monetary) is justified. A clear case exists for stimulation of aggregate demand, either directly through government spending or indirectly through monetary expansion or incomes policy. The latter, in contrast to its purpose under regime A, would need to produce an *increase* in real wages, to increase purchasing power and thereby stimulate aggregate demand.

What are the inflationary pressures created by the targeted employment subsidy? The further unemployment of group 1 will add to the downward pressure on this group's wage. The downward pressure on the wage of the target group will be reduced insofar as their increase in employment exceeds the induced reentry of discouraged workers into the labor force. If relative wages are a determinant of wage inflation, the tendency of w_2 to rise relative to w_1 will reduce the upward pressure on w_2 and the downward pressure on w_1. In the long run, a lower relative wage for primary labor may lower the unemployment rate consistent with a stable inflation rate.[15]

The initial (presubsidy) inflationary pressure on product price will be weak because of the shortfall in demand. If it were not for the inability to sell the output, the subsidy would lead firms to expand supply, as in

15. See Baily and Tobin, "Macroeconomic Effects," and "Inflation-Unemployment Consequences," for an argument in support of this.

regime A. In this sense the existing excess supply is aggravated and the inflationary pressure reduced. If the net effect of the subsidy on aggregate demand is positive (negative), the reduction in inflationary pressure will be lessened (reinforced).

The employment and inflation effects just described will continue to hold if the labor types are substitutes in production, provided f_{12} is not too large. But if f_{12} is negative and sufficiently large, the subsidy might have the perverse effect of increasing e_1 and decreasing e_2. In general, when f_{12} is negative, nothing definite can be said about employment or output effects. The only unambiguous conclusion in this regime, regardless of the degree of substitutability, is that the subsidy cannot induce a general expansion of employment, as it might in regime A. Although expansion of e_1 and e_2 may be consistent with the first-order condition for employment, it would lead to a greater expansion of supply than of demand; that is, to excess supply.

In sum, then, a targeted employment subsidy does not appear to have any clear or reliable effects in regime C, though the target group's employment will be increased provided the elasticity of substitution between labor groups is "not too high." In this state of general excess supply, general expansionary policy is called for.

Regime D

The impact of a targeted employment subsidy is again quite different if the market for the nontarget labor group 1 is tight; that is, when there is excess demand for group 1 labor together with excess supply in the product market and unemployment in the target group 2. The usual initial effect on the target group, a substitution of targeted for nontargeted labor, will not occur in these circumstances. As long as there is the excess demand for group 1 labor, firms have no incentive to substitute at the initial level of output. For a given level of output, y, and a given (full) employment level, N_1, of group 1 labor, the quantity, e_2, of group 2 employment is completely determined by the technological requirement that $y = f(N_1, e_2)$. Therefore, the only way in which the subsidy itself can have any effect is if it can somehow alter the level of aggregate demand for goods.

The components of aggregate demand here are the same as those under regime B: the demands of employed group 1 households, the demands of employed and unemployed group 2 households, the demands of unemployed group 3 households, government demand, and investment demand. Because of the lack of incentive for substitution in production, as described above, there will be, other things equal, no endogenous change in the composition of demand by government and groups 1 and 2 households. If discouraged workers are induced, by awareness of the potential subsidy, to seek employment actively (necessarily without success, other things equal), and thereby qualify for an unemployment benefit transfer from the government, the net impact on aggregate demand will be negligible provided the marginal propensity to consume of these workers is close to one. So far as this propensity is less than unity, the transfer will further depress aggregate demand.

The only hope, therefore, for a positive response to a targeted wage subsidy is that it will somehow spark an increase in investment. (Such an autonomous increase might conceivably come about if firms anticipate improved economic conditions because of government intervention.) If this should happen for whatever reason, employment of the target group would expand—not as a replacement for group 1 labor, but as required to produce the additional output. A multiplier effect would then occur as the increased purchasing power of the newly employed target group workers further stimulates aggregate demand. But since there is no obvious reason for investment demand to be adjusted upward in the first place, here again a clear case exists for pump-priming, expansionary government policy.

It is also important to note that, even if there were an autonomous increase in investment demand, the subsidy itself would not influence the amount by which target group employment is expanded. Since this expansion is determined by the aggregate demand and technology, as described above, subsidizing it will simply result in windfall profits to firms. As regards output and employment, given the need for expanding effective demand, the government would clearly do better to engage in direct spending on goods (or on cash transfers and the like) rather than in financing a targeted employment subsidy. Indeed, it should either be expanding the former to initiate a multiplier recovery or stimulating investment for the same purpose.

No change in inflationary pressure occurs in this situation unless output is stimulated by an autonomous increase in demand. If the government budget deficit is to be increased to provide a higher level of government spending on goods, there is some benefit in combining this increase with a targeted employment subsidy. On the negative side, though the subsidy in itself will have no direct impact on production decisions with a *given* budget deficit, the cost of the subsidy will displace the directly effective spending on goods and thus reduce the stimulative impact. But as a trade-off for the smaller impact on employment, the subsidy will serve to reduce the upward pressure on prices and wages. In particular, it will reduce the excess demand for group 1 labor and, by reducing production costs for the firm, help to maintain the deflationary pressure of excess supply. These effects will in turn help to preserve the preexisting downward pressure of excess supply on the wage of the target group, by maintaining the target group's relative wage and also its real wage.

It is clear from the foregoing analysis that, as in regime C, the value of introducing a temporary employment subsidy in this regime is negligible. The indirect effects of a subsidy are relevant, however, if the subsidy is to remain in place in potentially all regimes.

Policy Implications and Prescription

What can be concluded from the preceding analysis about the efficacy of a targeted employment subsidy in reducing the unemployment of the target group and the inflationary pressure it creates in so doing? One thing is clear: the impact of a subsidy will depend, qualitatively and quantitatively, on aspects of the economic environment other than just unemployment in the target group. The various alternative effects on unemployment and inflation derived above are summarized in figure 1. Recall the underlying premise that induced government spending on the subsidy program replaces government spending elsewhere; tax and transfer rates (but not their total quantities, in general) and the money supply are all assumed to remain unchanged. A "bang-for-the-buck" comparison between the subsidy and government spending on goods is thus implicitly being made, accounting for induced adjustments in the composition of the government's budget.

At any time the nonfrictional unemployment of the target group will be a product of cyclical and structural factors. The potential advantage of a targeted employment subsidy, compared with general spending or a general wage subsidy, is its inherent ability to focus on the structural aspect of the unemployment. At the same time it focuses on a subgroup of the population whose spending propensities are more likely than those

Figure 1. Employment and Inflationary Effects of a Targeted Employment Subsidy[a]

	Employment		Inflation		
	Δe_1	e_2	$\Delta \dot{p}$	$\Delta \dot{w}_1$	$\Delta \dot{w}_2$
Regime A	+ / −	+ / +	− / ?	+ / −	+ / +
Regime B	0 / 0	+ / +	− / −	+ / −	+ / +
Regime C	− / ?	+ / ?	? / ?	− / ?	+ / ?
Regime D	0 / 0	0 / 0	0 / 0	0 / 0	0 / 0

a. For each combination of regime and change in an employment or inflation variable, the upper and lower triangles contain, respectively, the effects under the alternative conditions of complementarity and substitutability of the two labor factors. The variables are defined as follows: Δe_i = change in employment of group i; $\Delta \dot{p}$ = change in product price inflation; $\Delta \dot{w}_i$ = change in group i wage inflation.

of other groups to stimulate output and employment. This corollary focus may or may not be a good thing.

Employment Effects

The results summarized in figure 1 show that a targeted employment subsidy will be most effective in stimulating the target group's employment when the product market is tight. It is then that the price incentive for firms will be the primary determinant of both the level and the composition of employment. Within this context the effect on target group employment is stronger when both labor markets are slack, in which event there will also be a change in primary employment. On the other hand, if the primary labor market is tight, there will be no negative employment effects.

When all product and labor markets are slack, a targeted employment subsidy will tend to benefit the target group at the expense of the primary group, since the price incentive for firms is then primarily a determinant of the distribution of employment but not of its level. Only when a tight primary labor market is combined with slack product and target labor markets will the subsidy not have the potential to assist the target group. The price incentive is then inoperative because of the shortfall in demand.

Inflationary Pressures

Usually government expenditure on a targeted employment subsidy program rather than on goods will have a dampening effect on product price inflation. When the product market is tight, and consequently demand pressure on price the greatest, a subsidy serves to reduce the inflationary pressure by promoting output even more than demand. When a tight primary labor market coexists with slack product and target labor markets, any stimulation of output and target group employment by expansionary government policy will result in less inflationary pressure if accompanied by a targeted employment subsidy. The reason is that, for any given output stimulation, the subsidy reduces the firm's production costs and biases the employment demands in favor of the target group. This bias serves to moderate the overall level of wage inflation. Some inflation of real wages, particularly of the target group, is desirable in this context for its expansionary effect on aggregate demand.

The main exception to the rule that a subsidy will diminish price inflation is when all markets are slack. A redistribution of income in favor of the target group is likely to occur, but it is not clear in which direction the excess supply of goods will be shifted. Either way, the initial deflationary situation is unlikely to be significantly altered.

Practical Implications for Policy

Variety may be the spice of life, but it affords little reassurance for policymakers when it comes in the guise of alternative responses to a given action. It is clearly essential to be able to identify the several regimes that provide the alternative contexts for policy implementation and thus condition the response. To some extent this can be done by direct observation of economic conditions, though agreement is unlikely. The state of the product market can be inferred from the movements of orders and backlogs, sales, or inventories. The state of a labor market is most obviously indicated by unemployment and vacancy rates. But to provide a general perspective on the range of economic environments, it may help to obtain a heuristic association between the regimes that have been analyzed and the stages of the business cycle.

The purpose here is to identify stages with regimes, not to explain their evolution. We therefore suppose that the structure of prices and wages changes over time in such a way that the various regimes emerge in a pattern consistent with historical observation. We also take as given that (nonfrictional) unemployment of the primary group will never be observed in conjunction with excess demand for secondary labor. Theoretical support for this assumption is provided by the segmented labor market arguments relating to technological complementarities and to the costs of hiring, training, and firing, as described earlier.

There are then five admissible regimes, five alternative configurations of excess demands and supplies. Besides the ones already defined, there is regime E, in which all markets are tight. This regime has inflationary potential in all areas and is identifiable with the peak of the business cycle, though the existence of chronic structural unemployment would suggest that such a situation rarely occurs and that the peak is typified by regime B. At the other extreme, the situation of general deflation or depression, regime C, can be identified with the trough. Since the secondary labor market is the last to tighten and the first to slacken, regime B will lie on both sides of the peak, immediately preceding regime E on the upside and succeeding it in the downturn. Regimes A and D will then occur between regimes B and C. Relative to regime B, regime A involves a slackening of the primary labor market, whereas regime D involves a slackening of the product market. Alternatively, relative to regime C, regime A involves a tightening of the product market and regime D a tightening of the primary labor market. There is thus no natural ordering for regimes A and D. Their location in the cycle is determined by whether the economy is on the upswing, emerging from a trough, or on the downswing, approaching the trough. In the downswing, we hypothesize, the product market will tend to slacken before the primary labor market is afflicted with unemployment, because of firms' vested interest in their high-skill workers. Conversely, the product market will tend to pick up before the primary labor market in the upswing. The overall picture is shown in figure 2.

Figure 2. Location of Regimes in the Business Cycle

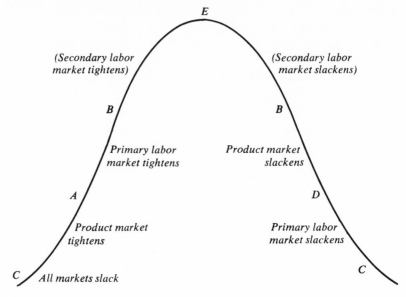

Prescription

At the bottom of the cycle (regime C) the economy is in need of general stimulation: expansion of employment and thence aggregate effective demand. This calls for expansionary fiscal or monetary policy. The concurrent introduction of a targeted employment subsidy will then twist the expansion of employment in favor of the target group. This bias will mitigate the tendency of wage-inflationary pressure to increase and will contribute to a more balanced recovery of the economy.

In the succeeding stage of the upswing (regime A), the tightening of the product market makes expansionary demand policy inappropriate. During this stage the flow of demand expenditure needs to be reduced. At the same time, the persistence of unemployment calls for a reduction in real wages as seen by firms. This can be effected by a targeted employment subsidy. Expenditure on a subsidy program, instead of on goods, will ease the upward pressure on prices. Furthermore, a subsidy that is targeted on high-unemployment labor will help to balance the employment expansion.

If the economy is nearing the peak of the cycle (regime B), with only the target group experiencing unemployment, the need to slow aggregate expenditure is concomitant with the need to shift labor demand to the target group. Accordingly, a reduction in government spending on goods together with a targeted employment subsidy is beneficial.

If the peak of the cycle occurs as regime E, actual employment and output will not at this stage be affected by a subsidy. In an economic state of general excess demand, a targeted employment subsidy will serve only to increase inflationary pressure on wages. Aggregate demand for goods needs to be reduced (by reducing government spending, for example) in order to reduce the inflationary pressure on product price.

In the downturn phase (regime B) it is again appropriate to be holding back government spending and to subsidize the target group. From the dynamic point of view, the situation of regime B on the downside differs from that on the upside in that the climate for government spending is becoming less rather than more demanding of contraction.

Once the product market has slackened, but the primary labor market is still in a state of full employment (regime D), expansionary government policy is necessary to counter the recession. Without it, a targeted employment subsidy will be ineffective in stimulating employment for the target group. At this stage, a combination of the two policies will be more effective in expanding employment with less inflationary pressure than will pure fiscal or monetary policy.

Conclusions

From our examination of the stages of the business cycle it is apparent that a targeted employment subsidy should not be regarded simply as a countercyclical policy instrument. Indeed, as a stimulus to target group employment, such a subsidy is likely to have greater impact in the upper part of the cycle. What the preceding investigation points to as an appropriate strategy for countering cyclical and structural unemployment, with minimal inflationary consequences, is a mix of aggregate demand policy and targeted labor market policy. Supported by countercyclical demand management, an employment subsidy, targeted on the structurally unemployed and maintained through the business cycle, may serve to balance the incidence of unemployment across labor groups and to moderate inflationary pressure.

Alternatively, a targeted employment subsidy program may be regarded as likely to be in place for only a short period, during which perhaps only one of the four unemployment regimes will be relevant, rather than for the duration of the business cycle. Its effectiveness in that case must be judged by its consequences in a particular regime. The choice of timing of the program, with allowance for organizational lags, must therefore be based on the relative policy weights given to the impact of the subsidy on the various employment and inflation variables.

On the basis of the analysis, the most obvious situation in which to apply a targeted employment subsidy is regime B, where the impact on target group employment and inflation are both in the right direction and adverse effects are minimal. Because of the difficulty of precise timing, it is advantageous that the regimes adjacent to B, namely A on the upside and D on the downside, are environments in which a subsidy is unlikely to have deleterious effects. Indeed, in regime A, apart from a reduction in primary employment if the labor factors are substitutes, in which case a compensating reduction in wage inflation occurs, the effects are particularly desirable.

Comments by Jeffrey M. Perloff

Burdett and Hool's paper is a clever analysis of the short-run disequilibrium effects of a targeted employment subsidy. By explicitly modeling the short-run adjustments firms make, the authors can determine the effects of the subsidy on employment, wages, and prices over the business cycle. The strengths of their paper are obvious: they are able to obtain a large number of results from fairly weak assumptions. My comments will concentrate on the realism of their model and its implications for policy.

Burdett and Hool, quite properly, consider the possibility that different labor groups may be either substitutes or complements in the production process. As they note, during certain stages of the business cycle, the desirability of a targeted employment subsidy depends crucially on this elasticity. But as the literature they cite and many other articles note, the sign of the cross-elasticity is uncertain. It depends on the groups being examined and the other inputs included in the estimated production function.[16]

16. See Ernst R. Berndt and David O. Wood, "Engineering and Econometric Interpretations of Energy-Capital Complementarity," *American Economic Review,* vol. 69 (June 1979), pp. 342–54, for a lucid discussion of the biases in elasticities introduced by having "too few" other factors in the estimated production function. Michael Wachter and I have recently estimated a production function with young workers (aged sixteen through twenty-four), adult workers (twenty-five years and

It is quite possible that the sign of this elasticity is different in the short run than in the long run. The short-run elasticity discussed in Burdett and Hool has been defined by Berndt and Wood as a gross price elasticity.[17] In technical terms, this is the logarithmic derivative of one labor group with respect to the wage of the other labor group, other inputs being held constant. The appropriate long-run concept, on the other hand, is the net price elasticity, which allows other factors to vary.

Given constant returns to scale in the production relationship, the net elasticity is smaller than the gross elasticity. For, again in technical terms, the net price elasticity equals the gross elasticity plus a term involving the product of the cost share of the variable inputs and the own-price elasticity of demand that is negative. Hence it is possible that labor groups are gross substitutes but net complements.

In Burdett and Hool's analysis, it appears that a subsidy is more likely to have desirable employment and price effects if labor groups are complements. It is therefore possible that undesirable effects may be observed in the short run when labor groups are gross substitutes, but desirable ones observed in the long run when the groups are net complements.

Of course, capital may be the input that is fixed in the short run, but variable in the long run. As a result, over time the subsidy may reduce capital investment, which may offset the desirable effects of labor complementarity.[18] Indeed, throughout this analysis, one must be aware that the subsidy induces a distortion at full employment that may make it undesirable during the peak phase of the business cycle.

In the long run, the subsidy may affect the wage and price differential equations.[19] Presumably, these equations are not stable over the long run

---

up), capital, and energy. As in the production-nonproduction worker literature, we find that youths and adults are complements. Jeffrey M. Perloff and Michael L. Wachter, "The Productivity Slowdown: A Labor Problem?" in *The Decline in Productivity Growth,* Conference Series 22 (Federal Reserve Bank of Boston, June 1980), pp. 115–42.

17. Berndt and Wood, "Engineering and Econometric Interpretations."

18. For example, if technological progress is embodied in capital, a targeted employment subsidy could slow technological progress. If this subsidy were combined with an investment tax credit, then both capital and targeted labor would be relatively cheap compared with skilled labor, which would induce complicated effects that might be more desirable than the ones discussed here. A reduction in capital could reduce the marginal products of certain labor groups and therefore reduce wages.

19. Burdett and Hool's equations 2 and 3 indicate that the price changes with excess product demand and the wage adjusts as a function of unemployment. Surprisingly, the authors show no relationship between the two rates of adjustment.

because of feedback effects across equations. As several contributors to the 1973 volume *Microeconomic Foundations of Employment and Inflation Theory* have noted, a stable inflation equation of the form used by Burdett and Hool could not persist, since profit opportunities would exist.[20] It is therefore uncertain if knowledge of the short-run effects of a subsidy on $\dot{w}$ and $\dot{p}$ (wage and price inflation rates) will help in predicting the long-run impact of the subsidy on the inflation-unemployment rate trade-off.

Thus the long-run effects of a targeted employment subsidy may be either more or less desirable than the short-run effects. Because their paper is explicitly a short-run analysis, Burdett and Hool do not examine these possible impacts. They suggest that a subsidy be used as a short-run tool during appropriate stages of the business cycle. Such a program could avoid the potentially distortionary effects of a subsidy during tight market periods and generate some desirable long-run effects as well.

Recent experience with the new jobs tax credit and the targeted jobs tax credit, however, indicates that firms do not quickly learn about or respond to tax credit subsidies.[21] Unless existing institutions are changed, this inertia will preclude the possibility of turning a subsidy on and off as needed. Moreover, there is no consensus, even for historical periods, on whether markets are tight or slack. Though Burdett and Hool are probably right in saying that a subsidy that was in effect only during slack periods would be desirable, the appropriate evaluation is whether the desirable slack-period and long-run effects outweigh the tight-period and long-run harms.

Burdett and Hool make this statement in their conclusions: "Supported by countercyclical demand management, an employment subsidy, targeted on the structurally unemployed and maintained through the business cycle, may serve to balance the incidence of unemployment across labor groups and to moderate inflationary pressure." But it should be realized that these desirable effects may not hold in the long run and may

20. This argument is analogous to the one that rational expectations theorists often make. Edmund S. Phelps and others, *Microeconomic Foundations of Employment and Inflation Theory* (Norton, 1970).

21. My paper in this volume presents descriptions of these programs and some summary statistics which indicate that few firms learned about the programs in their first year and few of the knowledgeable firms claimed the program in the first year. For a theoretical discussion of the implications of incomplete coverage of firms and targeted labor group members, see my paper and George Johnson's paper in this volume.

be offset by displacement of other factors, adverse income redistribution, and other harmful effects.[22]

Finally, it is worth emphasizing a point Burdett and Hool allude to in passing. If the subsidy does increase target group employment, measured productivity of the target group (and probably labor productivity as a whole) will fall. Similarly, in the long run, skilled labor and capital may be displaced. Thus if the program achieves its goals, it may create political pressure to end the program or to increase subsidies to investment tax credit in order to offset these effects.

In these comments I have stressed the costs and complications of a subsidy program that the model employed by Burdett and Hool does not address. Nevertheless, their paper provides a useful analysis of the short-run dynamic benefits of a subsidy, which have been largely ignored until now.

Comments by Karl-Gustaf Löfgren

I find the Burdett and Hool paper to be solid. It is essentially clear and correct. Moreover, it takes a general equilibrium approach, which is not common in the analysis of labor market policy.

The fact that the same economic-political means may have different impacts (which is one of the main points in the paper), depending on the kind of short-run equilibrium that prevails, is well known today from the works of Dixit, Malinvaud, and Baltensperger.[23] The Burdett-Hool paper is clearly inspired by Malinvaud's important book on unemployment theory. The answer to the question of when a targeted employment subsidy will cure unemployment follows from Malinvaud's analysis of when and why increased real wages can be used to cure unemployment. And the idea of investigating whether the market imbalances deteriorate or improve when employment improves is more or less explicit in Malinvaud's book. Besides developing these ideas for the targeted employment subsidy

22. If coverage of the subsidy is not universal, the effects on the unsubsidized sectors and labor groups could be adverse even if the direct effects, as analyzed by Burdett and Hool, are desirable.

23. Avinash Dixit, "Public Finance in a Keynesian Temporary Equilibrium," *Journal of Economic Theory,* vol. 12 (April 1974), pp. 242–58; Malinvaud, *Theory of Unemployment Reconsidered;* and Ernst Baltensperger, "Government Expenditure Policies in Equilibrium and Disequilibrium," *Kyklos,* vol. 30, fasc. 3 (1977), pp. 421–42.

case—which means that Burdett and Hool work with two categories of labor in a segmented labor market setting—the paper contains an elegant "bang for the buck" comparison between the effects of a targeted employment subsidy and general fiscal policy, an analysis of the general short-run equilibrium distributional consequences of such a subsidy, and an interesting discussion of what the appropriate timing or phasing for it is in terms of the business cycle. There are several points made in the paper, however, that I find a bit unclear or misleading.

1. At the beginning of the paper the authors note that it has become evident that the labor market is not clearing in the traditional sense, through the mechanism of price adjustments. I will not disagree with that statement, even though I know people who would. But when Burdett and Hool add that the disequilibrium in the labor market can persist even if the money wage itself has the right level, I do not believe they are making a significant point. For one thing, money wages usually do not matter, and for another, either the price vector is a general equilibrium vector or it is not, at least for the kind of model they are considering.

There are, however, some interesting stochastic disequilibrium models in which the price vector might be consistent with a full-employment equilibrium, while at the same time both the labor market and the market for goods are in excess supply because of pessimistic and self-fulfilling expectations among firms. These models have the following strange property: if the government, when prices are "correct," promises to buy the goods not bought by the private sector, firms will automatically produce the general equilibrium output; hence full employment is created without the government having to buy a single good. For a model with this "placebo-effect" property, the reader is referred to a recent paper by Honkapohja and Ito.[24]

2. One might also question whether it is unambiguously positive—which is the implicit evaluation in the paper—to have the pressure on prices decreased and the pressure on wages increased. Since there is unemployment resulting from too high real wage rates under regimes A and B, the tendencies that are created might disturb the long-run market-clearing process.

On this point I think one could say that too little is known. First of all, short-run fixed price theory assumes that prices are more or less wrong in

24. Seppo Honkapohja and Takatoshi Ito, "A Stochastic Approach to Disequilibrium Macroeconomics," Discussion Paper 719 (Harvard Institute of Economic Research, August 1979).

the short run, yet cannot give any commonly agreed upon reason for the assumption. Two promising, more or less competing, theories have been advanced to explain short-run price rigidities outside the full-employment equilibrium. One is the implicit or explicit contract theory advocated, for example, by Gordon; the other is the so-called theory of conjectural equilibria recently introduced by Hahn.[25]

Second, prices move in the long run and the mechanism that governs price adjustments under a disequilibrium setting is in no way self-evident, even if it is reasonable—at the present state of knowledge—to assume, as the authors do, that prices respond positively to increased excess demands. Needless to say, this is a field in which more successful work has yet to be done if this kind of short-run equilibrium theory is going to survive as a neo-Keynesian paradigm.

Third, the way in which the authors analyze how the market imbalances are affected may not be the most illuminating and realistic way of doing so. Instead of investigating how the market imbalances are affected in a "bang for the buck" comparison with equivalent net budgetary impact, one might compare the difference between the inflation pressure created by a targeted employment subsidy and that created by general government spending, when used to increase employment of the targeted group by a given number. Under so-called classical unemployment—that is, unemployment and excess demand for goods—this more "realistic" comparison of gross budgetary impact should of course be to the advantage of a targeted employment subsidy.

3. As for the authors' prescription for policy, their main point is that general government spending should be used at the bottom of the business cycle, possibly combined with a targeted employment subsidy to support the weak groups in the labor market when relative prices begin to matter again, whereas the subsidy should be substituted for government spending at the upturn of the cycle. At the peak of the cycle, when all markets are tight, neither an expansionary fiscal or monetary policy nor a targeted employment subsidy should be in force.

I feel that this prescription presents some unresolved practical problems even if the Burdett-Hool argument is convincing. One problem is of course the diagnostic problem. How will policymakers know when

25. Donald F. Gordon, "A Neo-Classical Theory of Keynesian Unemployment," *Economic Inquiry,* vol. 12 (December 1974), pp. 431–59; Frank Hahn, "On Non-Walrasian Equilibria," *Review of Economic Studies,* vol. 45 (February 1978), pp. 1–17.

unemployment is classical, in the sense that relative prices really matter to firms?

I find the authors' diagnostic tests satisfactory; namely, that the state of the product markets can be inferred from the movements of orders and backlogs, sales, or inventories and that the states of the labor market are indicated by unemployment and vacancy rates. It is worth noting that the tests are based on quantity adjustments, which, according to the short-run equilibrium paradigm, should be the first signs of changing market conditions.

Apart from the problem that the United States has, to my knowledge, no vacancy statistics, it might, however, already be too late by the time the illness is recognized. A difficult timing problem clearly remains: because of different kinds of lags, it is necessary to be able to know something about the future state of the economy in order to conduct an acceptable economic policy. This is particularly important when the economic-political means employed is nonrobust; that is, when it will not work under all kinds of unemployment regimes.

4. Another question is whether classical unemployment could really be observed very often. If one believes Malinvaud, then short-term fluctuations tend to favor states of general excess demand and states of general excess supply, and a targeted employment subsidy should be impotent most of the time. Malinvaud shows that short-term demand fluctuations favor those states, whereas technological and other kinds of supply effects could result in classical unemployment.

I would like to be less categorical than Malinvaud on this last point, even if I buy his argument that short-run demand fluctuations are more common than short-run technological changes. There are several reasons for my optimism.

First, it is obviously true that the labor market does not always clear in the neoclassical sense, but I think the proofs of a nonclearing market for goods, or at least of short-run price rigidities, are less convincing. If the market for goods clears while the labor market does not, then it is evident that relative prices matter to firms, and a targeted employment subsidy could be potent. It would increase the employment of the subsidized group, and it could increase employment of all groups provided it were combined with an expansion of demand.

Second, even if the market for goods does not clear in the short run, most firms would probably have some expectations of future relative prices, and it should be possible, even under a general excess supply situation (regime C), to affect their intertemporal production decisions.

Finally, in a small open economy like, for example, Sweden, there will always be a sector of the economy, sometimes of considerable size, where employment under unemployment conditions could be affected by a targeted employment subsidy. For firms in the export sector, under the small open economy assumption, face an infinitely elastic demand curve, and therefore real wages will matter as long as price covers variable costs. If, for example, a subsidy were used in regional policy, it could be very potent because of the small open-economy properties of the particular region. But then unemployment would be "exported," which could create political problems.

George E. Johnson

Allocative and Distributional Effects

The purpose of this paper is to investigate from a conceptual point of view the longer-term effects of a targeted employment subsidy program. Such a program is one of several instruments of labor market intervention that can be used to attempt to lower the overall unemployment rate without accelerating inflation.[1] To the extent that Congress was serious when it enacted the Full Employment and Balanced Growth Act of 1978—the Humphrey-Hawkins bill—which established a 4 percent goal for overall unemployment by 1983,[2] there will be considerable interest in the potential of these alternative labor market policies for permanent job creation. Moreover, if both the taxpayer rebellion and the low growth of per capita income continues during the 1980s, much attention will be paid to the cost effectiveness of the alternative instruments.

Several specific questions about the targeted employment subsidy approach follow directly from these concerns. The most important is, who (if anybody) should be eligible for the program? The answer depends on how well the labor market for different groups of workers adjusts in response to changes in relative demand and supply conditions—in other words, who are the problem groups of workers for which such adjustment does not readily occur? In the first section of this paper I set out three

Much of the initial work on this paper was supported by the U.S. Department of Labor. The attention to the partial coverage issue is entirely due to Robert I. Lerman. Some of the ideas on the optimal subsidy rate were developed jointly with Richard Layard of the London School of Economics. I have also benefited from the comments on an early draft of this paper by Robert H. Haveman, Orley C. Ashenfelter, and Donald A. Nichols.

1. The others include public service employment, training programs, labor market information, and the elimination of labor market rigidities (such as discrimination, legal minimum wages, and the system of income transfers to the nonemployed).

2. The date for achieving this goal was subsequently postponed to 1985.

alternative models of labor market equilibrium of individual labor force groups: (a) the *structural unemployment model,* in which the real wage rates of a group are not able to adjust (because of, for instance, legal minimum wages; (b) the *forward-rising supply curve unemployment model,* in which, for example, the labor supply of a group is lower than it would otherwise be because of income-dependent transfer programs (that is, the *induced unemployment model*); and (c) the *frictional unemployment model,* in which the wages of a group are free to adjust, so that, cyclical aberrations aside, it experiences only turnover unemployment and its labor supply elasticity is at most trivially different from zero. In my judgment, most segments of the labor force fit best into the last model, but some groups (for example, minority youth and recipients of aid to families with dependent children) may be best analyzed by the structural or induced unemployment models.

In the second section I discuss the likely effect of a targeted employment subsidy on the structure of employment. The most important point is that the program *must* be directed toward a problem population (that is, one characterized by structural or induced unemployment) if it is going to have any effect on employment and potential output. Proper targeting in this sense, however, is only a necessary condition for effectiveness. If the problem population is subject to structural unemployment (as opposed to induced unemployment), the program must also cover a large part of the problem population. Otherwise, it will redistribute a fixed level of employment only to those who are fortunate enough to be eligible for the program and away from those who are not. One must therefore conclude that when structural unemployment exists, public employment programs are potentially superior to employment subsidies because they can be more effectively targeted and their size more readily adjusted. If, on the other hand, the problem population is subject to induced unemployment, a targeted employment subsidy with partial coverage will be as cost effective as one with universal coverage. Another difficulty with the subsidy approach may occur if there are multiple problem populations. For example, teenagers may be subject to structural unemployment and low-skilled adults to induced unemployment. In that case a subsidy that is directed toward one group will worsen the employment situation of the other group if the two problem groups are substitutes in production.

It is important to note that answers to these behavioral questions, crucial in assessing the efficacy of the targeted employment subsidy approach, are still in doubt. No one has the detailed knowledge of the relevant labor market adjustment and demand parameters that are necessary to perform a reliable evaluation of what a particular subsidy can do, or, to move ahead several years, what a particular program, such as the targeted jobs tax credit, has done. This is, of course, also a problem in the evaluation of other labor market programs, like training and public service employment.

In the third section I examine normative questions about the optimal size of a subsidy program. Where structural unemployment of the problem group exists, the socially optimal subsidy is that value which reduces its unemployment rate to the frictional value during normal times. The labor groups and other factors that are not the recipients of the subsidy will benefit directly from such a program as long as there is an income-transfer program for the unemployed, but they will not want the subsidy rate to exceed the replacement ratio of the income-transfer program. These conclusions, however, depend on the assumption that groups in the labor market that are subject to structural unemployment can easily be identified. Such an assumption is questionable. If "the universe of need" cannot be identified precisely enough, a targeted employment subsidy is an inadequate weapon with which to fight structural unemployment.

The optimal subsidy rate to be paid to employers to hire workers afflicted by induced unemployment is, assuming that the other factors supply their services inelastically, equal to the replacement ratio of the income transfer program. The reason is that the income transfer program causes a distortion in the marginal valuation of leisure on the part of those eligible for it, and the subsidy should exactly compensate for this distortion. Assuming that the total cost of government is paid as a proportional tax by all other factors, the aggregate net income of all factors except the problem group is maximized when the subsidy rate equals the replacement ratio less the reciprocal of the labor supply elasticity of the problem group.

The final section of the paper presents the implications of the paper for the evaluation of the targeted jobs tax credit program.

Causes of High Unemployment Rates among Some Groups

Any analysis of the benefits and costs of a targeted employment subsidy program must follow from a careful specification of the operation of the labor markets of both the target population and those groups that are ineligible for the program but have characteristics that are somewhat like those of the target population. This is, as I argue later, difficult to do with any empirical precision, since economists still do not agree about how these markets work. The purpose of this section, therefore, is to set out alternative specifications of the operation of these labor markets, which will enable me to present a range of reasonable values for the benefit–cost ratio of budgetary resources devoted to a targeted employment subsidy.

Throughout the paper I assume that the overall unemployment rate equals its value consistent with nonaccelerating inflation. Most groups in the labor force—especially those with high levels of experience and training—are neither in excess demand nor in excess supply, but some groups in the labor force—youth, adults with low levels of experience and training, and the like—may be subject to high levels of frictional unemployment. Some or all of this problem population is the potential target of the employment subsidy. I concentrate on situations in which unemployment cannot be lowered by monetary or fiscal policy without causing excess demand in most labor markets and a consequent acceleration of inflation, since I regard the targeted employment subsidy as a quasi-permanent rather than a short-run countercyclical policy.

As mentioned before, I explore three different models of the high unemployment rate of a typical group in the problem population: (a) the structural unemployment model, (b) the forward-rising supply curve unemployment model, and (c) the frictional unemployment model. Each has a different set of implications about the cause of the high unemployment rate of the group, as well as about the efficacy of an employment subsidy targeted on the group.

The Structural Unemployment Model

A particular labor market group is subject to structural unemployment if its wage (either in real terms or in its value relative to the wages of a set of other groups) is, in periods of normal overall unemployment, not free to fall to the level consistent with frictional unemployment. In figure 1, the L_i curve (which need not be vertical) represents the supply of labor of group i (the typical problem group) adjusted for frictional unemployment. Because of structural rigidities—which could be caused by minimum wage legislation, union influence, custom, or some other force—the wage is fixed at W_i', thus creating involuntary unemployment of the group equal to $L_i - E_i'$.

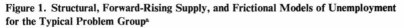

Figure 1. Structural, Forward-Rising Supply, and Frictional Models of Unemployment for the Typical Problem Group[a]

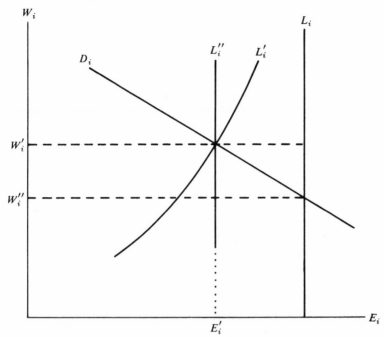

a. W_i, E_i, L_i, and D_i represent, respectively, the real wage, the employment level, the potential labor supply, and the demand for labor of group i.

An exogenous increase in the supply of the group, other factor inputs held constant, would shift the L_i curve to the right. Because the group's wage is institutionally fixed at W_i', employment cannot change. An increase in supply will therefore have no influence on the group's employment.

The Forward-Rising Supply Curve Unemployment Model

Here the explanation of the large observed gap between labor force and employment of the problem group rests on very different assumptions from those in the structural unemployment model. Because of the availability of income-dependent transfer programs (unemployment insurance, food stamps, welfare, and so on), the effective supply of labor of the group is reduced below what it would be without the programs, from L_i to L_i' in figure 1. The effective supply curve is upward sloping on the assumption that the benefit rate of these programs (π_i per unit of nonwork time) is fixed. Thus, as W_i rises relative to π_i, effective supply approaches what it would be if these programs were not available.[3] This type of unemployment can be termed "induced" unemployment; that is, it is caused by the existence of the income transfer programs.

A second variant of forward-rising supply curve unemployment is the Baily-Tobin model, in which the equilibrium unemployment rate of each group depends negatively on its wage relative to the wages of other groups.[4] Further, this specification is consistent with one in which the effective market labor supply depends positively on the wage relative to the returns to nonmarket activities (for example, petty crime).

A third variant is caused by wage rigidity for a *part* of the labor market for the problem group. Some jobs for which the problem group is eligible have relatively high, institutionally determined wages, but the wage rates of the jobs in the rest of the market are determined competitively. This may cause a high equilibrium rate of unemployment among those in the problem group who decide to join the queue for the high-paying jobs.[5] An increase in the wage of the lower-paying segment of the market will decrease the private returns to this type of job search and thus lower unemployment.

In these models an increase in the population of the group, other things equal, would be represented by a rightward shift in L_i by a certain proportion and a shift in the effective supply curve by the same proportion (such that the ratio $L_i - L_i'/L_i$ equals its initial value for all wage rates). This means that the equilibrium unemployment rate of the group would rise because of an increase in its population. However, because W_i falls to some extent, the increase in population would cause employment to increase above what it would have been otherwise.

3. See appendix B for a theoretical justification of the induced unemployment model.

4. The paper by Donald Nichols in this volume is based on the Baily-Tobin model. Martin Neil Baily and James Tobin, "The Inflation-Unemployment Consequences of Job Creation Policies," in John L. Palmer, ed., *Creating Jobs: Public Employment Programs and Wage Subsidies* (Brookings Institution, 1978), pp. 43–85.

5. For examples of this approach, see Mincer's analysis of minimum wages and Hall's analysis of the effects of unionism on unemployment. Jacob Mincer, "Unemployment Effects of Minimum Wages," *Journal of Political Economy,* vol. 84, pt. 2 (August 1976), pp. S87–S104; and Robert E. Hall, "The Rigidity of Wages and the Persistence of Unemployment," *Brookings Papers on Economic Activity, 2:1975,* pp. 301–49 (hereafter *BPEA*).

In subsequent discussion of the impact of a targeted employment subsidy, I consider only one variant of these models, the induced unemployment model. I do so because (a) the rationale for the kind of behavior assumed in the Baily-Tobin model is not convincing (unless it is the induced unemployment model as described above) and (b) the wage rigidity–search approach requires an analytical framework far too complicated for the present one. I therefore refer to the forward-rising supply curve model as the induced unemployment model, but it is important to remember that most of the conclusions about how employment and output will be affected by a targeted employment subsidy are the same in all three variants.

The Frictional Unemployment Model

A third possible reason for the high unemployment rate of the group in question is simply its extremely high job turnover due to weak labor force attachment. This explanation applies especially to teenagers—in general those still in school—and to part-year adult workers. As seen in figure 1, the frictional unemployment model can be represented by a vertical effective supply curve L_i'' that is well to the left of the L_i curve, which is the labor force adjusted for the extent of frictional unemployment associated with groups with a strong labor force attachment.

As in the induced unemployment model—but not in the structural unemployment model—the wage W_i' represents the equality of demand and effective supply. Unemployment of group i could not be reduced permanently by reducing the wage to W_i''; because of the high job turnover of the group, this reduction would create excessive job vacancies and lead to a restoration of the initial wage. An increase in the population of the group would be represented by proportional rightward shifts in both the L_i' and L_i'' curves, which would cause employment to increase in the same proportion and the equilibrium wage to fall.

Testing between the Explanations

These three alternative explanations of the cause of unemployment among the typical problem group have different implications about the benefits and costs of a targeted employment subsidy. It would be useful, therefore, to be able to separate all conceivable subsets of the labor force into the alternative explanations. In principle, this can be done by estimating the effect of proportionate changes in the potential labor force of each group on the proportionate changes in the group's employment. As seen in figure 1, each of the three models has a different implication about the effect of an increase of L_i on E_i. Algebraically, this effect may be represented as

$$\text{(1)} \qquad \frac{\Delta E_i}{E_i} = \lambda_i \frac{\Delta L_i}{L_i} + c_i,$$

where c_i represents several other variables, primarily common to all groups and interacted with $1 - \lambda_i$, and where λ_i is the proportionate increase in employment due to an increase in the potential labor force of the group, or coefficient of labor market adjustment. The three models of the equilibrium of labor market i have different implications about the value of λ_i. For the structural unemployment model, λ_i equals zero; that is, changes in the potential labor force of a group characterized by institutionally fixed relative or real wages have no effect on that group's employment. At the other extreme, for the frictional unemployment model, λ_i equals one; that is, a change in the potential labor force causes a proportionate change in the employment of group i. For the induced unemployment model, the value of λ_i is between zero and one. In this case, λ_i is

$$\text{(2)} \qquad \lambda_i = \frac{\eta_i}{\eta_i + \epsilon_i},$$

where η_i is the (absolute) wage elasticity of demand for the employment of group i and ϵ_i the wage elasticity of effective labor supply.[6]

Several attempts have been made to estimate λ_i's along demographic lines. With the use of age-race-sex breakdowns, clear evidence has

6. Let L_i be the potential labor force of the group and E_i the employment level. The proportionate change in effective supply is $d(\log E_i) = d(\log L_i) + \epsilon_i d(\log W_i)$, and the proportionate change in employment demand is $d(\log E_i) = -\eta_i d(\log W_i) + c_i'$, where c_i' reflects technological change and the growth in other factor supplies. Solving for $d(\log E_i)$ yields

$$d(\log E_i) = \frac{\eta_i}{\eta_i + \epsilon_i} d(\log L_i) + \frac{\eta_i}{\eta_i + \epsilon_i} c_i',$$

$$= \lambda_i d(\log L_i) + (1 - \lambda_i)c_i',$$

which is analogous to equation 1.

emerged that the relative wages of most individual demographic groups *do* adjust negatively to changes in relative supplies between periods of "normal" unemployment.[7] Gordon concluded that the extent of the adjustment of wages for secondary workers is about half that necessary to keep their unemployment rates at their equilibrium levels, which is consistent with a value of λ_i for secondary workers of about 0.5. Johnson and Blakemore, on the other hand, obtained estimates of λ_i much closer to unity for all groups except minority teenagers. A recent paper by Morse, which focused specifically on youth, suggested that the labor market for white teenagers is better described by the simple competitive model than by either the structural or forward-rising supply curve unemployment models.[8] The market for black teenagers, on the other hand, is best described by some variant of the forward-rising model.

It should be stressed that the problem of determining the appropriate disaggregation of the aggregate labor force into the various *i* groups is an unsettled question in labor economics. Ideally, one would split the labor force into all subgroups that are "almost identical" with each other (or, as in the approach of appendix A, perfect substitutes for one another). But because of data limitations and econometric difficulties, this is at present impossible. Hence questions like "How much structural and induced unemployment is there?" or "What is the potential of employment policy?" cannot be answered with precision. I believe the historical experience of the U.S. labor market decisively refutes the view that there has been much structural or induced unemployment.

7. See Robert J. Gordon, "Structural Unemployment and the Productivity of Women," in Karl Brunner and Allan H. Metzler, eds., *Stabilization of the Domestic and International Economy,* Carnegie-Rochester Conference Series on Public Policy, vol. 5 (Amsterdam: North Holland, 1977), pp. 181–229; Michael L. Wachter, "The Changing Cyclical Responsiveness of Wage Inflation," *BPEA, 1:1976,* pp. 115–59; and George E. Johnson and Arthur Blakemore, "The Potential Impact of Employment Policy on the Unemployment Rate Consistent with Nonaccelerating Inflation," *American Economic Review,* vol. 69 (May 1979, *Papers and Proceedings, 1978*), pp. 119–23.

8. Larry C. Morse, "Teenage Unemployment and Relative Wage Adjustment," Working Paper 124 (Industrial Relations Section, Princeton University, July 1979). See also Donald Nichols's paper in this volume; Arnold H. Packer, "Employment Guarantees Should Replace the Welfare System," *Challenge,* vol. 17 (March–April 1974), pp. 21–27; Ryuzo Sato and Tetsunori Koizumi, "On the Elasticities of Substitution and Complementarity," *Oxford Economic Papers,* vol. 25 (March 1973), pp. 44–56.

Impact of a Targeted Employment Subsidy
on Employment and Potential Output

The effects of a targeted employment subsidy on equilibrium employment and output depend on the nature of the unemployment problem of both the target population and the people in the labor force who are similar to the target population but ineligible for the program. Put differently, the likely impact depends on the extent to which the program covers all people who belong to groups that incur significant structural or induced unemployment. I ended the previous section by mentioning the considerable uncertainty that exists about how to identify these people empirically. In this section, therefore, I indicate how the effects of an employment subsidy vary with the degree to which it is effectively targeted.

Universal Coverage of All Persons Subject to Nonfrictional Unemployment

First, assume that there is a group of potential workers, arbitrarily designated as group 1, whose human capital is so low that all cannot be employed at the institutionally fixed minimum wage $\bar{W}_1$. This is the structural unemployment model. The other groups in the labor force, arrayed in order of ascending skill from 2 to N, are assumed both to be fully employed and to supply their services inelastically.

If all group 1 persons, a total equal to L_1, are eligible to participate in the targeted employment subsidy program, the employment and output effects of the program are straightforward. Since employers receive an effective subsidy of $s_1 \bar{W}_1$ for each group 1 worker they hire, the marginal costs of that type of worker are reduced by $100s_1$ percent. This means that the demand curve for the L_1s is shifted to the right by a proportion equal to $\eta_1 s_1$, where η_1 is the absolute wage elasticity of demand for that group. This is shown in figure 2 as the shift in the demand curve from $D_1(W_1)$ to $D_1[W_1(1 - s_1)]$. If the initial wage, W_1' in figure 2, is fixed at $\bar{W}_1$, the program causes an employment increase of $\Delta E_1 = E_1''' - E_1' = \eta_1 E_1' s_1$.

The budgetary cost of the program is $B_1 = s_1 W_1 E_1$. Thus the approximate cost per unit of net job creation is[9]

9. The actual budgetary cost per job of the program is
$$\frac{B_1}{\Delta E_1} = \frac{\bar{W}_1}{\eta_1}(1 + s_1),$$
which equals equation 1 for small subsidy rates.

Figure 2. Effects of a Targeted Employment Subsidy on Workers Subject to Nonfrictional Unemployment

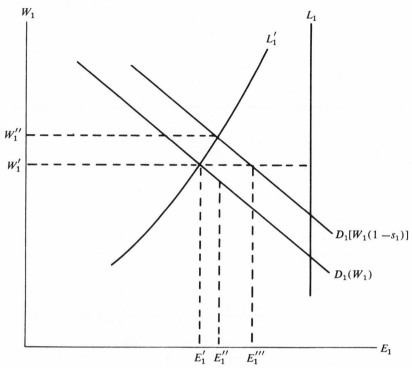

a. The subsidy rate for each gr oup 1 worker is denoted by s_1.

$$(3) \qquad \frac{B_1}{\Delta E_1} = \frac{\bar{W}_1}{\eta_1}.$$

The increase in potential output per unit of job creation is approximately equal to the wage of the L_1s, $\bar{W}_1$. Thus the increase in potential output (y) per unit of budgetary expenditure is $\bar{W}_1$ times the reciprocal of equation 1, or $y/B_1 = \eta_1$, which means that potential output will rise by more (less) than the budgetary cost of the program if the elasticity of labor demand for the target group is greater (less) than one.

Second, assume that the labor market for the L_1s is described by the induced unemployment model rather than by the structural unemployment model. Now the initial wage W_1' reflects the intersection of the effective labor supply curve L_1' in figure 2. The targeted employment subsidy causes the wage of group 1 workers to increase from W_1' to W_1'' and their employment to increase from E_1' to E_1''. The net increase in employment is

(4) $$\Delta E_1 = \frac{\epsilon_1 \eta_1}{\eta_1 + \epsilon_1} E_1' s_1,$$

where ϵ_1 is the wage elasticity of effective labor supply. The subsidy is obviously the more effective in increasing the employment of the target group the higher the elasticity of supply (the flatter the L_1' curve in figure 1). For a small value of the subsidy rate, the approximate cost of one unit of net additional job creation is $W_1 E_1'$ divided by equation 2, or

(5) $$\frac{B_1}{\Delta E_1} = \frac{W_1(\eta_1 + \epsilon_1)}{\epsilon_1 \eta_1}.$$

Notice that as the supply curve becomes perfectly flat ($\epsilon_1 = \infty$) the cost effectiveness of the subsidy under the induced unemployment model approaches that of the structural unemployment model given by equation 3. Of course, as the labor market for the target group approaches the simple competitive model ($\epsilon_1 = 0$), net job creation becomes rather expensive.

To give an idea of the range of values of the cost of creating an additional job by a targeted employment subsidy with universal coverage, I have calculated the value of equation 3 for selected values of η_1 and ϵ_1. First, direct estimates of the demand elasticity for specific labor market groups vary enormously, for the methods of estimating all the relevant cross partial elasticities of substitution are severely limited by data availability. Though values ranging from 0.5 to 2 for η_1 are used in table 1, the most likely value is about 1.5. The plausible values of ϵ range from zero to infinity, and the range used in the table reflects this. If the labor market for L_1s is best described by the minimum wage model (that is, $\epsilon_1 = \infty$), the budgetary cost per unit of net job creation is less (greater) than the wage rate as the demand elasticity is greater (less) than unity. With a finite value of ϵ_1, however, the condition for this to be true is obviously more stringent, for by equation 5 the ratio $B_1/\Delta E_1 < W_1$ only if $\eta_1 > \epsilon_1/(\epsilon_1 - 1)$, satisfaction of which necessarily requires that both η_1 and ϵ_1 are greater than one.

It is interesting to compare the cost effectiveness of a targeted employment subsidy with that of its leading competitor in the employment policy area, public service employment. Assuming that in the latter all the

Table 1. Budgetary Cost per Unit of Net Job Creation Due to a Targeted Employment Subsidy, for Selected Values of Demand and Supply Elasticities of Target Group[a]

Dollars

Demand elasticity for employment (η_1)	Supply elasticity of labor (ϵ_1)			
	0.25	1	2	∞
0.5	36,000	18,000	15,000	12,000
1.0	30,000	12,000	9,000	6,000
1.5	28,000	10,000	7,000	4,000
2.0	27,000	3,000	6,000	3,000

Source: Author's calculations.
a. Annual wage = $6,000.

participants (whose number is P_1) are taken from the ranks of the L_1s and receive the same wage as in the private sector, an additional participant in the program reduces the effective supply of labor to the private sector by one. By the structural unemployment model, this increases the total employment of the L_1s by one, and the cost per unit of net job creation is simply W_1. By the induced unemployment model, an additional participant shifts the effective supply curve to the private sector by one and thus drives up the wage rate (however incrementally) and reduces private sector employment of the L_1s. The budgetary cost of an additional unit of net job creation is thus

$$(6) \qquad \frac{B_1^{PSE}}{\Delta E_1 + \Delta P_1} = \frac{W_1(\eta_1 + \epsilon_1)}{\epsilon_1}.$$

When this result is compared with 5, the implication is that, given the assumption of perfect targeting of both programs (as well as costless administration of both programs), the targeted employment subsidy approach is superior (inferior) to the public service employment approach on the basis of cost effectiveness if the private sector demand elasticity is greater (less) than one.

In most problems considered throughout the paper I continue to assume that the other groups of workers supply their services inelastically. This assumption is convenient for analysis and, as an approximation, correct on empirical grounds but is not necessary. If it is assumed that there is one other group of workers (the E_2s), which (a) is fully employed, (b) has a labor supply elasticity of ϵ_2, and (c) pays all the taxes in the economy,[10] the budgetary cost of a targeted employment subsidy per unit of net job creation of the problem group is

$$(7) \qquad \frac{B_1}{\Delta E_1} = \frac{W_1}{\epsilon_1 \eta_1} \left[\eta_1 + \epsilon_1 + \epsilon_2 \frac{E_1}{E_2} \left(\frac{1 - \rho \epsilon_2}{1 - \frac{t}{1-t} \epsilon_2} \right) \right],$$

where $\rho = \pi / W_1$ is the replacement ratio of the income-transfer program. If $\epsilon_2 = 0$, equation 7 reduces to equation 5.

As shown in the next section, the taxpaying factors gain (lose) from a targeted employment subsidy on the E_1s as $\rho \epsilon_1$ is greater (less) than one. If the supply elasticity of the E_2s is positive, a subsidy is less (more) expensive if it yields a profit (loss) to taxpayers. On the other hand, if ϵ_2 is less than zero, these conclusions are reversed. However, because E_1 is likely to be small relative to E_2 (in addition to the likelihood that ϵ_2 is small), the quantitative magnitude of this effect is probably trivial.

Incorrect Targeting and Partial Coverage

The targeting of an employment subsidy may be imperfect for two reasons. First, its rules may be such that it provides subsidies to some people who are not in fact subject to structural or induced unemployment, and second, it may not cover all those who belong to the population subject to these types of unemployment.

The first imperfection is easy to handle. If, for example, some people who are in fact L_2s are certified eligible, they will receive an income transfer under the program, but output and employment will be unaffected. By assumption the L_2s are fully employed and supply their services inelastically, so the initial wage is W_2' and the initial employment is equal to L_2 (see figure 3). If L_2' of the group 2 workers are eligible for the subsidy, employers will bid for their services until their wage rises by the amount of the subsidy, $W_2'' - W_2'$. Thus the shaded area of figure 3 represents both the gain to those L_2s mistakenly made eligible and the cost to taxpayers of the mistake. If all the true L_1s were also covered by the subsidy, the effect on E_1 per budgetary dollar *correctly* allocated would be identical to

10. In appendix C, I set out the algebra of this model. For another paper based on this approach, see John H. Bishop, "The General Equilibrium Impact of Alternative Antipoverty Strategies," *Industrial and Labor Relations Review*, vol. 32 (January 1979), pp. 205–23.

Figure 3. Effects of a Targeted Employment Subsidy in the Case of Incorrect Targeting of Workers Subject to Nonfrictional Unemployment

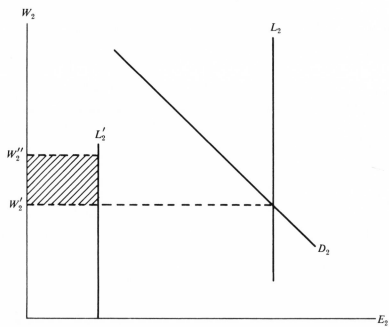

that derived in the preceding subsection. However, if μL_2s are deemed eligible for each L_1, then the budgetary cost per unit of net job creation, given by equation 3, must be multiplied by $1 + \mu$.

The effects of a targeted employment subsidy that covers only part of the problem population of the L_1 group depend on whether the structural unemployment or induced unemployment model is the correct diagnosis of the malaise in that market. With the former model, the effects of the program on employment and potential output depend on how many of the L_1s are covered relative to both the initial employment level (E_1' in figure 4) and the employment level that would prevail under the subsidy given universal coverage (E_1''). If the number of L_1s covered is less than E_1', as is the case with L_1' eligibles in figure 4, the program has no effect on the total employment of the L_1s. As with the L_2s who may mistakenly be deemed eligible for the subsidy, employers give first preference to the L_1s who are eligibles and then bid among themselves for this restricted pool. This means that excess unemployment of the eligibles will disappear, and their wage will be bid up to $W_1' = \bar{W}_1/(1 - s_1)$. The L_1s who are not

Figure 4. Effects of a Targeted Employment Subsidy in the Case of Incomplete Coverage of Workers Subject to Nonfrictional Unemployment

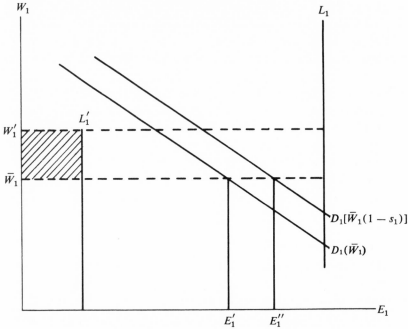

covered will suffer increased unemployment, but, as long as $L_1' < E_1'$, some of them will continue to be employed at a wage $\bar{W}_1$.

If the number of eligibles exceeds $E_1'' = E_1' (1 + \eta_1)s_1$, which is the employment level that would occur if the subsidy covered all L_1s, the employment subsidy has the same effect on total employment as it does under universal coverage. The wage remains at $\bar{W}_1$, and all the ineligibles who were employed before the program began are no longer employed.

These arguments imply that for the structural unemployment model a targeted employment subsidy is ineffective as a job creation device unless it covers more of the problem population than were employed at the initial level. A small program (in this sense) merely redistributes the fixed number of jobs from the ineligibles to the eligibles. It should be pointed out that the per-unit net employment creation potential of a similarly targeted public service employment program is (over the relevant range) independent of the scale of the program. Nonparticipants, in fact, have a better chance of finding jobs in the private sector labor market because the program participants have been removed from the market. Thus if it is difficult to identify the members who are subject to structural unemployment, a properly targeted public service employment program would, on this basis, be superior to a targeted employment subsidy.[11]

For the induced unemployment model, the conclusions about the net employment effects of a targeted subsidy under partial coverage are very different from those derived for the structural unemployment model. Only L_1' of the L_1 members of the problem population are eligible for the subsidy, and profit-maximizing employers bid among themselves to hire as many eligibles as they can. This drives up the wage of the eligibles and thus increases their effective supply and employment. As more eligibles are employed, some ineligibles become unemployed and their wage falls. Such an adjustment process continues until the wage paid by firms that employ ineligibles equals the wage paid by firms that employ ineligibles divided by $1 - s_1$.

Therefore, in equilibrium the eligibles will be spending more of their time in employment and the ineligibles less of their time in employment. But because there is a net subsidy to employers as a whole, the wage of eligibles will rise by more than the fall in the wage of ineligibles, and consequently the increased employment of the eligibles will outweigh the decreased employment of the ineligibles.[12] The changes in the employment levels of L_1s covered by the targeted employment subsidy (E_{1c}) and those uncovered (E_{1u}) per unit of expenditure on the program are given by

(8)
$$\frac{\Delta E_{1c}}{B_1} = \frac{\epsilon_1[\eta_1 + \epsilon_1(1 - k)]}{(\eta_1 + \epsilon_1)W_1}$$

$$\frac{\Delta E_{1u}}{B_1} = - \frac{\epsilon_1^2(1 - k)}{(\eta_1 + \epsilon_1)W_1},$$

where $k = E_{1c}/(E_{1c} + E_{1u})$ is the fraction of the L_1s covered by the program. The net effect of the subsidy on job creation is the sum of these two

11. This would also be true of temporary employment programs to combat cyclical unemployment.

12. Consider a program in which the subsidy of the employment of the eligibles was financed entirely by a tax on employers of the ineligibles. Then the supply reduction of the ineligibles would exactly offset the supply increase on the part of the eligibles. The financing of the targeted employment subsidy described above comes from outside the labor market for the L_1s—from exactly where is discussed in the next section—and thus increases *net* employment.

Table 2. Effects of a Targeted Employment Subsidy Expenditure of $6 Million (1,000 Jobs) on the Employment of Covered and Uncovered Members of Problem Group, for Selected Values of Demand and Supply Elasticities and Coverage Rate[a]

Demand elasticity of labor (η_1) and problem group	Change in employment level								
	$k = 0.25$			$k = 0.50$			$k = 0.75$		
	$\epsilon_1 = 0.25$	$\epsilon_1 = 1$	$\epsilon_1 = 2$	$\epsilon_1 = 0.25$	$\epsilon_1 = 1$	$\epsilon_1 = 2$	$\epsilon_1 = 0.25$	$\epsilon_1 = 1$	$\epsilon_1 = 2$
0.5									
Covered members	230	833	1,600	209	666	1,200	188	500	800
Uncovered members	−63	−500	−1,200	−42	−333	−800	−21	−167	−400
1.0									
Covered members	238	875	1,667	225	750	1,334	213	625	1,000
Uncovered members	−38	−375	−1,000	−25	−250	−667	−13	−125	−333
1.5									
Covered members	241	900	1,714	232	800	1,428	223	700	1,143
Uncovered members	−27	−300	−857	−18	−200	−571	−9	−100	−286
2.0									
Covered members	243	917	1,750	236	834	1,500	229	750	1,250
Uncovered members	−21	−250	−750	−14	−167	−500	−7	−83	−250

Source: Author's calculations.
a. The coverage rate is denoted by k; and the supply elasticity of labor by ϵ_1.

effects, and the reciprocal of the result is the budgetary cost of the program per unit of net job creation, which is equal to equation 5, its value under universal coverage.

The impact of a targeted employment subsidy on the employment of the eligibles equals the net employment effect, $\epsilon_1 \eta_1 / (\eta_1 + \epsilon_1)$, per W_1 of budgetary cost, plus the employment loss of the ineligibles, $\epsilon_1^2 (1 - k) / (\eta_1 + \epsilon_1)$, per W_1 spent on the program. The latter effect, the degree to which the eligibles displace the ineligibles from existing jobs, is the greater the larger the supply elasticity (ϵ_1) is and the smaller the demand elasticity (η_1) and coverage rate (k) are. To discern the range of the possible quantitative magnitude of these two effects, I computed the changes in employment levels of eligibles and ineligibles for a budget of $6 million, which at $W_1 = \$6,000$ is the wage bill associated with 1,000 jobs (see table 2). The values of demand and supply elasticities have the same range as in table 1. The fraction of the problem population eligible for the program is arbitrarily set at 0.25, 0.50, or 0.75. The effect of the subsidy at, for example, $k = 0.25$, $\epsilon_1 = 0.25$, and $\eta_1 = 0.5$ is 230 on the employment of eligibles and -63 on the employment of ineligibles. This is a net employment effect of 167, or a budgetary cost of $36,000 per job created (see table 1). A perusal of table 2 suggests that for small values of η_1 and k and a large value of ϵ_1 the displacement effect can be larger than the net employment effect of the program.

Multiple Problem Populations

The above analysis assumes that those in the problem population who are covered and those not covered are perfect substitutes in the production process. I now change this assumption and specify two distinct groups of workers that are subject to structural or induced unemployment. It is, for example, often alleged that wage subsidies directed to teenagers (like the targeted jobs tax credit) will increase their employment at the expense of the employment of low-skilled adults and, likewise, that a private sector wage subsidy tied to a welfare reform program will exacerbate the problem of youth unemployment. These allegations actually contain some strong assumptions about the operation of the two labor markets *and* of the joint role of these two types of labor in the production process, and it is interesting to see just what these assumptions are.

I first assume that there are two separate groups that are subject to labor market difficulties. The employment levels of the two groups are E_1 and E_2. The supply elasticities of these two groups are ϵ_1 and ϵ_2, and I continue to assume that the supplies of the other factors of production are fixed (that is, the other elasticities are all zero). The final important feature of the problem is the effect of increases in the employment of one group on the employment demand curve of the other group. This is represented by the partial elasticity of complementarity (C_{12}) between the two groups; C_{12} is positive if they are complementary to each other and negative if they are substitutable for each other in the production process.[13]

A subsidy placed on one group will increase that group's employment by driving up its wage, but, depending on the sign of C_{12}, it will increase or decrease the employment of the other group. In general, the change in the employment level of each group in response to a subsidy on the other groups is

$$(9) \qquad \Delta E_1 = \frac{\epsilon_1(1 - \alpha_2 C_{22}\epsilon_2)}{A}\frac{B_1}{W_1} + \frac{\alpha_1 C_{12}\epsilon_1\epsilon_2}{A}\frac{W_2}{W_1}\frac{B_2}{W_2}$$

$$\Delta E_2 = \frac{\alpha_2 C_{12}\epsilon_1\epsilon_2}{A}\frac{W_1}{W_2}\frac{B_1}{W_1} + \frac{\epsilon_2(1 - \alpha_1 C_{11}\epsilon_1)}{A}\frac{B_2}{W_2},$$

where B_1 and B_2 are the budgets of the two subsidy programs, α_1 and α_2 are the output share of the two groups, and $A = 1 + \epsilon_1\epsilon_2(C_{11}C_{22} - C_{12}^2) - \alpha_1 C_{11}\epsilon_1 - \alpha_2 C_{22}\epsilon_2 > 0$. In the event that $\epsilon_2 = 0$, which is the case of universal coverage of all people subject to nonfrictional unemployment, equation 9 reduces to equation 5 because $\alpha_1 C_{11} = -1/\eta_1$. If the E_1s and E_2s are perfect substitutes in the production process ($C_{11} = C_{22} = C_{12}$) and have the same supply elasticities ($\epsilon_1 = \epsilon_2$), equation 9 reduces to equation 8, which is the partial coverage case (where the E_1s are covered and the E_2s are not).

The most important implication of equation 6 is that a subsidy on one of the groups *need not* imply a decrease in the employment of the other group, for C_{12} may be positive. To take a relevant example, suppose that the E_1s are teenagers and the E_2s low-skilled adults (or, more precisely, the population of potential welfare recipients). It could be argued that a subsidy on teenagers would cause employers to substitute them for adult labor, a clear case of $C_{12} < 0$. But it could also be argued that the lower costs to employers due to the subsidy would *increase* the demand for

13. In appendix A, I review the economics of complementarity in detail.

adults. For example, if the fast food industry expands because youth labor is cheaper, the demand for adult labor during the breakfast and lunch shifts will increase (because most teenagers are in school). Thus it is not obvious on conceptual grounds that these two types of labor are close substitutes.

One special case of the multiple problem group model was implicit in the discussions on welfare reform during the Carter administration, and was advocated, in particular, by representatives of the Department of Labor.[14] It is interesting because it helps to explain that administration's policy on welfare reform proposals, youth employment, and the adminis-tration of the targeted jobs tax credit program. Its major assumptions are that teenagers and low-skilled adults are perfect substitutes (that is, $C_{11} = C_{22} = C_{12} = C$), teenage labor is supplied very elastically ($\epsilon_1 = \infty$), and the supply elasticity of low-skilled adults is positive but finite ($0 < \epsilon_2 < \infty$). With these assumptions, the employment effects of the two potential employment subsidies—one targeted on youths, the other on low-wage adults—become

$$(10) \qquad \Delta E_1 = \frac{1}{\gamma} [\eta_u + (1 - \gamma)\epsilon_2] \frac{B_1}{W_1} - \epsilon_2 \frac{W_2}{W_1} \frac{B_2}{W_2}$$

$$\Delta E_2 = -\frac{1 - \gamma}{\gamma} \epsilon_2 \frac{W_1}{W_2} \frac{B_1}{W_1} + \epsilon_2 \frac{B_2}{W_2},$$

where $\gamma = \alpha_1/(\alpha_1 + \alpha_2)$ is teenagers' relative share of the unskilled wage bill and $\eta_u = -1/(\alpha_1 + \alpha_2)$ is the elasticity of demand for unskilled labor services. For increasing total employment, the subsidy targeted on teen-age workers is clearly superior to one targeted on low-wage adults. The second subsidy increases adult employment by ϵ_2 times the "number of jobs" the program could hypothetically buy, but it decreases teenage em-ployment by this amount times W_2/W_1, which is greater than one if adults are more efficient than teenagers. Thus an employment subsidy for low-skilled adults would, by the low-wage labor model implicit in the Depart-

14. The original published statement of what eventually became the Carter ad-ministration's proposed Program for Better Jobs and Income is by Arnold Packer. See his "Employment Guarantees." The specific assumptions about the partial elas-ticities of complementarity are my recollection of the welfare reform meetings of 1977–78. For evidence that the partial elasticity of complementarity between teenage and adult female labor is negative, see James H. Grant and Daniel S. Hamermesh, "Labor Market Competition Among Youths, White Women and Others," National Bureau of Economic Research Working Paper 519 (NBER, July 1980).

ment of Labor position, cause a slight reduction in total employment. An employment subsidy for teenage workers, on the other hand, would have a longer positive effect on E_1 than a negative effect on E_2. The effect of the two targeted employment subsidies on potential output (Q) is

(11) $Q = W_1 \Delta E_1 + W_2 \Delta E_2$

$$= \frac{1}{\gamma} \left[\eta_u + (1 - \gamma)\epsilon_2 \left(1 - \frac{W_1}{W_2} \right) \right] B_1 - \epsilon_2 \left(\frac{W_2}{W_1} - 1 \right) B_2 .$$

The coefficient on B_1 is always positive; the coefficient on B_2 is negative if $W_2 > W_1$. But the loss of adult employment may involve additional costs (such as family instability) that far outweigh the beneficial employment and output effects of a program like the targeted jobs tax credit.

Another option is to employ some low-skilled adults in a public service employment program, to get them out of the private sector labor market altogether. Since each additional adult public service job causes adult private sector employment to fall by one, teenage employment increases by W_2/W_1 per public service job. In terms of equation 11, then, such a program causes no loss of private sector jobs; the additional public output is produced at zero social cost. Hence, in the Department of Labor framework, public service employment is clearly a better device for adults than the targeted employment subsidy approach.

These conclusions do not follow, however, if teenagers and low-skilled adults are not perfect substitutes. If, for example, C_{12} is close to zero, then each participant in the public service employment program displaces $\eta_2/(\eta_2 + \epsilon_2)$ of a private sector adult employee, but teenage employment does not change as a result of the program. In this case an employment subsidy targeted on teenagers would be more cost effective than a public service employment program if the wage elasticity of labor demand exceeded unity. Similarly, as pointed out earlier, some evidence exists that the labor market for most teenagers (minority youth being the possible exception) is not characterized by the sort of wage rigidity consistent with $\epsilon_1 = \infty$.

Several extensions of this approach are possible, but they lead to conclusions about the effectiveness of a targeted employment subsidy that are similar to those of the partial coverage models. Specifically, one cannot tell just what will happen unless detailed information on both supply and complementarity elasticities are available.

The Optimal Size of a Targeted Employment Subsidy

In the preceding section I examined the effects of a targeted employment subsidy on the equilibrium level of employment in the economy under several alternative assumptions about the kind of unemployment problem and the degree of universality of the subsidy. The purpose of this section is to set out a framework for answering normative questions about this approach: under what conditions "should" a particular targeted employment subsidy program be established?

Structural Unemployment

How large should the subsidy rate be in the presence of structural unemployment of the problem group? At first glance the answer is straightforward. Since the marginal value of the leisure of the problem group is by definition less than the wage, the subsidy should be increased until these are brought into equilibrium. In figure 5 the waged is fixed at $\bar{W}_1$ rather than at the competitive equilibrium value W_1'. The subsidy rate should, then, be set equal to

$$(12) \qquad\qquad s = \frac{\bar{W}_1 - W_1'}{\bar{W}_1},$$

so that E_1 rises to L_1.

A major factor (indeed, some would argue, the *sole* factor) in deciding whether or not to introduce a targeted employment subsidy under these circumstances is the question of who incurs the costs and benefits of the program. I shall assume that all government spending is paid for by a proportional tax on the income of all the other factors. Total government spending is then equal to

$$(13) \qquad\qquad G = \pi(L_1 - E_1) + sW_1E_1 + G_0,$$

where G_0 is the total level of government spending on other than social programs. The first term on the right-hand side of 13 is the cost of the unemployment insurance program, the second term the cost of the subsidy program. On the standard assumption that the aggregate production function for the economy is of the constant returns variety (that is, linear

Figure 5. Distributional Implications of a Targeted Employment Subsidy under Structural Unemployment[a]

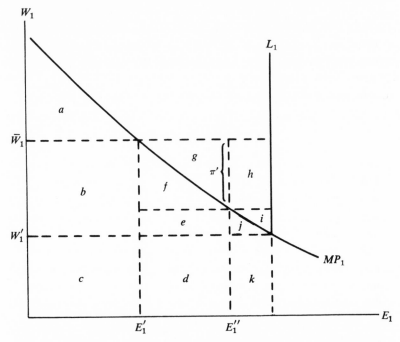

a. MP_1 denotes the marginal product of group 1, and π is the transfer payment to the unemployed.

homogeneous), the gross earnings of the taxpaying factors (that is, all but the E_1s) equal total output less the value added by the E_1s, that is

$$(14) \qquad\qquad Q_0 = Q - (1 - s)\bar{W}_1 E_1,$$

where Q is total output. Their income is their gross income less the cost of government, or 14 less 13:

$$(15) \qquad\qquad I_0 = Q_0 - G$$

$$= Q - \bar{W}_1 E_1 - \pi(L_1 - E_1) - G_0.$$

The total net income of the L_1s is their employment income plus their transfer income,

$$(16) \qquad\qquad I_1 = \bar{W}_1 E_1 + (L_1 - E_1).$$

Adding 15 and 16 gives aggregate disposable income, $Q - G_0$. I hereafter assume that G_0 is fixed.

To maximize Q, the government should obviously introduce a subsidy of a scale implied by equation 12; that is, all the unemployed L_1s would be hired. The L_1s are obviously better off with a subsidy so long as the replacement ratio is positive. The other productive factors, however, may not desire such a large subsidy. As E_1 increases, the net income of the other factors, given by equation 15, changes by

(17) $$\frac{\Delta I_0}{\Delta E_1} = MP_1 - \bar{W}_1 + \pi,$$

where MP_1 is the marginal product of the E_1s. At the initial employment level, E_1' in figure 5, the subsidy is zero and $MP_1 = \bar{W}_1$. A subsidy at this point increases E_1, and increases I_0 if there is a positive unemployment insurance benefit. The taxpaying factors will choose, solely on income-maximizing grounds, a subsidy rate that yields full employment if $\Delta I_0/\Delta E_1$ is not negative at $E_1 = L_1$. Otherwise, the subsidy rate desired by the taxpaying factors is equal to $\rho = \pi/W_1$, the replacement ratio of the income transfer program, since $MP_1 = W_1(1 - s_1)$.

The distributional implications of a targeted employment subsidy under structural unemployment are easily seen in the Harberger-type diagram in figure 5. The size of the payment to the unemployed L_1s is π', which is constructed so that it is less than $\bar{W}_1 - W_1'$. A subsidy of $s\bar{W}_1 = \pi'$ per worker increases employment of the problem group from E_1' to E_1''. The net income of the L_1s then increases by the difference between the increase in their labor earnings and the reduction in their transfer income, areas $d + e$. The cost of the program to the taxpaying factors is exactly offset by the reduction in the cost of the transfer program, but their gross earnings increase by area f (because their wages are driven up). Thus both the L_1s and the taxpaying factors gain by the targeted employment subsidy.

A further increase in the subsidy rate to that implied by equation 12 does not improve the welfare of both groups. The net income of the L_1s increases by area $i + j + k$. The increase in the cost of the program, $h + i + j$, is offset only by the reduction in transfer payments, h, plus the increase in the other factors' gross earnings, j. Hence the taxpayers lose area i because of the expansion. But since total output increases by area $j + k$, it might be possible to reduce $\bar{W}_1$ legislatively so that both groups benefit.

These conclusions need several qualifications. First, if the subsidy does not cover a sufficiently large fraction of the problem group, it does not, as was shown in the section on targeting and coverage, yield an increase in output. It will represent only a zero-sum transfer from the taxpayers and the unemployed L_1s to those in the problem group who are lucky to find jobs. The "optimal" subsidy rate in this case is zero—that is, no program at all.

Second, it is not necessarily true that *each* of the taxpaying factors is a net gainer from the imposition of the subsidy, even if the income transfer system involves large payments. For some factors (say, semiskilled workers) may be substitutes for the problem group in the sense discussed in the section on multiple problem population. To the extent that the subsidy increased the employment of unskilled labor, it would lower the wages of semiskilled workers. More skilled workers would gain more than their share, but this would be small compensation to the representatives of the semiskilled.[15] Indeed, if a policy were devised to maximize the net earnings of the groups that, though fully employed, are substitutable for low-skilled labor in the production process, it would involve negative subsidies on employment of the competition. Minimum wage legislation is, of course, an example of such a policy.

Third, one might ask why a subsidy policy should be introduced when exactly the same result could be achieved by legislation to remove the institutional barriers that keep W_1 at $\bar{W}_1$. Under the structural unemployment model, the targeted employment subsidy is, after all, only a remedial policy made necessary by other government policies (for example, minimum wage legislation). Part of the answer may lie in the fact that the L_1s will probably lose because of a reduction of their wage W_1'. In terms of figure 5, they would lose the area $b + f + g + h$ and gain only the area $d + k$.[16]

Induced Unemployment

Under the induced unemployment model the wage rates of the problem group adjust so that there is always full employment. This alters somewhat the determination of the optimal subsidy.

15. I go into this question in detail in "The Theory of Labour Market Intervention," *Economica*, vol. 47 (August 1980), pp. 309–29.

16. The aggregate net income of the L_1s increases because of a decline in W_1 only if $\eta_1 > 1/(1 - \rho)$.

The total net income of the other labor factors is still given by equation 15, but the true net income of the L_1s must also include a term $V(E_1)$ that reflects the economic value of their leisure. Given distributional weights of $1 + \delta$ for the L_1s and $1 - \delta$ for the other factors, the value of total income of the society is

$$(18) \qquad \phi = (1 + \delta)[W_1E_1 + \pi(L_1 - E_1) + V_1E_1]$$

$$+ (1 - \delta)[Q - W_1E_1 - \pi(L_1 - E_1) - G_0].$$

I continue to assume that all the other factors supply their services inelastically, so that terms for the value of leisure of the other factors can be ignored. If the weights assigned to the two groups are equal ($\delta = 0$), then social welfare is simply

$$(19) \qquad \phi = Q + V(E_1).$$

Maximization of social welfare in this case requires that a subsidy be paid such that at the resultant level of E_1 the increase in employment just offsets the loss in the value of leisure given by the L_1s. As shown in appendix B, the value of the marginal unit of leisure, given the existence of the income-transfer program, is $W_1 - \pi$. Thus

$$(20) \qquad \frac{\Delta\phi}{\Delta E_1} = MP_1 - (W_1 - \pi).$$

Since $MP_1 = W_1(1 - s)$, the optimal subsidy rate with $\delta = 0$ is $s = \rho$, the replacement ratio.

If no weight were placed on the welfare of the L_1s, that is, $\delta = -1$, the subsidy would be set so that the net income of the taxpaying factors is maximized. This requires that

$$(21) \qquad \frac{\Delta I_1}{\Delta E_1} = MP_1 - W_1 - E_1 \frac{\Delta W_1}{\Delta E_1} - \pi$$

$$= W_1\left(-s - \frac{1}{\epsilon_1} + \rho\right) = 0,$$

or, in words, the subsidy rate should equal the replacement ratio less the reciprocal of the elasticity of supply of the problem group. The reason for this rather curious result is that the taxpaying factors are in a monopsonis-

Figure 6. Distributional Implications of a Targeted Employment Subsidy under Induced Unemployment[a]

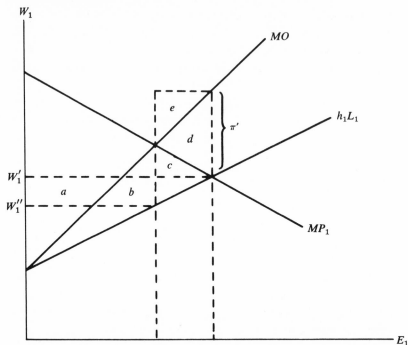

a. The employment-potential labor force ratio is denoted by h; and MO is the marginal outlay of group 1.

tic position relative to the L_1s. If there was no transfer program and the supply function was the same as if there were, the taxpayers would want the L_1s employed up to the point where their marginal outlay—in figure 6 the MO curve, which is equal to $W_1(1 - 1/\epsilon_1)$—equals their marginal product. In terms of figure 6, the taxpayers are willing to sacrifice area c to gain area $a + b$. This suggests that they would benefit from a negative subsidy on the L_1s (accomplished by, for example, a regressive payroll tax).

If, however, there is a cost to the taxpayers of more nonemployment of the L_1s, they will maximize their net incomes if W_1 is greater than W_1''. In figure 6 the income transfer payment is set at π' so that it just equals the difference between the MO and MP curves, a zero optimal subsidy from the point of view of taxpayers. If π is greater than π', the optimal subsidy from the point of view of the taxpayers is positive.

Implications for the Evaluation of the Targeted Jobs Tax Credit

If the targeted jobs tax credit is used to the extent anticipated at its inception, a strong effort should be made to evaluate its impact. For the targeted employment subsidy may be the *only* feasible instrument of long-run employment policy available in the United States. Public service employment may be of limited potential for shifting the demand curve for low-skilled labor because of the high-skill intensity of the public sector.

This paper shows that much of the evaluation of the targeted jobs tax credit must be done indirectly. Specifically, the analyst must have a clear idea of which identifiable groups in the labor force are subject to induced or structural unemployment. He or she must also have detailed information about the signs and magnitudes of the partial elasticities of complementarity between these different groups.

Without such information it will be difficult to conclude just what the impact of the tax credit was. If, for example, it is estimated that the total employment of the target population was 100,000 greater during 1980 than it would have been without the program, one must also know what happened to the employment of related groups not eligible for the subsidy. This depends on their supply elasticities and the extent of their complementarity elasticities with the target group. Very little is known about either of these issues.

Another problem in evaluating the targeted jobs tax credit regards its timing within the business cycle. Since the administration of the program did not get off the ground until mid-1980, most of whatever data that will be collected by, say, 1982 will refer to a period of rather severe recession. The appropriate model with which to analyze the labor market effects of a targeted employment subsidy under conditions of deficient demand unemployment is similar to the structural unemployment model with partial coverage discussed earlier. That is, one cannot necessarily assume that most noneligible labor groups experience continuous full employment. A detailed evaluation of the impact of the program during 1980 and 1981 might therefore conclude that much greater substitution of employment of the target group for that of noneligibles occurred then than would have occurred in the full-employment years of 1977 through 1979.

Appendix A: Complementarity and Substitutability among Factors of Production

One important question regarding a targeted employment subsidy is the extent to which the different factors of production are complements to or substitutes for the problem group. This question, which is central to the analysis of the effect of a subsidy program on total employment when there are multiple problem populations, is also critical in discerning the distributional implications of the program. The purpose of this appendix is to review the algebra of the partial elasticity of complementarity used in the text.[17]

Assume that the aggregate production function in the economy is homogeneous with degree one in the input levels of the N factors, that is

$$(22) \qquad Q = F(E_1, E_1, \ldots, E_N).$$

E_1 is the employment level of the problem group. The real wage (or rental price for nonlabor factors) of each factor equals its marginal product,

$$(23) \qquad W_i = \frac{\partial Q}{\partial E_i} = F_i(E_1, \ldots, E_n).$$

A change in each of the factors changes W by

$$(24) \qquad dW_i = F_{i1}dE_1 + F_{i2}dE_2 + \ldots + F_{iN}dE_N.$$

This can be rewritten as

$$(25) \qquad \frac{dW_i}{W_i} = \sum_{j=1}^{N} (F_{ij}E_j/F_i) \frac{dE_j}{E_j}$$

$$= \sum_{j=1}^{N} \left(\frac{F_j E_j}{Q}\right)\left(\frac{Q F_{ij}}{F_i F_j} d(\log E_j)\right)$$

$$= \sum_{j=1}^{N} \alpha_j C_{ij} d(\log E_j),$$

---

17. The standard reference for the theoretical development of this topic is Sato and Koizumi, "On the Elasticities of Substitution and Complementarity"; a review of the empirical knowledge about "substitution space" is Daniel S. Hamermesh and James Grant, "Econometric Studies of Labor-Labor Substitution and Their Implications for Policy," *Journal of Human Resources,* vol. 14 (Fall 1979), pp. 518–42.

where $\alpha_j = F_j E_j / Q$ is the output share of factor j and $C_{ij} = Q F_{ij} / F_i F_j$ is the partial elasticity of complementarity between factors i and j.

Because the marginal products are homogeneous of degree zero, the sum of the coefficients of equation 25 equals zero. For factor 1, this means that

(26) $$\alpha_1 C_{11} + \alpha_2 C_{12} + \ldots + \alpha_N C_{1N} = 0.$$

Factor i is complementary to (substitutable for) factor j if $C_{ij} > 0 (< 0)$. Since factor 1 is by definition substitutable for itself, $C_{11} < 0$, at least one of the other factors must be complementary to factor 1, and as many as all the other factors can be complementary to factor 1.

In the special case of the constant elasticity of substitution production function, the partial elasticity of complementarity is

(27) $$C_{ij} = \frac{1 - \alpha_i}{\alpha_i \sigma}, \quad i = j,$$

$$= \frac{1}{\sigma}, \quad i \neq j,$$

where σ is *the* elasticity of substitution. The one elasticity of demand for factor 1, all other factor inputs held constant, is

(28) $$\eta_1 = \frac{-d(\log E_1)}{d(\log W_1)} = \frac{-1}{\alpha_1 C_{11}}.$$

In the constant elasticity of substitution case this equals $\sigma / (1 - \alpha_1)$.

Appendix B: Labor Supply Assumptions

In the model of induced unemployment some fairly strong assumptions were made about the impact of income-dependent transfer programs on the labor supply behavior of the problem group. The purpose of this appendix is to expand on those assumptions.

First, in the section on the optimal size of a targeted employment subsidy, I stated that the marginal valuation of an additional unit of leisure by a potential recipient of an income transfer program is $W_1 - \pi$, the wage less the transfer payment per unit of time. In appendix C, I state that the equivalent for those factors not eligible for the transfer program is $W_1(1 - t)$, where t is their tax rate. These results come from the standard theory of labor supply. Utility per unit of time (say, a year) is a function of consumption (c) and leisure $(T - H)$, where T is the total potential labor force time and H is time at work. Consumption equals the effective wage, r, times hours plus unearned income, I. Thus

$$(29) \qquad U = \phi(rH + I, T - H).$$

Utility maximization requires that

$$(30) \qquad \frac{dU}{dH} = r\phi_1 - \phi_2 = 0,$$

subject to the convexity of ϕ. Around equilibrium an additional unit of H reduces utility by $-\phi_2$, and it would take an extra amount of I equal to r to compensate the person for this loss of leisure.

For recipients of the income transfer program, total consumption is $W_1 H + \pi(T_* - H)$, where T_* is "normal" hours. Thus $r = W_1 - \pi$ and $I = \pi T_*$, and their welfare (in terms of goods) decreases by $W_1 - \pi$ as H increases. For the taxpaying factors, $r = W_i(1 - t)$.

One utility function that yields labor supply behavior equivalent to that assumed in the text (but not in appendix C) is the Cobb-Douglas, that is,

$$(31) \qquad U = \beta \log \left[(W_1 - \pi)H + \pi T_*\right]$$

$$+ (1 - \beta) \log (T - H).$$

It is easily shown that if $T = T_* = 1/\beta$, satisfaction of 30 implies that

$$(32) \qquad H = 1 - \frac{1 - \beta}{\beta} \frac{\pi}{W_1 - \pi}$$

$$= 1 - \frac{1 - \beta}{\beta} \frac{\rho}{1 - \rho},$$

where $\rho = \pi/W_1$ is the replacement ratio. For those not eligible for the transfer program, $H = 1$, and the labor supply elasticity is zero. For $\rho > 0$, however, the supply elasticity is

$$(33) \qquad \epsilon = \frac{d(\log H)}{d(\log W_1)} = \frac{(1 - \beta)}{(1 - \rho)(\beta - \rho)}.$$

This is obviously larger the greater the replacement ratio is.

One implication of this approach is that the uncompensated labor supply elasticity will be quite large. For example, for $\beta = 2/3$ the value of ϵ in equation 33 is 2 at a replacement ratio of $\rho = 0.5$. Estimates of ϵ from the negative income tax experiments, however, have been much smaller than this—about 0.1 to 0.2 for women and essentially zero for men.[18] If these are close to the "true" elasticities rather than subject to severe downward bias because of the experimental framework, little potential exists for employment policy to increase the labor market activity rate of those subject to induced unemployment. A large targeted employment subsidy program would be primarily an additional transfer to participants in income transfer programs.

Appendix C: The Optimal Size of a Wage Subsidy in the General Case

The purpose of this appendix is to derive algebraically the conditions for an optimal wage subsidy when there are two groups of potential workers, both of which may have non-inelastic labor supply functions. As in the text, the L_1s are the targets of the employment subsidy, and all other employed workers, the E_2s, pay for all government spending in the form of a proportionate tax on their income.

The notation, which does not differ from that in the text, is as follows:

L_i = potential labor force of group i

E_i = employment level of group i

W_i = real wage per unit of time of group i

π = transfer payment available to group 1 nonemployed

Q = aggregate output

t = tax rate on income of E_2s

h_i = effective labor supply per worker

s = subsidy rate on the E_1s.

---

18. T. Johnson and J. Pencavel, "Utility-Based Hours of Work Functions for Husbands, Wives, and Single Females Estimated from Seattle-Denver Experimental Data" (Stanford Research Institute, August 1979).

The model is based on several assumptions. First, the aggregate production function is linear homogeneous in E_1 and E_2, that is

$$(34) \qquad\qquad Q = F(E_1, E_2).$$

Profit maximization implies that

$$(35) \qquad\qquad \frac{\partial Q}{\partial E_1} = F_1 = W_1(1 - s)$$

and

$$(36) \qquad\qquad \frac{\partial Q}{\partial E_2} = F_2 = W_2,$$

where s is, of course, the subsidy rate that the government pays employers as a fraction of their low-skilled wage bill.

Second, the effective supply of group 1 workers is assumed to depend, the real income transfer payment being held constant, on the wage, that is

$$(37) \qquad\qquad E_1 = h_1(W_1, \pi)L_1,$$

where $\epsilon_1 = \partial(\log h_1/\partial(\log W_1)$ is the wage elasticity of supply. The supply of group 2 workers is also assumed to depend on their net wage, $y_2 = W_2(1 - t)$, or

$$(38) \qquad\qquad E_2 = h_2[W_2(1 - t)]L_2,$$

where $\epsilon_2 = d(\log h_2)/d(\log y_2)$.

Third, the cost of government, which includes (a) the subsidy program, (b) the income transfer program, and (c) expenditure for other than social programs (G_0), must equal taxes collected from the E_2s. This means that

$$(39) \qquad tW_2E_2 = sW_1E_1 + \pi(L_1 - E_1) + G_0$$

$$= (W_1 - F_1)E_1 + \pi(L_1 - E_1) + G_0.$$

By setting the value of s in this model, the values of W_1, W_2, t, E_1, E_2, and Q are determined. To find the optimum value of s, it is necessary to reduce the number of variables to something more manageable. This can be accomplished by treating W_1 as exogenous (and s as endogenous, equal to $1 - F_1/W_1$). The trick is to manipulate equation 39 to eliminate t. First, add $Q = F_1E_1 + F_2E_2$ to both sides of 39 to obtain

$$(40) \qquad tW_2E_2 + Q = W_1E_1 + W_2E_2 + \pi(L - E_1) + G_0.$$

Second, when this equation is rearranged,

$$(41) \quad F[h_1(W_2)L_1, h_2(y_2)L_2] - W_1h_1(W_1)L_1 - y_2h_2(y_2)L_2$$

$$= \pi[L_1 - h_1(W_1)L_1] + G_0.$$

This implies that if one knows the value of W_1, one can determine the value of $y_2 = W_2(1 - t)$. W_1 and y_2 then determine the values of E_1 and E_2, which in turn determine the values of s, t, and Q.

Differentiation of equation 41 totally with respect to y_1 and W_1 yields

$$(42) \quad h_2L_2\left(1 - \frac{1}{1 - t}\,\epsilon_2\right) d(\log y_2)$$

$$+ h_1L_1\left[1 + \frac{\epsilon_1}{W_1}(W_1 - \pi - F_1)\right] d(\log W_1) = 0$$

of the income transfer program. Assuming that $\epsilon_2 < (1 - t)/t$, the sign of the effect of W_1 on y_2 is given by the coefficient on $d(\log W_1)$ in equation 42. The effect of a change in W_1 on E_2 is then

$$(43) \qquad dE_2 = -\epsilon_2E_1\left[\frac{1 + \dfrac{\epsilon_1}{W_1}(W_1 - \pi - F_1)}{1 - \dfrac{t}{1 - t}\,\epsilon_2}\right] d(\log W_1).$$

Of course, an increase in W_1 changes E_2 by

$$(44) \qquad dE_1 = \epsilon_1E_1d(\log W_1).$$

To obtain the socially optimal wage subsidy, first let social welfare be the level of output plus the value of the leisure of the L_1s and L_2s, that is,

$$(45) \qquad \phi = F(E_1, E_2) + V_1(E_1) + V_2(E_2).$$

Following the results of appendix B, the marginal valuations of leisure by the two groups are, respectively, $W_1 - \pi$ and $W_2(1 - t)$. The derivative of ϕ with respect to $\log W_1$ is then

$$(46) \qquad \frac{d\phi}{d(\log W_1)} = (F_1 - W_1 + \pi)\epsilon_1 F_1$$

$$- tW_1\epsilon_2 E_1 \left[\frac{1 + \frac{\epsilon_1}{W_1}(W_1 - \pi - F_1)}{1 - \frac{t}{1-t}\epsilon_2} \right].$$

The optimal subsidy is the s that makes equation 46 equal zero. Since $sW_1 = W_1 - F_1$, this is

$$(47) \qquad s = \rho - \frac{t\epsilon_2 \dfrac{W_2}{W_1}}{\epsilon_1 \left[1 + t\epsilon_2 \left(\dfrac{1}{1-t} + \dfrac{W_2}{W_1} \right) \right]},$$

where $\rho = \pi/W_1$ is the replacement ratio of the income transfer program.

If $\epsilon_2 > 0$, the optimal subsidy is less than ρ; if the L_2s' supply curve bends backward, the optimal subsidy exceeds ρ. The optimal subsidy from the point of view of the high-skilled population is simply the s that maximizes their after-tax wage, $y_2 = W_2(1 - t)$. This is found by choosing the s that makes the coefficient on $d(\log W_1)$ in equation 42 equal to zero, or

$$(48) \qquad s' = \rho - \frac{1}{\epsilon_1}.$$

This is obviously independent of the value of ϵ_2, and it is always less than the socially optimal subsidy so long as $\epsilon_1 < \infty$.

Comments by Donald A. Nichols

In his paper George Johnson uses a simple model of labor market equilibrium to derive many results about the efficiency and equity implications of targeted wage subsidies. Both the strengths and weaknesses of the paper stem from the simplifications of the model, which permit sharp results to be derived but also may distort the conclusions that are drawn. As Solow has said:

All theory depends on assumptions which are not quite true. That is what makes it theory. The art of successful theorizing is to make the inevitable simplifying assumptions in such a way that the final results are not very sensitive. A "crucial" assumption is one on which the conclusions do depend sensitively, and it is important that crucial assumptions be reasonably realistic. When the results of a theory seem to flow specifically from a special crucial assumption, then if the assumption is dubious, the results are suspect.[19]

Johnson derives an impressively long list of results from his simplified model, but several of these results flow specifically from a crucial dubious assumption and are therefore suspect.

Johnson's strategy is to divide the labor force into a small number of homogeneous groups that differ from one another in their productive abilities and in their roles in the production process. Results are derived that depend on the elasticities of substitution across these groups in the production process, on the relative sizes of the groups, on their equilibrium unemployment rates, and on their marginal productivities.

The problem with his approach is that the groups of workers are not in fact homogeneous, though the assumption of homogeneity is indeed a convenient one to make for most analytic purposes. If Johnson's results are divided into three categories, two are seen to be affected by this crucial assumption, one is not. The three categories can be described in terms of the distributions of characteristics each group possesses. First, those qualitative results derived for the means of distributions tend to remain intact. Second, quantitative results even for the means of distributions may be suspect. For example, results that claim that *all* of a group will be affected, that a policy will be *completely* ineffective, that *each* public service employment job will cause *one* private sector worker to be displaced are results that have to be softened when groups are viewed as nonhomogeneous. And third, and most important, results derived for members of the tails of distributions cannot be expected to be useful if they come from a model that considers only the means.

This third category of results is very important in a paper that deals with employment policies in the low-wage labor market. In that market, which contains the least productive members of any classification, some adults compete with some teens, some whites compete with some blacks,

---

19. Robert M. Solow, "A Contribution to the Theory of Economic Growth," *Quarterly Journal of Economics*, vol. 70 (February 1956), p. 65.

some males compete with some females. It is inappropriate to derive results for these low-wage people based, for example, on the assumption that *all* adults are more productive than *all* teens. If, in fact, some adults earn the minimum wage, or, worse yet, have difficulty finding jobs at the minimum wage, then it is important to consider the effect on this group of a subsidy that reduces the cost of teenage labor below the minimum. Johnson's methodology ignores effects of this kind.

It is important to note that my criticism is not leveled against the practice of working with models of homogeneous groups of workers. Few analytic models of labor markets would be immune to that criticism. In fact, the assumption of homogeneity is so convenient, it appears in one way or another in every paper in this volume. I am critical—to paraphrase Solow—not of analysts' making an assumption that is not true, but rather of their presenting final results that are sensitive to that assumption. Results not sensitive to that assumption, in this paper and in others, remain of interest.

A minor quibble concerns Johnson's labels of certain kinds of unemployment as "structural" or "frictional," when, in fact, those terms usually refer to a more general class of unemployment problems. Johnson's taxonomy neatly classifies the unemployment resulting from different kinds of labor supply behavior, but the use of structural or frictional labels to refer to several of these classes may confuse the reader who uses these labels differently.

With these qualifications, the paper is valuable, since it points out what a standard supply and demand model implies would be the effects of a targeted wage subsidy under a variety of assumptions about the slopes of the supply and demand curves of each labor class.

Jeffrey M. Perloff

Micro- and Macroeconomic Effects

In the late 1970s the United States instituted wage subsidy programs that encouraged firms to hire new low-wage or part-time employees. This paper surveys the theoretical effects of targeted, or categorical, employment subsidies under alternative assumptions. The survey suggests that such a subsidy is likely to increase welfare only if it offsets an already existing distortion or reduces unemployment.

Models like those described here should prove useful in evaluating programs such as the current targeted jobs tax credit by identifying the key issues that should be examined. The models also indicate indirect ways to test for various effects.

An important problem confronting researchers is which model to use. The two obvious candidates are the neoclassical general equilibrium model and an unemployment model. Both types of models are examined here within a common framework.

In the first section the major American targeted employment subsidy programs, the new jobs tax credit and the targeted jobs tax credit, are described, and the effects of a simple employment subsidy on firms is analyzed. In the second section a two-sector general equilibrium model is developed and used to examine the impact of an employment subsidy under various circumstances; and in the following section unemployment is built into the two-sector model. At the end, conclusions are drawn and the implications for empirical research are considered.

I am grateful to Costas Azariadis, John H. Bishop, Kenneth Burdett, David Crawford, Robert H. Haveman, Bryce Hool, Robert I. Lerman, Frank Levy, Kyle Shell, and Michael L. Wachter for helpful conversations and research materials. This project was partially funded under contract D9M9-3632 from the Office of the Assistant Secretary for Policy, Evaluation, and Research in the Department of Labor. Opinions expressed in the paper do not necessarily represent the official position or policy of the department.

95

Targeted Employment Subsidies

Several employment subsidy programs have been implemented in the United States in recent years, the two most important being the new jobs tax credit and the targeted jobs tax credit. Both programs encouraged firms to hire low-wage or part-time workers.

The New Jobs Tax Credit

The 1977–78 new jobs tax credit was the most widely used employment subsidy in U.S. history. It had four key provisions. First, the subsidy was paid to employers rather than employees.

Second, though not, strictly speaking, a targeted employment subsidy, the credit provided a larger subsidy for low-skilled and part-time labor than for skilled, full-time workers.[1] The tax credit was limited to the minimum of either half the amount by which Federal Unemployment Tax Act (FUTA) wages in the 1977 or 1978 tax year exceeded 102 percent of FUTA wages from the previous year, or 50 percent of the amount total wages exceeded 105 percent of the previous year's total wages. Although the second restriction prevented firms from firing all their full-time workers and hiring twice as many subsidized half-time workers, it did not prevent them from hiring part-time incremental workers. Furthermore, the credit could be no larger than 25 percent of FUTA wages or \$100,000, whichever was less.[2] Thus the credit (C) was

(1) $C = \min[\frac{1}{2}(4,200)(E - 1.02E_0); \frac{1}{2}(wE - 1.05w_0E_0); 100,000;$

$\frac{1}{4}(4,200E)],$ $w, w_0 \geq 4,200,$

$= \min[\frac{1}{2}(wE - 1.05w_0E_0); 100,000; \frac{1}{4}wE],$ $w, w_0 < 4,200,$

where E is current employment, E_0 is employment in the previous year, w is the current wage, and w_0 is the previous year's wage.

1. An extra credit was available for hiring the handicapped.
2. As of January 1, 1978, the FUTA maximum went up to \$6,000, but the new jobs tax credit subsidized only the first \$4,200 (the 1977 maximum) paid per employee.

Third, the credit, as shown by the formula above, was a marginal tax credit affecting incremental hiring rather than a subsidy covering total employment.[3] In firms whose employment growth exceeded the various subsidy ceilings, the marginal wage was unaffected and the program became a windfall, lump-sum reduction.

Some firms, if they were growing fast enough in the absence of the credit, may have received the maximum credit of $100,000 without taking any explicit action. Such a lump-sum credit could lower firms' average cost curves while leaving their marginal cost curves unchanged. If all the firms in a competitive industry were so affected, average firm output would fall and industry output would increase. Thus the credit may have encouraged an expansion of fast-growing industries and led to extra workers being hired at the margin by these industries.

Fourth, the credit had important dynamic properties, since it was only a two-year program, and a new worker generated wage savings for only one year. The one-year coverage may have created a saw-tooth employment pattern in which workers hired one year were fired the next.

A Bureau of the Census survey indicated that relatively few firms knew about and responded to the credit in its first year of operation.[4] Of the firms that responded to the questionnaire in full, 34.4 percent knew about it. But only 31.3 percent of firms with 0 to 9 employees were aware of the program, whereas almost three times as many (89.1 percent) firms with over 500 employees knew.

Even of those firms that knew about the credit, relatively few said they qualified for the program or made a conscious effort to claim the credit. Only 19.5 percent of the firms that knew of the credit believed they qualified for it, and approximately 25 percent did not know if they qualified. There was clearly a bias toward fast-growing firms qualifying for, and hence using, the credit. Only 6.1 percent of the firms that knew of the

3. For a cogent discussion of the significance of this distinction, see Jonathan R. Kesselman, Samuel H. Williamson, and Ernst R. Berndt, "Tax Credits for Employment Rather Than Investment," *American Economic Review*, vol. 67 (June 1977), pp. 339–49.

4. See U.S. Department of Commerce, Bureau of the Census, Economic Surveys Division, "New Jobs Tax Credit Survey, Covering the 1977 Tax Year," April 1978, for details of the survey. The survey was based on a Department of Labor–financed, Bureau of the Census questionnaire that was mailed to 4,266 for-profit firms in February 1978. All the important questions were answered by 1,473 firms. The statistics reported here are based on a weighted sample, in which the weights reflect a correction for the oversampling of large firms.

credit claimed they made a conscious effort to increase employment, whereas 36 percent said their employment growth was so high that they automatically qualified for the credit.[5]

Regression estimates indicate that firms which knew about the program in its first year of operation increased employment by 3 percent more than other firms, after controlling for industry, sales growth, and other variables.[6] Similar sizable effects of the program have been estimated using macro data.

The Targeted Jobs Tax Credit

The current targeted jobs tax credit program was designed to provide an incentive to private industry to hire certain economically disadvantaged people. To be eligible to be hired under the program, a worker must be certified by a certifying agency.[7]

A person is eligible if he or she belongs to one of the following seven groups:

—Youths, aged eighteen through twenty-four, who are certified as coming from an economically disadvantaged household. An economically disadvantaged household is one in which family income during the six months before the hiring date is less than 70 percent of the Bureau of Labor Statistics lower living standard on an annual basis.

—Economically disadvantaged Vietnam-era veterans. These veterans must be under thirty-five, have served active (nontraining) duty in the armed forces for more than 180 days or have been discharged or released

5. According to Larry Dildine of the Treasury Department, approximately 14 percent of all firms claimed the new jobs tax credit in the first year, and twice as many (28 percent) claimed it in the second year. Correspondingly, the dollar value of the credits claimed rose from $2.3 billion to $4.6 billion.

6. Jeffrey M. Perloff and Michael L. Wachter, "The New Jobs Tax Credit: An Evaluation of the 1977–78 Wage Subsidy Program," *American Economic Review*, vol. 69 (May 1979, *Papers and Proceedings, 1978*), pp. 173–79; and "A Reevaluation of the New Jobs Tax Credit," Discussion Paper 70 (Center for the Study of Organizational Innovation, University of Pennsylvania, April 1980).

7. To relieve potential employers of unnecessary paperwork and the burden of proving to the Internal Revenue Service that a person is a member of a target group, the secretaries of treasury and labor are required jointly to designate a single certifying agency in each locality that will make the determination and issue certificates. These certificates are sufficient evidence that a person is a member of a target group. The State Employment Security Agency has been designated as the certifying agency. Upon agreement of that agency, CETA prime sponsors and other agencies have the practical responsibility of certifying people.

from active duty for service-connected disability, and be a member of an economically disadvantaged household.

—Economically disadvantaged ex-convicts (felons), provided they are hired within five years after the date of release from prison or date of conviction.

—Vocational rehabilitation referrals.

—Supplemental security income recipients.

—General assistance recipients.

—Work-study youths who are sixteen through eighteen years old and high school or vocational school dropouts participating in a qualified cooperative education program.

Since a household's economic status is based on family earnings six months prior to hiring, the credit favors families whose fortunes have temporarily declined as well as those with long-run problems. If one family member temporarily withdraws from the labor force, transitory earnings may dip. Thus subsidized workers may be drawn disproportionately from families in which, say, the mother dropped out of the labor force to give birth. A comparable bias was observed in the negative income tax experiment.

An employer may claim a tax credit of 50 percent of "qualified first-year wages" and 25 percent of "qualified second-year wages" for newly hired target group employees. Qualified wages are those due to services rendered by a member of a target group during the first or second year of employment from the date employment began. In general, the credit applies to wage costs between January 1, 1979, and December 31, 1980, for certified employees hired after September 26, 1978.[8] The credit for any one worker is limited to $3,000 in the first year and $1,500 in the second. Because FUTA wages are now the first $6,000 of annual earnings, this limit is equivalent to applying the credit to FUTA wages only.

Since employees may be hired on a part-time basis if full-time employees earn more than $6,000 a year, firms have an incentive to limit employees to part-time work and hire more people. Since only new employees are eligible, firms have an incentive to fire old workers and hire new workers every year or two if this program is continued after 1981. Firms that invest in training employees (that is, specific human capital) or have high hiring costs should have less turnover of their labor force than other firms. This problem should be less pronounced under the tar-

8. The starting date for handicapped people and disabled veterans was January 1, 1977.

geted jobs tax credit than under the new jobs tax credit, which encouraged a zig-zag hiring pattern by giving credits only for FUTA wages in excess of 102 percent of FUTA wages for the previous year.

The targeted jobs tax credit is elective. The election may be made applicable (or revoked) at any time up to seven years after the return filing date or three years before that date. There is no limit on the amount of credit each employer may claim other than it must be no more than 90 percent of the firm's tax liability after the liability has been reduced by other nonrefundable credits. Although no refund may be claimed on this credit, any unused portion of it may be carried back three years or carried forward seven years.[9]

This program may be biased against small firms (unlike the new jobs tax credit, which was biased against large firms), because a credit cannot be claimed on qualified wages in excess of 30 percent of the aggregate FUTA wages paid by the firm in the preceding year. For example, this rule could eliminate the credit for firms with zero employees in the previous year and reduce the size of the credit for firms with few employees in that year. This limitation was designed to prevent displacement of non-target group workers.

Other important restrictions are that only for-profit firms are eligible and the credit cannot be taken on wages paid to an employee for whom the employer receives federally funded payments for on-the-job training or for whom he claims a work incentive tax credit. Although the targeted jobs tax credit is less restrictive than the new jobs tax credit in some ways, it is apparently less attractive to firms, since many fewer firms are claiming it.[10]

Employment Tax Credits and Firms

Because a typical targeted employment tax credit is given to firms rather than workers directly, it is convenient to analyze its impact within

9. This provision is more liberal than the new jobs tax credit. However, the survey of firms on the effect of the latter indicated that only 3 percent of the firms that knew about the availability of the credit were unable to use it because of insufficient tax liability.

10. According to Robert Lerman (formerly assistant secretary for policy, evaluation, and research of the Department of Labor), as of February 1980, 140,000 people had been certified under the targeted jobs tax credit program and obtained work. Approximately half were students in co-op education programs who were not subject to an income tax. Of the remaining 70,000, 50,000 were disadvantaged youths. Thus, aside from youths, virtually no other eligible group took advantage of the credit.

a model of firm behavior. All profit-maximizing firms, regardless of their possible monopoly power in product markets, attempt to minimize costs. Assuming that these firms have no monopsony power, costs will be minimized (in the absence of any tax or subsidy) when the ratio of the marginal products equals the factor price ratio for any pair of inputs. For example, the firms' marginal rate of substitution (ratio of marginal products) between target group labor, T, and nontarget group labor, N, equals the wage ratio:

$$(2) \qquad \frac{MP_T}{MP_N} = \frac{w_T}{w_N}.$$

A simple wage subsidy to firms would reduce the cost of a T-type worker, regardless of hours worked or other issues. If a firm were given a subsidy paying half a T-type worker's wage, it would minimize its costs when the ratio of marginal products equaled the new factor price ratio:

$$(3) \qquad \frac{MP_T}{MP_N} = \frac{\frac{1}{2}w_T}{w_N} = \frac{w_T}{2w_N}.$$

As shown in figure 1, the wage subsidy makes the isocost line flatter. Hence the subsidy will induce a firm to use a more T-intensive technology for any given level of output. This effect is the underlying motivation for a targeted employment tax credit. If all firms claim the subsidy, aggregate demand and w_T will rise.[11] This conclusion is subject to two important caveats.

First, any subsidy will have an effect only if it is not financed in a way that "undoes" its effect. For example, if, in order to pay for the subsidy, firms are taxed according to how much of the subsidy they claimed, the subsidy is undone. Alternatively, if the subsidy is paid for by lump-sum taxation, it will have the predicted impact. The targeted jobs tax credit is a credit against tax liability and therefore is not financed in a way that would obviously vitiate its effect.

Second, this analysis assumes that all firms are free to use the tax subsidy and that the economy may be viewed as a single-sector general equilibrium model. In the next two sections this assumption is relaxed. Specifically, the effects of a tax subsidy are analyzed in a two-sector general equilibrium model and in several unemployment models.

11. I am assuming here a full-employment model. The effects in an economy with unemployment are discussed later in the paper.

Figure 1. Effect of a Wage Subsidy on a Single Firm

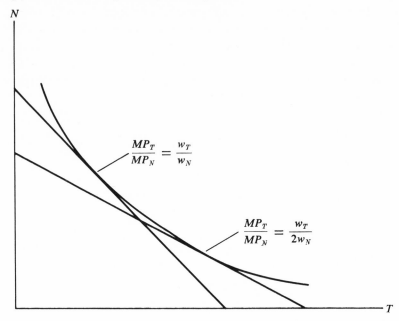

Two-Sector General Equilibrium Models

Because some firms can and will respond to a targeted employment subsidy while others cannot or will not, it is inappropriate to use a one-sector general equilibrium model to analyze the effects of the subsidy program. Probably the most important lesson of the new jobs and targeted jobs tax credit programs is that not all firms learn about and use a new tax credit, especially in the first year.[12] As noted above, only one in seven firms claimed the new jobs tax credit in its first year, and only twice that number claimed the credit in the second year.[13]

If these two programs are any guides, relatively few firms will take the trouble to find out about a new categorical employment tax credit, qualify for the credit, and make a conscious effort to use the credit. Most small

12. See Kesselman, Williamson, and Berndt, "Tax Credits for Employment Rather Than Investment," for a discussion of why some firms may not use a marginal employment tax credit.

13. An even smaller number are likely to claim the targeted jobs tax credit in its first year, as noted in footnote 10.

firms will probably not learn about the credit for at least a year.[14] Many firms (especially new ones) cannot qualify for programs which require that employment grow by a certain percent beyond the previous year's employment level (for example, 102 percent for the new jobs tax credit) before the firm becomes eligible for the credit. Limits on the credit ($100,000 for the new jobs tax credit and 30 percent of the previous year's FUTA wages for the targeted jobs tax credit), restrictions that the credit can offset only tax liabilities, the ineligibility of nonprofit firms, and other requirements will eliminate many firms. Small firms may not be able to handle the paperwork to qualify for the credit. Finally, many firms' production processes prevent them from using more target group employees.

As a result, it is reasonable to divide the economy into two sectors. In sector one, the targeted employment subsidy is not claimed; in sector two, it is claimed. These sectors may cross industry and occupational lines.[15]

The Basic Full-Employment Model

In the basic model, all wages and prices are assumed to be flexible so that all markets clear. To concentrate on the factor markets, I assume that firms are competitive.[16] These assumptions are relaxed later.

In general, there may be many factors of production. For the sake of graphic simplicity, the inputs are limited to two kinds: the target labor group (T) and the nontarget labor group (N). Initially, all the (homogeneous) members of each group are paid wages of w_T and w_N.

Since the credit will affect only firms in sector two, it will cause intersector substitution as well as intrafirm substitution in that sector. Again, for graphic simplicity, the credit is assumed to be simpler than the new jobs or targeted jobs tax credit: it merely lowers the per-dollar cost of T-type labor to the firms in sector two.

The output in sector i $(i = 1,2)$ is Y_i and is produced by a constant returns to scale production function:

$$(4) \qquad Y_i = F_i(N_i, T_i).$$

14. See the section on new jobs tax credit for evidence on that program.

15. See the preceding paper by George Johnson, who discusses the implications of a credit when only some members of a group are subsidized. His analysis is complementary to this one, in which only some firms claim the credit.

16. The analysis would also hold for monopolistic firms that face constant elasticity demand functions and hence pass along costs with a constant markup.

Figure 2. Effect of a Wage Subsidy on a Two-Sector Model

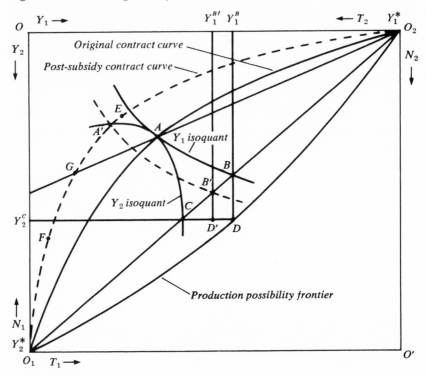

If the factors (N and T) are inelastically supplied, then their usage in the two sectors must add up to the total supply:

(5) $$N_1 + N_2 = N$$

$$T_1 + T_2 = T.$$

An Edgeworth-Bowley box may be used to demonstrate the general equilibrium solution for this economy. Initially, it is assumed that sector one is N-intensive and sector two is T-intensive, as shown in figure 2.

The vertical side of the box (O_1O) represents the economy's endowment of N; the horizontal side (O_1O') reflects the endowment of T. A Y_1 isoquant is drawn with reference to the origin O_1; a tangent Y_2 isoquant, with reference to the origin O_2. The tangency point, A, is the initial (presubsidy) equilibrium, and it lies on the original contract curve O_1AO_2, which consists of the tangency points of the two set of isoquants.

This curve is the locus of efficient production—that is, it reflects the factor allocations that maximize the amount of Y_1 that can be produced with various levels of Y_2.

By relabeling the axes, the production possibility curve can also be shown in figure 2.[17] Since production is constant returns to scale, the amount of output represented by any isoquant is proportional to the distance of that isoquant from the origin of the isoquant map (O_1 or O_2) along any ray from that origin selected as a reference line. The diagonal that runs through both sectors' origins serves as a convenient common reference for both isoquant maps.

The outputs measured along this diagonal (that is, the intersections of the isoquants with the diagonal) can be vertically projected to the sides of the box opposite to the origins of the isoquant maps on the northwest of the diagonal, given appropriate relabeling of the axes as described below. The resulting output combinations can be replotted in the interior of the box to make the production possibility curve that is related to the contract curve.

As an illustration of this technique, consider the output levels that correspond to point A on the contract curve. The Y_1 output at point B (which is determined by the intersection of the Y_1 isoquant through point A and the diagonal) is O_1B/O_1O_2 of the maximum amount, Y_1^*, that can be produced if the economy specializes in producing Y_1. Similarly, the Y_2 output at point C is O_2C/O_1O_2 as great as Y_2^*. These ratios can be transferred to the sides of the box: O_1B/O_1O_2 is projected to the top side of the box and O_2C/O_1O_2 is projected to the left-hand side of the box. The distance OO_2 now represents Y_1^*, and the distance OO_1 is Y_2^*. Thus Y_1^B (which is O_1B/O_1O_2 of the distance from origin O to Y_1^*) represents the output level of Y_1 corresponding to the point A on the contract curve.

The projections from Y_1^B through B and from Y_2^C through C intersect at point D. This point lies on the production possibility frontier O_1DO_2 and corresponds to point A on the contract curve. It can be shown that this frontier is concave to the origin O.

If sector two (the T-intensive sector) is now subsidized, the contract curve will swing out toward the O origin and away from the diagonal, as shown in figure 2 by the dotted line $O_1FA'EO_2$. The reason is that firms in sector two substitute toward T-type workers, as shown in figure 1. Thus

17. The method of showing both the contract curve and the production possibility frontier in one diagram was developed by K. M. Savosnick. See Melvyn B. Krauss and Harry G. Johnson, *General Equilibrium Analysis* (Aldine, 1974), pp. 67–68.

the post-subsidy contract curve represents intersections of isoquants rather than tangencies (for example, the intersecting isoquants at point A'). The difference in the slopes of the isoquants (that is, the marginal rates of substitution) reflects the difference in the price of T labor in sector one relative to that in sector two, as seen in figure 1.

If sector one (the N-intensive sector) were the only subsidized sector, the new contract curve would shift in the other direction. Indeed, in this case, if the subsidy were large enough, the factor intensities could reverse, and the first sector could become relatively T-intensive.

In either case the economy would be operating inside the original production possibility frontier (that is, closer to the O origin), since the economy's production potential is reduced by the subsidy-induced distortion. This reduction in output reflects the higher marginal productivity of T in sector one than in sector two. Suppose, for example, that the economy's tastes are such that the post-subsidy equilibrium is at point A', where the original Y_2 isoquant and the dashed Y_1 isoquant intersect.[18] The new output combination is point D', which corresponds to the same level of $Y_2(Y_2^C)$, but less $Y_1(Y_1^{B'} < Y_1^B)$.

Point E on the post-subsidy contract curve is the new equilibrium if relative demand is price inelastic; point F is the new equilibrium if demand is perfectly elastic.[19] Thus the new equilibrium must lie in the range from E to F.

If, after sector two is subsidized, the new equilibrium occurs at E, sector two will become more T-intensive; if equilibrium occurs at F, sector two will become less T-intensive.[20] If demand is elastic, the T/N ratio falls in both sectors and hence real w_T rises.[21] In this case, output in sector two rises, while output in sector one falls. If demand is inelastic, then w_T rises in terms of Y_1 (that is, w_T/p_1 rises, where p_1 is the price of the output in sector 1) and falls in terms of Y_2. These and other results are summarized in table 1.

18. As discussed below, this point would imply relatively inelastic demand; however, this analysis would hold for any type of demand.

19. At G, the output price ratio, p_1/p_2, is higher than at A. Since $MP_N^1 p_1 = w_N^1 = w_N^2 = MP_N^2 p_2$, $p_1/p_2 = MP_N^2/MP_N^1$, and MP_N^2 is the same at G and A, while MP_N^1 is lower at G. F is assumed to be the point where p_1/p_2 is the same as at A (it must lie below GAO_2). If demand were elastic, the economy would shift to point F, where relative output prices are unchanged. If demand were inelastic, y_1/y_2 would remain the same at A, or E, by construction. Since p_1/p_2 rises as one moves from F to E, the points in between represent intermediate cases.

20. Since E is above GAO_2, it must be more T-intensive.

21. If T_i/N_i falls, MP_T^i rises and hence $w_T/p_i (= MP_T^i)$ rises. Thus if T_1/N_1 and T_2/N_2 both fall, w_T increases relative to the price of either good, and so real w_T must rise.

If sector one (the N-intensive sector) is subsidized rather than sector two, and if demand is elastic, real w_T falls, since output in sector one falls and output in sector two rises, which increases the T/N ratio in both sectors. If demand is inelastic, w_T falls relative to p_1 and rises relative to p_2 (see table 1).

Supply Effects

So far, I have assumed that factors are inelastically supplied. It is possible to capture the effect of an upward sloping curve of T in this framework through the following argument. Suppose that in the short run, if demand were such that real w_T rises, the new (inelastic) supply of T will be larger if entry occurs.

This growth of the supply of T workers in the second period can be incorporated into the Edgeworth-Bowley diagram by expanding one axis, as shown in figure 3. The smaller box in the figure, O_1OO_2O', is the same as in figure 2. If new T-type workers enter, the box becomes elongated along the horizontal axes: $O_1'O''O_2O'$.

Given the constant returns to scale assumption, the relative output prices are unchanged. Since factor proportions in sector two depend only on these prices, the new equilibrium must lie on the ray $A'AO_2$. Similarly, the factor proportions in sector one are unchanged so that the new equilibrium, A', is determined by the intersection of $A'AO_2$ and $O_1'A'$ (which is parallel to O_1A).

In the figure, the increase in T leads to a shift from point A to A'. The relative increase in output in the second sector is $AA'/O_2A = HH'/O_2H$. The relative increase in T is $O_1O_1'/O'O_1$. Since $HH' > O_1O_1'$ and $O_2H < O'O_1$, the output of the second sector has grown by more than the T factor supply has grown. The output of the other sector has declined.[22] Thus, depending on demand effects, this supply effect may reinforce the output and other effects of the subsidy.

As an illustration of that effect, consider the following scenario. Initially, only large fast food chains and other service firms that employ a high ratio of T-type workers find that the fixed costs of claiming the credit are justified by the tax savings. This sector—sector two—hires additional T-type workers and expands (given favorable demand conditions),

22. This result is known as the Samuelson-Rybczynski theorem. See Harry G. Johnson, *Two-Sector Model of General Equilibrium* (Aldine/Atherton, 1971), pp. 37–38; Murray C. Kemp, *The Pure Theory of International Trade and Investment* (Prentice-Hall, 1969), pp. 14–16.

Table 1. Effects of the Employment Tax Credit in a Two-Sector, General Equilibrium Model[a]

Model	$\dfrac{w_T}{p_1}$	$\dfrac{w_T}{p_2}$	$\dfrac{w_N}{p_1}$	$\dfrac{w_N}{p_2}$	T_1	T_2	T	N_1	N_2	N	Y_1	Y_2	$\dfrac{N_1}{T_1}$	$\dfrac{N_2}{T_2}$	C	W
Inelastic supply; sector 2 subsidized																
Inelastic demand	+	−	+	+	−	+	0	+	−	0	−	−	+	−	−	−
Elastic demand	+	+	−	−	−	+	0	−	+	0	−	+	+	+	−	−
Inelastic supply; sector 1 subsidized																
Inelastic demand	−	+	−	−	+	−	0	−	+	0	−	−	−	+	−	−
Elastic demand	−	−	+	+	+	−	0	+	−	0	+	−	−	−	−	−
Elastic supply; sector 2 subsidized; elastic demand	+	+	−	−	−	+	+	−	+	0	−	+	0	0	+	−
Minimum wage (M_W) in both sectors; offsetting subsidy	−	−	+	+	n.a.	n.a.	+	n.a.	n.a.	0	+	+	−	−	+	+

n.a. Not available.
a. The signs for the offsetting investment tax credit model are the opposite of the two-sector, general equilibrium model.
W = welfare (efficiency effects only)
C = productive capacity (a positive sign indicates that the production possibility curve has shifted outward)
w_T = wage of T (target group) workers
w_N = wage of N (nontarget group) workers
T_i = target labor group in sector i $i = 1, 2$
N_i = nontarget labor group in sector i
Y_i = output in sector i
p_i = output price in sector i.

Figure 3. Effect of an Employment Tax Credit on a Two-Sector Model with an Elastic Labor Supply

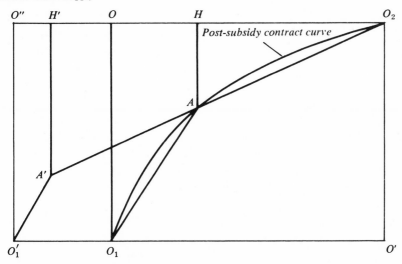

which drives up real w_T wages. The next period, as employment and wage opportunities look brighter, more teenagers drop out of school (hence qualifying for the credit) and become employed in sector two. Other resources are drawn from sector one to complement these new workers, and output of sector two expands further. Under the conditions assumed in this example, the larger the increase in the supply of T-type workers, the closer the economy will be to specializing in the sector two service industries.

This analysis suggests that empirical analyses of a targeted employment subsidy should look for a large number of effects. Table 1 indicates some of the effects that are likely to occur. Such subsidies may alter nominal and real wages, factor ratios, sector output ratios, and other economic variables. In the scenario presented above, both demand and supply effects are observed in the long run (that is, demand shifts along the aggregate supply curve).

Offsetting Distortions

In the above analysis, a targeted employment subsidy has adverse efficiency implications and therefore would seem to be justified only on equity grounds. But in the real world there are many distortions. To the degree that the subsidy offsets other distortions, it may increase efficiency.

If the other factor in the analysis is capital (rather than the non-target group labor), then the distortion caused by an equal percent investment tax credit may be offset by a targeted employment subsidy.[23] If the investment tax credit is exactly offset by the subsidy in terms of coverage and size, then the two tax credits will collectively have no effect on factor proportions. If the coverage of the two credits is not identical, complicated efficiency and equity effects may occur.[24]

Minimum wage laws usually affect T-type workers, but not N-type workers. If coverage of both the minimum wage laws and the targeted employment subsidy were universal, then an appropriate subsidy could exactly offset the harmful effects of the minimum wage (without necessarily interfering with the income redistribution effects of either program). Historically, minimum wage laws have not had universal coverage. If the minimum wage affects only one sector, a diagram very much like figure 2 could be used to show the effects.[25] The effects of the targeted employment subsidy in such a world is discussed later in this paper and in a discussion paper I prepared for the Center for the Study of Organizational Innovation in January 1980.[26] In general, the effects are quite complicated. But it is certainly quite possible that an appropriate subsidy can offset the harmful effects of a minimum wage with incomplete coverage.

General Equilibrium Models with Unemployment

As the previous discussion indicates, if the economy is fully employed and in a first-best (Pareto optimal) equilibrium, a targeted employment subsidy will cause distortions that lead to an inefficient equilibrium. If the economy is initially in a second-best (non-Pareto optimal) equilibrium because of other distortions, such a subsidy may or may not increase efficiency. Of course, in any case, it may be thought to have a bene-

23. This analysis disregards liquidity and other effects of the two credits and considers only their effects upon the scope of isocost lines. In particular, I am ignoring the investment impact, which is, of course, the key effect. It is difficult to examine investment effects in a static model.

24. These effects are discussed in Krauss and Johnson, *General Equilibrium Analysis,* pp. 266–72.

25. See ibid., pp. 142–48.

26. Jeffrey M. Perloff, "The Surprising Effects of Employment Subsidies on Unemployment and Welfare," Discussion Paper 68 (Center for the Study of Organizational Innovation, University of Pennsylvania, January 1980).

ficial effect on the distribution of income, though, as the previous section shows, under certain conditions it may not increase the real wage of target group workers.

The models so far described do not allow for unemployment. Yet one of the main reasons Congress created the targeted jobs tax credit was to help unemployed target group labor, whose members tend to have much higher than average unemployment. And in a world of unemployment, a targeted employment subsidy may increase efficiency by reducing unemployment.

In one sense, the problem economists face in analyzing unemployment issues is not that there are no models of unemployment but that there are too many. Although this assertion is clearly an overstatement, a large number of competing theories do exist—and many of these are consistent with one another, since they describe different types of unemployment.

How well a targeted employment subsidy will work in alleviating unemployment will depend on the causes of unemployment. Some of the better known models of unemployment are described here.

Disequilibrium models. These models have been surveyed by Drazen and include the well-known Barro and Grossman work. In these models, prices and wages are fixed and quantities adjust to equilibrate (but not clear) the markets. Though these models are quite powerful in their applicability, no strong theoretical or empirical justification for the stickiness of prices has been provided.[27]

Quasi-Walrasian models. These models have been surveyed by Calvo and include works by Solow and Stiglitz, Varian, and others. In these models, agents are not necessarily price takers and markets are usually incomplete.[28] In certain models, relative prices and wages remain constant in Keynesian fashion. Some models stress transactions costs in hiring, firing, or moving or cite institutional factors, such as implicit con-

27. Alan Drazen, "Recent Developments in Macroeconomic Disequilibrium Theory," *Econometrica*, vol. 48 (March 1980), pp. 283–306; and Robert J. Barro and Herschel I. Grossman, "A General Disequilibrium Model of Income and Employment," *American Economic Review*, vol. 61 (March 1971), pp. 82–93.

28. Guillermo Calvo, "Quasi-Walrasian Theories of Unemployment," *American Economic Review*, vol. 69 (May 1979, *Papers and Proceedings, 1978*), pp. 102–07; Robert M. Solow and Joseph E. Stiglitz, "Output, Employment, and Wages in the Short Run," *Quarterly Journal of Economics*, vol. 82 (November 1968), pp. 537–60; Hal R. Varian, "Non-Walrasian Equilibria," *Econometrica*, vol. 45 (April 1977), pp. 573–90.

tracts, to explain unemployment.[29] Others rely on imperfect information about workers' characteristics and institutional or legal constraints on labor contracts.[30] Although these models are analytically elegant, existing empirical evidence indicates that they can explain only a small fraction of total unemployment.[31]

Search models. Mortensen and others have shown that frictional unemployment could result from search. A variant of these models by Ross and Wachter and by Hall indicate that search could explain a significant amount of unemployment if workers search for administrative or government sector jobs (with high, sticky wages) and competitive sector jobs. Varian has indicated that Keynesian or other disequilibrium models can be used in conjunction with the Hall model. The minimum wage literature of the last decade, which includes Mincer's and Gramlich's work, is analytically similar.[32]

Structural unemployment models. Although structural unemployment has been out of vogue recently, it is conceivable that lack of substitutability between factors could lead to an excess of a factor. Salop has suggested other types of structural unemployment.[33]

The above models and several other theoretical ones are discussed in Varian.[34] Here I examine the structural and search (frictional) models

29. Costas Azariadis, "Implicit Contracts and Underemployment Equilibria," *Journal of Political Economy,* vol. 83 (December 1975), pp. 1183–1202; Martin N. Baily, "Wages and Employment under Uncertain Demand," *Review of Economic Studies,* vol. 41 (January 1974), pp. 37–50; and Arthur M. Okun, "Inflation: Its Mechanics and Welfare Costs," *Brookings Papers on Economic Activity, 2:1975,* pp. 351–90 (hereafter *BPEA*).

30. See Calvo, "Quasi-Walrasian Theories of Unemployment," and Steven C. Salop, "A Model of the Natural Rate of Unemployment," *American Economic Review,* vol. 69 (March 1979), pp. 117–25.

31. See, for example, Robert E. Hall, "The Rigidity of Wages and the Persistence of Unemployment," *BPEA, 2:1975,* pp. 301–35.

32. See, for example, Dale T. Mortensen, "A Theory of Wage and Employment Dynamics," in Edmund S. Phelps and others, *Microeconomic Foundations of Employment and Inflation Theory* (Norton, 1970), pp. 167–211; Stephen A. Ross and Michael L. Wachter, "Wage Determination, Inflation, and the Industrial Structure," *American Economic Review,* vol. 63 (September 1973), pp. 675–92; Robert E. Hall, "Rigidity of Wages and the Persistence of Unemployment"; Hal R. Varian, "Models of Unemployment," Department of Economics, MIT, February 1976; Jacob Mincer, "Unemployment Effects of Minimum Wages," *Journal of Political Economy,* vol. 84 (August 1976), pt. 2, pp. S87–S104; and Edward M. Gramlich, "Impact of Minimum Wages on Other Wages, Employment, and Family Incomes," *BPEA, 2:1976,* pp. 409–51.

33. Salop, "Model of the Natural Rate of Unemployment."

34. Varian, "Models of Unemployment."

by modifying the basic model described in the previous section. In their paper in this volume, Burdett and Hool discuss the disequilibrium model and the implications of a targeted employment subsidy in such a framework. The quasi-Walrasian models are also important, but the implications of a subsidy in such models are trivial or indeterminate.

Structural Unemployment

To determine the causes of structural unemployment, one must first define it.[35] The definition most consistent with the popular press's notion is as follows: unemployment resulting from a shortage of skilled workers or capital that prevents all unskilled workers from finding work.

Such unemployment could occur in the two-sector model described above if the isoquants have kinks. In that case, a tax credit would not induce firms to substitute toward the subsidized input. For each firm, factor proportions are fixed at the kinks. For specificity in this discussion, let the production functions be Leontief (fixed coefficient).

By appropriate choice of the units of measurement, the second sector uses one unit of T and one unit of N to produce one unit of output, Y_2. In the other sector, a unit of Y_1 is produced with one unit of T and k units of N. As before, sector two is T-intensive and sector one is N-intensive $(k > 1)$.

The usage of the factors is less than or equal to factor supplies:

$$(6) \qquad\qquad Y_1 + Y_2 \leq T,$$

$$(7) \qquad\qquad kY_1 + Y_2 \leq N,$$

where T and N are the factor endowments. The equations hold with equality if factors are fully employed; otherwise, factor prices equal their reservation wages.[36]

If both factors are fully employed, the economy is operating at point A on the kinked production possibility frontier, as shown in figure 4. Full

35. Salop, in "Model of the Natural Rate of Unemployment," shows that structural unemployment can result from having too few prices or inflexible prices—that is, he gives a quasi-Walrasian explanation. See Montek S. Ahluwalia, "Taxes, Subsidies, and Employment," *Quarterly Journal of Economics,* vol. 87 (August 1973), pp. 393–409, for the use of a two-sector model to examine the effect of subsidies on employment in a less-developed country.

36. Factor supplies are assumed to be inelastic above the reservation wage and zero below.

Figure 4. Production Possibility Frontier in the Fixed Coefficients Case

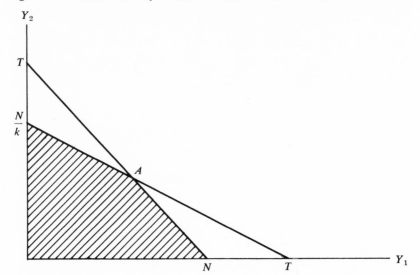

employment requires that factor supplies differ by not "too" much and that demand be appropriate (the community's highest isowelfare curve hits the production possibility frontier at the kink).

There might be, however, so little of one factor (say N) that the other factor is structurally unemployed. This situation is shown in figure 5. Here T's price, w_T, is driven to the reservation wage and there is structural unemployment: there is a strict inequality in equation 6. Note, however, that the amount of unemployment depends on demand conditions, though no shift in demand can lead to full employment.

If society consumes only Y_2, then $T - N$ of the T-type workers will be unemployed.[37] On the other hand, if society consumes only Y_1, then $T - (N/k)$ workers would be unemployed. Since $k > 1$, $N/k < N$, workers would be unemployed in the second case. Thus the structural unemployment problem is aggravated by adverse demand conditions. Up to $(T - N/k) - (T - N) = N(1 - 1/k)$ extra workers will be unemployed in the least favorable condition compared with the most favorable one.

In a competitive equilibrium, marginal cost would equal price:

(8) $$MC_1 = w_T + kw_N = 1,$$

37. If society consumes only Y_2, then N units of Y_2 can be produced and N units of T are hired for this purpose. As this figure shows, $T > N$, so $T - N$ units of T are unemployed.

Figure 5. Structural Unemployment in the Fixed Coefficients Case

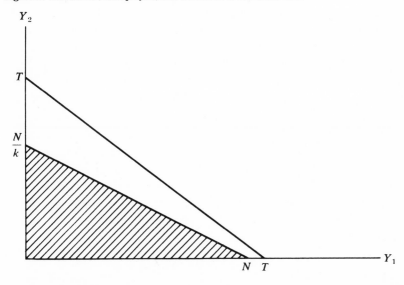

(9) $$MC_2 = w_T + w_N = \frac{p_2}{p_1},$$

where p_1 has been normalized to equal one. If the T-type workers' reservation wage is positive, the employment tax subsidy can reduce unemployment. By subsidizing workers in the T-intensive sector (or possibly both sectors), p_2 falls relative to p_1. This change in relative prices should stimulate demand for Y_2 relative to Y_1, and reduce unemployment. Of course, if the subsidy were placed in sector one, unemployment could increase.

In this model, there is no within firm (sector) substitution, but there is between firm (sector) substitution. In many industries, there may be little possibility of substituting in favor of T-type workers. If a targeted employment subsidy causes other industries to grow relative to those industries, they may be hurt by the credit.

Minimum Wage and Search

As noted earlier, if minimum wage coverage is incomplete, workers may be driven out of the covered sector into the uncovered sector, which will create a wage differential but no unemployment. In a world of imperfect information, however, a minimum wage–induced wage differential may cause workers to search for high-paying, minimum wage jobs, which will result in frictional unemployment. Mincer and Gramlich have discussed such models in the context of the minimum wage; Ross and Wachter, and Hall and Varian, have shown how sticky wages in the administered price sector or government sector could cause unemployment.[38]

Again, I assume that the minimum wage, w'_T, is paid in sector two, whereas a competitive wage, w_T ($< w'_T$), is paid in sector one. To simplify the model, I assume that a person cannot work full-time in the competitive sector and actively search for a high-paying minimum job at the same time.[39] As a result, the individual T-type worker decides what proportion of time to work in the competitive sector, q, and what proportion to devote to search (and/or work) in the noncompetitive sector, $1 - q$, in any time period.

The individual worker will attempt to maximize his expected utility through his choice of q:

$$(10) \qquad V[q(w_T, w'_T, \pi, r)] = \max \pi U[w_T q + (1 - q)w'_T]$$

$$+ (1 - \pi)U[w_T q + (1 - q)r w_T],$$

$$\equiv \max \pi U Y_1 + (1 - \pi)U Y_2,$$

38. See Mincer, "Unemployment Effects of Minimum Wages"; Gramlich, "Impact of Minimum Wages on Other Wages"; Ross and Wachter, "Wage Determination, Inflation, and the Industrial Structure"; Hall, "Rigidity of Wages and the Persistence of Unemployment"; and Varian, "Models of Unemployment."

39. For simplicity, I assume that one must start fresh in each period. That is, one cannot keep a high-paying job into the future. Alternatively, this is a model of a one-period economy (the discount rate is infinite). Relaxing this assumption would complicate the mathematics without adding any important insight; it would merely be necessary to consider several future periods. The only additional result that such a model would produce is that search diminishes with age. For analyzing the targeted jobs tax credit or a similar credit, this restrictive assumption is reasonable, since youths will grow out of the relevant job market quickly. Even though other target group members may not leave their groups so easily, credits usually last for a short time. Workers are also assumed to search or work for a fixed amount of time per period. This assumption could be relaxed so that workers could choose the number of hours to work. One possibility would be that people would choose not to work if welfare payments were high enough. Although this consideration is probably important for T-type workers, I am abstracting from it in this model. Finally, wages are implicitly expressed in real terms in the model.

where π is his (constant) expected probability of finding a minimum wage job, r (< 1) is the wage-income replacement rate from unemployment insurance, and Y_1 and Y_2 are the incomes in the two states. For $0 < q < 1$ (an interior solution), the first- and second-order conditions must be satisfied:

(11) $\qquad U'(Y_1^*)(w_T - w_T') + (1 - \pi)U'(Y_2^*)[w_T(1 - r)] = 0,$

(12) $\quad A \equiv \pi U''(Y_1^*)(w_T - w_T')^2 + (1 - \pi)U''(Y_2^*)[w_T(1 - r)]^2 < 0,$

where an asterisk indicates an equilibrium value. Given risk aversion, the second-order condition is always satisfied.

Changes in the variables that are exogenous to the individual worker (w_T', w_T, π, r) will cause him to adjust his labor supply to the competitive sector (q), as shown in the appendix. As the probability of finding a minimum wage job (π) increases, the fraction of time spent searching or working in the sector ($1 - q$) increases, and the fraction spent in the competitive sector (q) decreases. An increase in the unemployment insurance wage replacement rate (r) induces workers to decrease the fraction of time they work in the competitive sector. Because there are both "substitution" and "income" (or "insurance") effects, a change in either w_T or w_T' leads to ambiguous results. If the substitution effects dominate the income effects, an increase in w_T increases q, whereas an increase in w_T' decreases q.

It is clear that the unemployment in this model is due to search that results from a wage differential. If the minimum wage is not binding, all markets clear and no unemployment exists. If a targeted employment subsidy (financed through lump-sum taxes) reduces the minimum wage to the first-best general equilibrium wage level, then a first-best equilibrium can be obtained with no unemployment. Indeed, if only T-type workers are taxed to pay for the subsidy, the original equilibrium will be obtained.

In this model, the effect of a subsidy that does not exactly offset the minimum wage is unclear. The movement is from one second-best equilibrium to another, and no general welfare statements can be made. It is possible, however, to examine the comparative statics of such an economy. In order to complete the model, several equations in addition to 11 are needed. A simple general equilibrium model in which the prices of final goods and the other factor are constant (that is, final demand and the other factor's supply are elastic) is presented here.[40]

Equation 11 depends on the competitive wage and the probability of finding a minimum wage job. Two more equations are needed to explain these variables. The probability of finding a minimum wage job is the ratio of workers demanded in the minimum wage sector, T^2, to the number of people searching for such jobs, $1 - q$.[41] The number of workers demanded is determined by the equality between the wage and the value of the marginal product of T in each sector. Since output prices are given, the labor demand equations depend only on the wage in that sector and the subsidy to that sector. Thus the probability of finding a minimum wage job is

$$(13) \qquad \pi = \frac{T^2(w'_T, s)}{1 - q},$$

where s is the subsidy to the minimum wage sector. The partial derivatives of T^2 are $T^2_{w'_T} < 0$ and $T^2_s > 0$.

In the competitive sector, the competitive wage will adjust until supply equals demand:

$$(14) \qquad q = T^1(w_T, t),$$

where t is the employment subsidy to this sector and $T^1_{w_T} < 0$ and $T^1_t > 0$.

Unemployment (μ) is determined by the identity

$$(15) \qquad \mu = (1 - q)(1 - \pi)$$

$$= (1 - q) - T^2(w'_T, s).$$

The second line of equation 15 says unemployment equals the supply of labor to the covered sector less the demand in that sector (in the other sector, supply equals demand).

The formal comparative statics analysis is presented in the appendix, but some of the results are given below, where the signs of the derivatives

---

40. In "Surprising Effects of Employment Subsidies on Unemployment and Welfare," I present a general equilibrium, Cobb-Douglas model in which these elasticity assumptions are modified.

41. The total number of T-type workers is set equal to one by appropriate choice of units of measurement.

of the left-hand-column endogenous variables with respect to the top-row exogenous variables are shown.

	r	w'_T	s	t
w_T	+	?	+	+
q	−	?	−	+
π	−	−	+	+
μ	+	?	?	−

(The signs of dw_T/dw'_T and $d\mu_T/dw'_T$ are the same, and both are the opposite of dq/dw'_T.)

Heuristically, as the employment subsidy (s) is slightly increased in the minimum wage sector, the demand for labor in the minimum wage sector rises, which increases search and decreases the supply to the competitive sector. Because the demand increase outweighs the increased supply to the minimum wage sector, the probability of finding a minimum wage job increases. The reduced supply to the competitive sector increases the competitive wage. The overall unemployment level change is uncertain, since both the number of workers searching and the fraction who find minimum wage jobs increase.

An increase in the subsidy (t) to the competitive sector has surprising results. The increased competitive demand attracts labor to this sector (q rises). Since demand increases by more than supply responds, the competitive wage increases. Because fewer workers are searching in the minimum wage sector, the probability of finding a job there increases. The reduction in search causes the unemployment rate to fall.

The effects of changes in r and w'_T are similar. An increase in the unemployment insurance wage replacement rate encourages search and leads to an increase in unemployment. The effect of an increase in the minimum wage is unclear.[42] Once again, it should be noted that the welfare implications are unclear.[43] In my Cobb-Douglas, general equilibrium version of this model, three additional results are obtained: (1) only an optimally set subsidy that is equal in both sectors can eliminate the minimum wage–induced unemployment and result in a Pareto optimal equi-

---

42. This scenario has implicitly assumed that the subsidies were financed by lump-sum taxation of N-type workers or others. If targeted labor pays for the subsidy (either t or $sT^2/(1 - q)$ per worker), all the results reported in the text stay the same except for the following: the minimum-wage subsidy derivative $d\pi/ds$ would become negative; both dq/dt and $d\pi/dt$ would have the same (indeterminate) sign which is the opposite of $d\mu/dt$.

43. If workers differ in tastes, the welfare and other effects would be even harder to determine.

librium; (2) a subsidy just to the covered sector may actually increase unemployment and lower welfare; and (3) a subsidy just to the uncovered sector may do more good than one just to the covered sector.[44]

Conclusions and Implications for Empirical Research

This survey of theoretical models suggests that a targeted employment subsidy will probably increase efficiency only if it can correct a market imperfection such as might be caused by a minimum wage, or if it can reduce unemployment. It will probably increase welfare if it encourages firms to hire target group members who are unemployed or out of the labor market. It will probably reduce welfare if it merely causes firms that claim the credit to hire workers away from other firms that do not use the credit.

While this paper emphasizes efficiency considerations, equity effects are important. Although the models reported here indicate that, in the absence of serious offsetting distortions, a targeted employment subsidy will probably reduce efficiency, it may redistribute income in a desirable way. As table 1 indicates, under certain conditions the subsidy will cause target group wages to rise in real terms. A complete welfare analysis of a subsidy program (compared with no program at all) would have to consider the trade-off between equity and efficiency. The theoretical models show, however, that there is no guarantee that such a program will increase target group wages; positive equity effects are therefore not assured.

Such considerations indicate that indirect tests for the desirability of a targeted employment subsidy may be possible. For example, if the subsidy goes mainly to target group–intensive firms and demand for final goods is elastic, target group wages are likely to rise in real terms. If new hires come from the ranks of the unemployed, the program is more likely to be beneficial. If the program does not affect firms' factor proportions, it is unlikely to have much effect.

Such a program is more likely to be desirable if the increase in target group welfare is not offset by losses to other labor groups. Since such losses depend on the degree of substitutability in the production process, production function studies may provide valuable information. There have been several useful simulations of the effects of a targeted employ-

---

44. See Perloff, "Surprising Effects of Employment Subsidies on Unemployment and Welfare."

ment subsidy.[45] Unfortunately, none of them has considered its effects when only some sectors of the economy claim the subsidy.

Undoubtedly empirical studies are more useful for evaluating specific programs than simulations are; but because of data availability restrictions, empirical studies may be misleading if the results are not analyzed with care. For example, one might be tempted to contrast the wages of target group members who are hired under the subsidy program with those of other workers. Not only are there serious empirical difficulties with such a comparison, but also, as the theoretical models indicate, the program may benefit all workers, even though only some are hired under the program.[46] Since firms receive the subsidy rather than individuals, it may increase all target group wages equally.

In conclusion, this survey of theoretical models shows that the success of a targeted employment subsidy program will depend on which conditions in the economy prevail (that is, which model is relevant), which sector is subsidized, and whether demands are elastic, as well as on other conditions that can be determined only by empirical research. Without such information, the program is most likely to have desirable effects if it is designed to offset existing distortions in the economy.

Appendix: Formal Comparative Statics Analysis of Minimum Wage and Search Model

The effect of a change in market variable (w'_T, w_T, π, r) on a worker's time allocation decision (q) may be determined by totally differentiating the first-order equation 11. The resulting effects are

$$A1 = dq/dw'_T = -\pi[U''(Y_1^*)(1 - q^*)(w_T - w'_T) - U'(Y_1^*)]/A$$

$$A2 = dq/dw_T = -\{\pi U''(Y_1^*)q^*(w_T - w'_T) + \pi U'(Y_1^*)$$
$$+ (1 - \pi)U''(Y_2^*)[q^* + (1 - q^*)r]w_T(1 - r) + (1 - \pi)U'(Y_2^*)(1 - r)\}/A$$

45. For example, Gary C. Fethke and Samuel H. Williamson, *Employment Tax Credits as a Fiscal Policy Tool*, prepared for the use of the Subcommittee on Economic Growth of the Joint Economic Committee, 94 Cong. 2 sess. (Government Printing Office, 1976); Kesselman, Williamson, and Berndt, "Tax Credits for Employment Rather than Investment"; and Gary C. Fethke, Andrew J. Policano, and Samuel H. Williamson, *An Investigation of the Conceptual and Qualitative Impact of Employment Tax Credits* (Kalamazoo, Michigan: W. E. Upjohn Institute for Employment Research, 1978).

46. See the preceding paper by Johnson for a useful analysis of incomplete coverages of target group members.

$A3 = dq/d\pi = -[U'(Y_1^*)(w_T - w_T') - U'(Y_2^*)w_T(1 - r)]/A < 0$

$A4 = dq/dr = -(1 - \pi)[U''(Y_2^*)(1 - q^*)w_T^2(1 - r) - U'(Y_2^*)w_T]/A < 0.$

In general, only the last two effects can be signed, as discussed in the text. However, if the substitution effect dominates the income (or "insurance") effects, then an increase in w_T increases q while an increase in w_T' decreases q.

As mentioned in the text, I have elsewhere presented a general equilibrium, Cobb-Douglas version of this model. The Cobb-Douglas assumption is enough to sign the derivatives shown above. Suppose utility is

$$U(Y) = BY^{\beta_1+\beta_2},$$

where

$$B = \left(\frac{1}{\beta_1 + \beta_2}\right)^{\beta_1+\beta_2}\left(\frac{\beta_1}{p_1}\right)^{\beta_1}\left(\frac{\beta_2}{p_2}\right)^{\beta_2}.$$

For the worker to be risk averse, $\beta_1 + \beta_2 < 1$ is needed. Here, $A1$ may be rewritten as

$$A1 = dq/dw_T' = -\pi B(\beta_1 + \beta_2)(Y_1^*)^{\beta_1+\beta_2-2}\{w_T[(\beta_1 + \beta_2 - 1)(1 - q) - q]$$
$$- w_T'(\beta_1 + \beta_2)(1 - q)\}/A.$$

Since $(\beta_1 + \beta_2 - 1) < 0$, the term in the braces is negative; hence the numerator is positive, and $A1$ is negative.

Equations 11, 13, and 14 contain three unknowns (q, π, w_T) and four exogenous variables (w_T', r, s, t). With well-behaved functions, a unique equilibrium (q^*, π^*, w_T^*) exists and is stable. By totally differentiating this three-equation system, it is possible to study the comparative statics:

$$
\begin{bmatrix}
A2 & A & A3 & A4 & A1 & 0 & 0 \\
& & & & & & \\
& & & & & & \\
0 & \dfrac{-T^2}{(1-q)^2} & 1 & 0 & \dfrac{-T^2 w_T'}{(1-q)} & \dfrac{-T_s^2}{(1-q)} & 0 \\
& & & & & & \\
& & & & & & \\
-T_{wT}^1 & 0 & 0 & 0 & 0 & 0 & -T_t^1
\end{bmatrix}
\begin{bmatrix}
dw_T \\
dq \\
d\pi \\
dr \\
dw_T' \\
ds \\
dt
\end{bmatrix}
=
\begin{bmatrix}
0 \\
0 \\
0 \\
0 \\
0 \\
0 \\
0
\end{bmatrix}
$$

In general, very few of the comparative statics results can be signed. If, however, one is willing to assume $A1 < 0$ and $A2 > 0$ (as discussed above), then the results in the informal table on page 119 can be obtained by using Lancaster's algorithm.[47]

Comments by Kenneth Burdett

In his paper Perloff surveys the theoretical effects of targeted employment subsidies under a variety of assumptions. Specifically, he demonstrates how the predicted consequences of imposing a subsidy depend on the theoretical model under consideration. This is important groundwork. Nevertheless, I believe that Perloff does not address some of the main issues raised by his work.

Consider the major theoretical issue. It is well known that the models of the economy usually analyzed by economists imply that all people who want to work are fully employed. Specifically, assumptions are made which guarantee that full employment is the only possible equilibrium result. Four of the key assumptions are as follows:

(1) perfectly flexible prices;

(2) perfect mobility of the factors of production;

(3) perfect information about trading opportunities; and

(4) a production technology that allows for substitution among the various factors of production.

Different assumptions need to be made to generate an unemployment model; that is, a model in which unemployment may exist at an equilibrium.

Perloff puts unemployment models into four categories: disequilibrium models (fixed-price models is perhaps a better term), quasi-Walrasian models, search models, and structural unemployment models. Although this classification is not exhaustive, most unemployment models presented in the literature to date belong to one of these categories.

A typical unemployment model is the same as a full-employment model except that one assumption is changed. For example, in disequilibrium models assumption 1 above is replaced by the restriction that some prices are fixed in the short run. The fixed price assumption may be based on the idea that prices move less quickly than quantities, or on the existence of minimum wage legislation. In quasi-Walrasian models

47. Kelvin Lancaster, "The Solution of Qualitative Comparative Static Problems," *Quarterly Journal of Economics,* vol. 80 (May 1966), pp. 278–95.

it is assumed that labor is not perfectly mobile. In search models workers are assumed to be uncertain of the trading opportunities available, whereas in structural unemployment models factors of production are not substitutable. Thus, embedded in an unemployment model belonging to any of the four categories is a simple idea about the underlying cause of unemployment. Although the actual cause of unemployment in the United States has yet to be determined, the four potential causes just described are the primary suspects.

Perloff considers in detail a full-employment model and two unemployment models. One of the unemployment models is a structural unemployment model, and the other is a hybrid, since it includes some elements of a disequilibrium model, in that there is a minimum wage, and some elements of a search model. Not surprisingly, the imposition of a targeted employment subsidy has different effects in the three models. At first blush, this result is not encouraging. No one knows which of the three models is the most applicable to the real world problem, or if any one of the three models is applicable at all. Therefore, using a targeted employment subsidy scheme would appear to be a hit-or-miss affair. I think, however, that some progress can be made. For one thing, if there is full employment in the economy, the imposition of a subsidy will influence the distribution of incomes only. Indeed, if the economy is near enough to full employment that the full employment model is most applicable, the imposition of a subsidy does not seem to make much sense. In what follows I assume that there is unemployment in the economy and that the cause or causes of this unemployment is unknown.

A targeted employment subsidy scheme implies that the effective wage of workers covered by the scheme is lowered relative to other wages. Two crucial questions need to be answered. First, how many hirings of covered workers will be generated by a particular subsidy scheme? Second, what happens to the workers not covered by the scheme? It is not obvious to me that a full-blown general equilibrium model needs to be specified to answer these questions. What seems to be required is a more detailed understanding of a firm's demand for various types of labor; for example, whether high-skilled workers are complements to or substitutes for low-skilled workers in production. If a policymaker knew the answers to the two questions, then I conjecture that knowledge of the underlying cause of unemployment would be of marginal interest. This does not imply that some insight into the underlying cause of unemployment is not essential for many other problems. Policymakers have to make decisions without fully understanding the economy. Determining what is the minimal amount of information that a policymaker needs to evaluate a particular policy is perhaps the more relevant question to ask. Therefore, although I think Perloff's work is important, I feel that policymakers could spend their time more usefully by trying to find answers to simpler problems.

Comments by Frank Levy

Jeffrey Perloff should be commended for writing an interesting and difficult paper. In an early version of the paper, he extended his discussion to suggest how his theoretical analysis might be actually applied to evaluating the targeted jobs tax credit. Although that particular part is no longer included, the problem of evaluation remains important, and I focus most of my comments on it. And, in the process, I offer some suggestions about how the targeted jobs tax credit might be evaluated.

Perloff summarizes his analysis by saying that he would look to a targeted employment subsidy in general (or the targeted jobs tax credit in particular) for equity effects; the tax credit will not improve economic efficiency unless it offsets some already existing market imperfection. The conclusions are undoubtedly right, but, in practice, testing for both equity and efficiency effects will be quite difficult, owing to the small size of the program. The Department of Labor reports that as of February 1980, 140,000 people were certified for the credit and obtained work. (An additional number were certified and did not obtain work.) Of these, about 70,000 were students in co-op education programs (who are not subject to an income test). Of the remaining 70,000, 50,000 were disadvantaged youths. From my rough calculations, these 50,000 disadvantaged youths represent something less than 1 percent of all eighteen- to twenty-four-year-olds whose incomes are below 70 percent of the Bureau of Labor Statistics lower standard.

Given these small numbers, it seems unrealistic to examine the credit's efficiency effects or other subtle measures like employment displacement. Nonetheless, I believe some rough evaluation of equity per se is possible.

An initial strategy would be to focus on the credit's impact in a narrow way. Credit recipients, through their work histories, would act as their own controls, and the evaluation would show how much the credit had improved their employment prospects.

From the work of Akerlof and Main, Clark and Summers, and Ler-

Table 2. Employment Status in March 1978 and Weeks Worked in 1977,
Black Men, Aged Eighteen to Twenty-four[a]

Employment status in March 1978	Mean weeks worked in 1977
Employed	38.2 weeks
Unemployed	17.5 weeks
Not in labor force	4.8 weeks

Source: Special tabulation by the author, using the supplement to the *Current Population Survey* of the
U.S. Bureau of Labor Statistics.
a. The sample is restricted to men who were not in school in 1977 or 1978.

man, Barnow, and Moss, and from my own work with Lerman, it is clear
that unemployment statistics are disproportionately generated by a few
people in a far more concentrated fashion than simple Markovian models
would suggest.[48] A person who is unemployed today is far more likely to
be unemployed tomorrow than a similar person who is working today.
Even in the supposedly volatile youth labor market, this concentration
of experience holds, as can be seen in table 2.

Given this information, and the small sample sizes, it makes sense to
consider a rough-and-ready evaluation that does not require enormous
amounts of money and that can be grafted on to the kind of "recipient
audit" survey the General Accounting Office or some other agency might
do. In particular, one would like to identify a sample of disadvantaged
youths who were certified for the targeted jobs tax credit off the street.
That is, they came for certification on their own instead of being sent for
certification by a co-op program or by an employer for whom they were
already working. Assuming the sample was constructed from certification
records,[49] some time will have passed between the time of certification
and the time the youths were interviewed in the survey. This should then

48. George A. Akerlof and Brian G. M. Main, "Unemployment Spells and
Unemployment Experience," Division of Research and Statistics, Special Studies
Paper 123 (Board of Governors of the Federal Reserve System, October 1978);
Kim B. Clark and Lawrence H. Summers, "Labor Market Dynamics and Unem-
ployment: A Reconsideration," *BPEA, 1:1979*, pp. 13–60; Robert Lerman, Burt
Barnow, and Phillip Moss, "Concepts and Measures of Structural Unemployment,"
Office of the Assistant Secretary for Policy, Evaluation, and Research, "Technical
Analysis Paper 64 (U.S. Department of Labor, March 1979); and Frank Levy and
Robert Lerman, "Notes on Teenage Unemployment Rates and Targeting" (Urban
Institute, October 1979).

49. Presumably, information on how the young men decided to seek certification
—that is, whether or not they were sent by someone else—would come from the interview rather than from the certification forms.

make it possible to ask two kinds of questions: (1) How well are the youths doing at the time of the interview? And (2) how well were the youths doing before they were certified (as reconstructed from work history questions)?

Given the general persistence of labor market experience noted above, any sharp differences between the responses to the two questions could be attributed, at least in part, to the credit.

But what about selectivity bias? I did a lot of work in 1980 with selected sample estimators, and in this case I am not worried. My expectation is that young men who are savvy enough to seek out tax credit certification are also savvy enough to have developed a decent work history; that is, people who find employment under the credit are people who, in my argument, would have been employed anyway. If the data really show substantial employment for persons with ragged work histories, I am more than willing to give the targeted jobs tax credit program its due.

If my disdain of selectivity bias here is still unconvincing, the number of tax credit certifications is small enough to make it easy to assemble a sample of controls—people who were eligible for, but did not receive, certification. This set of controls would be combined with the certified group and examined from several perspectives, including a self-selected sample analysis. At the same time, it would be interesting to do a separate, perhaps more anecdotal analysis of the relation of the credit to co-op students. From the enrollment figures quoted above, it is clear that the co-op instructors made good use of the credit. My casual empiricism suggests that co-op students usually do pretty well in employment for two related reasons. First, the co-op instructor often does a fair amount of screening of students admitted to the program. Second, the potential employer knows he can complain to the co-op instructor if the student gets out of line, and the instructor—who wants to place future students—can act as an additional disciplinary force.

In this context, it is questionable whether the targeted jobs tax credit expanded employment at all—that is, did instructors take more "risky" applicants into the programs, or was the credit just subsidizing students who would have become employed in any case?

This discussion has taken me somewhat far afield from Perloff's paper, but it reflects the way in which circumstances have changed since Perloff began working on his topic. Had the targeted jobs tax credit been widely taken up, say, on the level of the new jobs tax credit, Perloff's theoretical development would have had much more relevance to the evaluation problem at hand. Conversely, had Perloff known when he began his work how small the take-up rate of the targeted jobs tax credit was going to be, I suggest he would have written a different kind of paper.

The cynical among us will conclude that Perloff's real mistake was in writing his paper on schedule. If he had put off writing his paper until, say, one week ago, he could have taken advantage of the most up-to-date data available. Speaking as Perloff's discussant, I find it unnecessary to dignify such a partial-equilibrium analysis with any comment.

Part Two

Empirical Evidence

Donald A. Nichols

Effects on the Noninflationary Unemployment Rate

The conceptual link between selective employment programs and the aggregate unemployment rate has been described by Baily and Tobin.[1] In this paper I provide preliminary estimates of that link for the case of a targeted employment subsidy. Although the procedure is straightforward, the estimates have many limitations and are subject to wide margins of error. Nevertheless, they are of interest because they constitute one of the first estimates of the potential effects of selective employment programs on unemployment that are consistent with macroeconomic constraints.

The subsidy considered here is one that reduces the cost to employers of hiring low-wage workers. The labor force is divided roughly in half and the subsidy is applied to the entire bottom half. The estimates indicate that with a subsidy of this kind the unemployment rate could be lowered between one-half and two-thirds of a percentage point with no increase in the rate of inflation. This subsidy is estimated to cost between $7.5 billion and $29.0 billion, depending on one's estimate of the elas-

I am grateful to the editors of this volume, to the discussants and participants at the conference, and to Burt Barnow, David Brazell, David Finifter, Donald Hester, Mead Over, Arnold Packer, and Eugene Smolensky for their comments on a version of this paper. I received able research assistance on various parts of the project from Constance Schnabel, Daniel McCollum, Judy Dawson, and Gregory Krohn. The research was supported by grants from the Labor Department to the Institute for Research on Poverty, University of Wisconsin, and from the National Commission on Employment Policy.
1. Martin Neil Baily and James Tobin, "Inflation-Unemployment Consequences of Job Creation Policies," in John L. Palmer, ed., *Creating Jobs: Public Employment Programs and Wage Subsidies* (Brookings Institution, 1978), pp. 43–75; and Martin Neil Baily and James Tobin, "Macroeconomic Effects of Selective Public Employment and Wage Subsidies," *Brookings Papers on Economic Activity*, 2:1977, pp. 511–41 (hereafter *BPEA*).

ticity of substitution between the two kinds of labor. Because of non-linearities, five-sixths of the unemployment reduction is available for three-fifths of the cost. Although this procedure could also be applied to public employment programs, only the wage subsidy issue is analyzed here.

The paper begins with a summary of the Baily-Tobin methodology and a description of the numerical computations to be made. Then comes a presentation of empirical estimates of the relation between wage inflation and the relative unemployment rates of different labor force groups. These relations imply a set of relative and absolute unemployment rates consistent with nonaccelerating wage inflation. The minimum overall rate of unemployment found in this set is computed along with its components. Estimates are then provided under a variety of assumptions of the size of the wage subsidy necessary to bring about the structure of unemployment found at that minimum. Finally, the effects of the subsidy on gross national product are computed. The paper closes with a discussion of the limitations of the computations and the possible ways they could be refined.

Reducing the Nonaccelerating Inflation Rate of Unemployment

The nonaccelerating inflation rate of unemployment (NAIRU), which was first defined by Phelps and Friedman, is the lowest possible unemployment rate consistent with a constant rate of inflation.[2] Sometimes called the natural rate of unemployment, it has become a more and more widely used concept over the past decade and now appears in popular macroeconomics textbooks despite a less-than-universal acceptance by leading economists.[3]

The NAIRU is a particularly convenient concept to use when estimating the effects of microeconomic (structural) employment programs on the unemployment rate. Since the macroeconomic policies that are used to reduce unemployment are substantially influenced by the rate of inflation, it has not been possible to estimate the full effect of structural pro-

---

2. Edmund S. Phelps, "Phillips Curves, Expectations of Inflation and Optimal Unemployment over Time," *Economica*, vol. 34 (August 1967), pp. 254–81; and Milton Friedman, "The Role of Monetary Policy," *American Economic Review*, vol. 58 (March 1968), pp. 1–17.

3. See, for example, James Tobin, "Inflation and Unemployment," *American Economic Review*, vol. 62 (March 1972), pp. 1–18; and Arthur M. Okun, "Inflation: Its Mechanics and Welfare Costs," *BPEA, 2:1975*, pp. 351–90.

grams on unemployment without knowing their effect on inflation, which will largely determine the level of offsetting or reinforcing macroeconomic policies likely to be adopted. Baily and Tobin have described a way to provide the needed estimate of the inflationary effect of structural programs as part of a procedure for estimating the level of the NAIRU.

The Baily and Tobin procedure first estimates the effect of unemployment in various labor force categories on its respective rate of wage inflation. The wage equations are then appropriately weighted and added up within the NAIRU framework to reveal an aggregate relation between the rate of wage acceleration and the levels of unemployment in those categories. Previous authors have estimated the NAIRU from equations that use a single unemployment rate to determine the rate of wage acceleration. In these relations NAIRU is the unemployment rate consistent with zero wage acceleration.[4] In the Baily-Tobin analysis a whole schedule of aggregate unemployment rates is consistent with nonaccelerating wage inflation, depending on how that unemployment is distributed across the various labor force groups. The empirical estimates provided by Baily and Tobin indicate that a lower NAIRU can be reached than the usual aggregate wage equations would imply if low-skilled employment could be increased and high-skilled employment decreased. One way to accomplish this change would be through a subsidy for employing low-skilled workers—a targeted employment subsidy.

This paper extends the work of Baily and Tobin in several ways: (1) an occupational classification of the work force is used rather than an industrial or demographic classification; and (2) an estimate is provided of the possible effect on the NAIRU of an employment subsidy focused on less-skilled occupations. The latter computation requires the use of admittedly strict and arbitrary assumptions, but the resulting estimate does not appear to be unreasonable.

Because a long time series of occupational wage rates does not exist, the relation is estimated in its aggregate form. The hourly earnings index is used to form the single dependent variable and two separate unemployment rates are used as independent variables, each representing roughly half the major occupational groups as defined by the Bureau of Labor Statistics. The classification is described in table 1. In this aggregated form the model is not the same as Baily and Tobin's, though it is consistent with their model in equilibrium.

---

4. See, for example, George L. Perry, "Slowing the Wage-Price Spiral: The Macroeconomic View," *BPEA, 2:1978*, pp. 259–91.

Table 1. Classification of High-Wage and Low-Wage Occupations in 1978

Occupation	Employment (thousands)	Unemployment (thousands)	Unemployment rate (percent)	Median wage rate, May (dollars per hour)
High-wage				
Managers and administrators	10,105	214	2.1	6.87
Professional and technical workers	14,245	381	2.6	6.74
Craft and kindred workers	12,386	603	4.6	6.50
Operatives, including transport	14,416	1,155	7.4	5.36
Total number or average rate	51,152	2,353	4.4	6.32
Low-wage				
Clerical workers	16,904	866	4.9	4.17
Nonfarm laborers	4,729	566	10.7	4.11
Sales workers	5,951	256	4.1	3.85
Service workers (except private household)	11,677	966	7.6	3.20
Farm workers	2,798	110	3.8	2.77
Private household workers	1,162	63	5.1	2.04
No previous work experience	...	868	...	...
Total number or average rate	43,221	3,695	7.9	3.71

Sources: Employment data are from *Employment and Training Report of the President, 1979*, pp. 260–61, 271; wage data are from *Current Population Survey*, May 1978.

The Baily-Tobin model can be described by the following three relations:

(1)
$$GWH = \alpha_1 + \frac{\beta_1}{UH} + \gamma_1 R$$

(2)
$$GWL = \alpha_2 + \frac{\beta_2}{UL} + \gamma_2 R$$

(3)
$$GW = \lambda GWH + (1 - \lambda)GWL,$$

where

UH = high-wage unemployment rate
UL = low-wage unemployment rate
WH = average wage rate for high-wage occupation
WL = average wage rate for low-wage occupation
R = the wage ratio WH/WL
G = the acceleration operator, that is,

$$GX = \frac{X_t - X_{t-1}}{X_{t-1}} - \frac{X_{t-1} - X_{t-2}}{X_{t-2}}.$$

The equilibrium requirements for this model are $GW = 0$ and $GWH = GWL$; aggregate wage acceleration must be zero and relative wages must be constant.[5] Solving the two equilibrium requirements together gives

(4)
$$O = A + \frac{B}{UH} + \frac{C}{UL},$$

where

$$A = \lambda\alpha_1 + (1 - \lambda)\alpha_2 + \frac{[\lambda\gamma_1 + (1 - \lambda)\gamma_2](\alpha_1 - \alpha_2)}{\gamma_2 - \gamma_1}$$

$$B = \frac{\beta_1\gamma_2}{\gamma_2 - \gamma_1}$$

$$C = \frac{-\beta_2\gamma_1}{\gamma_2 - \gamma_1}.$$

It is equation 4 that is used below for estimating the possible change in NAIRU that can be accomplished by varying UH and UL.

Because of the lack of data on relative wage rates, however, the parameter estimates for equation 4 are derived in this paper from a direct estimation of the effect of the two unemployment rates on the rate of wage acceleration. This procedure may cause a problem of unknown significance. The nature of the problem is described in the comments on this

5. Technically, setting $GWH = GWL$ does not fix relative wages, since it is possible for each wage to be increasing at a different, constant rate. Except for the Cobb-Douglas production function, however, a change in relative wages would change λ in equation 3, which is the relative share of income of high-wage labor. As λ changed and the two separate rates of wage inflation remained constant, the aggregate rate of wage change would change, violating the other equilibrium condition. Thus the pair of conditions, $GW = 0$ and $GWH = GWL$, do lead to constant relative wages with the exception of the Cobb-Douglas production function.

paper by George Johnson; namely, that in this aggregated form the estimated relation is consistent with several alternative disaggregated models having different implications for employment policies. The conclusions drawn in this paper are warranted only if the Baily-Tobin model is the true underlying structure. There is no formal way to show that it is. But since that model has been shown to be consistent with demographic and industrial disaggregations of the labor force, it is also likely to be appropriate for occupational disaggregations. (If it is not, the interpretations of equation 4 that are provided below are not justified.) In addition to the unemployment rates shown in equation 4, a small number of special independent variables are used to represent the effects on wages of changes in the minimum wage and of the wage control program of 1971–72.

Because there are two unemployment rates in the estimated wage equation, it cannot be solved for a unique NAIRU. Instead, when wage acceleration is set at zero, as in equation 4, a relation emerges between the two unemployment rates that yields a schedule of NAIRUs, each corresponding to a particular set of unemployment rates for the two groups. Each NAIRU, along with the separate unemployment rates of its components, is called an unemployment structure. Several of these structures are presented and discussed later. In particular, the minimum possible NAIRU is computed along with its associated structure.

The minimum NAIRU is found to be one-half to two-thirds of a percentage point below the NAIRU likely to be attained from a normal macroeconomic expansion. The structure of unemployment at the minimum NAIRU has far less low-wage unemployment and slightly more high-wage unemployment than would occur at the higher NAIRU more typical of macroeconomic expansions.

Many policies could be used to attain the minimum NAIRU. Here its computation is based on the assumed introduction of a targeted employment subsidy—a subsidy to employers that reduces the cost of low-wage labor. For these computations, an aggregate constant elasticity of substitution production function is assumed, where output is produced by the two classes of labor. Elasticities of substitution of 0.5 and 2 are used, representing the boundaries of plausible estimates suggested by past research.[6] For these elasticities, separate estimates are computed of the

---

6. Daniel S. Hamermesh and James Grant, "Econometric Studies of Labor-Labor Substitution and Their Implications for Policy," *Journal of Human Resources,* vol. 14 (Fall 1979), pp. 518–42. This survey reports estimates varying from 0.2 to 7.5 (pp. 526–28).

size of the wage subsidy needed to reduce the NAIRU to its minimum level.

Although the minimum NAIRU is, by definition, the lowest noninflationary unemployment rate, its structure of unemployment rates is not the one that leads to a maximum level of GNP. This is because workers are given equal weight when unemployment is being minimized but are weighted according to productivity when GNP is maximized. At the minimum NAIRU, a further increase in low-wage employment would require an equal reduction in high-wage employment if inflation was not to be affected. From this level, however, an increase in high-wage employment, combined with the reduction in low-wage employment necessary to leave inflation unaffected, would cause GNP to rise.

Given any elasticity of substitution, it is possible to compute the effect of the various employment structures on GNP. A maximum for GNP is computed here that is consistent with nonaccelerating inflation. The NAIRU associated with this level of GNP is estimated to be only one-tenth of a percentage point higher than the minimum NAIRU, but it has a very different employment structure. A subsidy only 60 percent as large is needed to reach the maximum level of GNP consistent with nonaccelerating inflation as is needed to reach the minimum NAIRU.

Estimated Wage Equations

A rough labor force classification is presented in table 1 along with associated data for 1978. Although Baily and Tobin use the words *high-skilled* and *low-skilled* to describe their two groups, in their empirical work they deal with industrial and demographic classifications. The two main categories used here are high-wage and low-wage occupations. Each category includes workers with a wide range of wage levels, so that many high-wage workers are counted in the low-wage category and vice versa. Ideally what is wanted is a classification of workers according to the effect of unemployment in their group on the rate of wage inflation.[7] Use of the rough classification described here will lead to an underestimate of the potential effect of structural programs on the unemployment rate,

---

7. Robert Eisner and David Finifter have pointed out to me that a classification according to unemployment rate rather than wage level is more likely to accomplish this goal. Several readers have suggested that clerical workers be included with the high-wage rather than the low-wage groups, since structural employment programs are unlikely to be directed at them.

because an error in classification will bias the coefficients of the sectoral unemployment rates toward each other.[8]

The difficulty encountered in classifying workers casts doubt on the usefulness of dual theories of the labor market in which some workers have good jobs and some have bad. The difficulty arises because workers and jobs have smooth unimodal distributions of characteristics, so that it is hard to draw a line that cuts these distributions into two groups, one whose unemployment affects wage inflation substantially and another that does not.

An important limitation of the procedure followed is that it treats the wage equation as a structural relation. This is potentially a major weakness. The use of wage equations for policy purposes has been criticized since the original Phillips article appeared in 1958.[9] But despite criticism, use of the Phillips curve and its successors has grown because they fill a void in macroeconomic models. The fact is there is no more reliable way to divide the effect of a change in demand into real and inflationary components than to use a wage equation. Although the typical wage equation in macroeconomic models does not display as tight a fit as the consumption function or the demand for money, predictions of wage increases have been better in recent years than predictions of interest rates or productivity, and the unemployment rate is usually the most important explanatory variable in the prediction of wage change.

Wage equations were quickly adopted by Keynesian economists soon after Phillips published. Not only did the wage equation fill the void just mentioned, but under certain conditions it could be interpreted as a simple transformation of Keynes's aggregate labor supply curve in which

8. In future studies more careful disaggregations are proposed, and it is expected that a larger potential role for structural policies will emerge from that work. It should be noted, however, that no matter how carefully the data are classified, a perfect separation is probably impossible. For every classification will have distributions of skills within it and will have members who do not need structural employment programs as well as those who do. This classification problem is the same as the problem encountered when choosing eligibility criteria for structural programs. No matter how carefully the criteria are drawn, there will be some who are eligible who do not need the program and some who are ineligible who do. It is only appropriate, therefore, that the econometric work give an underestimate of the role that would be attributed to structural programs if an ideal classification were possible, since such a classification is usually impossible for policymakers or researchers to attain.

9. A. W. Phillips, "The Relation between Unemployment and the Rate of Change of Money Wage Rates in the United Kingdom, 1861–1957," *Economica*, vol. 25 (November 1958), pp. 283–99.

the money wage plays an important role. Since the Phillips version specified in terms of the rate of change of money wages fits the historical time
series data far better than an equation specified in terms of the level of
the money wage, it was easily accepted by Keynesian economists.[10]

Although monetarists were never content with the simple Phillips
curve, they quickly accepted the hypothesis of a natural rate of unemployment espoused by Friedman and Phelps. The existence of a natural rate
of unemployment is a maintained hypothesis in wage equations expressed
in terms of acceleration—where the dependent variable is the increase in
the rate of wage inflation. This hypothesis was found to be more consistent with the aggregate data of the late 1960s and 1970s than the simple Phillips curve expressed in terms of rates of change. Monetarists now
feel comfortable with wage equations expressed in accelerationist form
because these are consistent with certain important characteristics of
monetarist models, such as the neutrality of money and the inability of
macro policymakers to influence unemployment in the long run.

After some initial resistance, Keynesian economists have begun to use
wage equations in accelerationist form, perhaps in part because of the
convenience afforded by models having the very long run properties so
appealing to the monetarists. To a Keynesian, a wage equation in its
accelerationist form remains simply a transformation of the Keynesian
labor supply curve, and the appropriate order of the derivative of the
wage variable is now viewed as something to be determined empirically.
The short-run policy implications of models with wage equations are the
same regardless of the dimension of the wage variable.

The work reported here requires stability of the wage equation and
depends on the assumption that it will remain fixed while major changes
in the structure of employment are engineered. Since the changes considered below move the employment rates far beyond their range in the
sample period, it is especially difficult to place any confidence in the
numerical estimates provided.[11]

The estimated wage equations are reported in tables 2 and 3. First,
they were estimated in the nonaccelerationist, or Phillips, form, as shown

10. For a description of the role of the Phillips curve in postwar macroeconomic
thought, see Robert J. Gordon, "Postwar Macroeconomics: The Evolution of Events
and Ideas," National Bureau of Economic Research Working Paper 459 (NBER,
February 1980).

11. For a summary of wage equations and their policy implications, see Arthur
M. Okun, "Efficient Disinflationary Policies," *American Economic Review,* vol. 68
(May 1978, *Papers and Proceedings, 1977*), pp. 348–52.

Table 2. Determinants of Wage Inflation: Nonaccelerationist Form, 1958:1–1978:4[a]

Equation	Average change in dependent variable, previous 4 quarters	Average change in dependent variable, 8 quarters before that	Average change in CPI in previous 4 quarters	Average change in CPI in 12 quarters before that	Inverse of high-wage unemployment rate	Inverse of low-wage unemployment rate	Minimum wage[b]	Wage control dummy[c]	Guidepost dummy[d]	Inverse of unemployment rate	Ratio of high-wage to low-wage employment	Constant	R^2	Durbin-Watson	Standard error of estimate
2-1	0.712 (6.6)	0.323 (2.5)	...	...	0.071 (1.9)	−0.054 (−0.5)	0.021 (5.1)	2.66 (3.5)	...	...	...	−1.11 (−1.1)	0.85	1.83	0.84
2-2	0.712 (6.6)	0.340 (2.7)	...	...	0.053 (3.8)	...	0.022 (5.2)	2.69 (3.6)	...	...	...	−1.55 (−2.9)	0.85	1.81	0.83
2-3	0.742 (6.9)	0.335 (2.5)	...	...	...	0.127 (3.3)	0.022 (5.3)	2.74 (3.6)	...	...	...	−2.28 (−2.8)	0.84	1.76	0.85
2-4	...	...	0.325 (6.6)	0.230 (3.1)	...	...	0.013 (3.3)	2.58 (3.8)	0.98 (3.5)	0.046 (1.2)	0.711 (2.9)	−35.5 (−2.9)	0.87	1.77	0.76
2-5	...	...	0.403 (9.2)	0.342 (3.9)	0.081 (1.6)	−0.006 (0.0)	0.014 (3.5)	2.33 (3.3)	0.67 (2.1)	...	...	0.77 (0.6)	0.86	1.63	0.79
2-6	...	...	0.403 (9.3)	0.345 (6.4)	0.079 (6.4)	...	0.014 (3.6)	2.32 (3.3)	0.67 (2.7)	...	...	0.71 (1.7)	0.86	1.62	0.79
2-7	...	...	0.403 (9.1)	0.441 (7.2)	...	0.227 (6.3)	0.015 (3.7)	2.39 (3.3)	0.35 (1.4)	...	...	−1.15 (−1.7)	0.86	1.58	0.80

Source: The hourly earnings index, the consumer price index, and the data for the unemployment rates are from the U.S. Bureau of Labor Statistics.

a. The dependent variable is the quarterly percentage change in the average hourly earnings index. The figures in parentheses are t-statistics.

b. The percentage change of the level of the minimum wage with no adjustment for coverage.

c. Equals minus one in 1971:4 and plus one-half in 1972:1.

d. Equals minus one from 1962:1 to 1967:1 and zero in all other observations.

Table 3. Determinants of Wage Inflation: Accelerationist Form, 1958:1–1978:4[a]

	Independent variable							Summary statistic		
Equation	Inverse of high-wage unemployment rate	Inverse of low-wage unemployment rate	Minimum wage[b]	Wage control dummy[c]	Inverse of generated high-wage unemployment rate	Inverse of generated low-wage unemployment rate	Constant	$\bar{R}^2$	Durbin-Watson	Standard error of estimate
3-1	0.078 (2.3)	−0.081 (−0.9)	0.021 (5.2)	2.64 (3.6)	...	...	−0.70 (−1.2)	0.41	1.82	0.83
3-2	0.049 (4.2)	...	0.022 (5.3)	2.66 (3.6)	...	...	−1.19 (−3.9)	0.41	1.79	0.83
3-3	...	0.101 (3.6)	0.022 (5.3)	2.70 (3.5)	...	...	−1.60 (−3.4)	0.38	1.70	0.85
3-4	...	...	0.021 (4.9)	2.64 (3.5)	0.028 (2.6)	0.022 (0.6)	−1.04 (−2.3)	0.38	1.79	0.85
3-5	...	...	0.020 (4.9)	2.66 (3.5)	0.032 (3.7)	...	−0.81 (−3.3)	0.39	1.78	0.84
3-6	...	...	0.023 (5.4)	2.64 (3.4)	...	0.080 (2.7)	−1.19 (−2.5)	0.34	1.69	0.88

Source: Same as table 2. Several of these estimates were reported in testimony of Donald A. Nichols, *The Effect of Structural Employment and Training Programs on Inflation and Unemployment*, Hearings before the Joint Economic Committee, 96 Cong., 1 sess. (GPO, 1979), pp. 4–26. Figures in parentheses are *t*-statistics.

a. The dependent variable is the quarterly acceleration in the average hourly earnings index.

b. Percentage change of the level of the minimum wage with no adjustment for coverage.

c. Equals minus one in 1971:4 and plus one-half in 1972:1.

in table 2. The first three equations in that table have lagged dependent variables, and sums of the coefficients of these variables are not significantly different from unity in any equation. As other economists have found, this result is consistent with the accelerationist hypothesis just discussed. The remaining equations of table 2 use lagged values of the consumer price index as explanatory variables instead of using lagged dependent variables. In each equation the sum of the coefficients on the CPI variables is less than one.

Because of these results, the equations were also estimated in acceleration form, constraining the coefficients on the first two dependent variables described in table 2 to be 0.7 and 0.3 respectively. Table 3 reports the wage equations that were estimated in this accelerationist form, and these are used to compute the effect of a targeted employment subsidy.

Two alternative sets of unemployment rates are used in the equations reported in table 3. The components of the first set, used in the first three equations, are weighted averages of the actual unemployment rates of the occupational groups in each category, where the occupational labor forces are used as weights. An example of this average for 1978 is found in table 1. The second set was constructed from the Bureau of Labor Statistics estimates of employment for each category but with a smoothed labor force series that is simply a fourth-order polynomial of time. Its purpose was to avoid problems resulting from changes in labor force participation, a factor discussed further below. This second set is referred to in the table as *generated* unemployment rates. These rates are weighted averages of generated occupational unemployment rates, where the generated labor forces are used as weights. All unemployment rates in tables 2 and 3 are entered in inverse form, so positive coefficients are predicted by the theory. The unemployment rate is expressed as a percentage; the inverse of an unemployment rate of 5 percent is therefore 20. Wage terms are expressed in percentage points; a wage increase of 5 percent is therefore entered as 5.0.

The results confirm those of Baily and Tobin that high-wage unemployment is a more important determinant of wage inflation than low-wage unemployment. In all equations where actual unemployment rates of both variables are entered together in the same regression, the coefficient on low-wage unemployment is negative with the wrong sign. The coefficient of high-wage unemployment has the right sign and is often significant at the 5 percent level. These variables are highly correlated, of course, as can be seen by examining the several reported regressions in which the variables are entered separately. In these regressions the t-statistics are substantially lower, whereas the standard errors of the regressions are largely unchanged.

An alternative form for testing the Baily-Tobin position is described in equation 2-4. There the aggregate unemployment rate is entered along with the ratio of high-wage to low-wage employment. The coefficient of the aggregate unemployment rate is found not to be significant at the 5 percent level, though the employment ratio is.

The reported unemployment rates have several undesirable properties that led to the decision to construct new rates from generated estimates for the size of the labor force. The properties can be seen in the following participation equations:

(5) $$\Delta LH = 0.00003 + 0.478\Delta EH - 0.183\Delta EL$$
$$(11.1) \qquad (-3.6)$$

$\bar{R}^2 = 0.62$; Durbin-Watson $= 1.68$; standard error $= 0.0014$

(6) $$\Delta LL = 0.001 - 0.385\Delta EH + 0.880\Delta EL,$$
$$(-10.1) \qquad (18.6)$$

$\bar{R}^2 = 0.839$; $\rho = 0.219$; Durbin-Watson $= 2.01$; standard error $= 0.0013$
$$(-1.94)$$

where

$\Delta LH =$ change in high-wage labor force
$\Delta LL =$ change in low-wage labor force
$\Delta EH =$ change in high-wage employment level
$\Delta EL =$ change in low-wage employment level
$\rho =$ Cochrane-Orcutt autocorrelation correction.

First, low-wage employment is seen to be only loosely associated with low-wage unemployment. When low-wage employment increases by 100, the low-wage labor force grows by 88. This means low-wage unemployment falls by only 12. Since the same increase causes the high-wage labor force to fall by 18, it can be assumed that 18 of the new low-wage workers are drawn from the high-wage labor force. The remaining increase of 70 represents an increase in the total work force. Put differently, of every 100 low-wage jobs created, 70 will be taken by workers not currently classified as being in the labor force. This suggests that the low-wage unemployment rate is not a good measure of the pressure on wage rates that could result from an increase in low-wage employment.

Second, the unemployment of low-wage workers is substantially affected by high-wage employment. For every 100 new jobs created in high-wage occupations, the high-wage labor force will grow by 48. This means high-wage unemployment will fall by 52 workers when 100 high-wage jobs are created. The equations also show that when high-wage employment is increased by 100, the low-wage work force falls by 39. This means that 39 workers currently classified in low-wage occupations will be upgraded to high-wage ones as a result of the increase in employment.[12] With the high-wage labor force growing by 48 and the low-wage labor force shrinking by 39, a net increase in the labor force of only 9 workers is caused by the 100 additional high-wage jobs. This suggests that variations in high-wage employment have a larger effect on the low-wage unemployment rate than do variations in low-wage employment. It also suggests that variations in low-wage employment have a larger effect on the high-wage unemployment rate than on the low-wage unemployment rate.

For these reasons hypothetical labor forces were constructed as polynomials of time. The hypothetical labor forces are the predicted values from regressions of the actual labor forces on time, (time)^2, and so forth. Four powers of time were found to be significant and were used to construct the labor forces. Unemployment rates were then generated by the use of actual employment levels with the hypothetical labor forces. In table 3, regressions 3-4 to 3-6 utilize these generated unemployment rates.

The coefficients in these regressions are very different from those in the other equations. The multicollinearity problem is substantially reduced, as can be seen from a comparison of equations 3-4 and 3-5. That is, the addition of the inverse of the low-wage unemployment rate in equation 3-4 has a much smaller effect than before on the coefficient of the high-wage unemployment variable and on its significance. Although the coefficient on the low-wage unemployment rate remains insignificantly different from zero, it now has the right sign and a more plausible value.

---

12. For a detailed analysis of the upgrading phenomena, see Wayne Vroman, "Worker Upgrading and the Business Cycle," *BPEA, 1:1977*, pp. 229–50. See also Arthur M. Okun, "Upward Mobility in a High Pressure Economy," *BPEA, 1:1973*, pp. 207–52.

It is equation 3-4 that will be used below to estimate the effect of a wage subsidy on unemployment.

The remaining variables in equation 3-4 are the legislated change in the minimum wage expressed as percentage points and a dummy variable for the phase I wage controls of 1971–72. This latter variable is constructed by Data Resources and equals -1 in the fourth quarter of 1971 and 0.5 in the first quarter of 1972. The coefficients on these variables are affected very little by the model specification.

The Effect of Employment Structure on the NAIRU

To solve for the NAIRU, equation 3-4 is set equal to zero. Mean values are entered for the minimum wage and price control dummies to yield the following relation between the two unemployment rates:

$$(7) \qquad 0 = -0.991 + \frac{0.028}{UH} + \frac{0.022}{UL}.$$

UH signifies the unemployment rate of high-wage workers, UL of low-wage workers. The 1978 values of these variables are 4.40 percent and 7.88 percent respectively. When these values are entered into equation 7, they make the right-hand side add up to a total value of -0.075, indicating an unemployment structure with rates slightly above the NAIRU. Since wage acceleration is measured in whole percentage points, a value of -0.075 should be interpreted as a decline of 0.07 percentage point in the rate of wage increase.

Equation 7 can be used to calculate various combinations of UH and UL that are all consistent with an absence of wage acceleration. To compute the NAIRU, some assumption must be made about the proportion in which these sectoral unemployment rates would be reduced during an economic expansion. Several alternatives are reported here.

First, it is assumed that the ratio of unemployment rates at NAIRU will be the same as their ratio in 1978. NAIRU is then computed by solving equation 7 together with

$$(8) \qquad UH = 0.558\ UL,$$

which expresses the desired ratio. This assumption yields a NAIRU of 5.56 percent and constituent unemployment rates of 7.28 percent and

4.06 percent for low- and high-wage unemployment respectively. The low-wage unemployment rate is therefore reduced by 0.6 percentage point from its actual 1978 value, and the high-wage rate falls by 0.34 percentage point.

Second, it is assumed that the *employment* ratio will be the same at NAIRU as in 1978. This assumption is expressed in

(9) $$EH = 1.18 \, EL,$$

which is solved with equation 7 numerically by decomposing the unemployment rate and holding the labor forces constant at their 1978 rates. This yields a NAIRU of 5.64 percent and high- and low-wage unemployment rates of 4.01 and 7.50 percent respectively. With this assumption the decline in both unemployment rates from their 1978 levels is about the same—0.38 percentage point for low-wage unemployment and 0.39 percentage point for high-wage unemployment.

Third, it is assumed that the change in high-wage employment will be the same percentage of total employment growth as it has been over past cycles. This historical ratio is derived from the regression

(10) $\Delta EH = 16.01 + 0.6335 \, \Delta(EH + EL) - 1.119 \, TIME.$
              (0.35) (11.257)   (−1.169)

$\bar{R}^2 = 0.6157$; Durbin-Watson $= 2.18$; standard error $= 197.9$

Rearranging this equation and ignoring the constants gives the relation $\Delta EH = 1.7285 \, \Delta EL$. This can be solved with equation 7 to give a NAIRU of 5.68 percent. Unemployment rates for low- and high-wage occupations are 7.61 and 3.99 percent respectively.

The range of estimates of NAIRU just described is quite small—5.56 percent to 5.68 percent. Although these estimates are within the range normally ascribed to the NAIRU, and although they seem reasonable enough to provide the basis for the calculations I performed below, a problem does exist with the method generally used to calculate these values.

The estimation procedure assigns coefficients to the explanatory variables so as to minimize the squared deviations of past values of the wage variable from its explained values. This procedure has certain well-known desirable properties if its objective is to determine the rate of wage change that would normally be caused by a given level of unemployment. Tradi-

tionally the NAIRU is determined from these equations, as shown above
—by setting the rate of wage acceleration to zero. But if the purpose of
the estimation is to find the level of the NAIRU, a different estimation
procedure would be implied—one that presumably had optimal properties for predicting the sign of wage acceleration rather than its level. This
procedure would presumably give more weight to observations near the
NAIRU than to observations near the tails of the unemployment distribution. Perhaps a discriminant function would be necessary.

It is generally accepted that the NAIRU has increased over the postwar
period. Other economists have explained this shift by a changing demographic composition of the work force.[13] The equations reported in tables
2 and 3 disaggregate the work force by occupation, which can be viewed
as an alternative way to model the shift in the NAIRU, if any, that has
taken place. Because the decomposition used is so crude, it is unlikely
that this shift has been captured, but it should be possible to do so in
future work with further disaggregation.

The three estimates of NAIRU just developed differ from one another
because different ratios of unemployment of high- and low-wage occupations are involved. Next, I solve for the unemployment ratio that minimizes the NAIRU by using the following LaGrangian equation:

$$(11) \qquad L = UH\,53505 + UL\,46916 + \lambda\left(-0.991 + \frac{0.028}{UH} + \frac{0.022}{UL}\right)$$

$$\delta/\delta UH = 53505 - \frac{0.028\lambda}{UH^2} = 0$$

$$\delta/\delta UL = 46916 - \frac{0.022\lambda}{UL^2} = 0$$

$$\delta/\delta\lambda = -0.991 + \frac{0.28}{UH} + \frac{0.022}{UL} = 0$$

$$UH = 5.17 \text{ percent}$$

$$UL = 4.89 \text{ percent}$$

$$NAIRU = 5.04 \text{ percent.}$$

13. See, for example George L. Perry, "Changing Labor Markets and Inflation,"
BPEA, 3:1970, pp. 411–41; and Michael L. Wachter, "The Changing Cyclical Responsiveness of Wage Inflation," *BPEA, 1:1976*, pp. 115–59.

Essentially, unemployment is minimized subject to the constraint expressed in equation 7, namely, that wage acceleration be equal to zero. The large coefficients multiplied by the unemployment rates in equation 11 are the 1978 values of the respective labor forces. These results imply that the marginal contributions to inflation of reductions in the sectoral unemployment rates must be proportional to the size of the respective labor forces. Put differently, the marginal increase in inflation from hiring one more worker must be the same regardless of his classification.

The minimum NAIRU derived in equation 11 is 5.04 percent, which is 0.5 to 0.67 percentage point below the estimates of NAIRU just presented, in which it was assumed the employment structure would retain its normal historical relationship. With high- and low-wage labor forces of roughly equal size, the difference in their rates of unemployment at the minimum NAIRU is due largely to the difference between their coefficients in the wage acceleration equation. Although it is interesting to note that at the minimum NAIRU there is a slightly lower unemployment rate for low-wage workers than for high-wage workers, it should be emphasized that since this relation is so different from what is historically observed, the estimates should be used with caution.

Effects of a Targeted Employment Subsidy

To compute an estimate of the size of the targeted employment subsidy required to reduce the NAIRU to its lowest level, it is necessary to make some assumptions about the aggregate production function. I will use a constant elasticity of substitution function with only two arguments. This function, described by R. G. D. Allen, is shown in

$$(12) \qquad Q^{-\beta} = aEH^{-\beta} + bEL^{-\beta} \qquad \text{with} \qquad \sigma = \frac{1}{1 + \beta},$$

where σ is the elasticity of substitution between high-wage employment (EH) and low-wage employment (EL).[14]

Assuming wage rates paid by employers are equal to marginal products, the relation in the following equation can be used to compute the change in wages necessary to attain a particular employment ratio:

14. R. G. D. Allen, *Macro-Economic Theory* (St. Martin's Press, 1967), pp. 52–54.

(13)
$$\left(\frac{EL}{EH}\right)^{1+\beta} = \frac{b}{a}\frac{WH}{WL},$$

where WH is the wage rate for high-wage workers, WL the wage rate for low-wage workers.

First, equation 13 is solved for b/a by assuming a value for β and using the actual 1978 data for employment and wage rates. This is done for values of β equal to -0.5 and 1, which correspond to elasticities of substitution of 2 and 0.5 respectively. These represent the bounds of the range of estimates in the literature reported by Hamermesh.[15] The new employment levels are then entered into equation 13, and the resulting wage ratios computed.

Before I describe the results of this computation, one more NAIRU is computed, this one being the level consistent with the maximum level of GNP:

$$(14) \quad L = (aEH^{-\beta} + bEL^{-\beta})^{-1/\beta} - \lambda\left(-0.991 + \frac{0.028\,LH}{LH - EH} + \frac{0.022\,LL}{LL - EL}\right)$$

$$\frac{\delta}{\delta EH} = a\left(\frac{Q}{EH}\right)^{1+\beta} - \lambda\frac{0.028\,LH}{(LH - EH)^2} = 0$$

$$\frac{\delta}{\delta EL} = b\left(\frac{Q}{EL}\right)^{1+\beta} - \lambda\frac{0.022\,LL}{(LL - EL)^2} = 0$$

$$\frac{\delta}{\delta\lambda} = 0.991 - \left(\frac{0.028\,LH}{LH - EH} + \frac{0.022\,LL}{LL - EL}\right) = 0,$$

$$UH = 4.60 \text{ percent}$$

$$UL = 5.75 \text{ percent}$$

$$\text{NAIRU} = 5.14 \text{ percent}.$$

As the marginal conditions described in equation 14 show, at this NAIRU the ratio of marginal products must equal the ratio of the contributions to inflation of marginal increases in employment. As it turns out, this level of GNP requires a substantial reduction in the NAIRU from the range of estimates presented in the previous section, but leaves the NAIRU above

15. Hamermesh and Grant, "Econometric Studies of Labor-Labor Substitution," pp. 526–28.

Table 4. Alternative Estimates of the Level and Composition of the Nonaccelerating Inflation Rate of Unemployment[a]

Variable	NAIRU minimum (1)	GNP maximum (2)	1978 unemployment ratio (3)	1978 employment ratio (4)	Historical ratio of employment change (5)	Actual 1978 (6)
NAIRU (percent)	5.04	5.14	5.56	5.64	5.68	6.03[b]
High-wage unemployment rate (percent)	5.17	4.60	4.06	4.01	3.99	4.40
Low-wage unemployment rate (percent)	4.89	5.75	7.28	7.50	7.61	7.88
High-wage employment (thousands)	50,739	51,044	51,333	51,359	51,370	51,152
Low-wage employment (thousands)	44,622	44,218	43,501	43,397	43,346	43,221
GNP index	1.005	1.006	1.004	1.004	1.004	1.000

Sources: Columns 1–5 are author's computations. Data from column 6 are from Bureau of Labor Statistics.

a. The labor force and its composition are held constant at low-wage labor force = 53,505, and high-wage labor force = 46,916 for all computations.

b. The actual level of unemployment.

its minimum. GNP is maximized in equation 14 subject to the zero wage acceleration constraint.

Although the NAIRU consistent with the maximum level of GNP is only slightly higher than its minimum value, the constituent unemployment rates are quite different and, as a result, the required subsidy is far smaller. The levels of employment, unemployment, and GNP implied by the different estimates of NAIRU are shown in table 4.

The elasticity of substitution was found to have very little effect on the levels of GNP implied by the various employment ratios. The difference between the NAIRU-minimizing GNPs for elasticities of substitution of 2 and 0.5 was computed to be about 0.01 percentage point. This is not reported in the table because the computation is not accurate in the fifth digit. Accordingly, only one line is reported for GNP, though it was derived from two separate sets of computations.

The sixth column of table 4 shows the actual levels for the variables for 1978; the level of GNP for 1978 is normalized at one. The table indicates that a move to full employment through normal economic expansion would reduce unemployment by about 0.4 percentage point. Since GNP is computed from a production function with constant returns to scale, it too would be increased by 0.4 percentage point from such a move. These estimates, shown in columns 3 through 5, indicate the NAIRUs that would result from keeping fixed the ratio of 1978 unemployment rates, the ratio of 1978 employment levels, and the historical ratio of employment changes.

Table 4 also indicates that GNP can be increased a further 0.2 percentage point—roughly $5 billion at current levels—by changing the ratio of employment in favor of low-wage workers. This would reduce the NAIRU by about 0.5 percentage point. A still further reduction in the NAIRU by 0.1 point is possible, but comes at the expense of a 0.1 point reduction in GNP.

Table 5 presents estimates of the size of the targeted employment subsidy needed to reduce the NAIRU to its minimum and to the level that maximizes GNP. The table is computed as follows. The elasticity of substitution is assumed to be either 2 or 0.5, and the NAIRU is assumed to be either 5.14 percent—the level that maximizes GNP—or 5.04 percent —the minimum possible NAIRU.

The percentage subsidy is derived by entering employment values from table 4 into equation 13. Then the values of the left-hand side of 13 for the cases covered in table 5 are compared with the value based on actual

Table 5. Estimated Cost of a Targeted Employment Subsidy That Reduces the Unemployment Rate to Its Minimum Possible Level

Elasticity of sub- stitution	β	NAIRU (percent)	Subsidy		Annual cost (billions of 1978 dollars)	Cost per low-wage job (thousands of 1978 dollars)	Cost per job (thousands of 1978 dollars)
			Percent	Cents per hour			
2.0	−0.5	5.14	1.24	4.6	4.6	5.6	9.2
2.0	−0.5	5.04	1.98	7.3	7.5	6.1	12.3
0.5	1.0	5.14	4.86	18.0	18.0	22.1	35.0
0.5	1.0	5.04	7.69	28.5	29.0	23.7	48.0

Source: Author's calculations.

1978 data, to derive the required percentage changes in the wage ratio. Since all the calculations were derived under the assumption of a fixed labor force, that assumption is also maintained here. Labor supply responses to wage changes are not considered. The entire subsidy goes to lowering the cost of labor to employers rather than to raising the wages of workers, which will lead to an underestimate of the cost of the subsidy that depends on the elasticity of labor supply responses. But since supply issues have been ignored elsewhere in this paper, it would be inappropriate to adjust the estimates in this instance without making offsetting adjustments elsewhere.

Once the percentage subsidy is derived, the remaining columns can be computed directly. The size of the subsidy in terms of cents per hour is simply the average hourly wage rate in 1978 for workers in low-wage occupations ($3.71) multiplied by the percentage subsidy. The annual cost of the subsidy in 1978 terms is derived by multiplying the percentage subsidy by an estimate of total wages paid to low-wage workers in 1978. The latter estimate is derived from an estimate of total wages paid to all workers in 1978 ($1,100.7 billion)[16] multiplied by an estimate of the fraction of total payments going to low-wage workers. This number is adjusted by the increase from 1978 levels in the number of low-wage workers necessary to reach the NAIRUs indicated in table 5.

Table 1 was used to derive an estimate of the fraction of total wages going to low-wage workers. Total employment in each category was multiplied by the respective wage rate. This product for low-wage workers was divided by the sum of the products for low- and high-wage workers.

16. *Economic Report of the President, 1979*, p. 204.

This procedure makes no adjustment for different work weeks. If it can be established that the work week is lower for low-wage workers, the estimates of subsidy cost should be reduced appropriately. The last two columns in table 5 estimate the cost per job of the subsidy. The figures are derived by dividing the total costs by, first, the increases in low-wage employment and, second, the increases in total employment. Increases are computed by comparing employment levels in columns 1 and 2 of table 4 to those in column 4.

The cost of the targeted employment subsidy shown in table 5 indicates the extent of the diminishing returns to an increase in the subsidy. The subsidy needed to reduce NAIRU to 5.14 percent costs only 60 percent as much as the subsidy needed to reduce the NAIRU to 5.04 percent, yet five-sixths of the possible unemployment would be eliminated. Put differently, after reducing unemployment from 5.64 percent to 5.14 percent with a wage subsidy program, a further reduction to 5.04 percent would provide 20 percent more jobs yet would require a subsidy over 60 percent larger.

Table 5 also indicates the importance of the elasticity of substitution to the computations. A small elasticity means that low-wage workers are poor substitutes for high-wage workers and that a large subsidy is needed to change the ratio of employment. The table shows that to have the same effect on employment an elasticity of substitution of 0.5 would require a subsidy four times larger than that required for an elasticity of substitution of 2.

Summary of Limitations

The limitations to the reliability of the estimates that were mentioned in the paper are summarized here.

—The estimates of the NAIRU are derived from a procedure that is appropriate for explaining wage inflation, not for selecting one particular unemployment rate as the boundary between the regions of accelerating and decelerating inflation. Although this weakness is common to the literature, it is one that can be remedied in the future. This limitation calls into question the level of the NAIRU estimated here and in other works. It has less effect on the changes in NAIRU, which are the primary emphasis of this paper.

—The use of a wage equation as a structural relation is common in macroeconomic forecasting models, but its use is questionable when one puts as much emphasis as I do on changes in the structure. This limitation, combined with the fact that the computations are made for values far beyond the range found in the sample, indicate that the estimates should be treated with caution and should not become the basis for policy decisions without further study.

—As pointed out by George Johnson in his comments, the estimated equation is not an exact description of the Baily-Tobin model in disequilibrium, because it does not make use of relative wage rates. The aggregate form of the estimated equation may be consistent with several microeconomic structures having different policy implications.

—The classification procedure that determines which workers are high-wage and which low-wage is crude. Many workers are clearly misclassified. Therefore, the regression coefficients on the separate unemployment rates are biased toward each other in the wage equations reported earlier. A larger difference between these coefficients would result in a lower estimate for the minimum NAIRU.

—The estimates of the inflationary effect of the unemployment of low-wage workers vary substantially in different specifications of the wage equation. The estimate used to calculate the impact of a targeted employment subsidy on unemployment comes from an equation with a t-statistic of 0.6 on the low-wage unemployment variable (equation 3-4), one of the few equations where the coefficient had even the right sign. Although I find the estimate plausible, it clearly has a wide range of error.

—Actual unemployment rates for the two labor force groups were not used in the regression on which the final computation is based. The participation equations reported in the paper indicate that the two unemployment rates vary as much with employment in the other labor force group as with employment in their own. Unemployment rates were therefore constructed by combining actual estimates of employment with synthetic labor forces that are functions only of time. Although there is reason to prefer estimates from the regressions based on these constructed unemployment rates to those from regressions based on actual unemployment rates, labor force participation effects are ignored by this procedure. This affects all the computations in various, and sometimes offsetting, ways.

One way the results would be changed is predictable. If, for example, labor force participation in each labor group varied directly with employment in that group but was unaffected by employment in the other group, then the coefficients of the true unemployment rates in an estimated wage equation would be smaller than those for the constructed unemployment rates. This means that the computations reported in tables 4 and 5 would still be valid for employment but would overstate the possible effects on unemployment of a change in relative employment levels.

Since equations 5 and 6 indicate that the low-wage labor force is more responsive to changes in employment than the high-wage labor force, the effect on overall unemployment of a change in employment structure is probably overstated.

—The labor supply effects of a change in wage rates is also ignored. It is assumed that the wage subsidy would lower wage rates paid by employers for low-wage labor and that employers would change their employment ratios in response. These employment changes are assumed not to have any offsetting effects on relative wages. This means the estimates of the cost of the targeted employment subsidy are low for the changes considered, though the size of the possible reduction in the NAIRU is unaffected by this omission.

—Finally, because the work week of low-wage workers is probably shorter than that of high-wage workers, though it was assumed that both groups worked equal work weeks, the cost estimates are biased upward.

Comments by George E. Johnson

In this paper, a revision of the one presented at the conference, Don Nichols acknowledges my fundamental criticism of his approach; namely, that he estimates an incomplete version of his underlying model so that one cannot tell from his results whether employment policy could reduce the NAIRU. But he has not corrected the problem. I shall therefore indicate here why his numerical estimates of the potential effects of a targeted employment subsidy on the NAIRU, summarized in table 4, should be interpreted cautiously.

Let me first stress that Nichols's subject is of great importance to policy. Moreover, although one might quarrel over several details, Nichols's approach is both interesting and potentially fruitful. Unfortunately, however, the paper does not contain the necessary structure with which to answer confidently the significant questions he poses. To illustrate this lack, I take Nichols's equations 1, 2, and 3 and show how they relate both to his estimating equation and to the fundamental policy question.

First, for employment policies targeted on low-wage workers (the Ls) to influence the NAIRU, γ_2 in equation 2 must be positive. If γ_2 is zero, a subsidy on the employment of the Ls (or public service employment jobs for them) will merely drive up their wages and leave low-wage unemployment (UL) at its equilibrium value, $-\beta_2/\gamma_2$. If, on the other hand, γ_2 is positive, a subsidy will drive down R and hence lower UL. A negative value of γ_1 and a positive value of γ_2, the fundamental assumptions of the Baily-Tobin model, imply a trade-off between the equilibrium values of UH and UL given by the U curve in figure 1. A positive value of γ_1 and a zero value of γ_2 imply a trade-off between UH and UL given by V. Zero values of both γ_1 and γ_2 imply a single point of equilibrium, A, in the figure. A subsidy on the Ls will reduce the NAIRU if $\delta(UH)/\delta(UL)$ is not large in absolute value—a fact that is guaranteed as U approaches V. If, however, γ_1 and γ_2 are both zero, society is stuck with the two unemployment rates implied by point A.

Second, to estimate the curve in figure 1 (and hence discern the potential impact of employment policy), one must estimate the γs. If they are both zero, the only "positive" labor market policy that will influence the NAIRU is training (that is, to change the value of λ). Nichols does not, however, have data on occupational wage rates, so he estimates an equation of the form

$$(15) \qquad GW = A + B\left(\frac{1}{UH}\right) + C\left(\frac{1}{UL}\right).$$

He then goes on to infer a trade-off like U on the basis of these parameters by setting $GW = 0$ and to derive his "estimates" of the impact of the subsidy from this trade-off.

But this method may be seriously wrong. Suppose that $\gamma_1 = \gamma_2 = 0$, so that the real trade-off is simply point A. Substituting Nichols's equations 1 and 2 into 3 gives

$$(16) \qquad GW = [\lambda\alpha_1 + (1 - \lambda)\alpha_2] + \frac{\lambda\beta_1}{UH} + (1 - \lambda)\frac{\beta_2}{UL}.$$

This estimated equation would suggest a trade-off between UH and UL like U, but the trade-off is probably illusory, since only point A on the curve is consistent with labor market equilibrium. If that is indeed true, any estimates derived from such a procedure would be worthless.

Figure 1. The Trade-off between High-Wage Unemployment and Low-Wage Unemployment

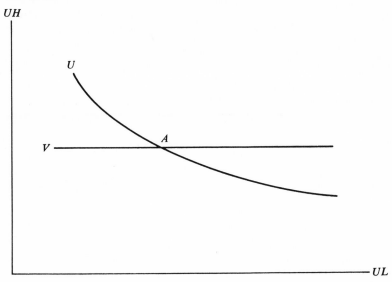

Suppose, on the other hand, that the L's wages are completely inflexible relative to those of the high-wage workers (Hs). Employers, by this view, set all wages in response to supply demand conditions for Hs. It then follows that

(17) $$GW + GWL = GWH = \alpha_1 + \frac{\beta_1}{UH}.$$

Estimation of equation 15 would yield a zero coefficient on $1/UL$, which implies that over the relevant range employment policy directed toward the Ls would lower the NAIRU. Interestingly, Nichols's estimates in table 2 are consistent with this scenario. But much evidence (for example, the absorption of the large increase in the labor supply of women over the past decade) suggests that we do not experience structural unemployment in the United States on such a grand scale.

What Nichols needs to do to reliably answer this important question about targeted employment subsidies and the unemployment rate is to develop his estimates for labor market grouping for which there are adequate wage data. Despite the obvious problems, industry data may be the most promising candidate: the use of occupational wage surveys from the Bureau of Labor Statistics is another possibility. Further, careful attention also needs to be paid to the issue of the appropriate level of dis-aggregation. Nichols admits that his is "crude"; all other studies of this question (including one by me) are likewise guilty. Nonetheless, one is not likely to generate useful results by, for example, lumping high-paid secretaries and minority teenagers in the same category.

In sum, Nichols has made an interesting start on a useful contribution in this area. But the results he obtains should be interpreted cautiously.

Robert I. Lerman

A Comparison of Employer
and Worker Wage Subsidies

The wage subsidy literature has proceeded along two tracks. Analysts of wage subsidies paid to employers have focused on employment effects,[1] whereas researchers dealing with wage subsidies paid to workers have looked most closely at the income distribution, wage rates, and labor supply effects.[2] This dichotomy has carried over into the government policy area. In the United States and Western Europe, governments have attempted to stimulate employment by subsidizing the costs of labor to employers.[3] Congress established the new jobs tax credit

I prepared most of this paper while working at the Office of the Assistant Secretary for Policy, Evaluation, and Research, U.S. Department of Labor. I am grateful to Bill Barnes, Gary Burtless, and Miles Maxfield for comments and Ed Fu for computer work.

1. See John Bishop, "Employment and Pricing in Construction and Distribution Industries: The Impact of the New Jobs Tax Credit," in Sherwin Rosen, ed., *Studies in Labor Markets* (University of Chicago Press, forthcoming); John Bishop, "The General Equilibrium Impact of Alternative Antipoverty Strategies," *Industrial and Labor Relations Review*, vol. 32 (January 1979), pp. 205–23; and Daniel S. Hamermesh, "Subsidies for Jobs in the Private Sector," in John L. Palmer, ed., *Creating Jobs: Public Employment Programs and Wage Subsidies* (Brookings Institution, 1978), pp. 87–122.

2. See Michael C. Barth, "Market Effects of a Wage Subsidy," *Industrial and Labor Relations Review*, vol. 27 (July 1974), pp. 572–85; Irwin Garfinkel, "A Skeptical Note on 'The Optimality of Wage Subsidy Programs,'" *American Economic Review*, vol. 63 (June 1973), pp. 447–53; and Robert I. Lerman, "JOIN: A Jobs and Income Program for American Families," in *Studies in Public Welfare, Paper 19: Public Employment and Wage Subsidies*, prepared for the Subcommittee on Fiscal Policy, Joint Economic Committee, 93 Cong. 2 sess. (Government Printing Office, 1974), pp. 3–67.

3. Robert H. Haveman and Gregory B. Christainsen, "Public Employment and Wage Subsidies in Western Europe and the United States: What We're Doing and What We Know," in *European Labor Market Policies*, a special report to the U.S. National Commission for Manpower Policy (The Commission, 1978), pp. 259–345.

in order to increase total employment and the targeted jobs tax credit and work incentive tax credit to raise the employment level of disadvantaged workers. In contrast, the earned income tax credit, the only U.S. subsidy paid to workers on the basis of earnings, has primarily an income maintenance role; payments go only to low-income families with children.

The main rationale for choosing employer wage subsidy programs to stimulate employment is that unemployment or nonemployment is caused by inadequate demand for workers at existing wage rates. Often the inadequate demand has been assumed to be caused by wage rigidities, like the minimum wage; a more recent view holds that the demand for labor (especially for low-skill labor) is too low because of an inability to increase aggregate demand during periods of inflation. In each of these situations, an employer subsidy could stimulate employment while exerting little upward pressure on wage rates.

For worker wage subsidy programs to increase employment, the effects must take place through supply-side changes. By raising the amount of labor supplied at presubsidy market wages, a worker subsidy can lower market wages paid by employers and thus raise employment. However, as a recent paper by Wachter and Kim shows, it is often difficult to determine the source of the underemployment problem.[4] Wachter and Kim analyzed youth employment trends over the last two decades to determine whether low youth employment has been largely caused by inadequate employer demand or by wages too low to attract young workers. Though hardly conclusive, their results indicate that wages too low to attract young workers are the primary cause. Therefore, they provide some empirical support for the idea that jobs can increase as a result of wage subsidies paid directly to workers.

Although either worker or employer subsidies might increase employment, only the employer subsidy approach has received serious attention as a job stimulus tool. The failure to consider the ability of the worker subsidy to raise employment is unfortunate, since employer subsidy programs have at best a mixed record. Not only have the employment effects per dollar of cost to the government of those programs been questionable, but also the number of eligible employers who have participated in targeted employer subsidy programs has been disappointingly small.

This paper attempts to widen the debate on subsidy programs by com-

4. Michael L. Wachter and Choongsoo Kim, "Time Series Changes in Youth Joblessness," National Bureau of Economic Research Working Paper 384 (NBER, August 1979).

paring the employment effects of worker and employment wage subsidies. The two approaches can have sharply different results, because of the structure of the programs, the nature of the labor market, and nonwage and administrative factors. The paper considers in turn each of these reasons for expecting differential employment effects. Although it does not demonstrate the superiority of one approach to the other, it does demonstrate that the employment effects of the two approaches are likely to differ for many reasons and that direct subsidies to workers can sometimes lead to a larger employment stimulus than equivalent-sized subsidies to employers.

The Structure of Alternative Subsidy Programs

There are usually considerable structural differences between employer and worker wage subsidy programs, largely because of their varying purposes.[5]

Since employer subsidy programs are intended to stimulate employment rather than increase wage rates, subsidies are often restricted to employers who hire workers from groups that have high unemployment rates. In the United States, two of the three employer subsidy programs (the targeted jobs and work incentive tax credits) limited eligibility primarily to low-income youth and welfare recipients. In France, such programs have been focused on youth. Britain has limited eligibility under its subsidy programs to firms in high-unemployment regions.

Two other features of employer subsidy programs highlight their employment-stimulus purpose. The first is the restriction of subsidy payments to new hires or to firms that increase total employment. Although only the new jobs tax credit in the United States required an increase in the firm's total employment, the targeted jobs tax credit pays credits only for workers hired after September 26, 1978. The limited duration of most employer subsidy payments is another indication that the subsidy is intended to induce firms to hire new workers rather than to subsidize wages of existing employees. Under the current targeted jobs and work incentive programs, firms may claim credits only for the first two years the eligible worker continues with the firm. Employer subsidy payments are always temporary because it is expected that once the worker remains with the

5. The information in this section comes mainly from Haveman and Christainsen, "Public Employment and Wage Subsidies."

firm for a reasonable period, he should be valuable enough for the firm to pay his full salary.

The design of worker wage subsidy programs usually reinforces their income-support purpose. The only major U.S. program paying subsidies to workers is the earned income tax credit, which limits payments to low-income workers who support children under eighteen. The proposals for wage rate subsidies have generally been part of an income maintenance package and often would limit payments to family heads.[6] Since family heads tend to have low unemployment rates relative to nonheads, it is clear that the objective has rarely been increased employment.[7] Given their income-support role, it makes sense that worker subsidy programs provide permanent subsidies instead of the temporary payments found in employer subsidy programs.

Differences also extend to the duration of the programs themselves. Often, the employer subsidies are enacted for a limited period to deal with a current, but not necessarily permanent, unemployment problem. In contrast, worker subsidies are envisaged as a permanent part of the income maintenance system.

Other differences in program design are in the formulas used to determine subsidy payments. Unlike employer wage subsidies, worker wage subsidies are designed with "clawback" provisions that reduce subsidy payments as wage rates, earnings, or income increase. (Although proposals have been made for employer and worker subsidy programs that base payments on wage rates, the actual programs have paid subsidies based on earnings.) For example, earned income tax credit recipients receive subsidies on the first $5,000 of earnings, but earnings beyond $6,000 cause reductions in the subsidy payments. The result is that a worker who receives $5.00 an hour will face a subsidy-inclusive wage of $5.50 for the first 1,000 hours and $4.40 for hours 1,200 through 2,000 per year. In worker wage subsidy proposals based on wage rates, the maximum sub-

6. See, for example, the paper by Betson and Bishop in this volume and the JOIN proposal (Lerman, "JOIN"), which called for a last-resort employment program alongside a worker wage subsidy program. Also see Richard Zeckhauser and Peter Schuck, "An Alternative to the Nixon Income Maintenance Plan," *Public Interest*, no. 19 (Spring 1970), pp. 120–30, for a proposal that would allow recipients to choose between a worker wage subsidy benefit and a negative income tax payment.

7. The low unemployment rates of family heads in general should not preclude serious efforts to raise employment among low-income family heads, especially among heads of one-parent families. Senators Howard H. Baker, Jr., and Henry L. Bellmon attempted to provide such a stimulus by including an employer wage subsidy program in their 1977 welfare reform proposal.

sidy per hour is at the lowest wage; as the worker's wage increases, the subsidy per hour falls until it reaches zero at some target wage rate.

It is not likely that employer wage subsidy programs would ever be designed with these kinds of clawback provisions. Under earnings-based formulas, such provisions would mean that after a worker's earnings with the firm reached some specified level, the firm's subsidy would decrease with any further increase in the worker's wage rate or hours of work. Under wage rate–based formulas, the subsidy would decrease as the firm increased the worker's wage up to the target level. Such programs would give rise to the objection that the government was providing too strong an incentive for firms to keep wages low. It is one thing to reward workers who can earn only low wages; it is much less acceptable to reward firms because they pay low wages, even if low-wage workers may benefit from the increased demand stimulated by the subsidy.

The absence of clawback provisions in employer wage subsidy programs virtually assures the need for categorical restrictions on the kinds of workers for whom employers can be subsidized. Consider, for example, a typical formula providing a subsidy of 25 to 50 percent of the worker's first $6,000 of earnings with the firm. If the subsidy were available with no categorical restrictions and no clawback provisions, then subsidies would be paid on behalf of all workers. Such a program would imply outlays of perhaps 10 to 20 percent of the nation's wage bill. Thus, unless the program had a very low subsidy rate, the employer subsidy with an earnings-based formula would have to be highly targeted.

Subsidy Programs in Alternative Labor Markets

The impact of any specific wage subsidy program will depend largely on the workings of the labor market. In this section I first consider simple programs in the context of simple models of the labor market, then examine the effects of more realistic program structures in more complex labor market settings.

The Static Models and Subsidy Effects

When economists think about wage subsidies, they instinctively envisage the kinds of effects illustrated in figure 1. The labor market model represented in the figure determines the wage and employment level in a

Figure 1. Wage Subsidy Effects in a Static Competitive Model

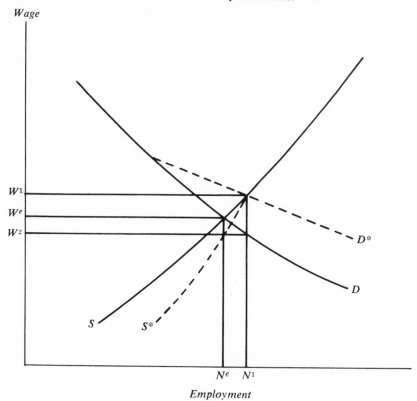

Wage

Employment

static equilibrium, competitive context. Initially, labor demand is depicted by D and labor supply by S; the market is in equilibrium at wage W^e and employment level N^e. Introducing an employer wage subsidy causes the employer's cost per worker to decline over a range of wages actually paid to workers. The result is a shift in the demand curve to the right to D^*. Note that at the presubsidy wage, W^e, employers now demand more labor than workers are willing to supply. This situation causes a bidding up of wages (to W^1), and an increase in available labor and overall employment (to N^1). The gap between W^1 and W^2 is the subsidy per worker paid by taxpayers.

If instead a worker wage subsidy were introduced, the wage received by workers would exceed the wage paid by firms, and the supply curve

Figure 2. Wage Subsidy Effects in a Rigid-Wage Model

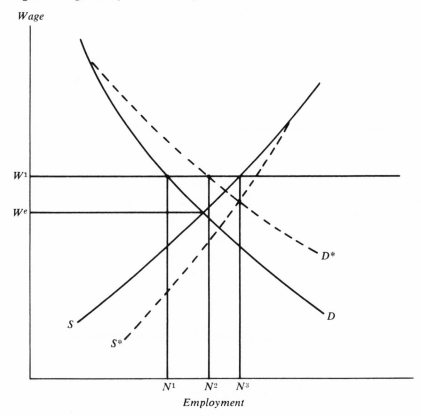

would shift to the right from S to S^*. Again the market comes to a new equilibrium at a higher level of employment, a lower effective wage paid by employers, and a higher effective wage received by workers.

The main trouble with this model is that (involuntary) unemployment, the problem for which employer subsidy programs are primarily intended, cannot occur. Wages can always adjust so that supply and demand are equated. A simple way to introduce unemployment is to assume wage rigidities that keep the market wage above the competitive equilibrium wage W^e. Figure 2 illustrates this case. Note that at wage W^1, the demand for labor is less than the quantity workers are willing to supply. Because some rigidity prevents the wage from falling to W^e, some workers remain unemployed even though they are willing to work at wages that make them attractive to employers. It is then that the employer wage subsidy can be an especially appropriate tool, whereas the worker wage subsidy is apparently counterproductive.

By shifting the demand curve to the right to D^*, an employer wage subsidy could stimulate additional employment without altering the wage received by workers. Each additional worker brings a corresponding decline in the number unemployed. Employment rises to N^2 and unemployment falls from $N^3 - N^1$ to $N^3 - N^2$. In contrast, a worker wage subsidy that shifts S to S^* would simply increase unemployment without raising the level of employment. The subsidy raises the number willing to work at wage W^1, but leaves the demand for workers at N^1.

The effects seen in this model underlie the common notion that the employer wage subsidy rather than the worker wage subsidy is the appropriate employment-stimulus tool. But how realistic is that illustration of subsidy effects?

Before complexities to the labor market model are added, it is useful to consider the effects of more realistic program structures. As noted above, the employer wage subsidy programs usually subsidize *earnings,* not wage rates, for some groups of workers with high unemployment rates. For example, the largest category of workers qualifying for the targeted jobs tax credit is low-income eighteen- to twenty-four-year-olds, a group that in recent years has experienced unemployment rates of more than 20 percent. Firms that hire these workers can claim tax credits worth 50 percent of their first year's earnings up to $6,000 and 25 percent of their second year's earnings up to $6,000. That subsidies do not cover the full-year earnings of full-time workers paid over $3.00 per hour provides firms an indirect incentive to hire more people from the low-wage pool. But this incentive alone is insufficient to ensure targeting on low-wage workers, because many workers stay much less than one year with the same firm. (The targeted jobs tax credit applies equally to all earnings of a worker paid $4.50 an hour for three-quarters of the year as the one paid $3.00 for a full year.) The credit is actually directed toward low-wage workers and possibly reduces rigid-wage unemployment partly because it is categorical —low-income youth usually earn low wages. In May 1978 the Current Population Survey showed that nearly half of low-income young workers eligible for the credit earned less than $3.00 an hour, an amount within 15 percent of the federal minimum wage. Only 17 percent earned over $4.00 an hour.

The low-wage status of target group members is therefore essential if

Figure 3. The Effects of Categorical Employer Wage Subsidies in a Rigid-Wage Model

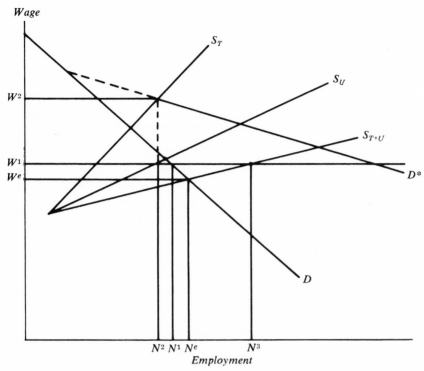

the targeted jobs tax credit is to lower rigid-wage unemployment, but by itself it is not enough. In addition, the program must cover a large proportion of very low wage workers. To understand this, consider figure 3, where S_T, S_U, and S_{T+U} represent the supply curves of target group workers, T, nontarget group workers, U, and all low-wage workers. S_T lies to the left of S_U and is more steeply sloped because it is assumed that group T is considerably smaller than group U. D is the presubsidy demand curve and W^1 is the minimum wage. In this case total employment is N^1, and unemployment is $N^3 - N^1$, divided up in unknown proportions (presumably randomly) between the T and U workers willing to work at the minimum wage.

D^* is the demand curve that would be applicable if all workers were eligible for this subsidy, in which case all unemployment would be eliminated. But since the subsidy applies just to T workers, the new demand curve actually follows D^* only until it intersects S_T, at which point it drops down to the presubsidy demand curve D. The impact of the subsidy is to raise the employment of T workers to N^2, to increase the wage of T workers to W^2, to limit employment of U workers to $N^1 - N^2$, to shift all unemployment to group U workers, and to leave total unemployment at $N^3 - N^1$. Only if S_T were to the right of S_U could the subsidy increase total employment; and, in any event, the minimum wage would still constrain the market from reaching a full-employment equilibrium unless the target group were very large relative to the size of the low-wage labor force.[8]

It turns out that most workers near the minimum wage are not members of the targeted jobs or work incentive tax credit target groups. Data from March–May 1978 Current Population Surveys indicate that only 20 percent of workers eighteen and over who reported wage rates less than the federal minimum were in low-income families. Although the targeted jobs tax credit covers some workers not in low-income families, even less than 20 percent of low-wage workers qualify for that credit or the work incentive tax credit. Thus it appears that both these tax credit programs cannot reduce rigid-wage unemployment, though they can redistribute this unemployment away from target group members.

This problem of coverage is likely to beset employer subsidy programs in general, especially those basing payments on earnings rather than wage rates. As noted above, subsidizing the initial $4,000 to $6,000 of a worker's earnings at a high rate requires tight categorical restrictions or an extremely large budget. But no set of categorical rules can simultaneously reach the bulk of low-wage workers and limit program costs.

The effects of the one actual worker wage subsidy program now in place (the earned income tax credit) also do not correspond to those illustrated in figure 2. Unlike a pure wage rate subsidy, the earned income tax credit *reduces* net wage rates of eligible workers as their annual family incomes increase above $6,000. As a result, the program may not increase labor supply or add to employment.[9]

Labor Markets with Low Wages and Frictional Unemployment

Most labor economists believe that the unemployment rate currently consistent with nonincreasing rates of inflation may be as high as 6 per-

8. See George Johnson's paper in this volume for a formal demonstration of these results.

9. Using a general equilibrium model, Bishop, "General Equilibrium Impact," finds that the earned income tax credit does not result in increased overall labor supply.

cent.[10] The inflationary push from the labor market when unemployment rates fall below 6 percent is said to come from several sources. One source already cited is rigid wages due to minimum wage laws and such other rigidities as restrictions on government-aided construction projects under the Davis-Bacon Act of 1931. Other sources often cited are the following: reported unemployment because nonmarket income sources lead workers to reject low-wage options, frictional unemployment associated with job search and the limited duration of jobs, and unemployment associated with statistical discrimination.

Some have argued that the growth of income transfer and illicit market alternatives has increased the number of workers who are unwilling to accept work at their market wage. In theory, these workers should be regarded as outside the labor force, or voluntarily unemployed. But in fact, many take enough informal, work-seeking actions to count as unemployed under the official Bureau of the Census definition. West has provided evidence from the Seattle-Denver income maintenance experiment that income transfers can induce this sort of unemployment both by making nonmarket income sources available and by lowering net wage rates. In one specification, with a sample of young men who started and continued in the experiment as relatives of the family head, West found that a one-dollar reduction in hourly net wages induced nearly an 8 percentage point increase in the time spent involuntarily unemployed and a 9 percentage point decrease in time spent in the labor force.[11]

Eisner has described a model in which those who cannot find work because they do not accept low-wage jobs can still be considered involuntarily unemployed rather than outside the labor force.[12] In this model, job vacancies and unemployed workers coexist when firms do not raise wage rates to attract adequate numbers of workers. Firms would be willing to raise the wages for the few vacant jobs high enough to attract unemployed workers, but in reality any such wage increase would have to be provided

10. See, for example, Jeffrey M. Perloff and Michael L. Wachter, "A Production Function–Nonaccelerating Inflation Approach to Potential Output: Is Measured Potential Output Too High?" in Karl Brunner and Alan H. Meltzer, eds., *Three Aspects of Policy and Policymaking: Knowledge, Data, and Institutions*, vol. 10 of the Carnegie Rochester Conference Series on Public Policy (New York: North Holland, 1979), pp. 113–63.

11. Richard West, "Labor Supply Response of Youth," in Phillip Robins and others, eds., *A Guaranteed Annual Income: Evidence from a Social Experiment* (Academic Press, 1980), pp. 73–84.

12. The description is the author's interpretation of Eisner's comments made at the conference.

to all similar workers. Were wages flexible in the short run, firms might be willing to provide such increases. But uncertainty about the future and the inability to lower wages if demand falls make firms too cautious to offer the wages necessary to reach equilibrium.

Another variant of low-wage unemployment comes out of models of job search. In these models workers are uncertain about their ability to obtain a good, moderate-wage job because of the wide range of wage rates paid to workers of equal skill. Initially, a worker might await a wage offer that is high relative to available alternatives. If he is lucky, he will receive a high-wage offer and take the job. If not, he might slowly adjust his wage expectations downward. As in the static case cited above, the availability of such alternate income sources as unemployment insurance can cause workers to delay returning to work, especially if the only available jobs are those at the low range of the worker's expected wage range.[13]

Frictional unemployment also occurs because the job duration that is optimal for firms and workers may be limited. Hall has developed a model in which firms face uncertainties about demand and the quality of workers. Under these conditions, there are trade-offs between the wage rate offer and the duration of the job offer. Given the preferences of workers and the cost structure of firms, one can find the equilibrium duration of jobs. With short job durations, frictional unemployment will be relatively high, since workers will have to spend frequent periods looking for new jobs.[14]

Subsidy Effects on Low-Wage Unemployment

In the simple, static case in which the equilibrium wage is low relative to nonmarket alternatives, both employer and worker wage subsidy programs can raise equilibrium wages and thereby reduce this reported unemployment. Since the government pays for the wage increase, employment gains can occur without increases in prices.

The employer wage subsidy might work as follows: an aggregate demand stimulus creates openings in moderate-wage positions; the subsidy permits firms to hire target group workers without raising prices; and the

13. See John M. Barron and Wesley Mellow, "Unemployment Insurance: The Recipients and Its Impact," *Southern Economic Journal*, vol. 47 (January 1981), pp. 606–16.

14. Robert E. Hall, "A Theory of the Natural Unemployment Rate and the Duration of Employment," *Journal of Monetary Economics*, vol. 5 (April 1979), pp. 153–69.

availability of jobs at moderate wages attracts workers out of welfare, unemployment insurance, and other alternatives into jobs. The worker wage subsidy would attract workers into existing jobs by raising net wages on jobs that formerly provided a low total return.

Where the low-wage unemployment results from uncertainty, short-run wage inflexibilities, and an inability to raise wages on only the vacant jobs, the worker subsidy approach is superior to the employer subsidy approach. Providing a wage subsidy to the workers most likely to be unemployed will encourage them to take the currently vacant low-wage jobs. Firms would be able to fill the marginal vacancies without altering their whole wage structures. The result would clearly be productive, since the marginal product of the new workers would be as high as their total payments (from firms and the subsidy combined). Spending an equal amount on an employer subsidy would probably not achieve such desirable outcomes. Lowering the cost of hiring marginal workers might not provide the firm with enough incentive to raise wages (of all workers) enough to fill existing vacancies. Although this subsidy might increase the firm's willingness to raise wages for the jobs that are currently vacant, it still would not permit net wages to rise for marginal workers without also rising for all similar workers.

The following example approximates the quantitative impact of an actual worker wage subsidy program. Suppose the program paid workers from low-income families a subsidy equal to 40 percent of the difference between $5.00 an hour and the worker's actual wage rate. Suppose further that the subsidy formula built in a maximum payment that assumed all eligible workers received presubsidy wage rates of at least the minimum wage. According to figures from the 1978 March through May Current Population Survey files, such a subsidy would have covered about 5 percent of workers. Over half of subsidized workers would have gained wage increases of 30 to 36 percent, or about $1.00 an hour. Nearly 70 percent of the very low wage workers (earning under $3.00 an hour) were youth (below age twenty-five) or adult women twenty-five to fifty-four. Since youth and women are groups whose labor supply and reported unemployment are highly sensitive to wage rates, the immediate effect of the subsidy should be to cause increases in hours worked and possible reductions in reported unemployment.

The second-round effects should go in the opposite direction as the increased labor supply leads to reductions in market wages. However, in this specific program, the labor supply increases would be small compared with the size of the entire low-wage sector, because only workers from low-income families would be eligible for the subsidies.[15] Within the very low wage group, subsidized workers would make up less than 20 percent of total employment. So if a 33 percent increase in the wages of subsidized workers were to stimulate even a very high (33 percent) increase in their labor supply, the overall increase in low-wage labor would amount to only 6 percent.[16] This 6 percent rise in labor supply would cause only a small reduction in market wage rates relative to the per hour subsidy payments; the reduction, however, would affect all low-wage workers, including those not eligible for the subsidy program. The 80 percent of low-wage workers from moderate- and high-income families would see only a decline in their net wage, and, by the arguments above, some rise in their reported unemployment along with reduced labor supply. On balance, the impact of the program will depend on the labor supply and unemployment responses of both low-wage groups to wage changes. In general, one would expect that the reported unemployment effects would be largest among workers from low-income families, since these workers are most likely to face the high marginal tax rates and work requirements from income maintenance programs.

Although the net impact on overall low-wage unemployment is uncertain, this worker subsidy program would be expected to help reduce the existing large differentials in unemployment rates among low-wage workers at different income levels. Current Population Survey data on the 1977 unemployment experience of low-wage (earning $3.00 or less an hour) workers from low-income families show that they averaged a 16.7 percent unemployment rate, or two and a half times the 6.4 percent unemployment rate of low-wage workers from moderate- or high-income families.

Subsidy Effects on Frictional Unemployment

Subsidy programs would have to induce different kinds of effects to lower frictional unemployment. In general, the subsidies would have to reduce the return to job search among workers and to raise the cost of turnover to firms. Consider first the return to job search. Employer and

15. Limiting the worker wage subsidy program to low-income workers could create serious administrative and incentive problems.

16. This estimate builds in a unitary elasticity of labor supply with respect to wage changes, which is almost certainly on the high end of empirical estimates. At lower elasticities the effect on market labor supply would be even smaller.

worker wage subsidies might exert different effects depending on the rigidities built into wage differentials. Suppose, for example, relative wages are rigid and unlikely to change in response to subsidies to employers. Then an employer subsidy might leave the overall degree of wage variation unchanged within firms. But firms might still try to take advantage of the subsidy by bidding for target group workers. If all employers who could benefit from the subsidy tried to participate, target group workers would move toward the jobs in the high wage range of those available. Such a process would narrow wage differentials among target group workers as well as raise the forgone earnings associated with job search. But for workers outside the target group, forgone earnings would fall and wage differentials would rise. Therefore, the employer subsidy would shift frictional unemployment away from target group members without reducing the total amount of frictional unemployment.

The effect of worker wage subsidies on wage differentials again depends on the specific program features. Under the earned income tax credit, wage differentials actually widen within the income range below $5,000 because the subsidy rate applies to the full wage. A 10 percent subsidy rate adds $.40 an hour to a $4.00 an hour job, but $.50 an hour to a $5.00 an hour job. But since the high-wage workers are more likely to have earnings in the $6,000 to $10,000 range, where subsidies decline with earnings, the earned income tax credit may narrow wage differentials overall.

Worker subsidy programs basing payments on wage rates would achieve narrowing of wage differentials even beyond the subsidy range. For example, a wage rate subsidy that paid half the difference between the actual wage rate and $5.00 would reduce the differential between a $3.00 an hour worker and a $6.00 an hour worker from 50 percent to 33 percent. This narrowing would occur without firms' having to alter relative wages paid for various jobs or widen differentials among workers outside the target group.

Such a program could reduce job search among the unemployed and job turnover among the employed. For both groups of low-wage workers, the wage rate subsidy would raise the cost of search (by raising net wages) and would lower the benefit of search (by reducing wage differentials among comparable skills). Mellow has documented the existence of wage dispersion for workers of similar characteristics and has attached the label "market differential" to the gap between the worker's actual wage and his expected wage based on the average of all workers with his characteristics. According to Mellow, workers with negative differentials quit more often than average and experience unemployment before finding jobs at wages closer to their expected wage.[17] Workers with positive market differentials tend to quit less often than average. Since the wage rate subsidy would tend to raise the wages of those with positive differentials, it would probably reduce the quitting rate.

Clear differences should emerge between the effects of employer and worker wage subsidies on firms' turnover costs. The former programs usually provide only temporary subsidies for any given worker. For example, the targeted jobs and work incentive tax credits provided their highest subsidy rate (50 percent) for first-year earnings, a lower rate (25 percent) for second-year earnings, and zero for third-year earnings. Such a scheme reinforces the firm's tendency to use the employer subsidy program to offer a high-wage, short-duration package to potential workers. The worker subsidy program would influence employers either in the opposite direction or would have no impact at all. If the market effect of such a program were to lower wages paid by employers, firms would have some tendency to shift to low-wage, long-duration packages for their work force. Thus, according to Hall's model, when frictional unemployment depends on the equilibrium duration of jobs, worker wage subsidies should do better than employer wage subsidies in lowering such unemployment.

In practice, even large subsidy effects on frictional unemployment will exert only a small impact on total unemployment. In separate studies, Clark and Summers and I have shown that turnover accounts for little of the total unemployment even among young workers.[18] Almost 75 percent of all weeks of unemployment experienced by male sixteen- to nineteen-year-olds during 1977 was borne by young workers with fifteen weeks or more of unemployment. The long cumulative amounts of unemployment did not usually occur because workers moved frequently from one job to another. Over 60 percent of those with fifteen weeks or more of unem-

17. Wesley Mellow, "Equilibration in the Labor Market," *Southern Economic Review*, vol. 45 (July 1978), pp. 192–203.
18. Kim Clark and Lawrence Summers, "The Dynamics of Youth Unemployment," in Richard Freeman and David Wise, eds., *The Youth Labor Market Problem: Its Nature, Causes, and Consequences* (University of Chicago Press, forthcoming); and Robert I. Lerman, "The Nature of the Youth Unemployment Problem: A Review Paper," Office of the Assistant Secretary for Policy, Evaluation, and Research, Technical Analysis Paper 69 (U.S. Department of Labor, March 1980).

ployment had at most one employer; only 17 percent had three or more employers. These data do not imply that youth stay in jobs for long periods. It does appear, however, that their frequent job movements do not by themselves account for much of the unemployment.

Statistical Discrimination and Wage Subsidies

Another plausible explanation for some structural unemployment is that employers use statistical discrimination to avoid groups of workers; that is, they apply group averages in judging all individual applicants from specific groups. As Aigner and Cain show, the discrimination occurs because employers have less reliable indicators of performance by which to judge disadvantaged relative to advantaged workers.[19] Even if group averages were similar with respect to available indicators, employers who want to avoid risk might discriminate against disadvantaged groups because of their higher variability. Low-income white and all black youth are groups that may suffer from this form of discrimination.

Consider the special case of young black men. Crime rates among this group are perhaps the highest of any group easily identifiable by employers.[20] Because of the high costs of a criminal incident, employers try to avoid the risks of crime by not hiring workers who are most likely to commit crimes. Many employers do not consider whether individual workers are likely or not likely to commit crimes; instead, they simply discriminate against all young black men. This tendency is probably heightened by the limitations on employer access to arrest and even conviction records.

An employer wage subsidy program aimed at target groups suffering from statistical discrimination is likely to exert a positive effect on their employment opportunities. First, by raising the costs of discrimination, the subsidy may stimulate firms to spend more resources distinguishing among applicants individually. Under these conditions, "creaming" for the most qualified of the target group can still raise target group employment. Second, firms that had discriminated before the subsidy may find

19. Dennis J. Aigner and Glen G. Cain, "Statistical Theories of Discrimination in Labor Markets," *Industrial and Labor Relations Review,* vol. 30 (January 1977), pp. 175–81.

20. See M. Wolfgang, "From Boy to Man: From Delinquency to Crime," paper presented at the National Symposium on the Serious Juvenile Offender, September 1977.

the gains from hiring eligibles enough to outweigh the expected value of their added costs. At least the subsidy may convince some employers to reassess their policies toward target group workers. Third, firms that already hire target group members may improve their competitive position and increase employment of these workers.

From another standpoint, a targeted employer wage subsidy may actually add to statistical discrimination by labeling eligible workers as undesirable enough to require government subsidies. For example, in a few cases work incentive placement officers reported that they decided against mentioning the tax credit to prospective employers so that it would not be known the workers were on welfare. The potential labeling effect varies by program and by target group. In cases where eligibility depends solely on age, employers gain little new information from worker eligibility. In other cases, as in subsidies for hiring low-income ex-felons, the labeling effect on workers may more than offset the positive effects expected from the subsidy's reduction in wage costs. In general, the impact of labeling should be most pronounced when statistical discrimination is the primary determinant of unemployment. Moreover, the labeling effect should be larger the narrower the category of worker subsidized is and the more new information on workers is provided by eligibility criteria.

Worker wage subsidy programs cannot exert any direct positive impact on unemployment caused by statistical discrimination. In fact, the subsidies could worsen the problem by increasing the number of workers looking for jobs that are available because of discrimination. Further, if the program requires special employer cooperation, it also could result in some undesirable labeling effects like those in employer wage subsidy programs. On the other hand, worker wage subsidy programs might reduce statistical discrimination if they encouraged workers to put additional energy into distinguishing their expected job performance from that of other target group workers.

Nonwage Aspects of Wage Subsidy Programs

Several elements affecting the performance of wage subsidy programs do not fit neatly into economic models. How workers and employers respond to nonwage factors is poorly understood but appears to depend on the design and administration of the program.

The information on program participation makes clear the importance of nonwage factors.[21] It turns out that many firms do not claim credits that they could receive without any change in the workers they hire or in the wages they pay. Under the work incentive tax credit, credits claimed amounted to about 15,000 person years of employment; data from aid to families with dependent children surveys show actual employment of potentially eligible workers in the range of 500,000. Thus only a small fraction of employers claimed credits for which they were eligible. The cumulative number of newly hired disadvantaged youth for whom employers claimed the targeted jobs tax credit through March 30, 1980, was about 60,000. This figure is less than 4 percent of the nearly 2 million disadvantaged youth hired by private firms during the year. European subsidies have sometimes reached a larger share of potential eligibles. Schwanse, in his paper in this volume, reports on a West German subsidy that reached 22 percent of eligible workers overall and 70 to 75 percent in some areas.

Under the earned income tax credit (the only U.S. worker wage subsidy program), a large share of eligible taxpayers have claimed the credit. This high participation rate has been partly due to efforts by the Internal Revenue Service to highlight the credit when providing tax forms.

Given the wide range in observed participation rates, and the fact that the subsidies cannot stimulate employment if they are unused, it is important to examine how design and administrative features affect participation. Apparently, each step that increases the number of required changes in worker or employer behavior lowers the expected participation and potential effectiveness of the subsidy. Ideally, administrators should require only those changes that directly serve the purposes of the program. For example, the new jobs tax credit, a program intended to stimulate increases in employment, permitted firms to claim credits simply by filling out a one-page form to include with the firm's tax forms. The firms did not have to alter their recruitment policy, but did have financial incentives to expand employment and to focus their hiring on workers with low earnings per year. Similarly, the British temporary subsidy in depressed regions allowed firms to qualify for credits without altering their basic recruitment procedures.

21. For background data, see Jan Parkinson, *Employment Tax Credit Utilization* (Minneapolis: IMPACT, 1977); Social Security Administration, *Aid to Families with Dependent Children, 1975 Recipient Characteristics Study* (U.S. Department of Health, Education, and Welfare, 1977), and supplemental data from the March 1978 Current Population Survey.

Under categorical employer wage subsidy programs like the targeted jobs tax credit, firms qualifying for subsidies must encounter eligible workers accidentally or must make special efforts to locate them. As a result, the firms most likely to take advantage of the work incentive and targeted jobs tax credits are those that use the employment service, work incentive program, or CETA services as part of their normal recruitment practices. Employers hiring at the gate or through personal contacts may not often encounter eligible workers and may not know when they do encounter one, because of the worker's lack of knowledge of the program. This problem is especially likely to occur unless the public agencies actively promote the program and eligibility is broad enough to cover more than a very small percentage of workers.

Since almost all the European and U.S. employer wage subsidy programs have been enacted as temporary measures, many firms are deterred from making substantial changes in recruitment practices or in their mix of labor and capital inputs. When firms do not have to alter their recruitment policies to take advantage of the subsidies in the short run, the temporary nature of the subsidies may not severely reduce their effectiveness. But it is probably quite harmful when firms must make costly changes in recruitment or production processes.

The method of certifying workers and the orientation provided to eligible workers can also influence the outcomes of categorical employer wage subsidies. Given the various attitudes about the efficacy of subsidies to employers and the demands on personnel in public employment agencies, a local agency may choose to reach and certify virtually all or very few eligibles. As part of the certification process, some agencies may explain how the subsidy can benefit employers and how workers can make use of eligibility in looking for a job. Other agencies may provide vouchers to workers with little or no explanation. Field experience under the targeted jobs tax credit indicates that many officials in local employment service and CETA offices have devoted little effort and resources to reaching eligible workers with vouchers or to stimulating firms to participate in the program.

Under a worker wage subsidy program, the problem of giving information to employers about the subsidy need not arise. Unlike employer wage subsidy programs, in which participation may depend on unusual actions by both workers and employers, the worker subsidy program must reach only the worker. Moreover, since workers should see the worker wage subsidy as a direct benefit and the employer wage subsidy as only a potential benefit, the share of eligible workers choosing to participate should usually be higher for the former than for the latter. This factor takes on special force because the percentage of the worker's income covered by worker subsidies is higher than the percentage of the employer's income covered by employer subsidies.

A final reason for expecting higher participation rates under worker subsidy programs than under employer subsidy programs has to do with the ethics of the labor market. As Robert Solow recently pointed out, workers usually do not approach employers and offer to work at wages below those paid to existing workers.[22] People are simply not accustomed to compete in the labor market by using the price competition visible in the market for goods. This reluctance of workers to underbid existing workers and to engage in direct wage competition can be somewhat undermined by categorical employer subsidy programs. Employers may also be reluctant to engage in the antisocial process of accepting low-wage bids. In contrast, the worker wage subsidy approach operates only through indirect effects on a worker's willingness to take low-wage jobs. Instead of offering firms a reduction in labor costs for choosing one worker over another, such programs simply encourage workers to make themselves available for jobs whose wages are already set at low levels.[23]

Conclusions

This comparison of the expected employment effects of worker and employer wage subsidy programs raises doubts about the apparent superiority of the employer-oriented approach as an employment stimulus tool. The structure of employer subsidy programs probably limits their effectiveness. Given the difficulty of imposing clawback provisions in such programs, the subsidies must usually be limited through categorical restrictions or through low subsidy rates. But any plausible categorical limitation is likely to result in a program that covers only a small portion of low-wage workers. This, in turn, implies that a categorical employer subsidy program is unlikely to make a substantial dent in unemployment resulting from rigid wage policies.

As for unemployment resulting from labor market factors, it appears

22. Robert M. Solow, "On Theories of Unemployment," *American Economic Review*, vol. 70 (March 1980), pp. 1–11.
23. This point was developed in conversation with Gary Burtless.

that worker subsidy programs are likely to do better than employer subsidy programs when unemployment is due to frictional causes, like short job duration and job search associated with wage dispersion for equal-skill jobs. On the other hand, the latter approach has clear potential for helping workers who are subject to statistical discrimination, though the labeling effects of the subsidy may outweigh its value in bribing firms to consider disadvantaged workers.

Nonwage factors may be at least as important as labor market conditions in determining the effectiveness of subsidies. Experience with categorical employer subsidy programs in the United States shows that only a small percent of employers take advantage of the subsidy, even when they claim the subsidy would require no change in hiring behavior. Often, however, these programs require employers to alter their recruitment practices to make substantial use of the subsidy. In those cases, a worker subsidy program would have an advantage. If the subsidy is paid directly to workers, favorable employment effects can occur without any change in employer recruitment behavior.

The potential employment stimulus from worker wage subsidy programs suggests the need for further research. Of course, one key element is improved understanding of the labor market. I believe that specific research relating to worker subsidy programs could be best pursued in field experiments. Analysis with micro data sets would be useful for gauging the overall potential of such programs, but would provide little information on the important role of nonwage factors.

Comments by David M. Betson

Should the goal of increasing the employment of a group of disadvantaged workers through the use of wage subsidies be pursued by making payments directly to the workers or to the firms that hire them? I imagine that if this question were put to the average citizen, not to mention the average economist, an overwhelming majority would answer that payments should be made to firms, as "bribes" to hire such workers.

This is not a new policy question. Earlier societies have been faced with high levels of unemployment and have tried both approaches. In the sixteenth century, the town of Lyons, France, subsidized manufacturers on the condition that training would be provided to pauper children. Later, in the seventeenth century, the sheriff and magistrates of Berkshire, England, designed a subsidy scheme that supplemented the wages of agricultural workers if their wages fell below a published scale. Much more recently, the U.S. Congress adopted two tax credit programs, the new jobs tax credit and the targeted jobs tax credit, which make payments to employers. Although these programs still await extensive evaluation, it is Lerman's belief that they were not very successful. This has led him to reexamine the wisdom of subsidizing employers' wage bills to increase employment of a target group.

In his paper Lerman compares the employment effects of wage subsidies paid to employers with those of wage subsidies paid directly to workers along two important and interrelated dimensions: the working of the low-wage labor market and the design of the particular program. What kinds of problems a program seeks to correct and how well the program addresses these problems are crucial elements to its success. For wage subsidy programs, the policy objective that Lerman considers paramount is the improvement of the employment levels of a group of disadvantaged workers who have abnormally low, unacceptable levels of employment. Obviously the choice of the policy instrument used to raise the group's level of employment should depend on the cause of the group's employment problem. In contrast to Lerman, I begin my comments with this issue, which, in my opinion, is the pivotal one in choosing between employer and worker wage subsidies.

Lerman attempts to identify the cause of the low rates of employment for the target group of workers by examining various models of the low-wage labor market. The basic question he addresses is, in effect, are target group workers not getting employment offers or are they not responding to the offers they receive? In all, Lerman considers five models or characterizations of the low-wage labor market. Each is analyzed with respect to its predictions about the ability of the two subsidy schemes to raise the employment levels of the group of disadvantaged workers. The models examined fall into two main classes. One class suggests that the existing wage offers are too high and are constrained from falling to clear the market; hence a subsidy paid to the firm would be preferable for raising the disadvantaged group's employment level. The other class of models suggests that the existing wage offers are too low for the workers to accept them and hence a worker wage subsidy would be preferable. Unfortunately, economists have not been able to demonstrate which of these models captures the dominant causes of low-wage unemployment. Thus one comes away from Lerman's discussion with an appreciation of the economic rationales for selecting one method of subsidy over another, but with no clear-cut guidance on which method should be preferred.

The general rubric of wage subsidies covers many different schemes that vary considerably in design. But in analyzing policy alternatives, the specifics of program design are frequently overlooked. Lerman correctly argues that differences in design may also determine the final effects of the subsidy program even if the program correctly addresses the real cause of the problem. To examine this point, consider the textbook wage rate subsidy that has served as the design for much of the theoretical analysis of the effects of wage subsidy programs. The total subsidy is equal to a percentage of the difference between the actual wage and some specified target wage of the worker times the number of hours he worked. If this formula is used, payments could be made to either the firm or the worker. But by discussing the characteristics of actual programs, Lerman implicitly shows that the final design of either an employer or worker wage subsidy program will differ substantially from this textbook design formula. For example, the textbook example assumes away the problem of administrative feasibility. Since policymakers must face these realities, departures from the textbook design may be made that can diminish the potential employment effects of the program.

When designing employer wage subsidy schemes, policymakers will depart from the textbook design because of several practical and political considerations. First, Lerman points out that commonsense logic would indicate that the duration of the subsidy for any given spell of employment of a worker with a given firm should be temporary: if a worker remains with a firm for a reasonable amount of time, then he must be of some value to the firm and the firm should be expected to pay his full salary. Second, Lerman questions the political feasibility of constructing a subsidy scheme that would "reward" firms paying low wages or having high rates of turnover. If policymakers believe that such designs are politically infeasible, they will reject schemes that would subsidize firms for the employment of workers who earn less than some specific target level, in favor of schemes that would subsidize part of the wage of *all* workers. The potential costs of the second kind of subsidy would be so prohibitive that policymakers would be encouraged to introduce categorical restrictions to limit the costs of the program and to increase the targeting of the monies on the disadvantaged workers. The introduction of these categorical restrictions are not without their own effects on total employment. As is pointed out in many papers in this volume, categorization may well shift employment toward the targeted group but only at the expense of reducing the employment of another group of workers. All these departures from the textbook design can be seen in the design of the targeted jobs tax credit, which gives to firms that hire welfare recipients, ex-convicts, and disadvantaged youths tax credits equal to 50 percent of the worker's first-year wages (limited to the first $6,000) and 25 percent of his second-year wages.

The overriding problem with the implementation of the textbook design for a worker wage subsidy is the administrative complexity of having individuals report their wage rates and hours of work, to compute the benefit from the program. If convinced of the infeasibility of requiring such reporting, policymakers must construct schemes that are operable with information, such as earnings, currently available to the Internal Revenue Service. One way to use only earnings data, and to satisfy the goals of not subsidizing the entire population or creating notches in the program, is to subsidize earnings up to some level and then reduce the payment for earnings above it. This departure from the textbook case is a major shift from the notion of a wage rate subsidy and has been regarded more appropriately in the literature as an earnings subsidy. The earned income tax credit, which was adopted in 1974 to supplement earnings of low-wage workers with dependent children and to correct for the disincentives caused by the transfer system, is the only earnings subsidy in place in the United States and hence is the program closest to a worker wage subsidy that we now have.

Since Lerman seems dismayed about the lack of success of the current employer wage subsidy programs, his conclusion that more should be learned about worker wage subsidy schemes, preferably within an experimental context, is not surprising. Although I concur with him in this, I disagree with his rationale. In justifying his proposal, Lerman states that it is our lack of knowledge about take-up rates and administrative issues that prevents us from examining the full potential of the worker wage subsidy relative to the employer wage subsidy. In contrast, I believe the chief obstacle is our inability to identify the primary cause of low levels of employment among the targeted group. Perhaps the main reason for the apparent lack of success of the targeted jobs tax credit is that the targeted workers are getting employment offers, but not ones with wages that match their expectations. Thus I would argue that the major benefit from experimenting with worker wage subsidy schemes would be twofold. First, we could gain some valuable insight into how people would change their search behavior in response to an exogenous increase in their expected wage rate. Second, the experiment would provide for a test of the administrative feasibility of schemes that would subsidize wage rates rather than earnings.

I have two final comments. First, the distinction between a wage subsidy and an earnings subsidy like the earned income tax credit is important: the "clawback" part of the earned income tax credit program decreases the returns to work just as any welfare or tax program would. Since most of the family units that receive the credit are in this part of the program, the presence of the clawback provision actually causes a lowering of the incentives to work. Simulations produced by the model used in my paper in this volume confirm this conclusion. The labor supply of those receiving the credit fell 1.5 percent to 2.3 percent (depending on the labor supply parameters chosen) from the level that would have existed without the credit. Also important is the enormous difference in the filing unit definitions between the earned income tax credit and the typical worker wage subsidy. Unlike the subsidy schemes presented in my paper that use the individual as the filing unit, the earned income tax credit is calculated on the basis of family earnings. Consequently, the credit should be viewed as subsidizing families with low earnings rather than individuals with low earnings.

Second, I find Lerman's separation of the income maintenance role of the subsidy from the employment effects to be artificial. Perhaps this separation arises from the partial equilibrium framework in which the author has chosen to analyze the two subsidies. But it should be noted that programs that transfer money from one segment of the society to another may alter not only the level of total aggregate demand but also change the composition of the final demand so as to increase total employment. Using the regional input-ouput model (RESIND) developed by Haveman and Golladay,[24] I have estimated the effects of a fully financed worker wage subsidy program on total employment. The results, which are tentative, show that the program would increase total employment by 71,000 jobs, with 63 percent of this increase in employment for earnings groups similar to the group initially targeted by the program.

Comments by Michael C. Barth

Two tools of income maintenance and labor market policy have been developed and variously implemented. One, the employer wage subsidy,

---

24. Frederick L. Golladay and Robert H. Haveman, *The Economic Impacts of Tax-Transfer Policy: Regional and Distributional Effects* (Academic Press, 1977).

is a payment to employers designed to reduce the price of a set of workers and thus increase their employment. The other, the worker wage subsidy, is a payment to workers designed to increase incomes in a way that does not reduce work incentives, or at least reduces them minimally.

As Robert Lerman shows, in a standard, static competitive model of the labor market, the two subsidies have identical effects on net wages and employment. Unfortunately, such models are not representative of the real world. Lerman sets out to modify the standard model by introducing several old and new ideas in labor economics, such as rigid (read minimum) wages, voluntary unemployment, search or frictional unemployment, human capital, turnover, implicit contracts, and statistical discrimination. One refinement not discussed by Lerman is, in my judgment, critical; namely, the lag with which an employer or worker wage subsidy policy would operate. As I argue below, an ex ante comparative evaluation must be explicit on this matter, especially if the two policies are likely to have different lag structures and the lags are potentially long.

Lerman then examines the relative employment effects of the two subsidies to determine if the predicted effects will differ. He finds that the effects do differ and concludes that doubts are raised about the apparent superiority of the employer subsidy over the worker subsidy as a tool to stimulate employment.

The policy implication of this moderate conclusion is not that policymakers should immediately reallocate resources from the targeted jobs tax credit and the work incentive tax credit to the earned income tax credit or to a wage rate subsidy; rather, they should open their minds to the idea that a worker wage subsidy can have important employment-creating, or at least employment-redistributing, effects and that they may wish to experiment with one.

Since I have no great quarrel with Lerman's innovative qualitative analyses, let me turn to the question of how one might move toward more interesting policy implications. First, one would need a manipulable model of the labor market and guesses about reasonable ranges for its parameters. Such a simulation model could then be "run" under the employer subsidy and worker subsidy effects hypothesized by Lerman, and the resulting changes in employment and net wage rates compared. Let me illustrate. Implicit in Lerman's analysis, and in those of many others, is the notion that some people's supply price (acceptance wage) exceeds the market wage for a person of their skill and experience. What is the size of the gap, and how does it vary over the duration of unemployment? At what wage rate–hours worked bundle does the labor supply curve resume its upward slope? If one knew the answers to these questions and also knew the elasticity of demand, the elasticity of substitution between subsidized and unsubsidized workers, and the appropriate lag structure, one could specify and solve a model for before-and-after wage rates and employment situations under employer and worker subsidies. One could similarly model the other facets of the labor market that Lerman describes.

I am aware that the results of such a model would be only as good as the hypotheses and parameters incorporated in it. Moreover, such a model could quickly become complex. The simple model in my 1974 paper could easily be modified to include rigid wages,[25] but bringing in segmented markets and labor market flows would be difficult, though not impossible, since the data and parameters exist. The results of such an exercise, given the current understanding of the labor market, would suggest whether Lerman's theoretical musings could lead to interesting policy implications. Moreover, the sensitivity analyses I have in mind would suggest what variables are most important to study or hold constant should field experiments be undertaken. Lerman's work does not indicate to policymakers whether, on employment-creation criteria, they should increase the size or coverage of the earned income tax credit or seek substantial research funds to experiment with a worker wage subsidy.

My guess is that the employment effects of worker wage subsidies will probably be as small, or as difficult to observe, as those of employer wage subsidies have been. Lerman's analysis clearly shows that current employer subsidy programs won't work for a variety of administrative and policy reasons. My own explanation is that labor-capital ratios are determined by fundamental technological, legal, economic, and sociological factors that do not change quickly, and certainly not in response to the government's latest whim. For this reason I hypothesize that lags under employer wage subsidies are likely to be longer, perhaps much longer, than those under worker wage subsidies. The positive feature of a worker subsidy is that at least part of its social payoff—higher income to a low-wage worker—exists irrespective of any employment effect. If the latter should exist, so much the better.

25. Michael C. Barth, "Market Effects of a Wage Subsidy," *Industrial and Labor Relations Review,* vol. 27 (July 1974), pp. 572–85.

David M. Betson and John H. Bishop

Wage Incentive and Distributional Effects

Several years ago the negative income tax seemed to be an idea whose time had come. There was strong support for it in the economics profession and in the Department of Health, Education, and Welfare, and both Republican and Democratic presidents had proposed similar kinds of approaches to comprehensive welfare reform, to provide income-related cash assistance to all low-income persons and eliminate the aid to families with dependent children (AFDC) and food stamp programs. Such proposals, however, have always been defeated in Congress, except for supplemental security income, which covers only the aged and disabled population. The main reason for political and public resistance to their implementation has been the fear that they would have a detrimental effect on the labor supply of employable persons.

Consequently, politicians and economists have been led to search for ways to raise the income of working poor families without seriously weakening incentives to work. Solutions to this dilemma have centered on designing programs whose benefits would be positively correlated with the amount of work performed by the recipient. For example, the earned income tax credit, a refundable tax credit that increases with the amount of earned income, was implemented after the defeat of President Nixon's negative income tax–like proposal, the family assistance program. Not only direct cash supplements to recipients, but also policies that have sought to increase work opportunities for the poor have been proposed. These solutions have taken the form of either retargeting current Comprehensive Employment and Training Act (CETA) jobs on the poor or providing direct cash subsidies to employers who hired the poor. Examples of this latter strategy that have passed Congress and were being implemented at the time of this writing are CETA on-the-job training subsidies, the work incentive program, and the targeted jobs tax credit paid to employers who hire welfare recipients or young members of low-income families.

In this paper we analyze one such alternative to the negative income tax scheme, the wage rate subsidy. Under wage subsidy programs the government makes payments to either employers or employees based on their levels of employment: the higher the level, the higher the payment. Programs that pay employers are usually called job or employment incentives, subsidies, or tax credits. Programs that pay employees according to their hours worked and their wage rate are usually called wage supplements or wage rate subsidies. We focus on the latter, and, in particular, we present results from some preliminary microeconomic simulations of the cost, output, and distributional effects of various wage rate subsidy schemes and compare these to the effects of a negative income tax. The main results are the following:

—A negative income tax causes a reduction in labor supply. The earnings reduction is about 30 percent of net cost for each of the three labor supply functions used in the simulations.

—An equal cost wage rate subsidy reduces labor supply less than a negative income tax. And under some labor supply assumptions it causes labor supply to rise. So on efficiency grounds a wage rate subsidy is preferred to a negative income tax.

—The wage rate subsidy that is most effective at raising the income of the needy subsidizes the wages of primary earners in families with children and has a target wage that depends on the number of children.

—When the distributional goals of the program are appropriately defined—families are ranked by the budget constraints they face (not by current income) and the objective is specified as raising the family's income—the wage rate subsidy conditioned by family size is more distributionally effective than a negative income tax.

In the first section of the paper, we review the literature on wage subsidies paid to the employee. Next we describe the specifics of the plans that are to be simulated. In the third section we give the results of our simulations, and finally we summarize these results and make suggestions for future research in this area.

Wage Subsidies Paid to the Employee

A wage rate subsidy is a government supplement to a worker's hourly wage. The hourly payment is equal to a percentage (the subsidy rate) of the difference between some target wage and the worker's actual hourly wage. The total payment made to the worker would then be equal to the hourly subsidy times the number of hours he or she worked. Although eligibility for the subsidy is limited to the workers whose wage rate is below the target wage, eligibility can be further restricted or defined by categorical requirements, such as limiting it to the primary earner of a family with children.

Since a wage rate subsidy does not provide an income guarantee for families with no working members, it is not a comprehensive system of income support. The subsidy must therefore be thought of as part of a system of income support that would divide people into those expected to work and those not expected to work. Families in which no members were expected to work would receive support from supplemental security income and a reformed AFDC program. For families headed by someone expected to work, unemployment-induced reductions in income could be dealt with by a reformed unemployment insurance system, public service jobs, and targeted subsidies for private employment. A universal income guarantee could be implemented, if desired, by offering low-wage public jobs to the long-term unemployed. A wage rate subsidy integrates well with a job guarantee.[1] It can be manipulated to make private jobs more attractive than public service jobs, thus reducing the number of public service jobs that must be created to make the job guarantee effective.

Comparison of the Work Incentive Effects of the Wage Rate Subsidy and the Negative Income Tax

Early analysis of the wage rate subsidy by economists established that its effects on work incentives would be less detrimental than those of a negative income tax.[2] Since our paper attempts to explore the issue empirically, through the use of simulation analysis, we will briefly review the theoretical basis for that claim. Work incentive, or disincentive, is a relative term and takes on meaning only when a counterfactual is chosen. Because the counterfactual we use is the current system of taxes and transfers, we propose answering the following questions. Do the changes

1. John Bishop and Robert Lerman, "Wage Subsidies for Income Maintenance and Job Creation," in Robert Taggert, ed., *Job Creation: What Works?* Proceedings of a conference sponsored by the School of Labor and Industrial Relations, Michigan State University and the National Council on Employment Policy (Salt Lake City: Olympus, 1977).

2. Jonathan Kesselman, "Labor-Supply Effects of Income, Income-Work, and Wage Subsidies," *Journal of Human Resources,* vol. 4 (Summer 1969), pp. 275–92.

in the current system implied by the addition of a wage rate subsidy or implementation of a negative income tax increase or decrease incentives to work and by how much? And which alternative has the larger impact?

In analyzing the effects on work effort of changes in the tax-transfer structure, economists have decomposed the effects into two parts. The impact of changing the family's disposable income is referred to as the income effect. Common sense and the empirical literature on labor supply suggest that if the program causes the worker's income to rise (fall), then he will work less (more). The second part of the decomposition is called the substitution effect, which states that if the program raises (lowers) the net wage rate of the worker without changing his or her income level, then he or she will tend to work more (less).

Under a negative income tax the government guarantees a family a specified amount if it has no income from other sources. If the family has some other income, this amount is reduced by a percentage (the benefit reduction rate) of this nontransfer income until the payment diminishes to zero. Thus eligible families experience an increase in disposable income and a decrease in the net return to work. In this case, since both income and substitution effects are operating in the same direction, one would expect the individual to work less than under the current system.

In contrast, when a wage rate subsidy is implemented, the family experiences a rise in both its disposable income and in the net return to work of the family members that are eligible. Like the negative income tax, the subsidy has an income effect that will tend to diminish work; unlike the negative tax, however, its substitution effect operates in the direction of encouraging more work. Thus under the subsidy the income and substitution effects operate in opposite directions, so that one cannot assign a priori the direction of change in work effort with respect to the current system without attaching relative magnitudes to these two effects. Since the wage rate subsidy's substitution effect operates in the opposite direction from that of the negative income tax, families receiving the same net benefits initially from both programs will work more if the payment is received from the subsidy than from the negative tax.

Early analysis of the wage rate subsidy has focused on the effects of the program on the work effort of the recipient. But members of his family may also be affected by the implementation of the program. The effects of the subsidy on their work effort have two components: an income effect—the extra income received from the subsidy will tend to decrease the work effort of all family members—and a cross-substitution effect—the work

Table 1. Effects of the Negative Income Tax and Wage Rate Subsidies on Work Effort in Relation to the Current System

Subsidy	Income effect	Substitution effect	Cross-substitution effect	Total
		Effect on recipient of transfers		
Negative income tax	−	−	+	−
Wage rate subsidy (only one member of family eligible)	−	+	0	?
Wage rate subsidy (more than one member eligible)	−	+	−	?
		Effect on other members of family		
Wage rate subsidy	−	0	−	−

effort of one member of a family is related to the net return to work by another member. Economic theory does not specify the sign of the latter relationship, but the few empirical studies that have examined the question suggest that higher wage rates received by husbands lower the amount of labor supplied by their wives. If this is generally true, then the cross-substitution effect of a wage rate subsidy on other members of a family will be to reduce work.

Table 1 summarizes the effects of wage rate subsidies and negative income tax on work effort. As can be seen in the table, the claim that a wage rate subsidy strengthens work incentives clearly rests on the implicit assumption of a large substitution effect on those that receive the subsidy. For if the substitution effect is not large, it is quite possible that work incentives may fall from their level under the current system and may be close to those of a negative income tax.

Other Comparisons between the Wage Rate Subsidy and the Negative Income Tax

Garfinkel has demonstrated that, relative to a negative income tax or to laissez-faire, a wage rate subsidy reduces incentives to sacrifice work time in order to invest in human capital.[3] But other policy instruments, such as scholarships and free schooling, are available to counteract this effect.[4]

3. Irwin Garfinkel, "A Skeptical Note on 'The Optimality of Wage Subsidy Programs,'" *American Economic Review,* vol. 63 (June 1973), pp. 451–53.
4. Koichi Hamada, "Income Taxation and Educational Subsidy," *Journal of Public Economics,* vol. 3 (May 1974), pp. 145–58.

Both the subsidy and the negative tax tend to encourage on-the-job training. Workers that choose to invest heavily in such training are compensated for an initially lower wage by future wage increases and promotions. Meanwhile, the subsidy and the negative tax reduce the income sacrifice that must be made during the training period. If the job for which the employee is training is in the range of subsidy, the wage rate subsidy and the negative income tax lower the payoff by an equivalent amount, which leaves the benefit–cost ratio of the on-the-job training unchanged.[5] If the job is above the range of subsidy, the cost-reducing effects of the wage rate subsidy and the negative income tax are proportionately larger than their payoff-reducing effects, which raises the benefit–cost ratio and presumably stimulates on-the-job training.

A wage rate subsidy should also reduce the level of search or frictional unemployment, because it raises the costs of searching for another job while it simultaneously reduces the payoff from searching by lowering wage differentials. A negative income tax, by contrast, tends to increase search unemployment. Since the social cost of unemployment greatly exceeds the private cost,[6] the tendency of the wage rate subsidy to reduce the time spent unemployed is desirable. Although search behavior is not explicitly modeled, most of the effects on durations of unemployment are captured by the simulations.[7]

In three of the four negative income tax experiments undertaken in the 1970s the experimental families experienced significantly higher rates of marital dissolution. Bishop, in his review of the social psychological and economic literature on marital instability, suggests that the stigma of being on a welfare-type program may have been responsible for the greater separation rate among experimental families.[8] Keeley attributes the phenomenon to the experiment-induced decline in the primary earner's net wage.[9] Since a wage rate subsidy raises the net wage of the primary

5. John Bishop, "The General Equilibrium Impact of Alternative Antipoverty Strategies, *Industrial and Labor Relations Review,* vol. 32 (January 1979), p. 223.

6. Martin Feldstein, "The Private and Social Costs of Unemployment," Harvard Institute of Economic Research Discussion Paper 602 (January 1978).

7. The only aspect of the wage rate subsidy's impact on unemployment not captured is that which results from a narrowing of wage differences.

8. John H. Bishop, "Jobs, Cash Transfers and Marital Instability: A Review and Synthesis of the Evidence," *Journal of Human Resources,* vol. 15 (Summer 1980), pp. 301–34.

9. Michael C. Keeley, "The Effects of Income and Wage Changes on Divorce," a research report performed pursuant to contract with the states of Washington and Colorado (January 1980).

earner and can be paid in a way that does not stigmatize its recipients (by manipulating withholding tax rates), it is not likely to destabilize marriages.

A wage rate subsidy has several characteristics that make it easier to administer than a negative income tax: no assets tests, no work tests, no need to measure unearned income or the earnings from unsubsidized jobs. But it also has one feature—the necessity of measuring hours of work—that makes it harder to administer. Further administrative complications are introduced if eligibility for the subsidy is limited to primary earners or heads of households. Thus, in the absence of practical experience, no definitive statement is possible on which program is easier to administer.

A Description of the Programs

In this section we describe the negative income tax and wage rate subsidy plans that we have simulated in this paper. Since reliable estimates of labor supply parameters for nonheads of families with children and for people over sixty-five were not available, we have limited eligibility for the simulated plans to families with children headed by someone under sixty-five. Comparability of the simulated plans was maintained by requiring them to be of equal net cost.

We began the exercise by constructing a negative income tax plan that provides an income guarantee of 75 percent of the poverty line and reduces the benefit by 50 cents for every dollar of earned income and by one dollar for every dollar of income from other sources.[10] Although this program was designed to replace six current federal and state programs— AFDC, AFDC-U (unemployed parent), food stamps, general assistance, supplemental security income, and the earned income tax credit—a hold-harmless provision was implemented so that no family unit would have its disposable income lowered through the implementation of the plan.

To review, the three major design characteristics of a wage rate subsidy scheme are (1) the subsidy rate, (2) categorical eligibility definitions, and (3) the target wage rate. In all our wage rate subsidy simula-

---

10. In 1975 the poverty lines were $3,505, $4,298, $5,505, $6,498, $7,311, and $8,975 for families with from two to seven members. Other sources of income counted in the benefit determination were social security benefits, unemployment compensation, workmen's compensation, pension income, alimony, child support, interest, dividends, and rental income.

tions, we chose a subsidy rate of 50 percent. This choice represented a compromise between two conflicting goals: on the one hand, providing more subsidy to low-wage workers, and on the other, maintaining incentives to obtain a higher-wage job and minimizing the incentives in the system to underreport one's wage rate to get a larger subsidy. To minimize administration and enforcement problems, we made only those persons who were not self-employed eligible for a subsidy. And to increase the target efficiency of the subsidy plans and also to limit the costs of the plans, we further narrowed eligibility to the primary earners in families with children.

The final design characteristic, the target wage, was then chosen so that the net cost of the scheme would equal that of the negative income tax simulation. In the first set of wage subsidies, the target wage is set at $4.40 an hour. Since the benefits of the program do not depend on family size, this wage rate subsidy will be more generous (relative to the poverty line) to smaller family units. To assess the effects of conditioning the target wage on family size, we simulated a second subsidy scheme with a target wage starting at $3.10 and an additional 60 cents for every dependent child.

To minimize the incentive for workers to increase their subsidies fraudulently by overreporting hours and underreporting wage rates, a wage subsidy would probably place lower limits on the wage rate that would be subsidized and upper limits on the hours that could receive subsidy. The first ensures that there is a market test on the value of the work being subsidized and also should serve as a magnet to pull wage rates up to the minimum subsidizable level; the second turns off the subsidy when hours worked reach some socially agreed maximum. In this paper we assume that this socially agreed maximum is 3,120 hours a year (60 hours a week). The wage rate subsidies simulated here do not place an absolute ban on the subsidy of jobs paying extremely low wages. Where the wage rate is below the legal minimum wage, $2.10 an hour in 1975, the subsidy is a flat percentage of earnings.

In summary, workers whose average wage rate, W, is between the target wage, TW, and the legal minimum, MW (equal to $2.10 in 1975), and who worked H hours are paid a subsidy of

$$\frac{TW \cdot H - ER}{2} \quad \text{for} \quad MW < W < TW,$$

where *ER* is equal to the worker's reported earnings. For workers below the minimum wage, the subsidy is equal to

$$\frac{TW - MW}{2MW} ER \quad \text{for} \quad W < MW.$$

If the person worked more than 3,120 hours, 3,120 is substituted for *H*.

Our two wage subsidy schemes are incremental in the sense that except for the elimination of the earned income tax credit, the rest of the tax-transfer system is left intact. To facilitate the integration of the wage rate subsidy with other programs, we treat it as taxable earned income by the positive tax system and by transfer programs like AFDC, supplemental security income, and food stamps.[11]

Results

In this section we show the results from simulations of the one negative income tax and two wage rate subsidy schemes described above.[12] These results were derived from a large microeconomic simulation model designed especially to simulate the effects of President Carter's comprehensive welfare proposal (The Better Jobs and Income Act, 1977) on trans-

---

11. If the wage rate subsidy is treated as earned income, the incentive for working more hours will be smaller than if it is treated as unearned income. But the former will ensure that people receiving both welfare and the subsidy benefit when they find better paying jobs.

12. Several assumptions favorable to the negative income tax and unfavorable to the wage rate subsidy were made in defining programs and designing the simulation model.

—The wage rate subsidy is not pure. The 5 percent of eligible workers who work more than sixty hours are effectively in the recapture range of an earning subsidy and therefore are predicted to reduce their labor supply.

—The 100 percent tax on unearned income under the negative income tax makes that program more target efficient. By assumption, there are no effects on reporting unearned income, on saving and borrowing, or on labor supply. These assumptions are almost certainly invalid. The wage rate subsidy, by contrast, does not tax unearned income and so leaves incentives to save and to report the income from saving intact.

—Unemployment insurance payments are assumed not to respond to changes in labor supply. If this response had been modeled, the net cost of the negative income tax would rise and the efficiency advantage of the wage rate subsidy would widen, especially under the alternate labor supply assumptions.

fers, taxes, and private and public sector earnings and use data for 1975.[13] In the first subsection we present aggregate data on the gross and net costs and the labor supply response to various alternative subsidy schemes using three different sets of labor supply coefficients; in the second subsection we report on the distributional impact of the programs.

Costs and Labor Supply Response

The first column of table 2 shows the estimated gross costs (before the labor supply response) of the three simulated programs, which all have roughly equivalent net costs after labor supply response. Gross costs vary considerably: from $18 billion for the negative income tax to $9.7 billion for the wage rate subsidy with a fixed target wage. Since these programs displace existing programs, the net cost of these reforms is considerably smaller. The negative income tax displaces all existing welfare programs aiding families with children, so the net increase in costs before the labor supply response is $4.6 billion, roughly one-quarter of the gross costs. The net cost of the wage subsidies before the labor supply response is roughly 55 percent of their gross cost because the subsidy substitute for the earned income tax credit reduces payments in existing transfer programs and increases tax yields.

The two subsidy schemes spread their benefits much more widely than the negative income tax does. More than 11 million families would receive benefits from either of the subsidies. Gross payments per family are roughly $850, and net benefits are roughly $500. The negative tax payments go to 6.6 million families with an average gross payment of $2,700 a family, and the average increase in net benefits is $860 a family.

Table 2 also shows simulation results based on three alternative sets of labor supply specifications. The first specification of labor supply parameters comes from the analysis by Keeley and others of the Seattle-Denver income maintenance experiment.[14] The principal advantage of this study

13. A description of this model can be found in David Betson, David Greenberg, and Richard Kasten, "A Microsimulation Model for Analyzing Alternative Welfare Reform Proposals: An Application to the Program for Better Jobs and Income," in Robert H. Haveman and Kevin Hollenbeck, eds., *Microeconomic Simulation Models for Public Policy Analysis,* vol. 1: *Distributional Impacts* (Academic Press, 1980).

14. Michael C. Keeley and others, "The Labor Supply Effects and Costs of Alternative Negative Income Tax Programs," *Journal of Human Resources,* vol. 13 (Winter 1978), pp. 3–36.

Table 2. Estimated Costs of Negative Income Tax and Wage Rate Subsidy Programs in 1975

Costs in billions of 1975 dollars

Subsidy	Gross cost[a]	Net cost[a]	Number of families receiving benefits (millions)	Seattle-Denver experiment I (linear)	Seattle-Denver experiment II (non-linear)	Alternative labor supply
					Net cost[b]	
Negative income tax	18.0	4.6	6.6	5.7	5.6	5.7
Wage rate subsidy: $4.40	9.7	5.5	11.6	5.7	5.9	5.4
Wage rate subsidy: $3.10 + $0.60 a child	10.0	5.5	11.3	5.7	6.0	5.5

Source: Authors' calculations.
a. Before labor supply effects are considered.
b. After labor supply effects are considered.

(Seattle-Denver I) over cross-sectional studies is that the parameter estimates were derived from data generated from families that underwent controlled and observed changes in their budget constraints. From these observed changes in employment and earnings, the researchers were able to estimate the substitution and income effects needed for the simulations.

The second specification of labor supply parameters is also derived from the same income maintenance experiment. These unpublished parameter estimates (Seattle-Denver II), made by the Stanford Research Institute, use different assumptions about the variance of income and substitution effects across the income distribution. This specification was included to test the sensitivity of the simulation results to the choice of functional form of the labor supply function. In general, it yielded smaller substitution effects for the recipient population than did Seattle-Denver I.

Although the labor supply estimates from the Seattle-Denver income maintenance experiment are consistent with the cross-sectional estimate for males, the estimated parameters for females contrast sharply with the parameters estimated by studies using cross-sectional data. The cross-sectional literature on female labor supply usually estimates higher substitution effects and smaller income effects than those obtained by analyses of negative income tax experiment data. From the literature we selected Masters and Garfinkel's parameter estimates of female labor supply response.[15] These estimates were combined with the Seattle-Denver I estimates of male labor supply response, and the resulting model was called the alternative labor supply model. A more detailed discussion of the labor supply assumptions can be found in the appendix.

Net costs after labor supply response are tabulated in the last three columns of table 2 for each of our alternative labor supply assumptions. A comparison with the net costs before labor supply response, tabulated in the second column, shows that accounting for that response substantially increases the net cost of the negative income tax plan. Costs rise because the reduction in earnings induced by the negative tax is partially replaced by increases in the negative tax payments. For the wage rate subsidy the change in net costs after the labor supply response is considerably smaller. The simulations that use the high-substitution elasticity labor supply assumptions predict a slight decline in net costs, whereas the simulations that use parameters derived from the Seattle-Denver income maintenance experiment indicate that the labor supply response slightly increases the net costs of a wage subsidy. The reasons for these contrasts are discussed shortly.

In table 3 we present our predictions of the labor supply response to the three program prototypes. The first two columns show estimates of the change in hours worked and earnings by the "primary" direct recipients. The third and fourth columns show estimates of the labor supply response of the other adult members of the family. Under a negative income tax, eligibility is determined by family income, so that all family members are primary recipients. Consequently, for the negative income tax the first two columns in table 3 report the sum of the labor supply responses of both the primary and secondary earners and the third and fourth columns are blank. Under the wage rate subsidies simulated, the wage rate of the family's primary earner determines eligibility, so that he or she is the primary recipient, while the other adult members of the family are the secondary recipients. In the fifth column we summarize each program's impact on earnings and disposable income by tabulating its efficiency ratio, defined as the ratio of the change in disposable income to the net cost of the program. Subtracting one from the ratio gives the per dollar effect of the program on output in the economy.

The addendum to the table presents our estimates of the aggregate hours of work and dollars of earnings of the members of recipient families

15. Stanley H. Masters and Irwin Garfinkel, *Estimating the Labor Supply Effects of Income-Maintenance Alternatives* (Academic Press, 1977).

**Table 3. Labor Supply Response to the Negative Income Tax and Wage Rate
Subsidy Schemes**

Hours in billions; earnings in billions of dollars[a]

Model	Direct recipients		Secondary recipients		Effi-ciency ratio (5)
	Change in hours (1)	Change in earnings (2)	Change in hours (3)	Change in earnings (4)	
Seattle-Denver experiment I (linear)					
Negative income tax	−0.57	−1.73	...	...	0.70
Wage rate subsidy: $4.40	0.04	0.07	−0.22	−0.43	0.94
Wage rate subsidy: $3.10 + $0.60 a child	0.05	0.10	−0.23	−0.40	0.95
Seattle-Denver experiment II (nonlinear)					
Negative income tax	−0.83	−1.52	...	...	0.73
Wage rate subsidy: $4.40	−0.31	−0.92	−0.37	−0.84	0.70
Wage rate subsidy: $3.10 + $0.60 a child	−0.29	−0.90	−0.39	−0.83	0.71
Alternative labor supply					
Negative income tax	−0.52	−1.63	...	...	0.71
Wage rate subsidy: $4.40	0.40	1.00	0.01	0.31	1.23
Wage rate subsidy: $3.10 + $0.60 a child	0.37	0.93	0.01	0.33	1.23
Addendum:					
Totals before response					
Negative income tax	7.76	17.75	...	...	...
Wage rate subsidy: $4.40	16.75	51.58	4.17	11.16	...
Wage rate subsidy: $3.10 + $0.60 a child	16.30	51.18	4.06	10.67	...

Source: Authors' calculations.

a. Measured over a one-year period.

before any response to the incentives of the program. Percentage changes
in hours or earnings may be calculated by dividing the changes tabulated
for the programs by the totals tabulated in the addendum.

The predicted labor supply response to a negative income tax does not
seem to be very sensitive to which set of parameter estimates is used.[16]

16. A 1980 paper on the Seattle-Denver income maintenance experiment reports
that labor supply responses to the five-year treatment were considerably larger than
responses to the three-year treatment and that parameters estimated on the behavior
of the five-year treatment group imply considerably larger labor supply responses
than those simulated here. Michael Keeley and Hoi Wai, "Labor Supply Response
to a Permanent Negative Income Tax Program," Stanford Research Institute memo-

The efficiency ratios range from 0.70 to 0.73. The total decline in earnings is between $1.5 and $1.7 billion. Recipient families lower earnings by 9 percent and reduce their hours of work by 7 to 11 percent.[17] Turning to the results for the two wage rate subsidy plans, we see that there is no significant change in the labor supply response when the target wage is conditioned on the number of children. This generalization holds for all sets of the labor supply assumptions. But what is most striking is the extreme sensitivity of the wage rate subsidy simulation to the set of labor supply parameters used. Efficiency ratios range from 1.23 with alternative labor supply assumptions (implying an output rise of 23 percent of net cost) to 0.70 for the nonlinear parameters of the Seattle-Denver experiment (implying an output decline of 29 percent of net cost).

When the linear assumptions of the Seattle-Denver experiment are used, the wage rate subsidy is predicted to cause a very small increase ($100 million) in the earnings of primary recipients and a somewhat larger decrease in the earnings ($400 million) of other family members. When the nonlinear assumptions of the experiment are used, the income effects dominate completely, and all members of subsidized families reduce their work effort and earnings—primary earners by 2 percent or $900 million and secondary earners by 8 percent or $830 million. The alternative labor supply assumptions predict that substituting a wage rate subsidy conditioned by family size for the earned income tax credit will raise the earnings of the primary recipient by 2 percent or $930 million and the earnings of other adult family members by 3 percent or $330 million. The labor supply of secondary earners increases because ending the tax credit raises the net wage of secondary earners and outweighs the income effect of the wage rate subsidy paid to the family's primary earner.

The comparison between the negative income tax and wage rate subsidy is quite sensitive to the choice of labor supply specification. If the

---

randum, August 1980. Using the Keeley-Wai parameters lowers the efficiency ratio from 0.7 to 0.5. In a recent paper Bishop argues that this and other problems result in the simulations significantly understating the size of the labor supply response to a permanent, pure negative income tax. John Bishop, "The Labor Supply Response to the Seattle-Denver Income Maintenance Experiment: A Reinterpretation," paper presented at the Western Economics Association meetings in July 1981.

17. The nonlinear specification produces an unusual pattern of results. The percentage decline in hours (10.7 percent) is substantially larger than the percentage decline in earnings, 8.6 percent. This occurs because the nonlinear specification assumes that low-wage workers are more responsive to the negative income tax program than other workers.

alternative labor supply assumptions correctly represent people's preferences, the subsidy will raise the disposable income of its recipients by nearly twice as much as a negative tax of equal cost. Under the linear assumptions of the Seattle-Denver experiment, the subsidy will raise the disposable income by 1.4 times what the negative tax does. Under the nonlinear assumptions of the experiment, the negative tax and subsidy do not differ significantly in how much they raise the income of recipients.[18] The small differences are nevertheless interesting. The reduction in hours worked is 830 million for the negative income tax and 680 million for the two wage rate subsidy plans. But the earnings reductions of $1.7 billion under the subsidy are larger than the $1.5 billion reductions under the negative tax. This seeming contradiction of our theoretical predictions occurs because lower-wage workers reduce their hours more than higher-wage workers.

Distributional Impacts

We report the distributional impacts of the programs in tables 4 and 5. Column 1 of table 4 tabulates the proportion of net benefits going to two-parent families. Two-parent families receive 64 percent of the net benefits of the negative income tax limited to families with children, 78 percent of the net benefits from the wage rate subsidy with a fixed target wage, and 83 percent of the subsidy conditioned by family size. Since benefits from a subsidy are proportional to hours worked, and since the primary earners of two-parent families usually work longer hours than single parents, two-parent families receive a larger share of the benefits from the subsidy than from the negative tax. Because two-parent families are usually larger, conditioning the subsidy target wage on the number of children tends to increase the share of benefits going to two-parent families.

The next two columns of table 4 present estimates of target efficiency: the proportion of each program's benefits that are paid to the needy. In column 2, we define the target group in the traditional way by reference to the family's current income before transfer. The only difference is that

18. The wage rate subsidy's larger number of beneficiaries includes many families with current incomes that are too high to be eligible for a negative income tax. As a result, the nonlinear specification asserts that the typical subsidy recipient has a more powerful income effect than the typical negative tax recipient. This compositional effect is strong enough to overcome the fact that under the subsidy substitution effects operate to increase rather than decrease labor supply.

Table 4. The Distribution of Net Benefits under Negative Income Tax and Wage Rate
Subsidy Programs
Percent

	Net benefits going to two-parent families (1)	Benefits going to needy		Reduction in number of needy[c] (4)
Program		Current income criterion[a] (2)	Earnings capacity criterion[b] (3)	
Negative income tax	64	100	87	25
Wage rate subsidy: $4.40	78	42	61	10
Wage rate subsidy: $3.10 + $0.60 a child	83	54	73	15

Source: Authors' calculations.
a. See text for explanation. Target group constitutes 18.6 percent of population.
b. See text for explanation. Target group constitutes 28.8 percent of population.
c. Measured by current income.

the threshold defining the target group was set higher than usual: current pretransfer income below 1.5 times the poverty line. This target group constitutes about 19 percent of the people living in families with children.

Current pretransfer income, however, is a poor measure of a family's level of economic welfare. Families with identical budget constraints (that is, wage rates and nonemployment income) often have dramatically different incomes. In some families the wife works and the husband has two jobs; in others no one is working. A further problem is that the programs being simulated are incremental to the existing set of transfer programs, yet income receipts from the latter programs are not counted in defining need, even though the receipts may already have induced a cutback in work effort by the family or pushed the family above 1.5 times the poverty line.

If, for a given budget constraint, variations across families in current income are primarily due to differences in tastes for work and to the stigma of being on welfare, a ranking of budget constraints is a better measure of economic welfare than current income. Circumstances that prevent the family from having all adult members working full time—involuntary unemployment and child care responsibilities—should be incorporated in the budget constraint index in a systematic manner.

For this paper we have assumed that the number of weeks during which a person reports that he or she is unemployed accurately measures the amount of involuntary unemployment experienced by that individual. Consequently, the earnings capacity of a family member was defined as

$$EC_i = \text{(expected hours}_i\text{)(hourly wage}_i\text{)} \left(\frac{52 - \text{weeks unemployed}}{52} \right).$$

All persons who do not have primary responsibility for the care of a young child—single persons, both the husband and wife when there are no children, the primary earner in two-parent families, and mothers (whether wife or single parent) whose children are over fourteen—have an expected 2,080 hours of work a year. Mothers (and single-parent fathers) with younger children were assigned expected hours that roughly corresponded to the number of hours worked by wives with children of that age: 1,080 when the youngest child is six to fourteen, and 680 when the youngest is under six. When a mother with children under fourteen is working, we also deduct child care costs of 90 cents an hour for the first child under six, 45 cents an hour for the second and third children under six, and 30 cents an hour for children aged seven through thirteen.

The earnings capacity of the family is defined as the sum of the earnings capacities of its adult members, plus all unearned nontransfer income minus the cost of child care.[19] As in the current income definition of the target group, we defined this target group as those families that had earnings capacity less than 1.5 times the poverty line. By this criterion, about 29 percent of the people living in families with children fall into the target group.

The "need" criterion so defined has several desirable characteristics. Most important, it treats as equally needy families that would have the same income level if they chose to supply the same amount of market labor. The college graduate who earns almost nothing while skiing in Aspen is not considered needy. The family that scrapes its way out of poverty only when the primary earner works more than sixty hours a week would be considered needy even though its current income might be more than 1.5 times above the poverty line.

Table 4 shows that, as one would expect, when current income is the basis for defining the target group, the program that uses current income to define eligibility is most target efficient. Under the negative income tax 100 percent of the net benefits go to the target group. The two wage rate

19. This "need" criterion can be thought of as Becker's full income concept applied to the family and given a welfare interpretation. It is also closely related to the net earnings capacity notion used by Garfinkel and Haveman. See Irwin Garfinkel and Robert H. Haveman, *Earnings Capacity, Poverty and Inequality* (Academic Press, 1977).

subsidy schemes do not do nearly as well, though conditioning the target wage on family size does improve its target efficiency. In the last column we estimate the percentage of people whose current post-transfer income is below the poverty line that would be brought out of poverty (measured by current income). Again, as one would expect, the negative income tax induces the largest reduction in the poverty population.

Contrasts between the programs are not so sharp when we use the earnings capacity concept of need to define the target group. The target efficiency of the subsidy conditioned by family size is 73 percent. The higher target efficiency of the negative income tax, 87 percent, is largely due to the 100 percent tax on nonlabor income. If this form of income had been taxed at 50 percent, the target efficiency of the negative tax would have been roughly 75 percent.

But the distributional impact of a program is not well described by reporting the proportion of its first-round benefits that accrue to some target group. Programs often produce behavioral responses that can inhibit or enhance the achievement of their objectives and these responses must be considered. The distributional objective of income maintenance programs is raising the income of families felt to be in need.[20] If recipients respond to an income maintenance program by reducing their earnings, distributional as well as efficiency goals are compromised. One way to measure the success of a program in achieving distributional objectives is to calculate the ratio of the change in disposable income of the target group to the net cost of the program.[21] These ratios are shown in table 5.

Since in our opinion earnings capacity is a more valid criterion of neediness than current income, we emphasize the distributional effectiveness ratios that use earnings capacity to define the target group. As seen in the table, a wage rate subsidy with a target wage conditioned by family

20. The optimal income tax literature assumes that raising the utility level of low-income people is the objective of a negative income tax. An examination of the public debate about income maintenance programs demonstrates, however, that the public views reductions in labor supply in response to a transfer payment as an undesired outcome. Zeckhauser has developed this argument at greater length. See Richard J. Zeckhauser, "Optimal Mechanisms for Income Transfer," *American Economic Review,* vol. 61 (June 1971), pp. 324–34.

21. We do not recommend that this criterion be the only basis for evaluating a program. An exclusive focus on the distributional effectiveness ratio, as we have called it, implies the judgment that a rise in disposable income of lower-middle-income recipient families that are outside the target group has zero social value. If raising the incomes of this group has a social value equal to raising target group incomes, the criterion to focus on would be the efficiency ratio.

Table 5. Ratio of the Change in the Target Group's Disposable Income to the Net Cost of Program

Criterion for target group and program	Seattle-Denver experiment I (linear)	Seattle-Denver experiment II (nonlinear)	Alternative labor supply
Earnings capacity			
Negative income tax	0.63	0.65	0.64
Wage rate subsidy: $4.40	0.61	0.49	0.81
Wage rate subsidy: $3.10 +			
$0.60 a child	0.71	0.65	0.92
Current income			
Negative income tax	0.69	0.73	0.71
Wage rate subsidy: $4.40	0.48	0.36	0.61
Wage rate subsidy: $3.10 +			
$0.60 a child	0.59	0.44	0.72

Source: Authors' calculations.

size has higher distributional effectiveness than a wage rate subsidy with an unchanging target wage. Also, the former type of subsidy is equal to or better than a negative income tax in distributional effectiveness. The two programs are equal only under the nonlinear assumptions of the Seattle-Denver experiment. When the linear assumptions are used, the distributional effectiveness ratios are 0.71 for the wage rate subsidy and 0.63 for the negative income tax. Under the alternative labor supply assumptions, the increase in disposable income of the target group is equal to 92 percent of the net cost of the subsidy and 64 percent of the net cost of a negative tax. When current income is used to define need, the negative tax is more effective in achieving distributional objectives under the two sets of labor supply assumptions based on the Seattle-Denver experiment and equally effective under alternative labor supply assumptions.

Conclusions

We have presented simulation results of a negative income tax and of various wage rate subsidy schemes to analyze their relative impact on labor supply, cost, and the distribution of income. We now offer the following observations:

—Though under some labor supply assumptions the wage rate subsidy adversely affects work effort in the recipient population, the reduction in output is not as severe as for a comparable negative income tax.

—When estimates of female labor supply behavior obtained from the cross-sectional literature are used in the simulation, replacing the earned income tax credit with a more generous wage rate subsidy produces a significant increase in output.

—Since the wage rate subsidy has only modest negative effects on labor supply, it is a more effective means of raising the recipient's income than a negative income tax.

—Since heads of single-parent families with young children are often outside the labor force, a wage rate subsidy scheme is not an effective means of further aiding this group and could not substitute for AFDC. But a subsidy scheme is an efficient way to aid two-parent families with young children without seriously affecting work incentives.

—Regardless of how distributional goals are defined, a wage rate subsidy with a target wage conditioned by family size is preferred on distributional grounds to a subsidy with a fixed target wage.

—When the distributional objective is to raise the incomes of families in need according to the budget constraints they face, the wage subsidy conditioned by family size is more distributionally effective than a negative income tax.

In assessing how well we were able to address the efficiency effects of the negative income tax and wage rate subsidy schemes, one must wonder about the results shown in table 3. All three labor supply specifications imply that under a negative income tax for two-parent families about 30 percent of the dollars transferred will be lost to the consumption of leisure. The estimates of labor supply response produced by a wage rate subsidy vary dramatically—an increase in earnings equal to 23 percent of dollars paid out under one set of assumptions and a decrease equal to 30 percent of net costs under another. Even more surprising is the sensitivity of our results to the choice of functional form of labor supply functions that have been estimated on the same data base. It would seem that despite nearly a decade of work, there is still no consensus on the relative size of income and substitution parameters of the labor supply function. Under the negative income tax these two effects operate in the same direction, so that our inability to estimate these parameters separately does not seriously affect predictions. For the wage rate subsidy, however, income and substitution effects work in opposite directions, so that their relative size is critical in making accurate predictions.

Unfortunately, more intensive analysis of currently available cross-sectional or negative income tax experiment data is not likely to settle the controversy about the relative importance of income and substitution effects. What are needed are before and after data both on people who experience unexpected increases in their wealth and on people who are experiencing an unanticipated exogenous permanent increase in their after-tax wage rate. Since retrospective data on previous labor supply are adequate, and it is possible after the fact to identify people who are experiencing unexpected changes in wealth, studies focusing on the income effect are feasible. Unanticipated exogenous wage rate changes do not occur frequently, and when they occur other qualities of the job usually change as well. Since our objective is to learn how people will respond to changes in tax and transfer policy and not to promotions, experimental manipulation of these policies and careful studies of the results are desperately needed.

Appendix: Specification of Labor Supply Behavioral Relationships

In this paper we used three alternative specifications of labor supply behavior. Although these specifications do not exhaust all the possible configurations of empirical representations of labor supply behavior, we hoped that our choices would yield predictions that would span the probable range forthcoming from the literature. In general, the specification of labor supply behavior is limited to stating the functional relationship between hours of work and its determinants: the net return to work and the amount of income from sources other than a person's own earnings. But individual studies of labor supply behavior differ considerably because of the choices analysts make—particularly their choice of functional form, measurement of variables, selection of estimation sample, and the econometric techniques used to estimate the relationship.

Our choice of the labor supply estimates of Keeley and others reflects a view that the Seattle-Denver income maintenance experiment is the best data source for estimating labor supply functions of low-wage workers.[22] Keeley and others chose the following functional form for the labor supply relationship:

$$h_{i1} = \delta_i + \alpha_i W_i + \beta_i(W_i h_{i0} + W_j h_{j0} + y),$$

22. Keeley and others, "Labor Supply Effects."

Table 6. Labor Supply Coefficients Used in Simulations

Simulation	α	β
Seattle-Denver experiment I		
Males	83.2	-0.0344
Wives	168.0	-0.1429
Female heads	125.8	-0.1011
Seattle-Denver experiment II		
Males	-178.2	-0.0459
Wives	-145.5	-0.1561
Female heads	-129.2	-0.1112
Alternative labor supply		
Males	83.2	-0.0344
Wives	121.1	-0.0206
Female heads	296.1	-0.0583

Sources: For Seattle-Denver experiment I, Michael C. Keeley and others, "The Labor Supply Effects and Costs of Alternative Negative Income Tax Programs," *Journal of Human Resources*, vol. 13 (Winter 1978), p. 12; for Seattle-Denver Experiment II, unpublished memorandum, 1978.

where

h_{i1} = the ith person's labor supply,
W_i = the ith person's net wage rate (per hour),
W_j = the ith person's spouse's net wage rate,
h_{i0} = initial hours of work of the ith individual,
h_{j0} = the ith person's spouse's initial hours of work,
y = nonemployment income, and
$\delta_i, \alpha_i, \beta_i$ = parameters to be estimated,

where α_i can be interpreted as the substitution effect and β_i the income effect. This model was estimated for three demographic groups: males in two-parent families, wives, and female heads of families. The Keeley and others estimates of α_i and β_i appear in the top section of table 6.

Upon request from HEW, the researchers from the Stanford Research Institute estimated another functional form of the labor supply that would predict that an individual would stop working if the net return to work were zero. This functional form, which we called Seattle-Denver experiment II, is expressed as follows:

$$h_{i1} = \delta_i + \frac{\alpha_i}{W_i} + \beta_i(W_i h_{i0} + W_j h_{j0} + y).$$

The Stanford Research Institute's estimates of α_i and β_i for the three demographic groups appear in the middle section of table 6.

Finally, to determine the generality of predictions from the Seattle-Denver experiment estimates, we chose to simulate a third set of labor supply functions that were taken from the cross-sectional literature. In the construction of this third set of labor supply estimates, we used the following methodology. First we chose the labor supply function that had been used by Keeley and others. We then went to the literature and selected from various studies wage elasticities (η_w) and total income elasticities (η_I) for the three demographic groups. We attempted to select studies whose estimated substitution elasticity at the mean (the difference between the wage elasticity and income elasticity) represented the upper end of the estimates in the literature. For males, the Keeley and others study met this criterion and was used. For female heads and wives we used the estimates of Masters and Garfinkel.[23] Once elasticities were selected, we imputed the parameters α_i and β_i from these elasticities, using the following equations:

$$\alpha_i = (\eta_{wi} - \eta_{I_i})\bar{h}_i / \bar{W}_i$$

$$\beta_i = \eta_{I_i} / \bar{W}_i,$$

where

$\bar{h}_i$ = mean hours worked by the demographic group in the simulation sample

$\bar{W}_i$ = mean net wage of the demographic group in simulation sample

η_{wi} = wage elasticity of demographic group from cross-sectional study

η_{I_i} = total income elasticity of demographic group from cross-sectional study.

The coefficients α_i and β_i that were used in the simulations for this third method appear in the bottom section of table 6.

Comments by Robert I. Lerman

Betson and Bishop's paper reopens a long-standing debate over the desirability of alternative income maintenance strategies. Comparisons between the negative income tax and the wage rate subsidy have often

23. Masters and Garfinkel, "Estimating the Labor Supply Effects," chaps. 7 and 8.

appeared in the literature, but without moving policymakers to take the subsidy as a serious policy option. No social experiments have tested the wage rate subsidy, no congressmen or senators have proposed a subsidy program, and no subsidy proposal has been included among favored options for a cabinet member's consideration. Perhaps the optimistic findings in the Betson-Bishop paper about some wage rate subsidy proposals will help bring the subsidy idea closer to the center of income maintenance policy debates.

The straightforward appeal of the wage rate subsidy is that it helps those who help themselves by working long hours. Unlike the negative income tax and other income maintenance programs, which provide the greatest benefits to those who do not work and lower the recipients' return to work, the wage rate subsidy pays bonuses only to those who work and raises the net wage of low-wage workers. While noting this basic appeal, Betson and Bishop want to go beyond the incentive differences and answer two empirical questions about the negative income tax and wage rate subsidy. How much would hours of labor actually supplied differ in the two programs? And how much would the percentage of benefits going to families most in need differ?

In attempting to answer these questions, Betson and Bishop compare negative income tax and wage rate subsidy programs that would go beyond existing welfare programs. Since existing programs already provide income guarantees to nearly all poor one-parent families, the authors are actually addressing the issue of how well the two income maintenance programs perform when covering the working poor.

It has long been recognized that wage subsidy programs can exert work-reducing effects (through the added income they provide) as well as work-increasing effects (through the added return to each hour of work they provide). Policy analysts have also realized that such programs are likely to provide less help to the most needy families than would negative income tax–type alternatives, since those families do not often have regular workers. Several empirical studies have produced estimates similar to those made by Betson and Bishop.[24] For example, Samuel A. Rea, Jr., has presented estimates that generally support the efficiency ad-

---

24. A good summary of these studies appears in Jack Habib and Haim Factor, "Job and Cash Transfer Approaches to Income Maintenance—Complements or Substitutes?" a paper presented at the 36th Congress on Public Finance and Public Employment, International Institute of Public Finance (Jerusalem, August 25–29, 1980).

vantages and distributional disadvantages of the wage rate subsidy approach.[25] Using data on 1967 incomes, Rea attempted to simulate the effects of wage rate subsidy and negative income tax alternatives after taking into account the labor supply effects induced by the programs. Rea drew the following conclusions about equal-cost wage subsidy and negative tax plans:

The NIT plan . . . lowers hours worked by 12 percent while the WS . . . reduces work by only 1.7 percent. However, only 39 percent of those receiving the WS were initially below the poverty line compared to 56 percent for the NIT. . . . The wage subsidy induces more work but is less efficient in transferring income to the poor.[26]

Although it would have been useful for Betson and Bishop to draw on the findings from earlier studies, their new simulation results are interesting in themselves, since the authors have used recent data on earnings, hours, and income maintenance payments; labor supply parameters based on experimental findings; and a new concept of need based on earnings capacity. Their primary comparisons are among programs of approximately equal net outlays. In light of the data differences and the enhancements in the Betson-Bishop model, it is interesting that their labor supply results are similar to those made by Rea and others. For example, Betson and Bishop project that a negative income tax would reduce hours worked by recipients by 7 to 11 percent, or slightly less than the 12 percent reduction predicted by Rea. When using two of their three labor supply parameters, Betson and Bishop estimate either slight increases or slight decreases in labor supplied by families receiving wage subsidies—a result that is also similar to the Rea finding. A third set of parameters yields results indicating that a wage subsidy may induce as large a work-reducing effect as the negative tax. But Betson and Bishop report that in this case the subsidy would raise the family incomes of its recipients by much more than the negative tax would for its recipients.

The surprising results presented by Betson and Bishop concern the distributional comparisons. Unlike Rea and the authors of other conventional studies, Betson and Bishop find that under one of the three sets of labor supply parameters a wage rate subsidy produces income gains for the poor that are as high as the income gains produced by an equal-cost

25. Samuel A. Rea, Jr., "Trade-Offs Between Alternative Income Maintenance Programs," in *Studies in Public Welfare, Paper No. 13: How Income Supplements Can Affect Work Behavior,* prepared for the Subcommittee on Fiscal Policy, Joint Economic Committee, 93 Cong. 2 sess. (GPO, 1974), pp. 33–63.
26. Ibid., p. 56.

negative income tax. Moreover, when Betson and Bishop define need in terms of earnings capacity instead of current income, they find that under all three sets of supply parameters the wage rate subsidy would help the needy as much as or more than the negative income tax.

One broad issue that Betson and Bishop do not confront is whether the comparisons might depend on the size of the program. As Habib and Factor point out, raising the negative income tax guarantees or the wage rate subsidy target wage tends to reduce the share of benefits going to the poor. However, it is not clear from either the Betson-Bishop or Habib-Factor papers whether the negative tax or the subsidy would be differentially sensitive to the guarantee levels.

Estimates of the kind produced by Betson-Bishop and Rea are interesting, but since they are based on average responses, the projections understate the true differences between the impact of wage rate subsidy and negative income tax programs. When one takes account of the distribution of responses, one would expect the wage subsidy to look better in terms of incentive effects and worse in terms of distributional effects. Whereas the negative tax could induce some recipients to quit work altogether and collect maximum benefits, the wage subsidy would end up paying zero benefits to those with zero hours of work. On the distributional side, the negative tax would provide substantial amounts to those unable to find many hours of work and those with the lowest incomes, whereas the wage subsidy would do best for low-wage workers able and willing to work many hours. Although labor supply analyses have usually not estimated the distribution of responses, these probable consequences should not be ignored on grounds that they cannot be measured precisely.[27]

A second program difference outside the scope of the Betson-Bishop paper concerns reporting effects. Recent evidence from income maintenance experiments suggests that negative income tax recipients understate their earnings substantially.[28] Any such understatement adds to program

27. For a rare attempt to examine the distribution of labor supply responses, see Gary Burtless and Jerry A. Hausman, "The Effect of Taxation on Labor Supply: Evaluating the Gary Negative Income Tax Experiment," *Journal of Political Economy,* vol. 86 (December 1978), pp. 1103–30.

28. See, for example, David Greenberg, Robert Moffitt, and John Friedman, "The Effects of Underreporting on the Estimation of Experimental Effects on Work Effort: Evidence from the Gary Income Maintenance Experiment," Office of Income Security Policy, Technical Analysis Paper 19 (U.S. Department of Health, Education, and Welfare, January 1980).

costs in the same way as labor supply reductions do. In the Gary income maintenance experiment, apparently several women recipients who reported no earnings to the experiment were actually working. In fact, what appear as labor supply effects were largely reporting effects. In the case of the wage rate subsidy, no recipient could receive benefits who reported no earnings. Although wage subsidy recipients could overstate hours to obtain extra benefits, the requirement that the recipient earn at least the minimum wage would severely limit the extent of possible overpayments to a particular recipient. Moreover, hours reports made by the wage subsidy recipient could always be verified with the employer, whereas negative tax recipients who report no earnings would require the auditors to find the recipient's employer to determine the recipient's earnings.

Because of these distributional and reporting differences, the wage rate subsidy is much less likely than the negative income tax to lead to the extreme labor supply responses or overpayments sometimes found in welfare programs. Although large numbers of wage subsidy recipients may each work slightly fewer hours or slightly overreport hours, the chance of any one participant stopping work entirely or misreporting large amounts of income is lower for the wage subsidy than for the negative tax. For this reason alone, the former could be more popular with the public and the Congress than the latter.

Let me close by pointing to a few technical limitations of the Betson-Bishop paper. The authors mention the possible difference between program effects on hours that workers are willing to supply and on hours actually worked. But they do not deal with the large biases that may result from their use of data measuring work and earnings patterns in 1975, a year in which the average unemployment rate was 8.5 percent. The use of data from a more typical year (when low-income families could find more hours of work) might have improved the distributional impact of the wage rate subsidy.

Second, Betson and Bishop, like many other microsimulators, do not adequately consider their reliance on wage rate data constructed from the preceding year's statistics on weeks worked, earnings, and usual weekly hours. Because wage rate data are critical to wage rate subsidy benefits and to negative income tax labor supply responses, it is important to correct for errors created in constructing the data. Betson and Bishop do take some account of the current population survey overstatement of those with below-minimum wages, but they do not make any other corrections for potential errors in wage data.

Comments by Marvin M. Smith

In view of the public interest in negative income tax and wage rate subsidy schemes, Betson and Bishop are to be commended for performing a valuable task (particularly for policymakers) by providing a rigorous yet readable comparison of these two types of programs with respect to their cost, effects on output, and distributional impacts. But the quality and usefulness of their resulting estimates hinge on the assumptions underlying their analysis and on the specific parameters used in the simulations. It is the choices exercised by the authors in these two areas and the implications of targeting wage rate subsidies that serve as the stimulus for my comments.

The subsidy rate of 50 percent, as the authors note, represents a compromise between two conflicting goals—on the one hand, providing more subsidy to low-wage workers and, on the other hand, minimizing the incentives in the system to underreport one's wage rate to get a larger subsidy. While this concern is duly noted, it would have been more informative—and more useful for policy purposes—to have considered, in addition, subsidy rates greater and less than the 50 percent rate (for example, 30 percent and 70 percent rates).

In their simulations Betson and Bishop use two sets of labor supply coefficients that are derived from the Seattle-Denver income maintenance experiment. In light of the limitations and qualifications associated with similar estimates from earlier income maintenance experiments (namely, the rural and New Jersey experiments), this exclusive reliance on the Seattle-Denver experiment coefficients would be grounds enough for skepticism. But it seems that the authors may have compounded the situation by using the coefficients estimated from one target group—those qualifying under the eligibility rules for the Seattle-Denver experiment—to represent the labor supply behavior of a seemingly different group—those included in some of the categories considered in their study. If in fact these coefficients are inappropriately used in the analysis, the resulting estimates are seriously compromised.

The authors' mention of the effect of a wage rate subsidy on investment in human capital—namely, that, relative to a negative income tax, a wage subsidy reduces incentives to sacrifice work time in order to invest in human capital—stimulated my curiosity about the implications for various demographic groups. Though a wage rate subsidy might not have adverse effects on the work careers of most low-wage workers, I wonder about the effects, if any, on the hard-to-employ or disadvantaged teenagers. A subsidy program targeted on such teenagers might seem an efficient way to assist them in the labor market but in the long run might prove counterproductive. A growing body of literature suggests that the early labor market experience of these teenagers influences their subsequent labor market performance and that their early labor market problems are largely due to nonexistent or less than adequate accumulation of human capital. Therefore, the accessibility of a subsidy program might exacerbate the situation by providing an incentive to shun efforts to accumulate human capital.

Finally, Betson and Bishop's discussion of the impacts of a wage rate subsidy and a negative income tax on job search raises some questions. If it is maintained that searching for employment is a productive activity, then it is not immediately clear whether the decreasing effect of a wage subsidy on search unemployment is preferable to the augmenting effect of a negative income tax unless some a priori "socially optimal" level of frictional unemployment is agreed upon. Moreover, the nature and extent of frictional unemployment, which are important in gauging the overall social and private costs of unemployment, may be conditioned on the assumptions governing the process by which wage adjustments are made during the search period. In addition, the demographic characteristics of those undertaking the search may strongly influence their search behavior. Thus, unless these factors are considered, the resulting overall impact on search behavior of a wage rate subsidy and a negative income tax cannot be judged accurately.

All in all, I remain somewhat skeptical about accepting the authors' results. I am reluctant to embrace their findings fully because of the high sensitivity of their results to the particular functional form of the labor supply functions chosen. This is especially crucial in estimating the wage rate subsidy schemes, where the income and substitution effects operate in opposite directions, and therefore their relative magnitudes are critical for predictive purposes. The significance of this concern is clearly reflected in the words of the authors, who aptly observe that "it would seem that despite nearly a decade of work, there is still no consensus on the relative size of income and substitution parameters of the labor supply function." Nonetheless, the comparative evidence provided by the authors is instructive in showing the relative merits of a wage rate subsidy scheme as an alternative to a negative income tax program.

Part Three

Program Design and Evaluation

John H. Bishop and Charles A. Wilson

Effects on Firm Behavior

The simultaneous appearance of high rates of inflation and unemployment throughout most of the western world has led several nations to experiment with a variety of employment subsidy schemes. In many of these schemes, firms are subsidized if they increase employment over a threshold that is based on the firm's employment level in some period before the subsidy is initiated. Ireland's premium employment program subsidizes in certain areas of the country 25 to 50 percent of the wage costs of increases in employment above what pertained on a stipulated base date. Britain's small firms employment subsidy started as an experimental program subsidizing small firms (under 50 employees) in a limited geographic area. Studies that made use of its experimental design pronounced it successful, and starting in January 1979 it was expanded to small- and medium-sized (under 200 employees) non-manufacturing firms in high-unemployment areas and manufacturing firms throughout the United Kingdom. Firms that increase employment received a subsidy of $45 a week for new full-time workers and $22 a week for new part-time employees.

The French incentive bonus for job creation offered all private firms a subsidy of approximately $750 per worker for expansion over and above the firm's employment level on June 4, 1975. Designed to last only until November 30, 1975, it was extended through 1977 for firms with fewer than ten employees. In 1977 the threshold was brought forward to the firm's employment level of January 26, 1977. France's second em-

The research reported on here has been funded in part by the Rockefeller Foundation, by the National Science Foundation, and by funds granted to the Institute for Research on Poverty by the Department of Health, Education, and Welfare pursuant to the Economic Opportunity Act of 1964. The views expressed are those of the authors and do not necessarily represent the position of any of the funding agencies.

219

ployment pact (1978) established a marginal subsidy that is targeted on youth. One-half of the social insurance taxes of youthful (under twenty-five) workers hired between July 1978 and December 1979 were forgiven. To be eligible the firm had to increase its total employment. Since this requirement often constrains how much subsidy the firm can receive, the scheme also acted as a marginal stock subsidy of total employment.

The largest of these marginal wage subsidy programs was in the United States—the new jobs tax credit. In 1977 and 1978 firms that increased employment could receive a tax credit of 50 percent of the increase in each employer's wage base under the Federal Unemployment Tax Act (sum of wages paid up to $4,200 per employee) above 102 percent of the wage base in the previous year. The employer's deduction for wages was reduced by the amount of the credit. A limitation of $100,000 on the amount of credit any one firm could receive effectively eliminated the incentive effect of the credit on large firms, which provide nearly 30 percent of the nation's jobs. Even though the Treasury Department and other public agencies made little effort to publicize and promote the new jobs tax credit, 1.1 million of the 3.5 million employers in the nation (more than 50 percent of those eligible) claimed a credit on their 1978 tax returns. Over its two-year period of operation, subsidies were claimed for more than 3.95 million employees at a cost to the Treasury in reduced federal tax revenues of approximately $5 billion. Three separate studies using different methods and data sets have found evidence supporting the hypothesis that the new jobs tax credit had a major impact on employment during 1977 and 1978.[1]

The marginal employment subsidy schemes implemented thus far have usually aimed to reduce cyclical unemployment and are thus intended to be temporary. But the problems they are designed to counter sometimes persist for long periods of time; renewals (frequently with important modifications) are therefore common. Furthermore, marginal employment subsidies are increasingly seen as potential tools for dealing with

1. See John Bishop, "Employment and Pricing in Construction and Distribution Industries: The Impact of the New Jobs Tax Credit," in Sherwin Rosen, ed., *Studies in Labor Markets* (University of Chicago Press, forthcoming); Statement by James D. McKevitt, in *Jobs Tax Credit,* Joint Hearings before the Subcommittee on Administration of the Internal Revenue Code and the Senate Select Small Business Committee, 95 Cong. 2 sess. (Government Printing Office, 1978), pp. 179–96; and Jeffrey M. Perloff and Michael L. Wachter, "The New Jobs Tax Credit: An Evaluation of the 1977–78 Wage Subsidy Program," *American Economic Review,* vol. 69 (May 1979, *Papers and Proceedings, 1978*), pp. 173–79.

longer-term problems—the labor supply and employment disincentives created by high marginal rates of taxation, structural unemployment of youth and other low-productivity workers, and poor export performance, for example. A marginal employment subsidy program designed to attack such problems would necessarily be in effect for many years and might eventually become a permanent feature of economic policy.

In any case, as was seen in the French experience, the renewal of a marginal subsidy usually results in the threshold being updated. For instance, the new jobs tax credit based the firm's threshold for the 1977 credit on its 1976 employment and its threshold for the 1978 credit on its 1977 employment. Unfortunately, such a policy of regularly updating the threshold according to individual firm experience creates additional problems. If employers anticipate that their current employment level will be used to establish the threshold for future subsidies, they have an incentive to reduce employment in the current period. Such anticipatory reactions seem to have occurred in France during the months immediately preceding the announcement of the second employment pact in July 1978.[2]

In this paper we address two critical policy issues in the design of permanent marginal subsidies. (1) Should the threshold above which the subsidy is paid be updated to reflect more recent experience? And (2) if so, how should this updating be implemented? To answer these questions, we must first be able to show how the firm's knowledge of the rule by which its threshold will be updated affects its response to the subsidy program. In the first section of the paper, we discuss three alternative methods of defining and updating the threshold for a marginal subsidy and the criteria by which we will compare the effectiveness of different marginal subsidy programs. The following two sections contain the principal findings of the paper: we describe how the different programs affect the response of an intertemporal profit-maximizing firm and report some of our results on the relative cost-effectiveness of these programs. We then examine several implications of introducing uncertainty into the analysis and discuss the implications of some alternative programs. Our main conclusions are summarized in the final section.

Although this paper focuses on employment subsidies, they are not

2. See G. Rehn, "Employment Premiums in Economic Policy" (Center for Public Policy, University of California, Berkeley, 1979); and Patrice DeBroucker, "La Politique Française de l'Emploi" (Ph.D. dissertation, Université de Paris, IX, Dauphiné, 1979).

the only programs with a marginal feature and therefore not the only programs for which defining firm-specific thresholds is a critical design issue. The tax subsidies of exports currently provided by the domestic international sales corporation provisions of the Internal Revenue Code are marginal in design. When the investment tax credit was first proposed by President Kennedy, it was to have been a subsidy of an investment that exceeded a threshold equal to half the firm's investment in some base period. Many senators and congressmen are promoting marginal tax credits for increases in dividend and interest income as ways to promote saving. Tax-based incomes policies are marginal taxes on increases in a firm's average wage. The windfall profits tax is a marginal excise tax on increases in the price of crude oil from certain types of wells. Grant-in-aid formulas with maintenance-of-effort provisions often amount to marginal subsidies of certain types of state and local expenditure. The issues discussed in this paper are common to all these programs.

The Programs, Model, and Measures of Cost Effectiveness

The primary objective of a targeted employment subsidy is to increase the employment of a target group of workers by lowering the cost to employers of hiring eligible labor. If this is the sole objective, then it is desirable to design the subsidy so that a given expansion in employment can be achieved at least cost. A marginal subsidy, which subsidizes only those workers who would otherwise not have been employed, comes closer to meeting this ideal than a general subsidy of all workers in the target group. Unfortunately, it is difficult to find an administratively feasible way of measuring how many of these workers would have been hired in the absence of the subsidy. Since the subsidy payment is made to the firm, it must be possible to define a separate threshold for each of the 3.5 million firms in the nation that have employees. The key to constructing a cost-effective targeted employment subsidy, therefore, hinges on finding an efficient way of defining the threshold above which the subsidy is paid. It is on this problem that we focus our attention.

Programs

We examine three marginal subsidy programs with contrasting ways of defining the subsidy threshold: a fixed threshold, a yearly updated threshold based on previous year's employment, and a threshold based on the firm's peak employment over all previous years.

The first and simplest program fixes a threshold in the initial period at some level, $\bar{L}$, and lets it grow (or decline) in each period by a constant factor, q ($\bar{L}_t = q\bar{L}_{t-1}$). While such a policy may be effective on a temporary basis, it is not necessarily desirable over a period of several years. A firm's 1981 employment level is a reasonable predictor of its 1982 or 1983 employment level but a poor predictor of its employment level in 1990 and 2000. By 1990 many employers doing business in 1981 will have gone out of business, and many new firms will have been started. Some employers will have increased their employment by factors of 5, 10, or 20; other firms will have had stagnant or declining employment. If the threshold that determines a subsidy of 1985 employment is equal to a firm's 1981 employment (or an average of employment in 1981 and previous years), some firms will be receiving subsidies for 80 to 100 percent of all their workers and other firms will be receiving no subsidy at all. Such a subsidy program may be perceived as unfair by the businessmen not receiving subsidies and by the general public. If the rate of subsidy is maintained, the cost of such a marginal subsidy will grow very quickly. After five years, costs will have at least doubled; after twenty-five years, costs will have been multiplied by a factor of 10.[3] Political pressure is likely to build to revise the thresholds so that they are based on more recent firm experience.

Although a fixed threshold program may not be politically feasible over the long run, it can nevertheless serve as a benchmark for evaluating the efficiency of alternative programs. Its primary virtue is that the actions of an individual firm in one period do not affect the subsidy it can collect in the following periods. Consequently, in the absence of adjustment costs, the effect on the employment level of the firm in any period is the same as it would be if the program were only temporary.

The second commonly proposed marginal subsidy program is the subsidy of the increase in employment over the previous year.[4] One might

3. John Bishop and Robert Lerman, "Wage Subsidies for Income Maintenance and Job Creation," in Robert Taggart, ed., *Job Creation: What Works?* Proceedings of a conference sponsored by the School of Labor and Industrial Relations, Michigan State University, and the National Council on Employment Policy (Salt Lake City: Olympus, 1977), pp. 62–67.

4. Jonathan R. Kesselman, Samuel H. Williamson, and Ernst R. Berndt, "Tax Credits for Employment Rather Than Investment," *American Economic Review*, vol. 67 (June 1977), pp. 339–49.

also incorporate a growth or depreciation factor into the update rule, so that the threshold in each period is merely some multiple of the previous period's employment level. In this case the threshold in each period t, $\bar{L}_t$, is defined by $\bar{L}_t = pL_{t-1}$, where p is some positive constant, and L_{t-1} is employment in the previous period. If, for instance, the new jobs tax credit of 1977 had been made permanent without any change in structure (as was voted by the Senate), this is the kind of program that would now be in place, with p equal to 1.02. As we argue later, such a subsidy program tends to be inefficient. Since a reduction in employment in one year lowers the threshold in the next, firms may have an incentive to adopt a two-period employment strategy in which they alternately increase and decrease their employment, collecting the subsidy every other year. This tends to generate a relatively large subsidy receipt but little net increase in employment.

A third method of updating the threshold, which eliminates any incentive to decrease employment, is to base the threshold on the firm's peak employment level since the beginning of the program. A slight generalization of this idea is to define the threshold by $\bar{L}_t = q \max(L_{t-1}, \bar{L}_{t-1})$, where q is a positive constant. If employment exceeds the threshold in any period, the threshold is automatically raised for future years. If employment stays below the current threshold, then the future threshold is unaffected: it simply grows (or declines) by a factor of q. Setting $q = 1$ yields a *pure* peak-employment threshold program.

The Model

We use a standard intertemporal model of firm behavior to analyze the responses of firms to the various kinds of marginal subsidies. The firm is assumed to choose its employment level in each period so as to maximize the discounted sum of its profits over an infinite planning horizon. The firm's profit in any period is a quadratic function of its employment, with no costs of adjustment. We also assume that, in the absence of any subsidy program, the firm's profit-maximizing employment level grows or declines in each period by a constant factor g, which is perfectly anticipated. A formal development of the model is presented in appendix A.

The purpose of the model is to calculate the partial equilibrium responses of the firm to the introduction of a permanent marginal subsidy program. We therefore assume that other aspects of the environment—the wage rate of labor and the revenue function—are unaffected by the subsidy program. In regard to the wage rate, this assumption is consistent with the need for a subsidy program. If, because of wage rigidities, there is an excess supply of labor at the market wage, the industry essentially faces a horizontal supply curve for labor at that wage. The assumption of a constant revenue function, however, is more restrictive. A subsidy program that increases the aggregate employment level may cause a rightward shift in the demand curve facing the firm. Also, to the extent that the program helps subsidize firms to grow at the expense of unsubsidized firms, the latter may experience leftward shifts of their demand curve. These are important considerations, but since they are discussed elsewhere in this volume, they need not be taken up here.

Measures of Cost Effectiveness

Besides analyzing the impact of these three alternative marginal subsidy programs on firm behavior, we also compare their cost effectiveness. As one might expect, the marginal costs of inducing firms to hire an extra worker increase with the size of the employment response desired. For a given program design, the larger the desired increase in employment, the less cost efficient the program will be. Consequently, when we make comparisons across program types, we adjust subsidy rates to produce equal increases in employment. The firm-specific cost effectiveness of the different marginal subsidy programs also depends on the rate at which the firm would have grown without the subsidy. Therefore, when we make comparisons between programs, we hold the underlying growth rate of the firm constant.

When calculating cost effectiveness, one must address at least two distinct types of cost. The first is simply the cost of the subsidy payments to the government. If the sole objective is to increase employment at the least cost to the taxpayer, this is the only measure of cost one would need to examine. From an efficiency perspective, however, it may also be desirable to subtract from the taxpayer cost the change in the total profits accruing to the firm. In this case the subsidy receipts by firms cancel the subsidy costs of the government, and all that is left is the partial equilibrium distortion costs of moving away from the firm's optimal employment level. Except for the gains to workers who would otherwise be unemployed, these costs correspond precisely to the deadweight loss associated with any subsidy in a partial equilibrium model with fixed wages and prices.

A second issue involves the comparison of subsidy programs that generate different streams of employment levels and subsidy costs over time. The discount rate, δ, which the firm uses to discount future profits, presumably reflects the rate at which the firm can borrow and lend real resources. If this also corresponds to the social rate of discount, then δ is clearly the appropriate factor for discounting both the subsidy and distortion costs. To the extent that different subsidy programs generate different employment streams over time, it will also be necessary to introduce a discount rate at which to evaluate employment gains over time. For want of a better measure, we also use δ as the employment discount factor. This would be the appropriate measure if the workers affected by the subsidy could borrow and lend in each period at a real interest rate equal to $(1 - \delta)/\delta$ and the opportunity costs of their labor were constant.

An Overview of Results

At this point it may be useful to present a brief overview of our results. The following list outlines the major points of the paper, and table 1 summarizes some of these points.

—There are essentially three patterns of response that firms may adopt upon the introduction of a subsidy program: (a) a *steady employment response*—employment is increased by a constant fraction over the no-subsidy level in each period; (b) a *weak cycling response*—firms periodically increase employment but never decrease employment below the no-subsidy level; (c) a *strong cycling response*—firms alternately increase then decrease employment every two periods relative to the no-subsidy level. The three subsidy types—fixed threshold, yearly updated threshold, and peak employment threshold—will generate different cycling response patterns.

—Once the subsidy rate is adjusted to generate a given employment response, the cost effectiveness of a program depends on how firms respond. Programs that induce the steady employment response are the most cost effective; those that generate the weak cycling response are less cost effective; and those that produce the strong cycling response are the least cost effective.

—For firms with sufficiently high growth rates, all three programs induce a steady employment response. For firms with lower growth rates, however, only the fixed threshold program continues to induce this response. Under a yearly updated program, most firms will adopt a strong

Table 1. The Employment Response and Cost Effectiveness of Alternative Marginal Subsidy Programs

| | Employment response | | Ranking of cost effectiveness[a] | |
	High growth rate	Low growth rate	High growth rate	Low growth rate
Program				
Fixed threshold	Steady	Steady	1	1
Yearly updated threshold	Steady	Strong cycle	1	3
Peak employment threshold	Steady	Weak cycle	1	2

a. Subsidy rates adjusted to generate the same employment response.

cycling response. Under a peak employment program, firms with low growth rates will adopt a weak cycling response.

—In general, a much higher subsidy rate is required under the yearly updated and peak employment programs than under the fixed threshold programs to obtain the same employment response.

—If firms are uncertain about the future life of the programs, the efficiency of the peak employment program may be substantially increased.

How Firms Respond: A Comparison

Before we evaluate the relative effectiveness of the three marginal subsidy programs described above, we need to explore in some detail the different ways firms respond to these programs. Besides the rate at which employment is subsidized, the major determinant of a firm's response to a given subsidy program is the size of its underlying growth rate relative to the rate at which the threshold depreciates. It is important, therefore, that we compare the firm's response to different programs for various growth rates. To simplify the exposition, we assume throughout that the threshold depreciation rate for each program is zero. The updating rule for the fixed threshold program is therefore $\bar{L}_t = \bar{L}_{t-1}$; for the yearly updated program, $\bar{L}_t = L_{t-1}$; and for the peak employment program, $\bar{L}_t = \max(L_{t-1}, \bar{L}_{t-1})$.

The response to the three programs of a firm with a very high growth rate is illustrated in figure 1. Under each program, the firm will respond by increasing its employment by a fixed percentage in each period. But the magnitude of the response will vary. Under a fixed threshold program,

Figure 1. Steady Employment Response of Firms with Very High Growth Rates to Marginal Subsidy Programs

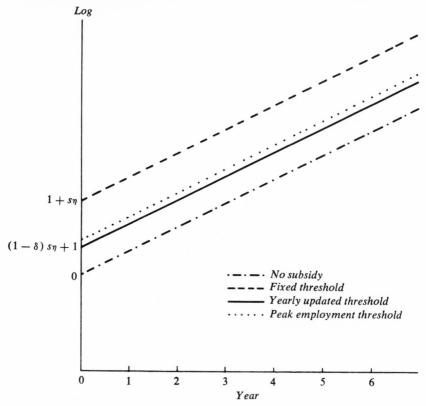

the firm's employment level in any period has no effect on the future threshold. Consequently, employment is increased by a factor of $1 + s\eta$, where s is the subsidy rate and η is the elasticity of labor demand. Under the two other programs, however, increasing employment in any period also raises the threshold in the next period. Therefore, the firm will choose an employment level that equates the marginal gain from increasing employment today with the marginal loss from raising the threshold in the next period. As a result, employment is increased by a factor of only $1 + (1 - \delta)s\eta$, where δ is the discount factor for future profits. This means that for a discount factor of 0.9, a tenfold increase in the subsidy rate is required to generate the same employment response under the yearly updated and peak period programs as under the fixed threshold program.

Inspection of the formulas in appendix B reveals that as long as firms follow a steady response to each program and the subsidy rates are adjusted to stimulate the same increase in employment, the distortion cost of each program is identical. Moreover, the subsidy costs are identical as well. Although yearly updated and peak employment programs require a higher subsidy rate, the threshold is continually updated so that a much smaller fraction of the labor is actually subsidized. Unfortunately, as the subsidy rate is increased, firms require a higher growth rate before they will show the steady response illustrated in figure 1. For a demand elasticity of 0.25, a subsidy rate of 0.4, and a discount factor of 0.9, the growth rate of firms under the yearly updated program must exceed 9 percent a year.

For a range of lower growth rates, firms under the fixed threshold or peak employment program will continue to adopt a steady response. But firms under the yearly updated program will adopt an employment strategy in which the subsidy is collected only once every two periods. In the first period, they will increase their employment by a factor of $1 + s\eta$; in the next period, they will decrease employment by a factor of $1 - \delta s\eta$. Then the cycle starts again. The result is illustrated in figure 2. Note that in those periods in which the subsidy is actually collected, the firm responds exactly as if the threshold were fixed. The reason is that since the firm does not plan to exceed the threshold in the next period anyway, the employment level today cannot affect future profits. In those periods in which the threshold is not exceeded, however, the firm *does* plan to collect the subsidy in the following period. It therefore decreases its employment below the presubsidy optimum in order to lower the next period threshold. Consequently, the gain in employment in the expanding periods is at least partially offset by the employment decline in the contracting periods. As one might expect, the net result is a relatively large increase in both the distortion and subsidy costs, to generate the same gain in employment as under the other programs.

For growth rates near zero, the employment of firms under a peak employment program will also begin to cycle, as illustrated in figure 3. After the firm initially increases its employment to collect the subsidy, the threshold in the next period may be so high that the firm will choose to remain at its presubsidy employment level. As the firm continues to grow, however, it will eventually choose to raise its employment beyond the threshold established in the initial period and collect the subsidy again, starting a new cycle. If the firm plans to wait n periods before collecting

Figure 2. Employment Response of Firms with Lower Growth Rates to Marginal Subsidy Programs

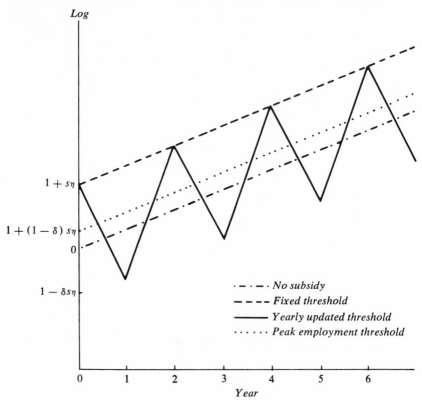

the subsidy again, the optimal employment in every nth period is increased by a factor $(1 - \delta^n)s\eta + 1$. In all other periods it remains unchanged. The length of the cycle is longer the lower the growth rate of the firm is, and goes to infinity as the growth rate goes to zero. For most parameters, however, the range of growth rates for which any cycling occurs is relatively small. For a subsidy rate of 0.4 and a discount factor of 0.9, cycling occurs only for growth rates between 0 and 1 percent. In figure 3, a three-period cycle is illustrated.

Note that even in the periods when the firm collects a subsidy, the response is less than it would be under a fixed threshold program. This occurs because any increase in employment today that exceeds the threshold imposes a cost in the form of a higher threshold in the future. As one would expect, however, the cost is less, and hence the employment re-

Figure 3. Employment Response of Firms with Near-Zero Growth Rates to Marginal Subsidy Programs

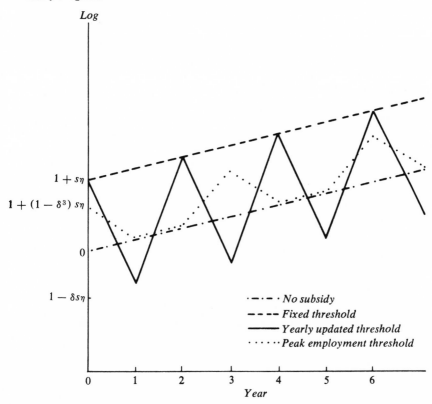

sponse is greater, the longer the firm plans to wait to collect the subsidy again. The important point to emphasize is that under the peak employment program the firm never has an incentive to reduce employment below the presubsidy level as it does under the yearly updated program.

If their growth rates are negative, firms under a peak employment program will collect the subsidy at most once. Firms under a fixed threshold program may choose to collect the subsidy for one or more periods, but eventually they too will stop responding to it. In general, the employment of firms under the yearly updated program will continue to exhibit the two-period cycle; however, if a firm's growth rate is sufficiently negative, it may choose to begin the cycle by first decreasing employment. Since later employment is discounted, it usually turns out that whenever this strategy is adopted, the present value of the employment gain is negative.

Figure 4. Employment Response of Firms with Negative Growth Rates to Marginal Subsidy Programs

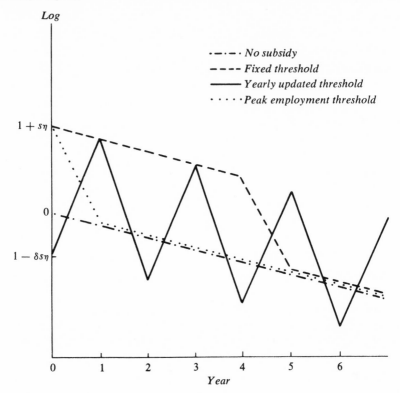

For a subsidy rate of 0.4 and a discount factor of 0.9, the gain is negative when the growth rate lies between −1 percent and −9 percent. Typical employment responses under the different programs for growth rates in this range are illustrated in figure 4.

Except under a fixed threshold program, the most efficient responses to these subsidies tend to occur at the higher growth rates. The effect of introducing a depreciation factor into the threshold updating rules is to increase the range of growth rates at which firms respond most efficiently.

Cost Effectiveness of the Programs

The relative cost effectiveness of the three programs may be sensitive to the level at which the threshold is set when the programs begin. For instance, if the initial threshold is set very low, the fixed threshold program essentially becomes a nonmarginal subsidy. Clearly, for that program, raising the threshold will result in a dramatic reduction in the subsidy costs. For the other programs an increase in the initial threshold will also lower the subsidy costs, but the decrease will not be as significant. If the initial threshold is set too high, however, firms may not respond at all, or in some cases may even respond by initially reducing their employment. It is therefore important that our calculations be based on the appropriate initial threshold level.

Last year's employment is just about the best predictor of this year's employment level one can find. For this and other reasons the government would probably base the period 0 threshold for each firm on its employment level in the previous period. In implementing our updating formulas, therefore, we equate the threshold in period -1 with the presubsidy optimal employment level of that period. The updating rules are then completely defined.

It is also important to recognize that the cost per unit of stimulated employment will usually be sensitive to the level of the employment increase. The greater the increase in employment, the greater is the cost *per unit* of employment. To better compare the programs, therefore, we adjust the subsidy rate for each program so that, given growth rates for which firms respond with a steady increase in employment (see figure 1), present discounted employment rises by 1 percent. In general, this will imply different subsidy rates for different programs.

Fixed Threshold Program

As long as the growth rate of the threshold does not exceed that of the firm, a firm will respond to a fixed threshold program exactly as it would to a nonmarginal subsidy program. For a subsidy rate of s, the firm will increase employment in each period by a factor of $1 + s\eta$, where η is the elasticity of demand for subsidized labor. The distortion costs are also the same. The major difference between the two programs is in the size of the subsidy costs.

We define the *subsidy–employment ratio* of any program as the subsidy cost divided by the increase in the firm's wage bill, and, similarly, the *distortion–employment ratio* as the distortion cost divided by the wage bill increase. Then, using the formulas reported in appendix B, we find that a nonmarginal subsidy generates a subsidy–employment ratio of

Table 2. Subsidy–Employment Ratios for Marginal Subsidy Programs[a]

Exogenous growth rate (percent)	No threshold	Fixed threshold		Yearly updated threshold			Peak employment threshold			
							$\pi = 1.00$[b]		$\pi = 0.75$[b]	
		$q = 1.0$	$q = 0.95$	$p = 1.0$	$p = 0.95$	$p = 0.90$	$q = 1$	$q = 0.95$	$q = 1$	$q = 0.95$
10.0	4.04	3.67	3.80	3.67	3.80	3.88	3.67	3.80	1.13	1.54
5.0	4.04	1.94	2.67	5.89c	2.67	3.05	1.94	2.67	0.60	1.07
1.0	4.04	0.44	1.68	3.89c	3.05c	2.37	0.44	1.68	0.13	0.68
0.5	4.04	0.24	1.55	3.68c	2.91c	2.25	0.40d	1.55	0.18e	0.63
0	4.04	0.04	1.42	3.48c	2.77c	2.15	0.40f	1.42	0.40f	0.57
−1.0	4.04	g	1.15	*e,h	2.51c	1.96	0.40f	1.15	0.40f	0.46
−5.0	4.04	g	0.04	*e,h	1.57c	1.15	g	0.40f	g	0.40f
−10.0	4.04	g	g	g	*e,h	0.87c	g	g	g	g
Addendum										
Subsidy rate[i]	0.04	0.04	0.04	0.40	0.276	0.211	0.40	0.276	0.123	0.111

Source: Authors' calculations.

* Negligible.

a. These results are based on a discount factor $\delta = 0.9$, and elasticity of labor demand $\eta = 0.25$.

b. π is the probability of continuing the program.

c. Two-period cycle.

d. One-period cycle.

e. Four-period cycle.

f. Response in first period only.

g. No response.

h. Present value of employment increase is negative.

i. Rate that increases employment by 1 percent when exogenous growth rate is 10 percent.

$s + 1/\eta$, whereas a fixed threshold program that grows at the same rate as the firm generates a subsidy–employment ratio of s. This means that for an elasticity of labor demand equal to 0.25 and a subsidy cost of 0.04, the subsidy costs generated by a nonmarginal subsidy are at least four times the amount by which the wage bill increases, whereas the subsidy–employment ratio for the fixed threshold program is only 0.04. In both cases employment is increased by 1 percent. If the firm grows faster than the threshold, the fixed threshold program is less efficient. For a fixed threshold the subsidy–employment ratio rises to 0.44 if the firm grows at 1 percent, 1.94 if the firm grows at 5 percent, and 3.67 if the firm grows at 10 percent. Other comparisons are presented in table 2. Except for firms with very high growth rates, however, the fixed threshold program is much more cost effective than the nonmarginal subsidy.

Yearly Updated Threshold Program

As we showed earlier, the response of firms to a program that bases the threshold on employment in the previous year depends on their rate of growth relative to the threshold depreciation factor. The updating rule can be written $L_t = pL_{t-1}$. Consider first the case in which the threshold depreciation factor, p, is equal to 1. Assuming a discount factor of 0.9, an elasticity of labor demand equal to 0.25, and a 40 percent subsidy rate, a firm growing by more than 9.8 percent a year will adopt a steady employment response and increase employment by 1 percent. For these firms, the costs of the program are identical to those of the fixed threshold program. Thus, as seen in tables 2 and 3, a firm growing at 10 percent a year will generate a subsidy–employment ratio of 3.67 and a distortion–employment ratio of 0.02.

Firms with growth rates between −9 percent and 9.8 percent will adopt an employment response that exhibits a two-period cycle. If the growth rate exceeds −1 percent, the firm will begin by increasing employment. In that case, the net increase in the present discounted value of employment will still be positive but usually less than 1 percent. In spite of this, the subsidy–employment ratio and, in particular, the distortion–employment ratio rise dramatically relative to these ratios under the fixed threshold program. Firms growing at 5 percent a year increase present discounted employment by only 0.76 percent but generate a subsidy–employment ratio of 5.89 (compared with a ratio of 1.94 for the fixed threshold program) and a distortion–employment ratio of 2.36 (com-

Table 3. Distortion–Employment Ratios for Marginal Subsidy Programs[a]

Exogenous growth rate (percent)	No threshold	Fixed threshold		Yearly updated threshold			Peak employment threshold			
							$\pi = 1.00$[b]		$\pi = 0.75$[b]	
		$q = 1.0$	$q = 0.95$	$p = 1.0$	$p = 0.95$	$p = 0.90$	$q = 1$	$q = 0.95$	$q = 1$	$q = 0.95$
10.0	0.02	0.02	0.02	0.02	0.020	0.020	0.020	0.020	0.020	0.02
5.0	0.02	0.02	0.02	2.36[c]	0.020	0.020	0.020	0.020	0.020	0.02
1.0	0.02	0.02	0.02	1.91[c]	1.030[e]	0.020	0.020	0.020	0.020	0.02
0.5	0.02	0.02	0.02	1.86[c]	1.010[e]	0.020	0.137[d]	0.020	0.049[e]	0.02
0	0.02	0.02	0.02	1.82[e]	0.993[c]	0.020	0.200[f]	0.020	0.200[f]	0.02
−1.0	0.02	g	0.02	*[c,h]	0.957[c]	0.020	0.200[f]	0.020	0.200[f]	0.02
−5.0	0.02	g	0.02	*[c,h]	0.834[c]	0.020	g	0.138[f]	f	0.20[f]
−10.0	0.02	g	g	g	*[c,h]	0.470[e]	g	g	g	g
Addendum										
Subsidy rate[i]	0.04	0.04	0.04	0.40	0.276	0.211	0.40	0.276	0.123	0.111

Source: Authors' calculations.
* Negligible.
a. These results are based on a discount factor $\delta = 0.9$, and elasticity of labor demand $\eta = 0.25$.
b. π is the probability of continuing the program.
c. Two-period cycle.
d. One-period cycle.
e. Four-period cycle.
f. Response in first period only.
g. No response.
h. Present value of employment increase is negative.
i. Rate that increases employment by 1 percent when exogenous growth rate is 10 percent.

pared with a ratio of 0.02 for the fixed threshold program). Inspection of tables 2 and 3 reveals similar results for growth rates of 1 percent, 0.5 percent, and 0 percent. For growth rates between -9 percent and -1 percent, firms will also adopt a cycling employment strategy, but then they will begin by decreasing employment. As we noted in the previous section, this actually leads to a reduction in present discounted employment.

The performance of the yearly updated program can be improved by setting the threshold equal to a fraction of last year's employment. For instance, by setting $p = 0.95$, firms growing at 4.1 percent or higher will adopt the steady employment response. Thus for a firm growing at 5 percent a year, both the subsidy costs and the distortion costs become comparable to those under the fixed threshold program; only those firms growing at less than -5 percent respond by initially decreasing employment. With lower threshold depreciation factors even more firms adopt the steady response strategy, but the subsidy–employment ratio begins to rise as a greater fraction of a firm's employment becomes subsidized. Some comparisons for a threshold depreciation factor of 0.9 are also presented in tables 2 and 3.

Peak Employment Threshold Program

For a given threshold depreciation factor, the cost effectiveness of a subsidy program can be substantially improved by basing the threshold not on the employment level of the previous year but on the peak employment level of all previous years. In this case the threshold updating rule can be written $\bar{L}_t = \max(L_{t-1}, \bar{L}_{t-1})$. The gain from using this rule rather than the yearly updated rule comes from two sources. First, under the peak employment threshold program, many more firms will respond with a steady increase in employment. Second, the response of those firms that adopt a cycling employment response is much more stable than it would be under the yearly updated threshold program. Under the peak employment program, firms never have an incentive to reduce employment below the level that is optimal without a subsidy.

We assume, as before, a discount factor of 0.9, an elasticity of labor demand equal to 0.25, and a 40 percent subsidy rate. Then any firm that grows by more than 1 percent a year will adopt a steady response strategy, increasing employment by 1 percent in each period. This contrasts with the 9.8 percent growth rate required to induce firms to adopt this response under the yearly updated program. We emphasize again that firms which adopt the steady response strategy generate the same subsidy–employment and distortion–employment ratios as they do under the corresponding fixed threshold program.

Firms with growth rates between 0 percent and 1 percent a year will adopt the cycling strategy illustrated in figure 3. For instance, if the firm grows at 0.5 percent a year, it will expand employment once every eleven years, generating a 0.98 percent increase in present discounted employment, with a subsidy employment ratio of 0.40 and a distortion–employment ratio of 0.137. Both these numbers are higher than they would be under the fixed threshold program, but they are also considerably lower than under the yearly updated program.

One of the drawbacks of a pure peak employment program is that only firms with positive growth rates will respond after the first period. One way to reach more firms is to let the threshold depreciate each period by a constant factor q. This has the additional benefits of inducing more firms to adopt the steady response strategy and of generating greater employment from each firm at the same subsidy rate. For instance, if $q = 0.95$, the subsidy rate required to induce firms following the steady response strategy to increase employment by 1 percent is lowered to 0.28. Furthermore, the steady response will now be adopted by any firm growing by more than -4 percent a year. In addition, the distortion–employment ratio is lowered for those firms that previously responded but not with a steady response. Unfortunately, lowering the threshold depreciation factor tends to increase the subsidy–employment ratio. In fact, the percentage increase is substantial for firms with growth rates near zero. We should point out, however, that the higher the subsidy rates (and hence the increase in employment), the less will be the proportionate increase in the subsidy–employment ratio. Nevertheless, these results suggest that the optimal depreciation factor will be sensitive not only to the distribution of firms according to growth rates, but also to the program designer's intentions, that is, whether he is concerned primarily with subsidy costs or distortion costs.

Finally, we should note that although this program is substantially more cost effective than the yearly updated program, a relatively large subsidy rate is still required to produce even a 1 percent increase in employment. This suggests that no feasible permanent program will have much impact. However, as seen in the next section, when firms are uncertain about the duration of the program, the same subsidy rate tends to induce a much larger employment response. Under these conditions, therefore, the program may be more effective.

Uncertainty

Thus far, the analysis has dealt with the optimal employment response of firms to various subsidy programs under the assumption that there is no uncertainty on the part of firms. There are at least two ways that uncertainty might be incorporated into the analysis. First, firms may be uncertain about how long the program will remain in place. This uncertainty will not affect the behavior of the firm under fixed threshold programs, but, as discussed below, it may have a dramatic effect on the cost effectiveness of other subsidy programs. The second kind of uncertainty that we might wish to examine is the firm's uncertainty about its future profit function, or alternatively, its optimal employment level. Although we believe that this kind of uncertainty may be important, a detailed analysis of firms' behavior under those circumstances is beyond the scope of this paper. We will therefore confine ourselves to a few brief remarks.

Uncertainty about the Life of the Program

Under most circumstances a subsidy program is likely to have a limited duration. If the firm takes this strong possibility into account, it will usually revise its employment response. Perhaps the simplest way to model this type of uncertainty is to assume that there is a fixed probability, $1 - \pi$, that the program will be discontinued in any period, given that it was still in place in the previous period and that the firm learns of its discontinuance at exactly the time this occurs. In terms of the firm's objective function, an increase in this probability merely acts to lower the discount factor used by the firm to evaluate future gains from the subsidy program.

As we noted above, this kind of uncertainty should not affect the behavior of any firm under a fixed threshold program, since the employment response of firms then depends only on the level of the threshold in the current period, not on the return to the firm in any future period. Under any other program, however, the firm will respond by increasing its level of employment; the firm now puts less value on future subsidy revenue, which is no longer certain.

In the evaluation of the employment gains and program costs, a difference exists between lowering the discount factor and increasing the *subjective* probability for the firm that the program will be terminated. If the government really intends the program to be permanent, then the social gains and costs of the program should be evaluated at a discount rate that does not incorporate the possibility that the program will end. The net effect of an increase in the subjective probability for the firm that the program will be discontinued, therefore, is to generate more employment for the same subsidy rate, or alternatively, the same employment at a lower cost. These gains can be quite significant.

Suppose a pure peak employment threshold program ($q = 1$) is in place but that firms believe there is a 25 percent chance that the program will be terminated in any year, if it is still in place in the previous year. Again assuming the discount factor is 0.9 and the elasticity of labor demand elasticity is 0.25, a subsidy rate of only 12 percent is required to induce firms adopting the steady response strategy to increase employment by 1 percent. This is much smaller than the 40 percent subsidy rate required under the pure peak employment program with no uncertainty but still three times higher than the 4 percent rate required under the fixed threshold program. The growth rates for which firms adopt a cycling employment response still lie between 0 percent and 1 percent, and the distortion costs are also unchanged. But the subsidy costs are lower. For firms growing at 10 percent a year the subsidy–employment ratio falls from 3.67 to 1.13; for firms growing at 5 percent a year, it falls from 1.94 to 0.60; and for firms growing at 1 percent a year, it falls from 0.44 to 0.13.

If a depreciation factor of 0.95 is introduced into the threshold updating rule, the cost effectiveness of the peak employment program for growing firms is reduced. Nevertheless, it still compares reasonably well with the fixed threshold program even without a depreciation factor. Except when growth rates are near zero, the subsidy–employment ratio is lower under the peak employment program and more firms respond to the program. A systematic comparison of the cost effectiveness of the three subsidy programs under uncertainty is presented in tables 2 and 3. These results suggest that the peak employment subsidy program may be considerably more effective than the other programs if firms are even a little bit uncertain about the permanence of the program.

Uncertainty about Future Optimal Employment Levels

The basic principles that govern the firm's response to a subsidy program under perfect certainty do not change when one introduces uncertainty about its future optimal employment level. Again the firm's response under a fixed threshold program depends only on the relation between its optimal employment level and the threshold in the present period. Similarly, under the other programs, the firm faces the same trade-off between increasing employment today and raising the threshold in the future. The difference is that the size of the future threshold relative to the firm's future optimal employment level is now a random variable.

Although consequently there may be more fluctuations in the employment response under uncertainty than under perfect certainty, one would still expect a peak employment program to be more cost effective than a yearly updated one. The reason is the same as before. Under the latter program, an incentive sometimes exists to lower present employment below the optimal level in order to lower the threshold in the next period. Under the former program, the future threshold can be affected only if the threshold is exceeded in the current period. Since future profits are discounted, the firm will never choose to lower employment below the optimal level in the current period.

Other Subsidy Programs

The three programs discussed above by no means exhaust all the programs that might be examined. Each of the three programs could be varied in several ways and sometimes combined. In this section we briefly discuss several alternative programs.

First, we could have considered an even more general version of the peak employment threshold updating rule by weighting last period's employment differently from last period's threshold. The threshold in period t may then be defined by $L = \max(pL_{t-1}, qL_{t-1})$. Letting $p = q$ yields the peak employment–based program; setting $p = 0$ yields the fixed threshold program, and setting $q = 0$ yields the yearly updated threshold program. Alternatively, setting p equal to one and q equal to some number less than one generates a program that is a mixture of the yearly updated and peak employment programs. It allows for a large depreciation of the threshold as long as it is not exceeded by the employment level in the current period. When the next period's threshold is required to be at least as large as this period's employment rate, however, growing firms will not be able to generate an excessively large spread between their level of employment and their threshold.

Unfortunately, this program suffers from the same defects as the pure yearly updated program. When $p > q$, it is possible for the firm to choose an employment level that is less than its threshold but large enough to increase the future threshold. In such cases, the employment level in that period will be less than it would be without a subsidy. For values of q very near p, this problem may not arise, but we have found no examples to indicate that such programs are more effective than a peak employment program with a depreciating threshold.

A second possible modification of the peak employment program is to set the subsidy threshold rate equal to the maximum employment of the last n years. Setting $n = 1$ reduces the program to the yearly updated program and setting $n = \infty$ yields the peak employment program. In a sense, therefore, the n-period updating program is a generalization of both of the programs we have already examined.

For an arbitrary threshold horizon, n, the optimal employment response to this kind of program may take on several different forms, depending on the growth rate of the firm. But the basic principles that underlie these responses are identical to the principles that determine the response to programs with the peak employment and yearly updated rules. We confine our attention, therefore, to a brief description of how the optimal responses depend on the threshold horizon.

As with a yearly updated program, firms will follow the steady response if they have very high growth rates. But as the threshold horizon is lengthened, this response is adopted by firms with lower growth rates. For threshold horizons that are sufficiently large, some firms may even adopt an n-period cycling strategy like the strategy they would use under the peak employment program. As long as n is finite, however, the firms whose growth rates range around zero follow an n-period employment cycle in which, during some of the periods, employment falls below the firms' optimal levels. For these growth rates it is always optimal for the firms to wait until the program "forgets" the employment levels established when the subsidy was last collected before they increase employment enough to collect the subsidy again. If a firm is growing, the typical cycle is to raise employment by a factor of $1 + s\eta$ in the first period, return to the nonsubsidy growth path for some (possibly empty) interval of periods, and then begin to decrease employment in each period so that the threshold stays constant. In period $n + 1$, the firm increases employment again by a factor of $1 + s\eta$ and collects the subsidy. If the growth rate of the firm is negative, the pattern is similar, except that the negative employment response begins in the period immediately after the one during which the subsidy was received rather than toward the end of the cycle.

We have also examined the cost effectiveness of this kind of program for various threshold horizons. As one might expect, the program usually tends to be more cost effective the longer the horizon. Again the peak employment program appears to be the most efficient, even though a pure program may exclude too many firms from its benefits. Apparently the better way of including more firms in the program is to introduce a depreciation factor into the threshold updating rule rather than to introduce a finite horizon for the threshold.

Conclusions

In sum, it appears very difficult to devise subsidy programs that are more cost effective than a simple marginal subsidy program with a fixed threshold in each period. If the optimal size of the average firm is growing (or declining) over time, it may be desirable to introduce a depreciation factor into the program. Alternatively, the threshold of each firm might be adjusted in each period on the basis of aggregate data from the previous period. So long as the individual firm cannot affect its threshold, however, its employment decision will not depend on how the threshold is updated.

A fixed threshold program also generates the maximum employment gain for a given subsidy rate. For a discount factor of 0.9, the employment response in the absence of uncertainty is *ten* times higher under such a program than under any other updating rule. Because there are no intertemporal trade-offs when the threshold is fixed, firms respond to the subsidy as if there were a permanent decrease in the wage. Therefore, to the extent that policymakers have reasonably accurate estimates of the labor demand elasticities, they may also be able to more accurately determine the subsidy rate that is required to generate a given employment level than they could under other, more complicated subsidy schemes.

In only one case have we been able to demonstrate the possibility of more cost effectiveness than under the fixed threshold program. This occurs when firms believe that the program will probably be terminated in some future period. Such a belief does not change the firm's behavior under a fixed threshold program. But the firm does modify its response under any program in which a trade-off can be made between more employment today and a lower threshold later. Since the firm cannot be certain of obtaining any future benefits resulting from the subsidy program, it tends to increase employment in each period, to be certain of obtaining its benefits while the program is still in place. As a result, the discounted sum of employment rises. Thus if firms are sufficiently uncertain about the future of the program, it is possible to use the employment history of each firm to update its threshold and eliminate excess subsidy payments without incurring a prohibitively high decrease in the employment response.

If it is decided that a subsidy program should include a threshold updating rule based on the individual firm's employment experience, then it is important to design the program in a way that reduces the fluctuations in the employment response. Our analysis suggests that a subsidy program which bases its threshold on the previous peak employment level (or the peak of some depreciating fraction of previous employment levels) will be most effective in meeting this objective. Unlike programs that base the threshold only on employment in the previous period (or the previous n periods), peak employment programs never provide an incentive to the firm to reduce employment below the firm optimal level. If there is no depreciation of the threshold, however, only firms with a positive growth rate will collect the subsidy more than once. When a depreciation factor is introduced into the threshold updating rule, not only will more firms respond to the subsidy but the employment response of each firm will be larger for the same subsidy rates. This effect tends to partially offset the higher subsidy–employment ratio resulting from the lower threshold.

Although we believe that our central conclusions will basically remain intact as more sophisticated models are examined, we should emphasize that the model on which the results of this paper are based does omit some important considerations. For instance, we ignored any effect the introduction of the program might have on the prices and wages faced by the firms. If the increased demand for labor raises the wage, the net employment gain will be less than is predicted here. Furthermore, if not all firms are eligible for the program, some of the employment gain by subsidized firms may be offset by a decline in the employment level of unsubsidized firms. Similar conclusions emerge if the subsidy program is targeted on only certain categories of workers.

In addition, some of our results depend on the simplified form of the firm's profit function. If we introduce adjustment costs, for example, the firm's incentive to adopt cycling employment responses may be dramatically reduced. And in that case the advantage of the peak employment program over the yearly updated program may not be so pronounced. In contrast, if we assume that firms may hold inventories at relatively low cost, the incentive to cycle may be increased. In that case the model may considerably understate the size of the employment fluctuations induced by the yearly updated program.

Finally, the question arises whether it is innocuous to suppose that the firm's underlying optimal employment level grows at a constant exogenous rate. Not only might there be random or cyclical fluctuations in the optimal size of the firm from period to period, but this size might itself depend on the employment level of the firm in previous periods.[5] Since we have not analyzed this possibility in detail, we confine ourselves to some brief remarks. First, the introduction of any subsidy program is likely to affect the growth rate of the firm. Suppose the optimal employment level of the firm in any period is larger the larger the firm's employment level in the previous period is. Then any program that induces a firm to raise employment (relative to the optimal no-subsidy employment level) in each period by some fraction will be increasing the growth *rate* of the firm by that same fraction. Second, for the same subsidy rate, the fixed threshold program should have a larger impact on the firm's growth rate than either the yearly updated or peak employment program. The reason is the same as the one described in the section comparing firms' responses. Under the yearly updated and peak employment programs any increase in employment beyond the threshold increases the firm's future threshold. This cost of increasing employment is not present under the fixed threshold program; hence that program induces a greater response. Third, although it is not possible to reach definite conclusions without further analysis, we should note that the same incentives that induced employment fluctuations in the model we analyzed are still present when the growth rate is endogenous. But we suspect that for the same parameters firms are more likely to adopt a steady response strategy if an increase in present employment also raises the optimal future employment level.

Appendix A: The Model

We assume that the objective of a typical firm is to choose its employment level in each period to maximize its discounted sum of profits. To obtain simple closed-form solutions, we assume that the value of output produced by the firm in any period is a concave function of this employ-

5. We thank Robert Eisner for directing our attention to this point.

ment in that period, L_t, given by $bL_t - (a/L_t^*) (L_t - L_t^*)^2$, where L_t^* is a parameter proportional to the optimal size of the firm in period t, and a and b are positive constants. The market wage rate is w, but if the firm receives a subsidy equal to sw for every employee it hires above some threshold $\bar{L}_t$, the net profit to the firm in period t is equal to

$$bL_t - \frac{a}{L_t^*} (L_t - L_t^*)^2 - wL_t + sw \max(0, L_t - \bar{L}_t).$$

With no loss of generality, we may assume that $b = w$.[6] Then, if the firm discounts profit in each period by a factor of δ, the problem of the firm is to choose L_t in each period to maximize

$$\sum_{t=0}^{\infty} \left[- \frac{a}{L_t^*} (L_t - L_t^*)^2 + sw \max(0, L_t - \bar{L}_t) \right] \delta^t,$$

where $\bar{L}_t$ is typically a function of L_{t-1} and $\bar{L}_{t-1}$.

It is clear from the previous equation that without any subsidy, the optimal policy of the firm is to set L_t equal to L_t^*. Thus L_t^* may be regarded as the optimal scale of the firm at time t. The profit function has been constructed so that the cost of a given percent deviation from the optimal employment level is proportional to the scale of the firm. To obtain steady state solutions, we assume that L_t^* grows each period by a constant factor g $(0 < g < 1/\delta)$. We also assume that both the wage rate and the revenue function are unaffected by the subsidy program.

By appropriately normalizing units and adjusting the value of a, we may set $L_t^*/g^t = L_0^* = 1$. Let $\lambda = g\delta < 1$ be the discount factor nor-

---

6. If $b \neq w$, let

$$a' = a + \frac{b - w}{2}$$

$$L_t^{*\prime} = \left(1 + \frac{b - w}{2a}\right) L_t^*$$

$$c_t = L_t^*(b - w)\left(a + \frac{b - w}{4}\right).$$

Then

$$\frac{a}{L_t^*} (L_t - L_t^*)^2 + (b - w)L_t = \frac{a'}{L_t^{*\prime}} (L_t - L_t^{*\prime}) + c_t.$$

Since c_t is a constant, it can be ignored in determining the optimal response of the firm.

malized for growth, and let l_t be the firm's employment level in period t, normalized for growth. Then the problem of the firm may be rewritten as

$$\max_{(l_t)} \sum_{t=0}^{\infty} \left[-a(l_t - 1)^2 + sw \max\left(0, l_t - \frac{\bar{L}_t}{g_t}\right) \right] \lambda^t.$$

In the absence of a subsidy, the firm will set $l_t = 1$ in each period to generate zero profits.[7]

Finally, we may show that at the no-subsidy optimal employment level the wage elasticity of demand for labor, η, is equal to $1/2a$. Ignoring the subsidy, the single period profit function for the firm is $- a/L^* (L - L^*)^2 = (b - w)L$. Differentiating with respect to L and setting the resulting expression equal to zero generates the optimal employment level,

$$L = \left(\frac{b - w}{2a} + 1\right) L^*.$$

Then

$$\eta \equiv \frac{-L}{w} \frac{\partial L}{\partial w} = \left(\frac{b - w}{2a} + 1\right) \frac{1}{2aw}.$$

Then if $b = w = 1$, $\eta = 1/2a$.

Appendix B: Formulas Used in the Text

We present here the general formulas for the *present value* of the increase in employment, distortion costs, and subsidy costs produced by the various subsidy programs discussed in the text.[8] The *distortion–employment* ratios presented in tables 2 and 3 are defined by the distortion cost divided by the employment gain. The *subsidy–employment* ratios are defined similarly.

1. Fixed threshold program: $\bar{L}_t = q\bar{L}_{t-1}$ $(q > 0)$.

   Assume that $\bar{L}_0 = qL^*_{-1}$.

   If $g \geq q$, the firm sets $l_t = s\eta + 1$ for all $t \geq 0$. In this case, we have

$$\text{Employment gain: } \frac{s\eta}{1 - \lambda}$$

7. We are ignoring any constant term in the profit function. See note 6.
8. The derivations are available from the authors upon request.

Distortion costs: $\dfrac{s^2\eta/2}{1 - \lambda}$

Subsidy costs: $s\left(\dfrac{s\eta + 1}{1 - \lambda} - \dfrac{q/g}{1 - \delta q}\right)$.

If $g < q$, then there is a $\hat{t}$ such that $\hat{t} = \max\,[t: p^t \leqq g^t(1 + s\eta/2)]$. Then $l_t = 1 + s\eta$ if $t \leqq \hat{t}$; $l_t = 0$ for $\hat{t} > t$. If $p > g(1 + s\eta/2)$, then $t < 0$ and there is no response. Otherwise, we have

Employment response: $s\left(\dfrac{1 - \lambda^{\hat{t}+1}}{1 - \lambda}\right)$

Distortion costs: $\dfrac{s^2\eta}{2}\left(\dfrac{1 - \lambda^{\hat{t}+1}}{1 - \lambda}\right)$

Subsidy costs: $s\left[(s\eta + 1)\dfrac{1 - \lambda^{\hat{t}+1}}{1 - \lambda} - \dfrac{q}{g}\left(\dfrac{1 - (\delta q)^{t+1}}{1 - \delta q}\right)\right]$.

2. Yearly updated threshold: $\bar{L}_t = pL_{t-1}$ $(p > 0)$.
   Define

$$\bar{g} = p\left(\frac{s\eta(2 - p\delta) + 2}{s\eta(1 - 2p\delta) + 2}\right)$$

$$\underline{g} = p\left(\frac{2 - \delta ps\eta}{2 + s\eta}\right).$$

Assume that $\bar{L}_0 = pL^*_{-1}$.
  For $1/\delta > g \geqq \bar{g}$, then firm sets $l_t = (1 - p\delta)s\eta + 1$. In this case, we have

Employment gain: $\left(\dfrac{1 - p\delta}{1 - \lambda}\right)s\eta$

Distortion costs: $\left(\dfrac{1 - p\delta}{1 - \lambda}\right)^2\dfrac{s^2\eta}{2}$

Subsidy costs: $s\left(\dfrac{(1 - p\delta)^2}{1 - \lambda}s\eta + 1 - \dfrac{p}{g}\right)$.

For $\bar{g} > \underline{g} \geq g$, the firm follows a two-period cycle. Employment alternates between $s\eta = 1$ and $-p\delta s\eta + 1$. Define

$$g_0 = \frac{2p}{s\eta[1 - (p\delta)^2] + 2}.$$

If $g > g_0$, then the firm responds by first increasing employment (that is, $l_0 = s\eta + 1$). In this case, we have

Employment gain: $\left(\dfrac{1 - \lambda p\delta}{1 - \lambda^2}\right) s\eta$

Distortion costs: $\left(\dfrac{1 + \lambda(p\delta)^2}{1 - \lambda^2}\right) \dfrac{s^2\eta}{2}$

Subsidy costs: $s\left(\dfrac{s\eta(1 + \lambda(p\delta)^2 + 1 - p/g}{1 - \lambda^2}\right).$

If $g < g_0$, then the firm responds by first decreasing employment (that is, $l_0 = -p\delta s\eta + 1$). In this case, we have

Employment gain: $\dfrac{\delta(g - p)s\eta}{1 - \lambda^2} < 0$

Distortion costs: $\left(\dfrac{(p\delta)^2 + \lambda}{1 - \lambda^2}\right) \dfrac{s^2\eta}{2}$

Subsidy costs: $s\left(\dfrac{\lambda(1 + s\eta) - p\delta(1 - p\delta s\eta)}{1 - \lambda^2}\right).$

For $g < g$, the firm does not respond.

3. Generalized peak employment threshold: $\bar{L}_t = q \max(L_{t-1}, \bar{L}_{t-1})$ $(q > 0)$.

Assume that $\bar{L}_0 = qL_{-1}$. As in the text, let π be the probability that the subsidy will not be discontinued in any given period, given that it has stayed in place up to that period.

If $g > q$, the firm will respond by setting $l_t = s\eta[1 - (\pi q\delta)^n]$ for $t = 0, n, 2n, \ldots$ and $l_t = 1$ in all other periods. The length of the cycle is determined by choosing an n that maximizes

$$F(m) = \left(\frac{1 - (\pi q \delta)^m}{1 - (\pi \lambda)^m}\right)\left([1 - (\pi q \delta)^m]\frac{s\eta}{2} + 1\right).$$

In this case, we have

Employment gain: $\left(\dfrac{1 - (\pi q \delta)^n}{1 - \lambda^n}\right) s\eta$

Distortion costs: $\left(\dfrac{1 - (\pi q \delta)^n}{1 - \lambda^n}\right)^2 \dfrac{s^2\eta}{2}$

Subsidy costs: $s\left[\dfrac{1 - (q\delta)^n}{1 - \lambda^n}\left(s\eta[1 - (\pi q \delta)^n] + 1\right) - \dfrac{q}{g}\right].$

If $q \geq g \geq 2q/(2 + s\eta)$, the firm will respond with $l_0 = 1 + s\eta$ and $l_t = 1$ for all $t > 0$. In this case, we have

Employment gain: $s\eta$

Distortion costs: $\dfrac{s^2\eta}{2}$

Subsidy costs: $s\eta + 1 - \dfrac{q}{g}.$

If $0 < 2q/(2 + s\eta)$, then there is no response.

Comments by Bryce Hool

Bishop and Wilson's paper makes a useful contribution to our under-standing of how the design of marginal wage subsidies can affect their employment incentive effects. The authors demonstrate, in particular, the way in which firms respond to such a subsidy and how this response de-pends on the revision rule that is used to determine, for successive years, the threshold above which employment is to be regarded as marginal.

The analysis has been neatly executed. Indeed, it is so neat as to belie the difficulty of the general dynamic problem, which Bishop and Wilson have successfully made tractable in a useful way. But because the authors have been explicit about the restrictions under which their results are formally derived, they are made vulnerable to attack on the grounds that some relevant influences on firm behavior have been excluded. Nevertheless, the general incentives exhibited in the analysis will still be present in more complex environments. In particular, the tendency of threshold updating rules based on the previous year's employment or the previous peak employment to induce a cyclical employment response will persist. In establishing precise conditions under which this will occur, Bishop and Wilson have rigorously confirmed what has previously been either overlooked or, at most, informally recognized.

Among the potentially important complications that have been explicitly assumed away are adjustment costs associated with varying the firm's work force, departures from a steady growth mode in the presubsidy period, endogeneity of the firm's growth rate, and movement of wages and prices over time.

The absence of adjustment costs is especially relevant to the possibility of a cycling employment strategy. Although there might be other factors that would tend to reinforce this type of strategy, it seems clear that the magnitude of employment fluctuations will be reduced by these costs. In this regard also, the employment decisions of the firm will be influenced by the increase in unemployment insurance contributions that would result from labor force reductions following a subsidy-induced expansion. Costs such as these must be weighed against the direct benefit of subsidized labor. It is conceivable that a firm and its associated workers could collectively benefit from the subsidy through employment fluctuations, with formal or informal contractual agreements that recognize the costs of these fluctuations. But such contracts would be likely to involve compensating wage adjustments, which have been ruled out of the analysis. More directly, the absence of wage and price adjustment over time is troublesome because of the infinite horizon assumed for the firm's optimization problem. This assumption is, of course, part of the price of tractability, like the assumption of an exogenously determined, constant growth rate for the firm.

The single most obvious alternative to steady growth in the presubsidy period is one of cyclical fluctuation. If one is interested in the long-run effects of a marginal subsidy, or if one denies the existence of cycles in the first place, then it is natural to focus on trend growth. In that case, the induced cycling response to thresholds based on previous employment levels is of less interest than the cost effectiveness of a program in achieving a specified increase in employment. On the other hand, limited duration of the subsidy program and belief in the existence of a business cycle both suggest a focus on short-run, about-trend responses.

The assumption that the subsidy program will be of infinite duration is a restrictive one, and the corresponding predicted response by the firm serves only as a benchmark. Bishop and Wilson have made some interesting progress by relaxing this assumption and allowing for uncertainty about the duration of the subsidy. They find specifically that uncertainty of this sort enhances the performance of the peak employment threshold program, making its effectiveness comparable to that of the fixed threshold program. This is useful information. Presumably, knowledge that the subsidy program would be of finite rather than infinite duration would similarly produce a greater short-run response by the firm—whether more or less so than with uncertainty would depend on the time profile of the probability of continuation. Further study of the effects of uncertainty would doubtless be difficult but enlightening. In the unlikely event that the authors seek a more challenging technical problem, they might consider the choice of the threshold rule as the optimization problem, taking as given the employment function of the firm or, more generally, its basic environment.

Finally, it is worth emphasizing the obvious point that the subsidy analyzed is marginal but not targeted. Imposing an eligibility requirement would alter the firm's response largely according to the degree of substitutability between targeted and nontargeted labor groups. In this context, departures from steady employment growth are more likely, and the assumption of long-run constancy of wages (now relative) and zero costs of adjustment would be even more troublesome than before.

Comments by Robert Eisner

Using several simplifying and in some instances critical assumptions, Bishop and Wilson compare the effectiveness and distortion of three basic kinds of marginal employment subsidy programs: fixed threshold, yearly updated threshold, and peak employment threshold. Among the critical assumptions are:

(1) the profit function is a quadratic in actual employment, L_t, and in optimal employment without a subsidy, L_t^*;

(2) there are no costs of adjustment: $L_t^* = (1 + g)L_{t-1}^*$, where g is a constant, exogenous rate of growth; and

(3) the wage rate, w, is assumed constant; the supply curve of labor to the firm is viewed as horizontal.

Given the explicit assumptions, the Bishop-Wilson analysis is impressive and informative. Under conditions where continuation of the given subsidy program and future optimal employment levels are certain, and with criteria of maximum bang for the buck and minimum distortion—a function of variance around L_t^*—the fixed threshold program usually comes out best. The yearly updated program may lead to cycles of higher and lower employment and even initial declines and generally lower employment than without the subsidy. The peak employment program may also lead to cycles, but without employment ever sinking below what it would be without the subsidy. Introducing uncertainty about whether the program will continue, which reduces the incentive to lower current employment to gain a greater subsidy later, can make this last program the most effective and least distortionary.

Bishop and Wilson's analysis is a useful, systematic presentation of possible implications of various subsidy programs which can be ignored only with peril. But the special nature of the explicit assumptions, the further unnoticed and implicit assumptions, and the limited criteria for evaluation can also be ignored only with peril.

First, the form of the profit function predetermines several results. As the relative amount of subsidized employment grows, its costs grow in greater proportion. Distortion costs in turn become implicity a function of assumed values of elasticities of labor demand, η, as the form of the profit function imposes particular relations between η and the parameter, a, of the quadratic expression in $L_t - L_t^*$. Both magnitudes of response and relative values of distortion costs, if not their ranking, are therefore affected.

Second, the ruling out of adjustment costs may seriously exaggerate the danger of cyclical responses from yearly updated and peak employment programs. Firms may not wish to accept what may be sharply added costs of fluctuating employment.

Third, the assumption of horizontal labor supply curves rules out the possibility of differences between short-run and long-run elasticities of labor supply. The probably lower short-run elasticity of supply will also tend to reduce cyclical tendencies, particularly with asymmetrical inelasticity of short-run supply for increases in employment. Firms will be less inclined to reduce employment or hold it down in anticipation of intermittent increases if such increases will be much more expensive than steady growth.

Fourth, employment is viewed entirely as a choice variable for the firm. But in fact, firms may well have reason to preset required qualifications and wage offers and then, in the short run, accept resultant rates of quits, hires, and employment. This stochastic nature of actual employment may mitigate further against planning cyclical variations.

Fifth, the implications of uncertainty about whether a program or its parameters will continue or remain unchanged are more complicated than indicated in the paper. On an analytical level it is disconcerting to suggest, without further explanation, that firms can long entertain a subjective probability of 0.25 that a program will be discontinued in the next year, which implies a 0.58 probability that it will be discontinued in the next three years, while analysts assume the program is permanent. Can they fool all the firms all the time? I would not want to force this analysis into a framework of rational expectations but the assumption of "irrationality" makes me uneasy. If one is trying to predict the effects of a continuing program, one would expect that firms' subjective probability of its continuance, π, will eventually approach unity.

Sixth, Bishop and Wilson implicitly rule out demand factors (and imperfect competition) in making the optimal nonsubsidy level of employment, L_t^*, exogenous. In fact, even aside from adjustment costs, the optimal level of employment in the next period may well depend upon employment in this period. Given positive storage costs and depreciation of the value of output, increased current employment may imply meeting potential future demand now. If a producer of durable goods is induced by an employment subsidy to produce and sell more now, his optimal employment later, without a subsidy, may be less. And decreased employment now may, conversely, reduce future demand and employment. In the terms of Bishop and Wilson, instead of writing $L_t^* = (1 + g)L_{t-1}^*$, where g is exogenous, one would have to write L_t^* or g_t as a function of L_{t-1} and of expected demand in year t. McDonald's is not likely to cut its employment and sales in year t in the hope of getting a bigger subsidy in year $t + 1$. And General Motors is unlikely to give up its share of the market in 1981 to Toyota or Chrysler in order to gain a greater share in 1982. Yet if it increases employment and production now, it may be able to realize sales only by "borrowing" its regular customers from next year.

Seventh, while the authors consider the possibility of firms with different growth rates, g, their analysis is exclusively microeconomic. They explore neither aggregative nor distributional implications, though they refer briefly to the latter. Yet these in the last analysis are the essence of the problem.

In fact, there is a distribution of g_i for the firms in the economy, and indeed a distribution of g_{it} for individual firms over time, where the growth rate of the ith firm in the year t is a variable, yet is not independent of the value of g_{it} for other firms or other years.

If one measures aggregate costs and benefits, one may then find low-growth firms with cyclical responses to yearly updated or peak employment programs. These responses would imply low effectiveness, that is, high ratios of subsidy to employment, and high distortion. But these firms, receiving subsidies in only some periods, will account for a small part of total subsidies. The growing firms with stable responses will account for most of the subsidies and employment increases. A yearly updated or peak employment program might then appear better in the aggregate than indicated by Bishop and Wilson, because the firms for which the program proves inefficient will have relatively little role in it.

Further, if only because of demand shocks, g_{it} may vary with t. In particular, growth may turn down in a recession. Fixed threshold and peak employment programs will then reduce sharply or eliminate the subsidies received by many firms just when it may be most important to support employment and aggregate demand. The yearly updated program in this situation appears more stabilizing, since, after one year of decline, firms will become eligible for subsidies to induce renewed growth in employment.

Finally, one must recognize important criteria of distribution, equity, and social costs for any program expected to be politically viable. Since firms do have different underlying growth rates, a fixed threshold program will offer major benefits to some firms and little or nothing to others. The distribution considerations here will loom large not only for individual firms but also for the states and regions in which they operate. A program that encourages employment most in firms or regions that are already growing suffers on grounds of both equity and economic efficiency. This may argue for a fixed threshold program with lower, aggregatively less-efficient thresholds (lower values of q). The yearly updated or peak employment program, by adjusting subsidies to each firm's past experience, may also serve to lessen what might prove unacceptable discrimination in favor of rich and successful firms. This discrimination is likely to be all the more acute when it is recognized that subsidies have income as well as substitution effects, offering advantages in greater wealth and liquidity.

One may or may not have any reason to ease the competitive struggle for survival of less rapidly growing firms. But one should not ignore the discriminatory implications of subsidy programs, which may help shove them under.

The Bishop-Wilson paper is enlightening in its exploration of certain implications of a useful, simplified model. Important complications await further recognition and analysis.

George J. Carcagno and Walter S. Corson

Administrative Issues

The administrative implications of policy choices are often overlooked or granted only cursory attention in the public debate about new government programs. Although administrative issues should not figure as prominently as the broader questions of public policy, neither should they be considered minor technical details that can be readily resolved by the administering agency once legislation is passed. Under many programs administrative problems have subverted the attainment of policy objectives.

In some cases, administrative issues may be so important that the manner in which they are resolved can result in a program that operates differently from what was intended. For example, the basic education opportunity grant program, which provides scholarships to college students in need of financial assistance, made erroneous payments in over half the cases in the 1978–79 school year, largely because of administrative difficulties. As a result, many ineligible persons received scholarships and some eligible students were underpaid.[1]

Some administrative matters might even rule out of consideration certain program or policy options that are desirable in themselves. For example, an employment subsidy could not be both administered within the income tax system and provide coverage to nonprofit organizations and units of state and local government.

In this paper we examine the impact on administration of alternative formulations of targeted employment subsidies. The intent is to identify the program approaches or features that complicate administrative processes or have high administrative costs relative to their program benefits.

We thank Larry Dildine, Isabel V. Sawhill, and John H. Bishop for helpful comments on a draft of this paper.
1. *New York Times*, December 14, 1979.

Since the precise design of an employment subsidy program depends on what policy goals are sought, a conscious decision could rightly be made to incorporate a program feature that is relatively difficult to administer. What should be avoided are design decisions that unnecessarily complicate program administration, for complicated administrative processes not only are costly to manage but also may result in such low participation rates by firms that policy objectives cannot be reached.[2]

A recurring theme of this paper is that program approaches in which many decisions must be based on the characteristics of particular individuals or firms introduce administrative complexities. At the very least, such complexities make it impossible to rely completely on the tax system as the administrative vehicle for the program. But also using the tax system raises some broad issues of public policy that must be addressed. The general principles underlying this discussion of program administration are relatively straightforward: keep the program as simple as possible, try to achieve the policy objectives as directly as possible, and avoid adding extraneous policy objectives to the program or its delivery mechanism.

In the first section we briefly review the recent U.S. experience with employment subsidy programs. Next we discuss the alternative administrative models that could be used to operate such a program. We then present the administrative implications of the most commonly discussed design elements of employment subsidy programs. In the final section we review the administrative issues involved in performing the operating

2. During the conference the possibility of using the participation or take-up rate in a program as an indicator of administrative effectiveness was raised. The shortcomings of such an approach make it an unreliable measure. An apparently low participation rate could indicate that the program itself is poorly designed, containing features that cause fewer people to be eligible than expected. Low take-up rates may result because a subsidy is too small to compensate employers for their real or perceived costs of employing the target population. The data available to estimate the number of people potentially eligible for a program are subject to large error or are simply unavailable. As a result, estimates of the eligible population, needed to calculate take-up rates, are suspect. Finally, one would also have to know something about the quality of administration—a high incidence of administrative errors often means that ineligible persons are determined to be eligible. Nevertheless, if take-up rates were available for different administrative jurisdictions, they could indicate the relative ability of agencies in different areas to administer the program (quality being held constant). Such comparisons, however, would not enable us to determine whether the design of the administrative process itself was flawed. Such determinations require more information than a single measure can provide.

functions common to these programs—the determination of eligibility, calculation and disbursement of the subsidy, enforcement, and outreach and publicity.

U.S. Experience with Employment Subsidies

Three employment subsidy programs have been tried in the United States in recent years that resemble the types of programs discussed in this paper. Each of them pays or has paid benefits through the income tax system in the form of nonrefundable credits.

The work incentive tax credit, enacted in the Revenue Act of 1971, was the first of these credits. Initially it paid firms that hired welfare recipients enrolled in the work incentive program and equaled 20 percent of the first twelve months' wages. Changes in the program were made in 1975 to extend it to all welfare recipients covered under aid to families with dependent children (AFDC) and, in 1979, to increase the subsidy to 50 percent of wages up to $6,000 for the first year of employment and 25 percent of wages up to $6,000 for the second year. Data on use of this program, reported in table 1, indicate that benefits paid under it have been low throughout its life. In its peak year (1977) $38.2 million in credits was claimed on 20,800 tax returns. Although a precise estimate of participation among eligibles cannot be made, available evidence suggests that it has been low.[3] Furthermore, evidence on the effect of this program on firms' hiring decisions, though far from conclusive, suggests that much of the employment that was eligible for the credit would have existed anyway.[4]

3. For example, data from the 1975 AFDC survey indicate that AFDC recipients earned $1.8 billion in 1975. (U.S. Social Security Administration, *Aid to Families with Dependent Children, 1975 Recipient Characteristics Study,* pt. 3: *Financial Circumstances* [SSA, 1978].) With a 20 percent credit and our estimate that 65 percent of all jobs are with employers with positive tax liability, $234 million in credits could have been paid in 1975 if all these AFDC recipients began their jobs during that year. (Others who left the program would presumably add to the total.) Although this is clearly an overestimate, 100 percent participation by employers would have required that only 5 percent of the AFDC recipients began their jobs in 1975, a figure that is much closer to the monthly average of accessions to jobs in manufacturing. (The number was 3.7 percent in 1975.)

4. For a discussion of this evidence see Daniel S. Hamermesh, "Subsidies for Jobs in the Private Sector," in John L. Palmer, ed., *Creating Jobs: Public Employment Programs and Wage Subsidies* (Brookings Institution, 1978), p. 96.

Table 1. Experience with the Work Incentive and New Jobs Tax Credits, 1972–78

	Work incentive tax credit			New jobs tax credit		
Year	Corporate returns	Individual returns	Total	Corporate returns	Individual returns	Total
	Number of returns (thousands)					
1972	1.9	4.8	6.7	...	...	...
1973	4.1	2.1	6.2	...	...	...
1974	4.2	2.9	7.1	...	...	...
1975	3.3	5.1	8.4	...	...	...
1976	5.3	5.7	11.0	...	...	...
1977	5.0	15.8	20.8	195.8	418.3	614.1
1978	5.3	5.1	10.4	365.3	776.5	1,141.8
	Amount of credit claimed (millions of dollars)					
1972	2.0	0.7	2.7	...	...	...
1973	9.0	0.7	9.7	...	...	...
1974	7.8	1.1	8.9	...	...	...
1975	5.3	1.8	7.1	...	...	...
1976	9.7	1.9	11.6	...	...	...
1977	29.7	8.4	38.2	1,614.0	744.4	2,358.4
1978	20.9	5.2	26.1	3,087.1	1,426.4	4,513.5

Source: Unpublished tabulations supplied by the Treasury Department. Data for the work incentive tax credit for 1977 and 1978 are preliminary, and the differences between those two years and previous years may result from the Treasury's method of estimation rather than from actual changes in individual and corporate response to the program. The new jobs tax credit was not available during the 1972–76 period.

The second program, the new jobs tax credit, was temporary, providing credits to firms for increased employment in tax years 1977 and 1978. The credits equaled the minimum of 50 percent of the first $4,200 paid each new hire in excess of a 2 percent annual growth rate for the firm's employment level or 50 percent of the excess of total wages over 105 percent of the previous year's wages. In addition, the credits were limited to 25 percent of the aggregate unemployment insurance wages under the Federal Unemployment Tax Act or $100,000, whichever was less. The program was considerably larger than the work incentive one, paying benefits of $2.3 billion in 1977 and $4.5 billion in 1978. Although little evidence on participation is currently available, the Treasury Department estimates that half of all corporations qualified for the credit in the first year and that less than half of these filed for benefits.[5] The 90 percent

5. Interview with Larry Dildine, deputy director, Office of Tax Analysis, U.S. Treasury, October 7, 1980.

increase in credits in the second year of the program suggests that the participation rate probably rose substantially with increased knowledge and visibility of the program. Available evidence indicates that the new jobs tax credit had significant effects on employment growth (3.4 percent) among firms that knew of the program.[6]

The third program, the targeted jobs tax credit (established under the Revenue Act of 1978), is also temporary; it was originally available for the 1979 and 1980 tax years and later extended to the 1981 tax year. This program provides a tax credit of 50 percent of wages up to $6,000 in the first year and 25 percent of wages up to $6,000 in the second year for certified employees hired after September 26, 1978. These employees can come from any of seven groups considered to be particularly disadvantaged.[7] Certification of workers is the responsibility of the U.S. Department of Labor, and the tax credits are paid through the income tax system. Certification requires the issuing of a voucher indicating eligibility (which can be done by many agencies, CETA [Comprehensive Employment and Training Act] prime sponsors and the U.S. Employment Service being the principal ones); once a worker is hired, a certification form is issued by the employment service and sent to the employer.

Experience in the first year indicates that the program was slow to get started. Only about 8,000 certifications had been issued by June 1979, but by the end of 1979 the total was 109,000, with a monthly average in the last three months of the year of about 30,000.[8] No evidence is yet available on participation rates or the employment effects of this program. But two facts suggest that many certifications in the first year may have been for employment that would have occurred without the program.

6. See Jeffrey M. Perloff and Michael L. Wachter, "The New Jobs Tax Credit: An Evaluation of the 1977–78 Wage Subsidy Program," *American Economic Review,* vol. 69 (May 1979, *Papers and Proceedings, 1978*), pp. 173–79; and Jeffrey M. Perloff and Michael L. Wachter, "A Reevaluation of the New Jobs Tax Credit," report to the Assistant Secretary for Policy, Evaluation, and Research, U.S. Labor Department, November 1979.

7. These seven groups are supplemental security income recipients, handicapped persons undergoing vocational rehabilitation, youths aged eighteen through twenty-four from economically disadvantaged families, Vietnam-era veterans under thirty-five who are members of economically disadvantaged families, recipients of general assistance, youths aged sixteen through eighteen who are participants in cooperative education programs, and ex-convicts who are members of economically disadvantaged families (92 Stat. 2831).

8. Data are from U.S. Employment Service, Office of Program Review, "Targeted Jobs Tax Credit Program (TJTC) Monthly Summary" (selected issues).

First, 50 percent of the certifications as of December 31, 1979, were for cooperative education students, a group that probably would have been hired in any event.[9] And second, many of the certifications (estimates by program administrators range from 60 to 90 percent)[10] have been retroactive; that is, they have been for persons already hired. Sizable employment effects of this program, if they occur, may therefore not appear until the second or even the third year of the program.

Choice of Administering Agency

The broadest administrative issue to consider is which government agency should administer the program. Three administrative models come to mind.

In the first model the program is administered wholly within the tax system.[11] This approach has a commonsensible appeal, given the ample precedent for using the tax system as a way to extend financial incentives to firms and individuals. The tax system already collects data of the type that would support at least some versions of an employment tax credit, so that only minor additions may be required. Furthermore, the tax system provides a convenient means of transferring funds to employers. Although there are limitations to the data that can be obtained—some questions about whether people who make hiring decisions are generally informed about incentives in the tax system, and problems in dealing with firms and organizations that either have no tax liability or are outside the tax system—this approach to administration has been used under the work incentive and new jobs tax credit programs.

The second model assigns administrative responsibility to the Department of Labor or a related state or local agency. This approach places responsibility for the program in the government department charged with defining and carrying out employment policy. It also provides the

9. Certifications for cooperative education students are issued directly to employers by the administrators of cooperative education programs without use of a prior voucher. This direct link between the employer and the certifying agency may explain the high proportion of total certifications issued for such students.

10. U.S. Department of Labor, Employment and Training Administration, Division of Staff Evaluation Studies, "Telephone Follow-up Survey on TJTC Development," February 1980.

11. At this point equal consideration is given to using the income tax, social security tax, or unemployment insurance tax as the administrative mechanism.

greatest flexibility in defining eligibility requirements and other program specifications, since there are fewer limitations on the kinds of data that can be obtained. On the other hand, a large expansion of staff would probably be required.

The third model combines the tax system and a program agency. The program agency establishes worker eligibility, and the tax system transfers the funds to employers. This method capitalizes on the relative simplicity of using the tax system for disbursements while permitting more complex eligibility rules to be used. This is the model for the targeted jobs tax credit.

Any choice of administering agency that uses the tax system as a disbursement mechanism raises the general policy issue of the quality of the review and oversight associated with tax expenditure programs compared with programs that are subjected to the budget review procedures of both the executive and legislative branches of government. It is generally agreed that the second process provides much more effective public oversight of expenditures and operations than the first, because the budget is reviewed annually, whereas subsidies embedded in the tax system are not reviewed in any systematic manner.

This problem could be avoided if disbursements were made through the social security tax (FICA) and unemployment insurance tax (FUTA) mechanisms, with worker eligibility determined by the Department of Labor or a related agency like the state employment service or the CETA prime sponsor. The budget for the program could then include an allocation for reimbursement of the appropriate trust fund and so be part of the regular budget cycle. Although such an unorthodox use of the trust funds would undoubtedly be controversial, in principle the integrity of the funds would not be compromised by such an arrangement.

In choosing an administrative model, it is important to consider the implications of having one agency perform eligibility determinations for another agency's program. In such cases the incentives for making accurate determinations are considerably diminished if there are no budgetary consequences for doing a poor job. A "poor job" may take the form of carelessness or may be the result of a one-sided emphasis on the service aspect of the program without any of the leavening usually provided by the budgetary constraint. It is too early to know whether this will be a problem with the targeted jobs tax credit, which relies on several different agencies to determine eligibility.

Administrative Implications of Selected Design Issues

In this section we discuss some of the important design options for
employment subsidy programs: incremental employment strategies, regional variations, different bases for subsidy calculations, and short-term
or cyclical programs.

Incremental Employment Strategies

One program design goal may be to maximize the impact of program
expenditures by attempting to pay a subsidy only for "new" employment
generated by the program. That is, one might try to avoid subsidizing
employment actions that would have occurred without the program. But
since "new" employment cannot be directly measured, an approximation
of this concept becomes necessary. Several mechanisms to limit the subsidy to new employment have been proposed. As under the targeted jobs
tax credit, a subsidy can be paid (1) only for incremental employment
above a base amount and (2) only for new hires among the target groups
(a hiring subsidy). Further, restrictions can be placed on this second
method to provide a subsidy only for net additions in the employment of
target group members or to require that overall firm employment be increased. This last restriction, which is also a part of the targeted jobs tax
credit, is aimed at minimizing the substitution of target group members
for other workers.

Implementing these mechanisms demands a set of complex regulations.
Each of the incremental employment strategies requires the definition of
base period employment (either the employment of all workers or only
target group members). The appropriate time period for this base must
be specified, and regulations that often raise difficult questions about program goals are needed for many special cases, including new employers
and new combinations of employers (that is, mergers and acquisitions).[12]

12. For instance, consider a situation with two employers (A and B), each of
whom employs 500 workers one year. If at the start of the second year employer A
sells half his business to employer B and doubles the remaining half, employer A
will have 500 workers in year 2 and employer B 750 workers. If an incremental subsidy is paid based on a comparison of employment in the second and first years, employer A would receive no subsidy and employer B would receive a subsidy. One
could argue that the reverse should be true, since employer B did not increase overall
employment whereas A did. Regulations that handle situations like this can and have

The measurement of base period employment is difficult even in firms that undergo no major changes in their structure. Ideally, the definition of base period employment should be uniform across employers. For example, if the subsidy were based on the "number of employees," one might want to define an employee as a person who works forty hours a week. Since firms do not have uniform work weeks of forty hours, further rules would be needed to define how to aggregate part-time employees into full-time equivalents and how to handle overtime hours. Although such rules can be based on the National Labor Relations Board standards for overtime, data to construct such estimates may be difficult for some employers to collect or may not be available (for example, under piece-work payment schemes).

An administratively simple, but partial, solution to this measurement problem is to calculate the employment base and any incremental change by using unemployment insurance or social security records, since these are already kept by employers. For example, the new jobs tax credit was based on changes in wages subject to the federal unemployment tax.[13] But since the FUTA tax base is $6,000 per employee, part-year or part-time workers may be counted as full-time equivalents with this mechanism. An increment in such workers could lead to a subsidy without an actual increase in full-time equivalent employment. This problem also exists for the social security tax base, though the wages subject to taxation are much higher ($22,900 in 1979; $29,700 in 1981). Since social security wage records are kept and reported separately for each employee, a count could be made of the number of workers employed over a year. This number would, however, also include part-time workers and be sensitive to variation in turnover rates. In addition, neither FICA nor FUTA taxes cover all employment for which one might want to pay a subsidy. For example, despite recent changes in coverage, some agricultural employees are not covered by unemployment insurance and social

---

been established for the new jobs tax credit. These regulations allow employer A to deduct employment in the sold-off portion of the business from his base period employment when computing the subsidy and require employer B to add the employment to his base. Thus employer A receives a subsidy. But if the transfer to employer B of part of A's business resulted in liquidation of that part of the business by B, the government might not want to pay the subsidy.

13. For a fuller discussion of the legislative history and problems created by this solution to the problem, see Emil M. Sunley, "A Tax Preference Is Born: A Legislative History of the New Jobs Tax Credit," in Henry J. Aaron and Michael J. Boskin, eds., *The Economics of Taxation* (Brookings Institution, 1980), pp. 391–408.

security, and some state and local governments have elected not to be part of the social security system. Furthermore, as we discuss in more detail below, state and local governments and nonprofit employers with workers covered by unemployment insurance are not required to file and make regular contributions to the unemployment insurance system. They never compute the federal unemployment tax and hence would not usually be computing base period employment if it were based on FUTA wages.

When limitation of an employment subsidy to a particular target group is combined with rules designed to limit the subsidy to incremental increases in employment, administration can become complex. If the incremental rules apply to aggregate employment, no problems beyond the definition and measurement of employment discussed above occur. But when the incremental rules apply only to target group members, administrative problems may be severe.

If an employment subsidy were paid only for net additions to the target group, old as well as new employees would have to be certified as members of that group. Once the program is established, this could be accomplished by counting each year's new subsidized employees as members of the employment base for a given number of years, if they continue to be employed. But in the first year or two of the program, certification of old employees would be necessary. If defining membership in the target group is at all complex (for example, as for some groups eligible for the targeted jobs tax credit), certification would be a large task, and it might not be clear how to deal with some potential eligibility requirements such as "economically disadvantaged." Current employees would be unlikely to be economically disadvantaged, but they might have been so categorized before being hired. The difficulty and expense of doing these certifications seems to rule out this option as administratively infeasible unless the definition of target group membership was very simple (for example, it was age-based). Furthermore, certification of current employees would probably lead to low employer participation because of the trouble involved. Current employees might also be resistant to being labeled as members of the target group.

Regional Variations

One often-discussed program option is to provide regional variations in subsidy levels or in the application of incremental rules to try to tilt the subsidy toward economically distressed regions. For example, incremental rules that exclude declining firms from receiving benefits might be waived in low-growth, high-unemployment regions but applied in those with high growth and low unemployment.

Several administrative problems occur under regional variations. For one thing, unless the regions that receive special treatment are defined by political boundaries, a problem of designation arises. If the regions are large (for example, the ten federal regions) and a well-known, clearly defined concept (such as the unemployment rate) is used as a measure, this task can be accomplished. But since large regions contain many subareas with both low- and high-unemployment rates, using broad geographic units would probably not ensure that most high-unemployment areas would receive special treatment. Therefore, policymakers are likely to designate regions by smaller areas, such as states or units within states —for example, standard metropolitan statistical areas or counties. If so, data problems are severe regardless of what concept is used to define the region's status—unemployment rate, level of personal income, poverty incidence—and hence it is difficult to make decisions objectively.

For example, although many current programs base their benefits on unemployment rates for local areas, two problems exist with such estimates. First, most statistics that could be used to define an area's status are defined for political divisions; yet a geographic definition that would make sense for an employment subsidy program would probably extend across political boundaries. In cities on state boundaries, labor market conditions in both states clearly define the labor market strength or weakness of these cities, but a program that allowed state-by-state variations could create two sets of rules for one urban area. Second, state and local area estimates of unemployment rates are not very accurate.[14] The Current Population Survey does not have a large enough sample to be used for local area estimates and even at the state level the sampling error is quite large.[15]

14. An extensive discussion of problems with state and local data is found in Harold Goldstein, *State and Local Labor Force Statistics,* Background Paper 1 (U.S. National Commission on Employment and Unemployment Statistics, May 1978).

15. The recently expanded survey provides state annual average estimates of unemployment rates with a coefficient of variation that averages 6.5 percent. This means that if the true state unemployment rate is 6 percent, the chances are about one in three that sampling error will cause the estimate to be less than 5.6 percent or more than 6.4 percent. See U.S. Census Bureau, *The Current Population Survey: Design and Methodology* (Government Printing Office, 1979), chap. 7.

To produce substate area estimates of unemployment rates, other data must be used. These estimates start with data on the insured unemployed (that is, people eligible for unemployment insurance) and add estimates for other groups (unemployment insurance exhaustees, new entrants, reentrants) to arrive at an estimate of total unemployment. Not only are the estimates for the latter groups difficult to make accurately, but the estimates of insured unemployment are also uncertain, since an unemployed person's likelihood of being eligible for unemployment insurance depends heavily on state law. People in states with short potential durations of unemployment insurance have, other things equal, a lower probability of being eligible for insurance during a week in which they are unemployed than people in states with longer potential durations.

The frequency with which area eligibility rules are adjusted also increases the administrative complexity. Frequent estimates (for example, quarterly or monthly) will add to the problems of obtaining accurate estimates for local areas and to the complexity of the benefit calculation. Moreover, the potential for changes in the status of an area may reduce participation in the program, since employers will not know how long a subsidy will last when making hiring decisions. If rules restricting the subsidy to incremental changes in employment apply during one time period and not another, an employer will need to calculate the subsidy separately for each time period. This means that employers must be notified of the appropriate benefit calculation or the information must be readily available to them. Separate calculations for each time period are not difficult if the frequency of filing and benefit computation corresponds to the time periods chosen for rule changes. This will happen if the program is administered as a stand-alone program but not if the tax system is used for benefit payments. Even if the status of an area is changed only once a year, differences between the annual definition chosen for the program and an employer's fiscal year will necessitate a complex benefit calculation procedure.

A final problem with regional or area program differences occurs when an employer operates in more than one locality. In such cases the employer will need to compute the subsidy separately for each site if benefit computation rules differ by site.[16] Even if they do not differ, an employer

16. A further problem arises when the site or office may not correspond to the actual place of employment—for example, railroads, trucking concerns, construction firms, and traveling salesmen. In these instances individual employees as well as the firm may be split among regions.

may want to elect to compute the benefit separately to maximize the subsidy (for example, he or she may want to isolate a site with a high growth rate in employment). Although administrative rules can be devised for these situations, they add to the complexity of filing and to the complexity of determining if applications for benefits are correctly prepared.[17] The problem is more severe if policymakers wish to use an existing system—that is, the tax system—to administer the program, since the tax filing unit will be likely to include more than one site.

In sum, regional variations in benefit computation rules are difficult to administer, cannot be determined accurately, and push administration toward the establishment of a separate administrative structure. Administrative considerations suggest, therefore, that there should be no regional variations in employment subsidy programs.

Basis for Subsidy Calculation

Employment subsidies, whether incremental or universal and whether or not they are targeted on particular groups, can be based on earnings, employment, hours, or wage rates. Probably the easiest basis to handle administratively is earnings, because earnings data are presumably collected for all employees and reported by each employer to the Internal Revenue Service. This means that calculation of the subsidy will not become an administrative burden for employers, and it also means that the auditing of the subsidy calculation is straightforward, since no new data need be collected. Furthermore, since these data are collected for various purposes (individual income, corporate income, social security, and unemployment insurance taxes), several options are readily available for the subsidy calculation. The calculations can use total earnings, earnings subject to FICA, earnings subject to FUTA (which would tilt the subsidy toward low-wage labor), or individual earnings. Therefore, the disadvantages of using earnings for the subsidy calculation are not administrative but relate to the fact that earnings may not accurately portray employment changes. For example, a subsidy based on FUTA wages might be paid when all that occurred was an increase in part-time employment.

Each of the other possible bases for the subsidy calculation—employment, hours, or wage rates—necessitates using data not regularly re-

17. The existence of regional variations also creates incentives for fraud. Employers may hire in one region but put the employee on the payroll in another to maximize the subsidy. Uncovering that kind of fraud is difficult.

ported for tax purposes by employers. Using such data may increase an employer's information needs and hence costs, and it limits the ability of the government to audit and control the program. For example, if a subsidy were based on employment or employment changes, it would be necessary to define who counts as an employee (for example, anyone working more than ninety days for seven or more hours a day). Since counts of employees are not usually made, doing so would increase employers' administrative costs. Furthermore, if the administering agency wanted to audit a subsidy calculation based on the number of employees, it would either have to spend considerable time with an employer verifying the calculation or it would impose much of this cost on the employer by asking for complete documentation. In addition, some employers may not be able to collect the necessary information. For example, hours worked and wage rates are not collected for persons paid on a piece-work basis or for those paid on commission for sales. Administrative considerations, therefore, argue for the use of earnings as the basis for subsidy calculation. Other bases should be chosen only if they clearly enhance program goals more than a subsidy based on earnings.

Short Duration or Cyclical Programs

Another option is to establish a program that lasts a limited time or that turns on or off with the business cycle. Clearly such a program should be as simple as possible, since, to be of use, it must be established quickly and knowledge of it must be disseminated as fast as possible. In this regard it is useful to examine the experience with the targeted jobs tax credit. This program required, among other things, that the vouchering and certification process be devised and instituted before the program could be implemented. That process took a long time, since agreements about administration had to be reached between the Department of Labor and the state employment service agencies and then between those agencies and the multiple agencies that handle the client groups (CETA, state vocational rehabilitation agencies and welfare departments, and so forth). Consequently, vouchers and certifications were not issued at all until three months after the program was expected to begin and not in any quantity until the nine- to ten-month point. A program of short duration that is intended as a countercyclical program must be available more quickly. Programs that involve complex administrative processes, such as the targeted jobs tax credit, will take time to become established.

Administrative Functions

In this section we address administrative issues related to (1) the determination of eligibility for individuals, (2) the calculation and disbursement of the subsidy, (3) enforcement, and (4) outreach and publicity.

The Determination of Eligibility

If a broad class of people is intended to be the beneficiary of a program—low-wage workers, for example—then some aggregate measure rather than the characteristics of individuals might be used to determine program eligibility. For example, in the new jobs tax credit, the subsidy was based on changes over a firm's previous year's total FUTA wages.

Although the FUTA wage base and other similar aggregate measures are imperfect mechanisms for identifying low-wage workers, they can be measured easily within the scope of the tax system and can be defended as a reasonable proxy for a more extensive method. But if policymakers choose to focus eligibility more narrowly, say on economically disadvantaged youth, then an aggregate measure is no longer sufficient. It becomes necessary to examine the characteristics of individuals in order to certify them as eligible to carry a subsidy. The collection and evaluation of such information far exceeds what is routinely dealt with by the tax system and must be handled by alternative means; namely, an agency or agencies charged with responsibility for making such individual assessments. In short, if specific target groups are selected, as under the targeted jobs tax credit, then an agency other than the Internal Revenue Service must administer the subsidy.

It should be noted that the potential range of choice of such other agencies is broad, since it derives from whatever target groups are included in any given program. Thus, in the targeted jobs tax credit, the inclusion of cooperative education students in the target population resulted in local school districts certifying program eligibility. If one is concerned about such issues as equity and the uniform application of program rules across jurisdictions, the matter of choosing these other administrative agencies should not be approached with indifference. In the example cited, the agents selected are ones that embody a strong tradition of local control. Though appropriate for some institutional settings, an orientation toward local control, with resulting differences in the way the program is defined and administered, would seem inappropriate within a national program like the targeted jobs tax credit.

Identifying people eligible for the program. If it is decided to focus an employment subsidy on specific, narrowly defined target groups, then the administrative implications of the target group definitions should be considered. Targeting a program on youth or high school dropouts, for example, creates no serious administrative problems. But if the objective were to target the subsidy on residents of neighborhoods with high unemployment, the administrative problems would be serious. The data for such small areas are even more inaccurate than those available for regions and are available only from census tabulations, which means they usually will be several years out of date. Seeking some objective means of identifying such areas is therefore even more problematic than defining a regional subsidy scheme. Once particular areas are defined, however, the administrative problems are reduced to verifying place of residence and dealing with people outside the area who attach themselves to the households of friends or relatives residing there.

It is likely that, in addition to the eligibility criteria described above, determining who is eligible will require measuring income in some way. If income level is chosen as a criterion, family or household income (besides the income of the applicant) will probably have to be determined, since persons from relatively well off families will most likely be excluded from the program (as under the targeted jobs tax credit). The agency may therefore have to contact someone other than the program applicant, who may not be privy to the required information. Additional contacts obviously involve additional administrative costs.

Defining eligibility in terms of economically disadvantaged households also raises the issue of an assets test. In many instances such a test would seem essential. For example, does the rural youth whose parents own a 2,000-acre farm but have a low net income as measured by their tax return come from a disadvantaged household? Probably not. But measuring net worth, which involves extensive data collection and the exercise of judgment about the current market value of assets, is a difficult task, and one to be avoided if possible.

Another issue in income measurement is the time period. Incomes of the low-income population are known to fluctuate over short time periods. Data from a longitudinal study of income dynamics show that from one-third to one-half of the people who had incomes less than the poverty level in one year had incomes above the poverty level in the next year.[18] In some jurisdictions, for programs like AFDC, which bases benefits on income, income data are collected on a monthly basis. But with an employment subsidy, for which eligibility may be limited to a specified time period, the amount of the subsidy is not a function of past income, and in any event the value of the subsidy is small compared with welfare benefits, so that frequent collection of income data is unlikely to be cost effective.

The choice of a measurement period should be guided by the program's intent. If policymakers seek to stimulate the employment of the long-term unemployed or of people who are structurally unemployed, then measuring income over a three- or six-month period provides an effective compromise between the administratively feasible and the fulfillment of the program objective. A measurement period of that length should exclude most people experiencing a recent fall in income because of, say, a temporary layoff and those who are seasonally unemployed, such as schoolteachers and school workers. On the other hand, if the objective were to stimulate employment generally, one might choose a longer measurement period.

Once eligibility is established, should there be a subsequent redetermination of income and eligibility? This question essentially asks how precise the eligibility determination must be at the time someone becomes employed. Since it is known that the economic circumstances of the low-income population are subject to frequent change, a one-time eligibility determination will mean that some people who carry a subsidy will become ineligible.

One approach would be to establish eligibility for a specific time period, six months, for example. After the worker was employed, the employer could collect the subsidy for as long as permitted under the program rules. Note that this last point is important to the effectiveness of the subsidy—hiring and training costs probably require that the subsidy be guaranteed over a substantial period.

Measuring other eligibility criteria. Eligibility for a targeted employment subsidy program can be defined by still other criteria related to policy objectives. Participants in particular programs, like AFDC, supplemental security income, and vocational rehabilitation, could be eligible

18. Unpublished data supplied by Richard O. Coe, Michigan Panel Study on Income Dynamics, Survey Research Center, University of Michigan.

for a targeted employment subsidy. Eligibility could be extended to the aged, youth, veterans, ex-convicts, and the disabled. Except for disability, all the criteria are straightforward and easily measured. The determination of disability is a complex and specialized task that must be performed by highly trained staff. Since such determinations are routinely conducted for the supplemental security income and vocational rehabilitation programs, the obvious approach is to use participation in those programs as the determining factor. Participation in income-conditioned programs, like AFDC, supplemental security income, and food stamps, may prevent the need for an independent determination of whether someone is economically disadvantaged. In such cases evidence of current receipt of benefits should be enough to establish eligibility. The agency administering the income-conditioned program could even certify recipients as eligible for the targeted employment subsidy. But for other possible target groups, such as youth, the aged, veterans, and ex-convicts, a separate determination of economic status would be necessary. As noted above, this is a complex undertaking.

Delegating the authority for making determinations of economic status for a targeted employment subsidy to various agents, like parole officers and the Veterans Administration, is likely to result in widely different applications of the eligibility rules. The easiest way to avoid this result would be to have one agency responsible for determining eligibility. Confirmation of a person's status—for example, veteran—would be necessary if he were not referred from the appropriate agency. This method seems preferable to fragmenting the responsibility for determining eligibility among several agencies. The targeted jobs tax credit experience should provide some information about the practical difficulties of administering a program in which many agencies make eligibility determinations.

Definition of eligible employer. Two aspects of this definition have implications for program administration. First, and most important, what constitutes an employer must be defined for program purposes. If the tax system is used for payment of benefits, the logical way is to define the employer as the unit that files a tax return. If the tax system is not used for disbursement, other definitions could be chosen that might better achieve program goals by more closely tying the subsidy to the unit within a firm that makes employment decisions. For example, if a firm has several independently run locations, one might want to calculate and pay the subsidy by location to reward each hiring unit directly for its decisions. A separate definition incorporating this concept would be difficult to construct, however, and it would not necessarily be a better approximation of the concept than the tax unit. Furthermore it might be open to abuse. An employer might be able to define multiple units purely for the purpose of applying for and maximizing the subsidy.[19]

Second, some employment subsidy proposals might restrict the program to certain industries. Subsidies of that kind require definition of the included or excluded industries, which, of course, leads to problems when firms may arguably fit more than one industry. Should a decision be made separately in each case or should the firm be allowed to divide employment into two groups, eligible and ineligible? Such rules obviously add to administrative complexity and increase the cost of administration; they may also push the choice of administrative structure away from use of the tax system.

Calculation and Disbursement of the Subsidy

In an earlier section the choice of an administering agency was discussed from a broad perspective. The advantages of using the Internal Revenue Service for payment purposes are considerable and mostly obvious. The service is an existing and experienced agency and the calculation and disbursement of the subsidies could be largely self-administered; the administrative cost to both the government and employers would therefore be minimized. Although use of a separate agency would allow greater flexibility in the computation of the subsidy and the breadth of coverage of employers, these relatively small advantages, compared with those of the tax system, do not seem to warrant the costs of setting up and running a separate payment operation. Here we discuss three special issues related to calculation and payment of the subsidy through the tax system: coverage, limits on the subsidy, and the use of vouchers.

Coverage. Using the tax system exclusively for disbursement of program benefits constrains the subsidy to a fraction of potential employers. If one assumes that the target for the subsidy includes state and local governments, nonprofit employers, and for-profit employers but excludes federal civilian and military personnel and the self-employed, use of the income tax system with a refundable credit would cover approximately

19. A tax unit definition would not create this incentive, since other considerations about the structure of an employer's business would outweigh any wage subsidy consideration.

77 percent of the employment base.[20] The refundability of the subsidy could also be administered rather easily, though the Internal Revenue Service has not had much experience with refundable credits. (The only such credit is the earned income tax credit for low-income people.)

If it were decided to restrict the credit to only those employers with a current positive tax liability, then coverage would drop to 65 percent of the employment base. But a larger group of employers would be affected within the income tax system with a nonrefundable credit if unused tax credits or deductions could be carried forward or backward to other years or, as indicated above, if the subsidy were made refundable. For example, the new jobs tax credit and the investment tax credit both have seven-year carry-over and three year carry-back provisions. These provisions require definition of the method of using up excess subsidies, but they present no special administrative problems.

Reaching well beyond the 77 percent of the employment base covered by the business income tax is possible, however, since payroll tax returns, federal unemployment insurance, and social security provide alternative methods of disbursing the subsidy. Although these tax returns have generally not been used in this way before, there appears to be no technical reason that they could not be.[21] The only extra step necessary would be to reimburse the unemployment insurance or social security trust funds by the amount of the subsidy.

Compared with use of the income tax system, use of payroll tax returns has three advantages. First, refundability is not a major problem, since all employers filing FUTA or FICA tax returns will have a positive payroll tax liability.[22] Only for FUTA might the amount of taxes not cover the

20. One could also include federal civilian employment, but to have an effect on employment, agencies that hired employees eligible for the wage subsidy would have to be allowed to increase their appropriations. Such incentives are out of place in a system where agency funding limits are established by acts of Congress.

21. Disbursements of the earned income tax credit made by employers to employees are credited against an employer's payment of withheld income tax payments. If these disbursements exceed the withheld income tax payments, a credit can be taken against payment of the employers' or employees' portion of social security taxes (92 Stat. 2774).

22. Since federal unemployment taxes are paid quarterly with an annual reconciliation, the subsidy would probably be paid as a reduction on the next year's taxes. That might also be necessary for social security taxes. If the wage subsidy were computed annually and applied to the last quarterly FICA payment, high-wage firms might find that the subsidy exceeded their last quarter's FICA payment.

amount of the subsidy.[23] Second, under both payroll taxes, more employees are covered than under the income tax system. However, although 97 percent of wage and salary employees in our defined employment base are covered by unemployment insurance, only 80 percent work for employers who pay the federal unemployment tax. Employees of state and local government and most nonprofit organizations are currently not covered by this federal tax.[24] Hence, if policymakers wished to make those groups eligible for the subsidy, the federal unemployment tax could not be used as the sole payment vehicle. Social security taxes currently cover the largest portion (93 percent) of workers in our employment base. The main group not covered are those state and local employees who have chosen not to be a part of the social security system. This group amounts to 30 percent of state and local government employees. The third advantage of using payroll tax returns is that reimbursement of the appropriate trust fund from a specific employment subsidy appropriation would provide for better oversight of the tax credit programs.[25]

One final method of payment might be to allow an employer to take a credit for the subsidy against any of his federal tax obligations, possibly including withheld individual income taxes of employees. All employers would presumably be covered if the credit could be taken against withholding. Such a scheme might work if the credit were paid with redeem-

23. The federal unemployment tax is 0.7 percent of the first $6,000 paid an employee. If a large portion of an employer's work force were eligible for the subsidy, the subsidy might exceed the tax.

24. State and local governments and nonprofit organizations do pay state unemployment insurance taxes, but in most cases payment is on a reimbursable basis; that is, they pay only for unemployment insurance benefits charged directly to them. They do not pay the federal unemployment tax that is used to pay for the administration of the program. If this tax exemption were to change, the federal unemployment tax system would then have the advantage of covering the largest number of employees.

25. One potential problem with the use of payroll taxes for disbursement is that the subsidy payment function should not interfere with unemployment insurance and social security program goals. It would be necessary to ensure that the payment function was isolated from these programs. Any conflict that might occur would probably concern how incorrectly claimed credits should be handled. Should the Treasury have responsibility for detecting and handling incorrect payments or should the employment subsidy agency? Furthermore, what happens while payment problems are being resolved? Which account—FICA or FUTA or the employment subsidy account—shows the payment discrepancy? It seems that however these questions are answered, it will still be possible to isolate the subsidy payment function from the social security or unemployment insurance program.

able vouchers (see below for a discussion of this option), which could be used to offset any tax payments. Alternatively, the tax form computing the subsidy could be submitted separately, and the employer's account with the Internal Revenue Service given a credit. In this case the credit could be used to offset any taxes owed by the employer.

The above discussion suggests that if policymakers wish to cover as much employment as possible (including state and local governments and nonprofit organizations) with an employment subsidy and use the tax system for payments, use of a system that allows the employer to apply the credit to any tax payment is the best alternative. Use of this system for disbursement is fairly straightforward and, relative to the alternatives, might also have the advantage of alleviating firms' cash-flow problems.

Limits on the subsidy. Many employment subsidy proposals limit the amount of the subsidy paid to any one employer to discourage substitution of subsidy-eligible persons for other employed workers. Both the new jobs tax credit and the targeted jobs tax credit have had such limits. The former program had four limitations on the credit. It could not exceed (1) 25 percent of FUTA wages, (2) $100,000, (3) 50 percent of the increase in wages over 105 percent of the preceding year's wages, or (4) the tax liability for the year. The targeted jobs tax credit limits the subsidy to 30 percent of FUTA wages and 90 percent of tax liability less all other credits.

Limitations like these are easy to compute and apply and present no major administrative problems,[26] particularly when the variables used to compute the limitations are defined and used for other purposes such as for payment of taxes. Only if the limits were defined in a complex way unrelated to current tax data needs would administrative and definitional problems arise. Consequently, the decision about subsidy limits should rest solely on whether or not limits are thought necessary to achieve program goals.

Voucher system. In the light of previous remarks it should be clear

26. Some minor problems are created by limitations if carry-overs of the credit to other years are permitted. The chief problem, which arises with the new jobs tax credit program, occurs because the credit is "taxable," that is, it reduces the deduction for wages. Under that program the decrease in the wage deduction occurs currently even though the credit is deferred, since there is no easy way to adjust the deduction for wages to the amount of credit used.

that we believe the most desirable administrative arrangement for a narrowly targeted employment subsidy is one that uses the Department of Labor or a related state or local agency to determine eligibility and the tax system as the disbursement mechanism. This arrangement lends itself well to some form of voucher, since the administrative system must link particular individuals to particular firms. The targeted jobs tax credit program uses one variant of a voucher system. After eligibility is determined, the applicant is given a voucher that is valid only for the calendar month in which it is issued. The voucher is given to the new employer, who then mails it to the state or local employment service office. The agency sends the employer the program certificate that is needed to claim the tax credit. This approach minimizes the opportunities for abuse and eliminates the possibility of a worker with two jobs providing a subsidy to two employers. At the same time, it is more costly to administer than other voucher schemes, since it requires both a voucher and a certificate and has a short eligibility period once a voucher is issued. It also presents some risk to employers because eligibility is not firmly established at the time of hiring.

A more streamlined voucher system might take the following form. The eligibility agency could provide eligible persons with a card certifying that they qualify for a subsidy. This card would contain an identification number that would also be transmitted to the Internal Revenue Service. Eligibility would be established for a limited period of time, say three months. The eligible person would then present this card to the employer, who would record the number and show it on the appropriate tax return along with the total wages paid to that person and the value of the subsidy. The card would be the property of the employee, who would use it for subsequent employers in the event he or she were to change jobs.[27]

27. One potential problem is that it is difficult to control use of the card if someone holds two jobs. But since only about 5 percent of the labor force holds two jobs, and an even smaller fraction both holds two jobs and has been economically disadvantaged, the problem is unlikely to be severe.

Another problem is that use of the card might be easily abused, with an employer continuing to claim a subsidy after an employee has left the firm (this is also a potential problem with the targeted jobs tax credit). One way to control this abuse would be actually to provide eligible persons with a book of vouchers. Each month they would tear one out and give it to the employer, who would attach it to the appropriate tax schedule. But the paperwork burden this would impose, along with the problem of misplaced or lost coupons, make it an undesirable alternative.

Enforcement

The allocation of resources for enforcement depends on the program rules. As pointed out earlier, regional differentials in the amount of subsidy can provide opportunities for abuse that will be difficult to control. The need for a precise measure of income or assets would also make administration difficult. Let us assume, however, that such problems are limited. Where, then, is the program vulnerable to abuse?

The potential for employer-employee collusion is often cited as a problem with employment subsidy programs. The employee agrees to accept a wage below that which he or she would normally receive and then splits the subsidy with the employer, so that they both come out ahead. It is difficult to understand why an employer would accede to this arrangement, since the firm would effectively get a smaller subsidy. Of course, if eligible workers were in short supply, an employer might make such an agreement; but given an eligibility determination by a government agency and the relatively small payoffs resulting from collusion, that is unlikely. In any event, so long as eligibility is properly determined, such collusion should not be a matter for concern.

A more remunerative form of collusion would be between an employer and a staff member of the agency responsible for establishing eligibility. This form of abuse could be controlled through supervisory review of work and by quality control sampling, though the sample sizes of quality control reviews that are conducted in existing transfer programs are usually too small to draw meaningful conclusions about the work of any particular employee.

Another problem could result from misreporting. What prevents an employer from continuing to collect a subsidy for someone no longer working for him? Coordinating the data on the subsidy return with wages withheld for individuals or performing computer matches of valid eligibles against employer reports are ways of handling this problem. Routine computer matching for masses of data is expensive, however, especially with the prevalence of transcription errors. The cost effectiveness of computerized matching could be determined by examining the incidence and magnitude of abuse as revealed by normal tax audit procedures. That is also the most appropriate strategy for determining what level of resources should be allocated to enforcement activities in general. Quality control and audit samples should provide guidance to program administrators about where enforcement efforts should be directed.

Outreach and Publicity

A necessary administrative function of any employment subsidy program is outreach and publicity. If the program is to have a significant effect on employment decisions, knowledge of the program must be widespread among potential employers. Furthermore, this knowledge must be available before employment decisions are made, and it must be available to the persons making the hiring decisions. For a general employment subsidy, such as the new jobs tax credit, the relevant decisionmakers are probably the management group that sets the overall level of employment in a firm; for a targeted employment subsidy, such as the targeted jobs tax credit, the relevant decisionmakers also include those actually making the individual employment decisions.

For any subsidy, some information will be distributed to the larger employers and to many smaller ones by the various personnel and accounting information services.[28] For example, such services have provided information on the targeted jobs tax credit explaining not only what the specifics of the law are, but also how an employer should claim a tax credit. This amount of information appears to be enough to make employers collect the subsidy if they happen to be eligible. Whether or not employers actually change their hiring decisions (for example, hire more workers in general or more of a particular group) in response to the subsidy will probably depend not on any additional information they receive but on their evaluation of the subsidy's expected effect on the firm.

The design of the employment subsidy program will have two implications for outreach policy. First, if the program is targeted like the targeted jobs tax credit, some outreach activity can be aimed at unemployed members of the target groups as well as at employers. This activity could be channeled through organizations that represent those groups—for example, community organizations, veterans' organizations, other programs designed for those groups, supplemental security income, vocational rehabilitation—or more general outlets could be sought for publicity—employment service offices, newspapers, radio, and so forth. This type of outreach activity could be effective. People looking for jobs may be willing to use the prospect of a subsidy to induce an employer to offer them a job, unless they are concerned about being stigmatized by the target group label.

28. Other information sources include various business and industry association publications and business-related periodicals.

Second, the complexity of an employment subsidy program will affect outreach activities. The more complex a program is, the more specialized and intensive the outreach activities must be. And this is especially true for programs with complicated administrative procedures. Publicity may be needed to counteract the presumed negative effect of complexity on participation.

Finally, some publicity and outreach is needed for program administrators as well as employers and employees. Such activity is particularly necessary for a program like the targeted jobs tax credit where most administrative work is done by people who have important aims and priorities outside the program. Under the targeted jobs tax credit, eligibility is in many instances determined for three target groups by the CETA prime sponsors as an offshoot of the CETA eligibility determination process. Administrators of CETA should therefore be made aware of the tax credit program and given incentives to direct applicants into it. In fact, for this program, some incentives have been offered—prime sponsors receive credit for program vouchers as part of their overall performance assessment—though no administrative funds have been given to prime sponsors for their efforts. Even so, one early evaluation of the program suggests that many local employment service and CETA staff question the usefulness of the targeted jobs tax credit.[29] The report states that staff members believe that most employers are not interested in tax credits and that time spent on eligibility screening and issuing vouchers will be wasted, since it will not lead to increased placements. In such instances publicizing the program among program staff is clearly important.

Conclusions

This review of the administrative issues confronting targeted employment subsidies leads us to two kinds of conclusions. First, administrative considerations suggest that certain design options should be either severely constrained or not considered at all. Only if there are strong policy arguments in favor of these options should they be considered. Second,

29. For a brief description of this evaluation of nine program sites, see U.S. Employment Service, "TJTC Monthy Summary" (period ending September 1979). Similar conclusions were found by a more recent study of twenty-five sites. See Ohio State University, Mershan Center, "The Implementation of the Targeted Jobs Tax Credit," Report 1 (July 1980).

our discussion describes the general administrative structure that we consider the most desirable for a targeted employment subsidy program.

Among potential policy options, regional variations in subsidy provisions are administratively the least feasible. We conclude that regional variations are difficult to define, that the data needed to implement them on a sound basis do not now exist, and that the cost of obtaining such data is prohibitively high. For these reasons regional variations cannot be implemented consistently, even though appealing economic arguments can be made in their favor. Another potential design option that administrative considerations argue against is an incremental employment subsidy paid for increases in the employment of narrowly defined target groups— for example, disadvantaged youth. Such a subsidy would require identification of employed as well as unemployed members of the target groups, a potentially difficult and expensive administrative task. We also present in the paper arguments against basing the subsidy on employment measures other than earnings. Earnings data are already collected for all employees, and the simplest approach administratively is to use these data to calculate the subsidy rather than other data, like hours worked, which are not currently reported to the government and may not be collected for some workers. In addition, we present arguments against using a definition of the economically disadvantaged that includes an assets test or that fixes income eligibility for short time intervals. Finally, in our discussion of vouchers, we conclude that a system of redeemable coupons should not be used as the payment mechanism.

The best and most likely administrative arrangement for targeted employment subsidies, we suggest, is one that uses the tax system for payments by making the subsidy a tax credit. If the employment credit does not require individual eligibility determinations, no other government agency need be involved in the administrative process. But if there is strong policy interest in targeting the subsidy on particular groups, certification of target group members will be necessary; the administration of that part of the program should probably be done by the Department of Labor or its related state agencies, as in the targeted jobs tax credit program. Although this arrangement requires close coordination among departments, a sometimes difficult task, it appears to be the most feasible alternative.

Disbursement of the subsidy through a tax credit should, in our view, be done by making the credit applicable to any federal tax obligation.

This could be done by having an employer file a separate form once a year that reported the subsidy calculation together with supporting data. Data used for the subsidy calculation should be made, insofar as possible, congruent with data used for other tax purposes. The subsidy amount would then be credited to the employer's federal tax account and could be used to pay any federal tax obligations. All other tax forms would then have a line for showing available credits when calculating the amount owed. This arrangement would maximize the coverage of employment by the subsidy but would probably require the cross-checking of tax forms to ensure that the amount of the subsidy was consistent with other reported data. Furthermore, when the credit was used, reimbursement of the applicable tax account (for example, corporate income tax, social security tax) from an employment subsidy program account could be required. Thus the program would be treated like a direct subsidy and its costs included in the federal budget, which would ensure continued legislative oversight of the program.

Comments by John H. Bishop

The paper by Carcagno and Corson deals with an important subject: the administrative considerations that should inform the design of targeted employment subsidies. At the beginning of the paper they lay down a principle with which everyone would probably agree—"keep the program as simple as possible." They go on to assess various design options—marginality, regionality, rules for individual eligibility, employer coverage, administering agency, and the definition of what is subsidized—primarily from this perspective, and they usually favor the least complicated alternative. I agree with the following judgments they make:

—All employers should be eligible for the subsidy.

—Payment should be made through the tax system as a credit against taxes owed rather than by a check from a government agency.

—Making the subsidy a credit against social security taxes seems the simplest way of achieving these two objectives.

—An employment subsidy cannot simultaneously be incremental and highly targeted.

—If an income test is used to define individual eligibility, it should be based on at least three-to-six months of income experience.

—Individual eligibility should not depend on an assets test.

Where I disagree with Carcagno and Corson is in the kind of simplicity that is considered important. Too much emphasis is given to keeping the program simple so that government workers do not make errors in determining eligibility. Not enough emphasis is given to keeping the program simple so that workers and employers know whether they are eligible and how they should apply for the credit. The authors do not even consider that a tax credit might be designed so that workers and employers recognize their eligibility and apply for the credit without having to visit a government office to make special application for the credit. The features of targeted employment subsidy schemes that require government mediation between employer and job seeker—the complicated eligibility rules and the requirement that certification forms signed by the government agency be filed with the tax credit claim—are not evaluated.

An employment subsidy scheme cannot be considered successful unless a high proportion of eligibles make use of it. When people eligible for large monetary benefits from a program do not bother to apply for them, the reason is likely to be that hidden costs of participation are large. Such costs—the trip to the office to apply, the loss of privacy, the stigma, and, for the firm, the costs of changing recruitment and hiring practices—are no less real for being hidden. When the net benefits of the program are calculated, these costs must be subtracted from the program's benefits. In his paper in this volume, Jeffrey Perloff shows that if some of the firms that normally hire target group workers are not eligible for subsidy, the main effect of the subsidy is to redistribute target group workers among firms. George Johnson, in his paper, demonstrates that if only some of the workers needing employment assistance are subsidized, the scheme helps the subsidized workers obtain jobs at the expense of the job prospects of equally needy unsubsidized workers. Thus when participation rates are low, displacement rates are high, and the net increase in demand for target group workers is very small.

By a participation rate criterion, all the targeted employment subsidy schemes tried in the United States—job opportunities in the business section, CETA on-the-job training, the work incentive program, and the targeted jobs tax credit—have failed. Only the mildly targeted incremental new jobs tax credit has been successful. Participation in the targeted jobs tax credit is higher than that in any of the previous targeted employment subsidies, but even so the credit reaches less than 10 percent of those it was supposed to serve.[30] In contrast, the new jobs tax credit attracted in its second year the participation of more than 1 million firms —more than 30 percent of all employers in the nation and more than half of those eligible.

There are three basic causes of the low participation rate in the targeted jobs tax credit.

1. Most job seekers and most employers are not aware of the program. A 1980 survey of employers found that only 17 percent of all employers, accounting for 33 percent of private sector employment, reported being "familiar" with the credit.

2. A stigma is attached to being a member of most of the credit's target groups, which reduces the likelihood that employers will ask CETA or the job service to refer workers eligible for the credit to their firm. Most employers do not ask job applicants whether they are on welfare or come from a poor family. Consequently, applicants may feel that telling prospective employers of their eligibility for the credit may hurt their chances of getting the job.

3. In most cases employers are unable to identify who is eligible on their own. Government certification of employee eligibility is necessary, and this has three consequences: (a) it often introduces red tape and delays into the hiring process, (b) it often forces a firm out of its traditional recruitment channels, and (c) it makes the program's success depend upon the enthusiasm and competence of government bureaucrats.

The first problem could be overcome by publicity and aggressive promotion of the program. The two other problems, however, arise from a mismatch between the structure of the employment subsidy scheme and the recruitment processes that predominate in the relevant labor markets. Each month the typical employer hires one employee for every ten it has on board. The probability that a new hire will still be with the firm a few months later is less than 50 percent. As a result, employers try to keep the costs of searching for new employees to a minimum. Studies of how people have obtained their last jobs found that 35 percent of all jobs were obtained by applying directly at the firm without suggestions or referrals

30. There are 7 million to 9 million new hires every month and 55 percent of these are under age twenty-five. Certainly at least 10 percent of the age group was eligible, so the average monthly certification rate, October 1, 1979, to September 30, 1980, of 22,000 implies a participation rate of 6 percent or less. See Malcolm S. Cohen and Arthur R. Schwartz, "New Hire Rates by Demographic Group," prepared for the U.S. Employment Service, Employment and Training Administration (Department of Labor, July 1979).

and that another 26 percent were obtained by applying directly at the firm at the suggestion of a friend or relative.[31] Most firms prefer to hire people who are recommended by current employees or who have shown their desire for the job by coming to the establishment and applying. Only a small minority of all employers ask the job service, CETA, or some other government agency for referrals. As a result, it was found that even though 34 percent of all workers had checked with the employment service during their last period of job search, only 5.1 percent had got their jobs through an employment service referral.[32] Employers prefer informal recruitment because (a) it is faster; (b) they do not become inundated with job applicants who must be interviewed; (c) prescreening is possible, so the number of applicants who are turned down is minimized; and (d) they can avoid dealing with government.

This preference acts to limit the market penetration of any program for finding jobs for the disadvantaged that depends on a labor market intermediary—the job service, or a CETA subcontractor like the Urban League. Such programs can overcome their inherent structural weakness only when unusually dedicated and competent people are running the intermediary. Under ordinary leadership the programs are bound to be only partially successful—assisting some of the people who approach the agency for help but failing to reach most of the eligible population.

A Department of Labor study during the summer of 1979 found "widespread skepticism about [the targeted jobs tax credit] and hesitation among many local agency staff to actually screen and voucher applicants or talk with employers about the credit." Usually CETA prime sponsors "have been and were still preoccupied with more pressing CETA program concerns." Employment service and CETA staff "doubt the value of the tax credit in increasing job placement among the targeted groups or in netting hires among them that would not have taken place anyway."[33] The staff comments seem to reflect a lack of desire to help firms receive a tax benefit to which they are entitled unless the firm reciprocates by changing its behavior (something the tax law does not require). Some employers perceive this attitude to be pervasive and therefore view many

31. Carl Rosenfeld, "Jobseeking Methods Used by American Workers," *Monthly Labor Review*, vol. 98 (August 1975), p. 41.

32. Ibid., pp. 40–41.

33. U.S. Employment and Training Administration, Office of Program Evaluation, "Evaluation Study of the Early Implementation of the Targeted Jobs Tax Credit Program," Report 51 (ETA, December 1979).

of the agencies responsible for improving the operation of the labor market as a hostile force not to be dealt with if it can be avoided.

The targeted employment subsidies that preceded the targeted jobs tax credit all required agency referrals of eligible job applicants. With the credit there are two alternative ways of bringing subsidy, employer, and job seeker together. One way is for job seekers to inform employers of their eligibility. This does not often happen because most eligible workers are unaware of the credit's existence and because most employment service offices do not routinely inform the eligibles that do come in for help that they are eligible. Also, as mentioned before, many job applicants are reluctant to advertise their eligibility for fear of being stigmatized.

The alternative way is for the employer, the one who most directly benefits from the tax credit, to take the initiative. This scenario envisions employers screening their job applications for eligible individuals and then sending them down to the employment service for vouchering and certification before or after they are hired. Presumably, if it is anticipated that A may be eligible for the subsidy and B is not, the probability that A is offered the job increases. But because family income and participation in welfare programs are used as targeting criteria, employers find it difficult to know who is eligible and are thus prevented from considering the tax credit when hiring. Sending job applicants over to the employment service before hiring is not likely to become popular, because it delays the hiring process, risks losing the worker altogether, and is thought unethical by many employers.

If high participation rates are to be achieved, the target group must be defined by nonstigmatizing criteria that are visible to the employers, and employers must be able to certify and calculate their own eligibility. Only a few targeting criteria would seem to meet this test: age, wage rate, and location of the firm or of the job seeker's residence. Carcagno and Corson raise two objections to using location as a targeting criterion. They correctly point out that selecting which locations should receive preference is difficult and that local unemployment statistics that have sometimes been used for this purpose are poor. This argument is not decisive, however, since it is the government that faces this difficulty, not the employer or the worker. Furthermore, the difficulty can certainly be surmounted, for hundreds of other federal programs award aid to localities on the basis of formulas. Accurate measurements of wage levels, per capita income, and employment are available for local areas and could be used to define counties or other political jurisdictions where the subsidy would apply.

From the perspective of the firm and the worker, subsidies keyed to an employer's location are easier to participate in than those based on worker characteristics like family income or welfare recipiency. Location-based subsidies do not stigmatize their participants. The ease with which they can be made incremental is also important, since incremental subsidies are significantly more cost effective than subsidies of new hires. The disadvantages of targeting by location are not administrative but stem from its lack of refined targeting: the aid it provides to many who do not need it and the exclusion from eligibility of many who do need assistance in finding a job. Other proposals for simpler destigmatized targeting raise the same issue.

Carcagno and Corson limited their analysis to only one class of subsidy, the recruitment subsidy. The options considered tied the subsidy to the hiring of persons with a particular set of characteristics. But there is an alternative way of defining and targeting an employment subsidy. A subsidy can be made a function of the aggregate characteristics of a firm or establishment, such as total hours worked, the wage bill, or the FUTA wage base, as was the new jobs tax credit, the only U.S. employment subsidy scheme to achieve a significant participation rate. This approach has several advantages:

—Firms can calculate and certify their own eligibility.

—To benefit from the scheme, workers and job seekers need not even be aware it exists.

—Targeting is accomplished by keying the subsidy to the firm's location and/or wage rate, so no one is stigmatized by participating.

—The scheme can be made marginal to increase cost effectiveness.

—Government need not be involved except to audit some share of the tax returns that are filed.

—The scheme can be designed to create incentives to lower the rate at which wage rates increase.

One class of such schemes makes the subsidy a positive function of increases in total hours and a negative function of increases in the firm's average wage. The latter feature places strong pressure on a firm to expand by hiring new workers at lower-wage, entry-level jobs, which automatically targets the employment stimulus on the unskilled.

How such a scheme would work is most easily understood by examining a concrete proposal. (Its specifications are merely illustrative.) Firms and nonprofit entities would receive a tax credit against employer social security taxes of $1.00 an hour for every hour by which total hours worked (including those worked by salaried management) at the firm in 1982 exceed total hours worked in 1980. A tax credit would also be provided in 1983 for increases in total hours worked beyond the 1982 or 1980 figure (whichever was higher). In 1984 the tax credit would be for increases in total hours worked beyond the 1983, 1982, or 1980 figure (whichever was highest). The tax credit for which the firm was eligible would be reduced if its average wage (calculated by dividing total compensation by total hours worked) in 1982 was more than 17 percent greater than its 1980 wage. The threshold for this deduction might be 24 percent in 1983 and 32 percent in 1984.

A general formula for the tax credit is

$$TC = s \sum_i \Delta H_{it} - u \sum_i (W_{it} - g\bar{W}_0) H_{it},$$

subject to the constraint that

$$TC \geq 0, \qquad \sum_i (W_{it} - g\bar{W}_0)H_{it} \geq 0,$$

where

H_{it} = hours worked by people in the ith job during time period t
ΔH_{it} = growth of employment in the ith job above the threshold
W_{it} = hourly wage rate of the ith job
$\bar{W}_0$ = the firm's average wage in the base period
s = hourly tax credit
g = wage growth standard, $g > 1$
u = subsidy deduction rate.

An increase in the wage rate is taxed at the rate u. This discourages wage increases above the standard. An expansion of hours that leaves the composition of employment unchanged is subsidized at the rate of s dollars an hour. Where expansions are not proportional and the firm has exceeded the wage increase standard, the tax benefit depends upon the wage rate of the jobs that are expanded:

$$\frac{d_tC}{dH_i} = s - u(W_{it} - g\bar{W}_0).$$

If, for instance, $s = \$1.00$ an hour, $u = 0.1$, and $g\bar{W}_0 = \$8.00$ an hour, expanding a job paying $\$4.00$ an hour would generate a tax credit of

$1.40 an hour, expanding a job paying $12.00 would generate a credit of 60 cents an hour, and expanding a job paying $18.00 an hour would generate no credit.

This type of a marginal employment subsidy has a number of attractive features:

1. Firms are encouraged to increase employment by hiring inexperienced workers and training them rather than by increasing overtime work or bidding experienced workers away from other firms by raising wages.

2. Within each firm the subsidy tends to target the employment stimulus on the least-skilled workers. (This occurs because hiring extra low-wage workers lowers the average wage of the firm, which helps the firm meet the wage increase standard.) The increase in demand at the unskilled end of the labor market should produce large reductions in the unemployment of youth and the disadvantaged.

3. Targeting on less-skilled workers is accomplished without giving low-wage firms a proportionately larger subsidy.

4. Firms are encouraged to slow the rate at which they increase wage rates.

5. Both marginal and average costs of production are reduced while simultaneously wage increases above the standard are taxed. Penalty tax-based incomes policies, in contrast, have the disadvantage of raising marginal and average costs and therefore prices of firms that violate the wage standard.

It is a balanced anti-inflation program. The subsidy component lowers price inflation and the subsidy deduction lowers wage inflation.

Comments by Isabel V. Sawhill

My comments on the Carcagno-Corson paper fall into three categories: (1) the paper's organization and data base, (2) its major conclusions, and (3) issues that might have been given greater attention.

Organization and Data Base

It is difficult to discuss the administrative issues for targeted employment subsidies unless one begins with certain assumptions about the objectives of the programs and the design options most likely to achieve these objectives. Only then can one focus on the compromises in design that may be needed for administrative reasons and evaluate whether reductions in administrative costs or increases in feasibility warrant tampering with the ideal design. The Carcagno-Corson paper covers a range of administrative issues quite well, but I believe it suffers from not having been set more explicitly within a broader policy framework. I am not always convinced that an option that the authors determine to be administratively infeasible is substantively desirable in the first place.

Another problem is how to define what one means by administrative issues. A broad definition—I think too broad—would include political constraints on the one hand and questions of managerial and staff competence within the delivery system on the other. A narrower definition would be limited to how to put program *rules* into effect and establish delivery systems and procedures. Put more concretely, these are the issues usually raised when a general policy is translated into specific legislation, regulations, and program operation guidelines and practices. The Carcagno-Corson paper might have benefited from an approach that simulated this process more systematically and selectively. For example, a distinction could be made between factors that should be considered in making decisions about *who is eligible* (a program design issue) and those that should be considered in deciding *who is responsible for eligibility* determination or certification (a program operation issue). Trying to cover both kinds of issues in the same paper may be overambitious.

A final problem is that the authors (and conference discussants!) have little or no first-hand knowledge of the subject; the conclusions therefore depend primarily on an armchair discussion of administrative issues. I would have preferred more emphasis on what little "data" exist, even if they are based on a nonscientific set of interviews with a small number of federal program administrators, local operators, and participating employers. For example, the staff of the Employment and Training Administration conducted an on-site review of the targeted jobs tax credit program during its first half-year of operation, and the Manpower Demonstration Research Corporation evaluated wage subsidies paid to private employers as part of the youth entitlement program.[34] Both studies con-

34. William A. Diaz and others, *The Youth Entitlement Demonstration: Second Interim Report on Program Implementation* (New York: Manpower Demonstration Research Corporation, March 1980); Employment and Training Administration, "Evaluation Study of the Early Implementation of the Targeted Jobs Tax Credit Program."

tain interesting preliminary evidence on the operation of two different targeted employment programs. They both suggest that the enthusiasm and priorities of local program operators are important determinants of program utilization (program design being held constant). Both studies have raised questions about the administrative feasibility or desirability of recertifying eligibility after initial entry into the system. They both suggest (the evidence is impressionistic) that employers have more favorable attitudes toward these programs than is often assumed. Any negative employer reaction has been caused more by the characteristics of the eligible population or a lack of new hiring than by the red tape or other administrative problems in dealing with program staff. Some employers do seem to fear an Internal Revenue Service audit if they participate in the tax credit program. This could be an argument in favor of using direct subsidies instead of tax credits. The low level of frustration with red tape in the entitlement program may well be a direct result of the way that program was structured. Not only were employers freed from the responsibility of determining eligibility, but they did not have to add participants to their own payrolls or worry about fringe benefits, insurance, or other personnel functions. Reporting requirements (for example, for attendance) were kept to a minimum.

The Paper's Conclusions

Apart from the difficulties mentioned above, I found the conclusions of the paper to be fairly sound and well reasoned.

The authors favor disbursing subsidies through the tax system but leaving the determination of eligibility to the Department of Labor or related state and local agencies. They suggest that the subsidy take the form of a tax credit that can be claimed against any federal tax liability—income, social security, or unemployment insurance taxes—and they provide some interesting data on the broad employer coverage that this would imply. They also advocate reimbursing the trust funds out of a special tax subsidy account that would be part of the Labor Department budget. This is a good way to preserve program accountability while utilizing the administrative efficiency of the tax system; however, it does gloss over the controversy about the extent to which the government should bend the tax system and the trust funds to purposes for which they were never intended.

There was some discussion in the paper and at the conference of whether a targeted incremental subsidy is administratively feasible. Although the authors correctly point out that an earnings ceiling will tilt a tax credit toward low-income workers, in an early version of their paper they concluded that it is not administratively feasible to have a subsidy that is simultaneously targeted *and* marginal. In the subsequent discussion of this issue at the conference, both Robert Eisner and John Bishop pointed out that *some* targeting criteria (for example, age) could be combined with an incremental approach—an important point that is noted in the current version of the paper.

The next issue the paper considers is whether regional variations in program parameters are feasible. Although I agree with their contention that sufficient data do not exist at the local level to put these variations into practice, the authors do not adequately show why these variations are desirable in the first place and thus worthy of such a long discussion.

The discussion of *what* should be subsidized—earnings, employment, hours, or wage rates—seems straightforward. I am convinced that full-time-equivalent employment or hours worked are clearly the preferred option and that administrative constraints may necessitate using earnings or earnings subject to some ceiling.

Finally, the paper deals with who should be eligible for the subsidy. Much of the discussion focuses on the measurement of income and concludes that too frequent and too refined an income certification process is not needed in an employment program as opposed to a welfare program. I think this is a valuable observation, especially in light of the evidence noted above on recertification problems in the targeted jobs tax credit and youth entitlement programs. A tendency exists to assume that family income is a good proxy for people with employment problems or that equity considerations dominate these programs. I would have preferred that more attention be given to some other eligibility criteria—duration of unemployment, a documented period of job search, age, prior labor market experience, and actual or potential wage rates. In the past I have argued that some thought be given to using *residence* in a low-income census tract as a criterion. Residence is much easier to verify than income. Also it would target more resources on the chronically poor, minorities, and those with little access to jobs. The administrative feasibility and costs of these broader-based eligibility criteria need to be compared with the family income criterion.

Other Issues

When targeted employment subsidies are discussed in policymaking circles, two issues always dominate the debate. The first is *windfall gain* (or as I have termed it elsewhere "revenue sharing for the private sector"). The second is the *take-up rate*. Policymakers would like to minimize the former and maximize the latter, but, of course, there is a trade-off between the two. Employers are not going to hire people they would normally reject unless they are given enough financial incentive to do so. And the more heavily targeted a program is (both categorically and incrementally), the less likely employers are to use it. But administrative arrangements can improve this trade-off or increase the elasticity of demand for subsidized employees. This elasticity may vary with (1) the extent to which firms know about the subsidy, (2) the extent to which they believe they are getting low-productivity workers (the degree of stigma or labeling associated with the subsidy), and (3) transactions and search costs (including the amount of bureaucratic red tape). It would have been helpful if the paper had given more attention to these kinds of problems and to the evidence that currently exists on their probable importance under different administrative arrangements (some of which was mentioned above). Unless these problems are resolved, targeted employment subsidy programs may continue to be plagued by low take-up rates.

Peter Schwanse

European Experience

Program evaluation in Europe is still in its infancy. And except in the United Kingdom, the academic community appears to show little interest in evaluating labor market programs. Even the general public does not seem to be worried about the success or failure of individual programs. All this is in striking contrast to U.S. attitudes and practice.

It is difficult to find reasons for the lack of interest. Perhaps one explanation is that labor market policies in Europe are usually designed, pursued, and budgeted, not as separately identifiable programs but rather as part of comprehensive policy packages, whose various elements are hard to disentangle. This is particularly true of employment subsidies adopted for anticyclical reasons. The German wage cost subsidy of 1974, for instance, was closely linked with a comprehensive (and unsuccessful) recovery program based on a coordinated strategy of aggregate demand stimulation through public investment programs and mobility and labor demand incentives. Similarly (though for a different purpose) the French national employment pact of 1977 was intended to cushion the effects on youth labor markets of severe, restrictive fiscal and monetary policies.

In other circumstances, employment subsidies have been part of a political deal, such as a trade-off against trade union demands for import controls, or simply were meant to demonstrate that governments were "doing something" in the face of a rapidly deteriorating employment situation. The stronger the political element, the weaker is the will to undertake impact evaluations on purely economic grounds. Even if the eco-

I am grateful to John Martin and Barbara Smith for helpful comments on a draft of this paper. The views expressed here are my own and should not be ascribed to the Organization for Economic Cooperation and Development, of which I am a staff member.

nomic value of the program should turn out to be negligible, the political advantage might be considerable, though more difficult to defend.[1]

Most of the European evaluations, therefore, are confined to relatively simple questions and methodologies. Impact evaluations are almost non-existent; most examinations of the working of employment subsidies do not try to estimate the effects of the programs on the economic environment, but rather to identify elements in program design, control, and administration that could be changed in order to increase the administrative effectiveness of the schemes.

It is rather difficult, therefore, to make comparisons between European and American evaluation research; nevertheless, this paper attempts to go some way toward that goal by discussing several European evaluation studies that explicitly aim to assess some economic effects of the program in question. Most of these evaluations were initiated by the Organization for Economic Cooperation and Development but have all subsequently been published in national sources. (These sources, cited in the footnotes, should be consulted for further details.) It should be noted that only a few schemes are reviewed here. Since most countries pursue several employment subsidy programs simultaneously, the evaluations reviewed do not cover all the subsidy policies of a particular country at a given time.

The first section of the paper summarizes six subsidy programs, and the next section reviews some evaluations of these programs. Then comes a critique of the evaluation methods applied, followed by a discussion of how evaluations—in the European context—could be improved.

Selected Schemes

Table 1 summarizes the main characteristics of the six selected schemes for which evaluations are available. Most of these programs were adopted at an early stage of the post-1974 downswing (note that most European labor markets, unlike the U.S. ones, never recovered after the 1974 downswing). They were designed, therefore, with a countercyclical objective in mind; namely, to preserve or create jobs during a period of temporary labor market slack. Under such circumstances one would expect that (a)

1. A more simple and straightforward reason is, of course, that research resources devoted to the preparation and control of political decisionmaking are much more limited in Europe than in the United States, though this is not necessarily true of the actual role of research advice in policymaking.

the schemes would apply on a temporary basis; (b) they would operate "at the margin," that is, subsidize net changes but not the total stock of employed workers;[2] and (c) they would attempt to achieve a wide and nondiscriminatory promotion of employment (as distinct from a targeted program to improve the employability of structurally disadvantaged groups).

While all schemes reviewed comply with points a and b, only the Swedish scheme and the U.K. temporary employment subsidy were non-selective (though the latter was limited to "assisted areas").[3] As is clear from the table, the other four were targeted on specific subgroups of the labor force. Even the British temporary employment subsidy and the Swedish scheme were *implicitly* targeted in that their flat-rate subsidies were a more effective incentive for low wage earners.

The marginal stock subsidies examined here can be subdivided into incremental subsidies—those based on net increases in the stock of employed over a certain base level—and redundancy-averting subsidies—those based on averting layoffs that would otherwise occur. The Irish, German, French, and the U.K. programs fall into the first category, the Swedish and U.K. programs into the second.

Most schemes were small, covering only a tiny fraction of total employment. The French and Swedish schemes, however, affected about 4 percent of the work force in those countries. And furthermore—especially since the U.K. targeted employment subsidy continued a long time—a substantial accumulated total of workers was at some time affected by the programs.

All programs were initially established for a short period (on average one year), pending a cyclical upswing of economic activity. When the expected upswing failed to materialize, the programs were usually rolled forward or replaced by new and similar schemes. Of the countries listed in the table, only West Germany (because of disappointing results) and, more recently, the United Kingdom (because of fiscal constraints) have discontinued their subsidy programs.

The Irish premium employment program described in the table has

2. In accordance with Haveman and Christainsen's terminology, these types of schemes will be referred to as "marginal stock subsidies." Robert H. Haveman and Gregory B. Christainsen, "Public Employment and Wage Subsidies in Western Europe and the U.S.: What We Are Doing and What We Know," in *European Labor Market Policies*, National Commission for Manpower Policy, Special Report 27 (The Commission, September 1978), pp. 259–345.

3. The Swedish scheme has subsequently become permanent.

Table 1. Summary of Six Employment Subsidy Programs

Program	Targeting	Base for subsidization	Amount of subsidy	Maximum length of subsidization	Workers affected Number	Workers affected Percent of civilian employment	Gross costs as percent of total public expenditure
Ireland Premium employment program, 1975–77	*Employees* Registered 4 weeks or more as unemployed, or on part-time work, or in certain training courses	Employment increase over base level at the start of the scheme; base readjusted monthly if premiums claimed for 10 employees or 10 percent of original work force	Weekly flat amount. Equivalent to 15 to 20 percent of average male earnings; 25 to 40 percent of average female earnings	18 months	8,157	0.8	0.08 (1976)
	Employers In agriculture and manufacturing						
Germany Wage cost subsidy, 1974–75	*Employees* Registered 3 months or more as unemployed	Employment increase over base level at the start of the scheme	60 percent of the wage paid as a lump sum after notification of new hiring	6 months	78,900	0.3	0.08
	Employers In regions of above-average unemployment						

Program	Coverage	Employment condition	Type of subsidy	Duration	Number		
France First national employment pact, 1977	*Employees* School leavers and young persons returning from military service; *Employers* Nationwide	Employment increase over base level at the start of the scheme except for natural attrition	(1) Total exemption from social security charges, equivalent to 25 percent of labor costs or 35 percent of wages; (2) total subsidization of work experience (*stages pratiques* and *stages de formation*)	12 months	550,000	3.8	0.6
Sweden Employment maintenance and training scheme; started in 1974, modified in 1977, now permanent	Nationwide	Number of workers at risk of being laid off	Hourly lump sum for workers assigned to on-the-job training instead of being laid off; equivalent to 50 to 60 percent of industrial earnings	960 hours per person	165,000 (1976)	4.0	0.3 (1976)
United Kingdom Temporary employment subsidy, 1975–1979	Initially in "assisted areas," later nationwide	Number of workers at risk of being laid off	Weekly lump sum, equivalent to 30 percent of average manufacturing wage costs	12 months per person at full subsidy; additional 6 months at half the subsidy rate	Cumulative total 1975–79, 518,000; at any one time, 170,000–190,000	2.1 0.7	0.25 (1978)
United Kingdom Small firms employment subsidy, 1977–80	Manufacturing firms with fewer than 50 employees in "assisted areas"; later extended to firms with up to 200 employees	Employment increase over base level at the start of the scheme	Weekly lump sum, equivalent to 30 percent of average manufacturing wage costs	6 months	c. 20,000 a year	0.1	0.02

meanwhile been replaced by a new program, the employment incentive scheme, which provides for a higher subsidy rate, longer duration, broader industrial coverage, and less-complicated eligibility criteria.

The first national employment pact of France listed in the table was followed by a second national pact (July 1978–March 1979) affecting 275,000 young people. This pact differed from the first one in three ways: a 50 percent (instead of 100 percent) exemption from social security charges, a restriction to enterprises of less than 500 employees, and the participation of employers (20 percent) in financing the *stages pratiques*. The second pact has been succeeded by a third pact, which extends the 50 percent exoneration from social security contributions to cover the hiring of all females with employment handicaps and also provides for a special employment premium for the hiring of older workers.

Although the Swedish scheme was also first designed as a temporary measure—partly to complement an inventory subsidy to protect employment—the government decided in 1979 to use the program whenever circumstances require it, subject to certain rules that prevent firms from getting support more than once for the same person.

Evaluations

In the evaluation studies carried out for these six schemes, the questions raised and the methods applied to answer them vary greatly. The following review focuses on the issues that best lend themselves to a comparison of the studies. This focus precludes doing justice to all issues dealt with in the evaluations, even though some might be important for other purposes, like national policymaking. Only the Irish and French studies are discussed in some detail, because they represent two different kinds of evaluation and because they have not so far been the subject of much attention in the literature.[4]

Ireland

The Irish premium employment program was an incremental employment premium available to employers in agriculture and manufacturing who increased their employment over the level existing at the inception

4. The German study by Günther Schmid and the two evaluations of the U.K. Department of Employment are discussed in *European Labor Market Policies*.

of the scheme in June 1975. The higher level of employment had to be maintained for at least four weeks. The return of part-time workers to full-time employment could also qualify employers for a partial premium. The program was in operation between June 1975 and January 1977. The premium, a weekly flat amount that was modified twice during the scheme, equaled between 15 and 25 percent of average male industrial earnings and between 25 and 40 percent of average female industrial earnings.

The rules for recalculating the base level of employment were complicated. If premiums were claimed in one month for more than ten employees (or 10 percent of the original work force), the effective base for the next month had to be recalculated to include *half* the workers for whom premiums were paid in the previous period. For employers to qualify for the premium, the additional employment had to consist of persons who were registered as unemployed (or were taking certain training courses) or who were working part-time during the previous four weeks *and* had received unemployment benefits (to which part-time workers are entitled as well) at some time since 1974.

The Irish program was evaluated by Rory O'Donnell and Brendan Walsh from the Economic and Social Research Institute in Dublin, and the net costs of the program accruing to the Exchequer were estimated by Brian Nolan.[5]

O'Donnell and Walsh first provided some general considerations on how the premium might be expected to operate, given the particular program design and the cyclical state of the economy over the lifetime of the program. Relating the highest weekly amount paid in premiums to the average weekly wage bill of manufacturing yields a reduction in average wage costs of only 0.4 percentage point. The authors conclude that the order of magnitude of the average wage cost reduction is such that the existence of the program is not likely to have had any measurable impact on a firm's level of output or prices.

In analyzing the available statistical records of the program, the authors focus on the industrial pattern of program uptake. Their main finding— supported by regression results—is that the program largely affected branches with strong output growth or low average earnings. These results are in line with prior expectations, since only expanding firms qualified

5. Rory O'Donnell and Brendan Walsh, *Survey of the Premium Employment Programme*, Memorandum Series of the Economic and Social Research Institute (Dublin, September 1979); Brian Nolan, "An Examination of the Premium Employment Programme," *Central Bank of Ireland Annual Report, 1978*, pp. 86–98.

for the subsidy; because of the flat-rate subsidy, firms with below-average earnings levels profited disproportionally from wage cost reduction.

O'Donnell and Walsh surveyed a sample of 100 participating firms and a comparison sample of 102 nonparticipating firms. Different, but closely interrelated, questionnaires were administered to the two samples. The sample of participating firms covered 16 percent of the firms in the program. The sample of nonparticipating firms was a judgmental sample chosen to control for size and industry, thus permitting comparisons between behavior of participating and nonparticipating firms.

In analyzing the results of the survey, O'Donnell and Walsh emphasize the following issues:

—What was the likely net impact of the scheme on employment and on hiring decisions in general?

—To what extent did narrow and complicated eligibility criteria hinder the achievement of the objectives of the scheme?

—What were the distributional effects on output growth?

One of the key questions to the participating firms was: "Did the existence of the premium employment program influence your hiring plans?" The distribution of firm responses was as follows:[6]

Response	Percent
No influence	46
Yes	54
"Brought forward hiring"	17
"Changed to full time"	5
"Hired more workers"	17
"Hired from the unemployed"	15

These answers, of course, may overstate the program's impact, since firms that obtained a subsidy may have felt some pressure to say the program did affect their behavior. Even so, almost half the respondents replied that the program had no influence. The 17 percent of firms that said they "hired more workers than they otherwise would have" represents, of course, the most interesting result. If one optimistically attributes all the subsidized employment of additional workers in these firms to the program and applies the proportion obtained from the survey to the total number of workers subsidized by the program, then 17 percent of the 8,157 affected employees, or 1,387, could be said to be the net increase in employment attributable to the program.

6. Respondents were free to mention more than one factor in replying to this question, but in fact only two firms did so. Both the latter mentioned "recruiting from the unemployed" in addition to "hiring more workers." The following tabulation does not include these two additional mentions of hiring from the unemployed.

However, bringing hiring forward, transferring part-time workers to full-time employment, and shifting recruitment toward the registered unemployed were equally important objectives of the scheme and must be considered along with the relatively small pure job-creating effect. Moreover, bringing hiring forward could be at least partly regarded as short-term job creation and should therefore be added to the pure job creation effect. Unfortunately, there is no information about how many hirings were brought forward and by how many months. Defining a short-term job as one that lasts at least six months and assuming—rather arbitrarily —that half of the "brought forward hiring" category represents jobs created six months earlier than otherwise (that is, without the subsidy) adds another 8 percent to the net employment effect and increases the net employment rate to 25 percent of the subsidized workers.[7]

The relatively small change in behavior by firms in response to the program is also apparent from the replies to another question: "Were all the additional workers hired during the period June 1975 to January 1977 eligible for the premium employment program?" A great majority of firms (78 percent) replied no; this suggests the rather limited extent to which employers were prepared to alter their hiring plans to qualify for the subsidy. However, 64 percent of the firms answering no—that is, those that hired "ineligible" workers—said they could not "get particular skills" from among the unemployed, and another 21 percent said they could not "get suitable workers" from among them. Therefore, part of the reason for the small change in hiring decisions may lie in the narrow eligibility criteria that had to be met to qualify for the subsidy.

In comparing the sample of participating and nonparticipating firms, O'Donnell and Walsh observe that the average level of employment increased by 17 percent in participating firms and decreased by 6 percent in nonparticipating firms over the period June 1975 to June 1977. Even so, employment rose in about 40 percent of nonparticipating firms; the obvious question, therefore, is why they did not also avail themselves of the subsidy. Thirty percent of those firms replied that they could not find particular skills from among the unemployed or that no suitable workers were available. Thirty-seven percent either did not know about the scheme or did not bother to find out if the workers they actually hired were eligible. Fourteen percent responded that the premiums were too small or

---

7. Throughout this paper the net employment rate is defined as the estimated number of genuinely created (or preserved) jobs as a fraction of the number of subsidized jobs. One hundred minus the net employment rate is defined as the displacement rate.

that there was "too much trouble" associated with applying for the scheme. These results confirm the earlier observation about the narrowly designed eligibility criteria and also suggest that ignorance of the program or of its precise details further diminished its impact.

As to the pattern of output growth, comparison between participating and nonparticipating firms reveals that the former produced relatively more for export than the latter. But the authors do not interpret this result as evidence that the program unduly subsidized and increased exports. Output and employment expansion in Ireland have traditionally been led by export growth, which implies that export industries will normally be overrepresented in the growth industries that alone qualify for the subsidy.

The evaluation of O'Donnell and Walsh has been complemented by Nolan, who estimated the net Exchequer costs of the program. He has calculated that the gain in revenue to the Exchequer resulting from the reemployment of a person receiving unemployment benefits is about £30 (£17 savings on unemployment benefits and £13 revenues in taxes), whereas the maximum premium is £15. This implies that if 50 percent of the premiums paid resulted in genuine job creation, the net cost of the program to the public treasury would be zero. Correspondingly, these net costs would be negative if the net employment rate were higher than 50 percent and positive if it were lower.

France

The French exemption of social security charges was available to private employers who hired workers or apprentices between July 1 and December 31, 1977. During that period the level of employment had to be at least maintained, and no dismissals for economic reasons were permitted. Therefore, even the firms that merely replaced workers lost through attrition could qualify for the subsidy. The exemption was applicable until July 1978, that is, for a maximum of one year (two years for apprentices). The exemption represented a reduction of about 35 percent in the wage costs of newly hired young workers and a reduction of about 25 percent in total labor costs. The scheme was targeted to school leavers and reentrants into the labor market after military service.

The exemption scheme was closely interlinked with two other schemes under which a lump-sum subsidy (90 percent of the minimum wage for young people over eighteen) was paid in favor of young workers hired by private firms for certain activities that would prepare them for normal employment. These activities provided either work experience outside a proper employment context (*stages pratiques*) or on-the-job training outside a proper apprenticeship context (*stages de formation*). The latter two schemes were not targeted on labor market entrants. All three schemes formed part of an administrative and political package, the first national employment pact. Only the exemption of social security charges strictly conforms to the definition of an employment subsidy; but for evaluative purposes—as will be further explained below—it was not possible to separate the "exemptions" from the *stages*.

The first pact was adopted to limit the increase of seasonal unemployment resulting from the large-scale inflow of school leavers into the labor market in the second half of 1977. The wide scope of the program and its application over a relatively short period make it quite different from the other subsidy programs discussed here. Furthermore, since the common attitude of demand management during that period was one of fiscal and monetary restraint, it was an interesting policy experiment to stimulate selectively the employment of a particularly vulnerable and structurally disfavored group—namely, youth—within a general context of economic restraint.

The first national pact has been evaluated by Jean-François Colin and Jean-Marc Espinasse, two researchers working with the Ministry of Labor.[8] Their evaluations are based on a statistical analysis of program and labor market data as well as on a qualitative review of the operation and effects of the program derived from interviews with local program administrators. In addition, Colin and Espinasse sought to simulate the effects of the program, using a macroeconomic model. They focused on the following questions:

—What were the net effects on employment and unemployment?

—What factors explained the industrial and regional distribution of take-up?

—What were the effects of the program on the subsidized and non-subsidized workers?

—What was the macroeconomic effect of the fiscal stimulus created by the program?

Net effects on employment and unemployment. Colin and Espinasse estimated the net employment effect of the exemptions by comparing the actual outflow from the unemployment rolls during the second half of

8. Jean-François Colin and Jean-Marc Espinasse, "Les Subventions à l'Emploi," *Travail et Emploi* (June 1979).

1977 with the outflow that would have been expected without the national employment pact. The authors first tried to estimate a regression relationship by using several cyclical variables as independent variables to explain the normal outflows from unemployment during the six-month period. Unfortunately, the results were disappointing. Since prima facie evidence suggested a declining trend of outflows over a number of years, the authors finally fitted an exponential time trend covering the period July 1974 to June 1977. On the basis of that, they estimated the creation of 19,400 jobs.[9] But if it were assumed that the outflow in the second half of 1977 was the same as in 1976, the job creation effect of the exemptions was estimated as 81,700. The authors believed that these two estimates spanned the lower and upper limits of the net employment effect of the exemptions. In relation to the total number of workers affected by the exemptions the estimated net employment rate ranged from 7 to 30 percent.

Conceptually, it would have been easier to limit the estimate of net employment effects to the exemptions, which are employment subsidies in the true sense. But the authors observed a high degree of substitutability between the different provisions of the pact, notably between the exemptions and the *stages pratiques*. Since the take-up at local level often depended on the preference of the individual program administrator for one or the other of the two schemes, Colin and Espinasse concluded that they should also consider the job creation effect of the *stages pratiques*. The *stages* were jobs for which the government paid almost 100 percent of the cost, and firms were not obliged to keep the workers after the program expired. These were obviously very favorable conditions, and it seems reasonable to assume, therefore, that workers hired under this program were truly "additional" ones. But from extensive interviews, the authors concluded that one-third to two-thirds of the participants would have been offered regular jobs without the program, and they assumed that only the remaining two-thirds to one-third of the *stages pratiques* were newly created jobs. Adding in these jobs gave a range for the net employment effect of 50,000 to 140,000 jobs, that is, a net employment rate of between 15 and 40 percent. To obtain the total estimated reduction of (recorded and nonrecorded) unemployment, the authors also included the persons participating in the *stages de formation*. This yielded an estimated reduction in unemployment of between 100,000 and 200,000 workers.

These results are supported by two other studies. The Diréction de la

9. The procedure requires a number of statistical adjustments and complementary estimates that are not reported here.

Prévision, a government agency, has estimated (in an unpublished study) that the net effect of the national employment pact on the reduction of unemployment amounted to between 100,000 and 120,000 young workers. The national statistical office estimated an additional cancellation of 100,000 young job seekers at the employment exchanges between August and December 1977 and assumed this to be the net impact of the national employment pact. All these studies agreed that the *stages* had a great effect on unemployment, whereas the exemptions had little.

Industrial and regional distribution of take-up. Colin and Espinasse also undertook a detailed econometric study of the sectoral and regional variations of the take-up rate (defined as persons affected per persons employed in the respective industry or region). The most important results were the following:

—The subsidy was in general used not by growth industries but by rather small industries with high staff turnover and relatively low earning levels.

—The subsidy was used mostly in depressed regions where there is little industrialization.

—If local labor markets were particularly sluggish, *stages de formation* were mainly adopted; if labor markets were reasonably tight, the exemptions were mainly adopted.

Colin and Espinasse also attempted to estimate the net employment effect of the program on a cross-sectional basis, using the variance in the take-up rate among twenty-one regions as the independent variable. The results, however, were not satisfactory.

Effects on workers. Since the program was targeted on youth, it is relevant to ask whether the employment opportunities of adult workers were reduced. Colin and Espinasse examined this question on a cross-sectional basis by comparing program take-up and outflow of adult workers from the unemployed rolls at regional levels. They found no significant correlation between the two and therefore rejected the hypothesis of displacement in hirings between subsidized youth and nonsubsidized adults.

One objective of the national employment pact was to improve the stability and quality of employment for young workers. But Colin and Espinasse argue that the pact may have had the opposite effect, largely because of the *stages pratiques*. From indirect evidence and discussions with program managers, they found that many *stages pratiques* may have replaced normal hirings and regular contracts. The latter protect the worker through both legal and collective bargaining provisions. By contrast, the institution of the *stages pratiques* gives the employer considerable discretionary power over the worker. These observations are supported by the empirical findings noted earlier, which suggest that the main take-up of the scheme occurred in small enterprises in the tertiary sector, characterized by a large proportion of relatively low wage earners and high labor turnover—all typical features of secondary jobs in a dual labor market. The authors, therefore, argue that, despite the large number of young workers affected, the pact may, in the final analysis, have made it more difficult for youth to become regularly employed.

Macroeconomic effects and net budgetary costs. The estimation of net budgetary effects was achieved by simulating the effects of the various additional public expenditure or forgone revenues resulting from the pact on a macroeconomic model used for short-term forecasting by the French authorities. This method allowed Colin and Espinasse to estimate the backflow of public revenues and thus the net costs of the program. But when the study was carried out, the final fiscal data were not yet available. Since then, it has become apparent that the gross costs of the pact were substantially higher (5 billion francs) than assumed earlier (3 billion francs). The macroeconomic simulations by Colin and Espinasse are therefore now of limited value. Nevertheless, the simulations suggest that the net costs amounted to 80 percent of the gross costs, a relationship that may hold for a higher absolute amount of gross costs as well. The main reason for the relatively low gross-net difference was the weak backflow of taxes from young workers. The simulations also showed a deterioration of the current account of the balance of payments (mainly because of higher imports arising from the stimulus to private consumption) and no inflation-accelerating effect. In fact, they indicated a slight reduction of overall prices.

Other Countries

Like the Irish evaluation, the Swedish study by Petersson and Vlachos and the British study by the *Department of Employment Gazette* relied on survey data from participating firms.[10] Except in regard to the British temporary employment subsidy, participating firms were specifically asked whether they had actually changed their behavior as a result of the subsidy. For the British small firms employment subsidy, a control group approach was used in addition to the questionnaire approach.

10. Jan Petersson and Vassilis Vlachos, *En granskning av utbildningsbidraget för permitteringshotade (25/15-kronan)* (Economics Institute of the University of Lund, October 1978); *U.K. Department of Employment Gazette,* July 1977, March 1978, May 1978.

The German study by Günther Schmid was like the French one in that regression models were used to measure the net effect by estimating what would have happened without the scheme.[11] Whereas the French study used time series data, Schmid relied on a cross-sectional analysis covering eligible and noneligible regional labor market units (defined by the jurisdiction of local employment service agencies).

None of these studies presented much information on the distributional effects and price effects of the various subsidies. In each study, however, some attempt was made to estimate the net effect on employment and budget costs. For the British temporary employment subsidy, only displacement resulting from the increased sales of subsidized firms was estimated. In the study of the British small firms subsidy and in the Swedish and Irish studies, the main emphasis was on possible windfall effects accruing to subsidized firms. As for the German study, in comparing employment growth in eligible and noneligible regions (and controlling for other influence), Schmid tried to estimate a more global net employment effect than just the behavior responses of participating firms. If his estimation techniques had been reliable, he would, in principle, have captured several types of displacement, including output displacement *within* eligible regions (not, however, output displacement between eligible and noneligible regions). The French study attempted to capture the net effect of the subsidy on the employment (and unemployment) of the total target group (youth); that is, to account for possible types of displacement of nonsubsidized members by subsidized members of the target group. The net effects of the Swedish scheme were especially hard to estimate. The number of (training) hours that qualified for subsidization was calculated from the number of persons threatened by dismissal. But since this approved number of subsidized hours could be spread over any desired number of workers in the firm, it was difficult to estimate the number of jobs actually preserved by the subsidy.

Critical Comments on the Estimated Net Employment Effects

Although the available evaluations have generated a wealth of useful peripheral information and data on the programs, not much progress has been made in achieving reliable results on the core questions: the actual

11. Günther Schmid, "The Impact of Selective Employment Policy: The Case of a Wage-Cost Subsidy Scheme in Germany, 1974–75," *Journal of Industrial Economics*, vol. 27 (June 1979), pp. 339–58.

net impact of the programs on employment, prices, and output. Since the overriding objective of all employment subsidy schemes is to raise or protect levels of employment, the most straightforward way to evaluate their effectiveness is to count the number of genuinely created or preserved jobs. For all six programs evaluated, some tentative estimate of this net effect on employment was undertaken (or can be derived from the findings). Expressing the estimated number of genuinely created jobs as a fraction of the total number of subsidized jobs suggests a range of 15 to 40 percent for the job creation subsidies of Ireland, West Germany, and France and the British small firms subsidy.[12] For the redundancy-deferring Swedish scheme and the British temporary employment subsidy, the estimates of the net impact are somewhat higher, but their underlying assumptions and methodologies are so weak that the available results must be regarded as more or less useless.

As mentioned before, in the French and West German studies the authors used regression techniques to derive statistical estimates, whereas the other evaluations were based on enterprise surveys. Neither the cross-sectional estimates for West Germany nor the time series analyses for France provided statistically powerful results. For example, the exponential time trend that Colin and Espinasse were finally forced to use can be regarded only as an unsatisfactory substitute for a behavioral model. The net employment effect derived from this time trend is the lower limit of the authors' estimate. The upper limit is based on the even more tenuous assumption that the normal outflow of 1977 might have been the same as in the previous year.

Most of the survey-based evaluations rely on responses from participating firms to the question of how much they actually changed their behavior (hired more workers or deferred redundancies). The reliability of responses to that question must be low if eligibility depends on such a change of behavior. Under employment protection schemes, for instance, firms qualify only if they can provide some proof that without the subsidy they would be compelled to lay off workers. If, on the other hand, a change of employment measured against a certain base level is the criterion for qualifying,[13] then there might be some justification for asking firms how

12. Although the estimated results were surprisingly close in most countries, this similarity must not be overvalued, since the underlying estimation methods varied, implying that different types of displacement were estimated in the different countries.

13. The base level may be below 100 percent of the level at the inception of the scheme, in which case the scheme is having the effect of both protecting existing jobs and inducing job creation.

much they changed their behavior to qualify for or to maximize receipt of the subsidy.[14] In this situation, firms may still feel some pressure to say the scheme did affect their behavior, but the bias will probably be much smaller than when they are virtually asked whether or not they violated the rules of the program to qualify for the subsidy.

For these reasons, a direct question on firms' behavior may have been justified for the Irish scheme and the U.K. small firms subsidy, but not at all for the redundancy-deferring schemes. Indeed, the question was deliberately not included in the U.K. questionnaire on the temporary employment subsidy. But the Swedish survey did include such a question, so that the reliability of the derived employment estimates must be regarded as particularly weak.

The evaluations of the Irish scheme and the U.K. small firms subsidy both used comparison groups. Unfortunately, in the Irish study, one of the nonmatched characteristics of the samples of participating and non-participating firms—employment growth—is one of the most important. To make relevant comparisons between the two samples, one would have needed to include in the sample of nonparticipants only firms that increased their employment without claiming the subsidy.[15] This latter approach was adopted in the U.K. survey, where the comparison group consisted of firms with rising employment (and with some other characteristics identical to those of participating firms) that were outside the assisted areas to which the program was targeted. Employment growth in the participating firms could then be compared with the natural employment growth in the nonparticipating firms, which provided a cross-check of the estimated net employment effect derived from the direct question to participating firms about their actual change of behavior. Such cross-checking was not possible in the comparison group design of the Irish survey.

14. Note, however, that in the West German scheme, besides demonstrating that the work force had increased, the employer also had to certify that (a) without the subsidy the worker would not have been hired and (b) the newly created jobs were permanent.

15. Ideally, however, one should compare the participating firms with *potentially* growing firms; that is, include those firms in the control group with stable employment as well as the tiny fraction of the declining firms for which a switch from contraction to expansion might have been an advantageous choice. Ashenfelter has shown that this latter "opting-in employment growth" depends on the size of the subsidy and the demand for labor elasticity. Orley Ashenfelter, "Evaluating the Effects of the Employment Tax Credit," *Conference Report on Evaluating the 1977 Economic Stimulus Package* (U.S. Department of Labor, 1978), pp. 1–14.

A final comment relates to the number of firms or number of jobs to be derived from survey results. Both the Irish enterprise survey and the U.K. survey on the effect of the temporary subsidy provide information only about the number of firms that can be put into categories such as "brought forward hirings" or "increased output at the expense of competitors." This, obviously, does not mean that the same proportion of subsidized jobs would fall into these categories. Yet that assumption was made in estimating the net employment impact, on the tenuous assumption that all subsidized jobs in the categorized firms have been (according to the above examples) "brought forward" or "maintained at the expense of competing firms."

By contrast, in the Swedish survey and the U.K. survey on the small firms subsidy, firms were asked to categorize subsidized workers according to whether or not they had been hired or maintained because of a change in the firm's policy. Although this approach is methodologically more appealing, the risk of biased replies is probably greater. In general, firms are more reluctant to respond the more precise and "policing" the question is. Moreover, many firms find it difficult, if not impossible, to distinguish neatly between the number of subsidized workers that they would have hired (or maintained) anyhow and the number of induced hirings (or hoardings).

How Evaluations Could Be Improved

Ideally an evaluation strategy should be developed from a theoretical and, if appropriate, empirical model describing how a given program can be expected to operate. It is therefore almost impossible to suggest a research strategy that would fit all six kinds of subsidy programs discussed in this paper. The following comments refer only to a few major elements that should be considered in future evaluations. Since the observations relate to types of subsidies that have so far not been experienced in the United States, some positive feedback on the evaluation research and future program design in the United States might emerge. However, with regard to technical and financial means, European evaluations will probably continue to be severely constrained. Thus there is not much point in developing elaborate research strategies for which the essential base is missing. For example, experiments in which a set of firms would be randomly assigned to treatment and control groups—now a widely used research tool in the United States—would be regarded as prohibitively expensive in most European countries.

Basically the same considerations would tend to rule out the use of general equilibrium or disequilibrium models to simulate the likely effect of a subsidy program. Such models would need to be highly disaggregated to fit the characteristics of the program,[16] but the rapidly changing policy environment and the need to adjust programs accordingly would probably result in a modeling effort that would still not meet actual needs. In addition, current macroeconomic models are useful for simulation purposes only when a program has a strong fiscal impact.

Against this background, program evaluations in Europe can at best be partial impact evaluations. But even to achieve a modest evaluation objective, major improvements are needed. In order to identify a reasonable set of evaluation objectives, it is useful to start with a theoretical perspective of how employment subsidies work.

A Theoretical Perspective

From a microeconomic perspective there are two ways in which the demand for labor may rise as a response to a marginal employment subsidy: (1) a *factor substitution effect* may occur as the price of labor is reduced relative to the price of other factors, notably capital; and (2) a *scale effect* may occur as employers pass on the decreased labor costs by reducing output prices, which in turn will increase sales and, subsequently, employment. However, casual examination of ex post employment data for firms that availed themselves of the subsidy does not indicate whether employers actually changed their behavior in the described ways—that is, substituted labor for other factors of production or decreased prices to expand output. They may simply have used the subsidy to finance hirings or hoardings in which they would have engaged anyhow. A first important requirement for estimating the real impact of a wage subsidy on employment,

16. For a proposal of such an equilibrium model, see Richard Layard, "The Costs and Benefits of Selective Employment Measures: The British Case," in *European Labor Market Policies*, pp. 99–138. Even this elaborate model, if it could be specified, would consider only the possible scale effects (expansion of output and employment resulting from subsidy-induced price reductions) and would ignore the substitution effects (subsidy-induced increase in labor input to produce a given output).

therefore, is to determine the extent of such financial displacement or windfall effects.

If labor supply is not infinitely elastic, some of the additional demand for labor will result in higher wages instead of higher employment. This wage offset will depend partially on the aggregate demand for labor and the level of unemployment when the program is introduced. It will also depend on the particular group to which the program is targeted. The Irish and German schemes were targeted to the long-term unemployed; the Swedish scheme and the two British ones were flat-rate subsidies largely affecting low-paid workers. The French scheme was targeted on young people seeking their first jobs. Only under the French scheme would one expect a relatively inelastic labor supply and hence an upward shift in wages. If, however, one assumes that the French minimum wage exceeds the market wage for young people, which seems plausible for part of that group, then there may have been little upward pressure on wages. Therefore, although a completely elastic labor supply certainly did not prevail in all cases, it can be assumed that short-term wage adjustments to the upward shift in labor demand have probably been negligible in the six programs reviewed and can be disregarded.[17]

If one leaves aside these possible countervailing labor supply effects, can the microeconomic demand effects be added up over the total economy? In principle, factor substitution effects could be added up, *provided* that the subsidy is not targeted to particular categories of the labor force.[18] If it is so targeted, one must also ask whether substitution between targeted labor and nontargeted labor inputs has taken place. The second important empirical task, therefore, consists of forming a view about possible labor market *displacement* in case of a categorical subsidy. As mentioned earlier, all the schemes under review were targeted explicitly or implicitly to particular types of labor. Labor market displacement also includes the possible increase in job opportunities for some members of the target group at the expense of other members. It is therefore relevant to establish whether displacement of other workers within and outside the target group has occurred.

17. Over the longer term, wage adjustments might become more important and thus gradually erode the employment effect. However, since the emphasis is on anticyclical programs and results, these longer-term effects can be neglected.

18. This consideration disregards possible negative effects on the demand for labor caused by the financing of the subsidy and reduced investments.

The microeconomic scale effects also cannot be added up over the whole economy, because an individual employer may be able to increase sales only at the expense of noneligible or ignorant or unwilling competitors. Thus a third task is to estimate the extent to which output *displacement* between subsidized and nonsubsidized (domestic and foreign) firms occurred. One might argue that, unless real aggregate demand increases, all microeconomic scale effects are bound to add up to zero, particularly if foreign competitors are included. But for at least two reasons that argument may not hold.

1. The relative price of labor-intensive goods will decrease and that of capital-intensive goods will increase, so that a given level of aggregate demand is likely to shift toward greater consumption of labor-intensive goods. The derived demand for labor will therefore rise even if the level of demand for goods and services remains constant.

2. If the overall prices fall because of the stiffer price competition resulting from the subsidy, a given level of nominal demand will buy more goods and services, thus increasing output and employment.

Ashenfelter has argued that it is necessary to adjust not only for the three common kinds of displacement (financial, labor market, and output), but also for intertemporal displacement: jobs may be created during the period of subsidization, but at the expense of decreased employment later.[19] However, a temporary scheme is bound to lead to reverse effects as soon as subsidization discontinues, since relative factor prices and marginal costs revert to their presubsidy level. A temporary program should therefore be judged on its short-term employment effects and not on its success or failure in creating (or maintaining) permanent jobs. Obviously, the creation of permanent jobs is the ultimate aim, but that will happen only if further changes occur in the economic environment like improved general demand conditions or a rise in the productivity of the newly hired (or maintained) workers. Thus the creation (or maintenance) of permanent jobs should be viewed as an additional, but not primary, criterion of evaluation. Then even brought forward hirings should be at least partly included among the newly created jobs, since one of the objectives of anticyclical subsidy programs is to bring forward hirings and to shorten (or reverse) the time lag between output and employment recovery.

19. Orley Ashenfelter, "Evaluating the Effects of the Employment Tax Credit," p. 9.

It is important to keep in mind that even if at the micro level employers do not alter their hiring or hoarding behavior, a program may still have a positive macroeconomic employment effect. For instance, a 100 percent financial displacement could still improve employment, since higher liquidity would stimulate new investments. To assess the total impact on employment, one must estimate the multiplier effects of the change in the fiscal deficit on incomes, demand, and employment. Such an exercise would require a simulation with a large-scale macro model, and the numerical solutions would probably depend on the existing structure of the model. But if the scheme is small relative to the total economy (like the Irish, West German, and U.K. small firms schemes), such general equilibrium repercussions are not very important.

Other Target Variables for Evaluation

So far, I have emphasized the core question: the actual impact of the subsidy on employment. But other variables, like output and prices, are affected by the subsidy, and they, too, are policy targets. In evaluating a subsidy program, therefore, one may also need to assess its effects on the rate of inflation and on total output growth. Since some subsidized firms are likely to produce for exports or compete with imports, the trade balance effect would be relevant as well.

Apart from these impacts on the macro variables of the economy, subsidies—by changing relative factor prices—will have important distributional effects on employment (in favor of target groups) and output (in favor of labor-intensive products).

Finally, some peripheral (though policy-relevant) effects must be considered in an overall evaluation strategy, such as: a thorough analysis of the take-up rates and their distribution across firms and regions; the impact of cyclical parameters on both the take-up rates of employers and their actual behavioral changes in making hiring decisions; the effects of the subsidy on job stability and on future or alternative employment opportunities for subsidized workers; possible repercussions on collective bargaining; and effects on labor force participation that might generate a wedge between employment and unemployment behavior.

Since this is a fairly broad menu, a detailed discussion is beyond the scope of this paper. I therefore focus only on a few issues that seem particularly relevant to the improvement and extension of evaluation studies, bearing in mind the constraints on data and intellectual and financial resources that are likely to persist in Europe.

A Strategy for Evaluation

A straightforward evaluation strategy would start with a detailed analysis of micro data from participating firms and affected workers. In particular, the analysis of data from these firms would shed light on several important economic and administrative aspects of the subsidy in operation. What kind of firms (their size, labor intensity, product mix, market power, export intensity, location, and so forth) availed themselves of the subsidy the most? The French study, for instance, identified a strong regional dispersion in the take-up rate of the subsidy that can be explained only partly by the variation in industry mix or demand pressure; therefore, the administrative procedures adapted in different areas to implement the program probably had a strong influence. In West Germany, by contrast, the subsidy was largely taken up by the construction industry; the coincidence of the subsidization period with that of normal seasonal employment growth suggests that the industry made major windfall gains. The two redundancy-deferring subsidies, the Swedish employment maintenance and training scheme and the U.K. temporary employment subsidy, overwhelmingly affected industries like textiles, clothing, pulp and paper, and steel that suffer from severe international market pressure, either because of slackening world demand or because of competition from new sources of international supply, or both. Thus output and employment in those industries were probably maintained at the expense of foreign output and workers.

It would be relatively easy to extend this kind of analysis by collecting more comprehensive data from participating firms, to facilitate, in particular, cross classifications of firms' characteristics and types of subsidized workers. An analysis based on such data could help explain why firms decide to participate in the program. The evidence would, however, be indirect.

To obtain a direct answer to the question why some firms participate, one should compare a randomly chosen group of participating firms with a group of randomly chosen nonparticipating, but eligible, firms. Differences in characteristics other than eligibility criteria could then be identified as having an impact on decisions to participate or not. But a simple statistical exercise based on existing statistical records would probably not be sufficient. Firms in the two groups would need to be surveyed to determine the relative importance of such factors as administrative complications, knowledge of the scheme, and availability and suitability of target group workers.

The next step would be to estimate how much participating firms changed their hiring (or hoarding) decisions in response to the subsidy. This is, of course, the same thing as estimating financial displacement or windfall effects, as described earlier. Here again a randomly selected control group of nonparticipating firms could be of value. If this is not possible, a comparison sample of nonparticipating firms, which presumably had the same characteristics as participating firms, could be selected. Such an approach would create some formidable technical problems. The danger of a self-selection bias accounting for differences between the participant and comparison groups is obvious. That is, firms that use the subsidy may differ in systematic ways from firms that do not, so differences in their behavior may stem from differences in their underlying characteristics, not from their participation or nonparticipation in the program.

The earlier discussion of the (appropriate) comparison group approach adopted for evaluating the U.K. small firms employment subsidy and the (inappropriate)[20] approach adopted for evaluation of the Irish scheme showed the difficulties of avoiding a systematic bias in the comparison group selection. For job creation subsidies the comparison group should consist only of actually or potentially growing firms; for a redundancy-deferring subsidy the comparison group should consist only of firms that are actually or potentially shedding labor. In that way actual employment growth or employment maintenance in participating firms can be compared with "natural" growth or maintenance in nonparticipating firms. But the conditions for a "natural experiment," like the one adopted for the U.K. small firms subsidy, are not always present.[21] It would therefore be more satisfactory to replicate an experimental setting

20. The approach was inappropriate for estimating the net employment effect of the program.

21. Perloff and Wachter also used this approach for evaluating the new jobs tax credit in the United States; they compared participating firms and firms that were eligible but ignorant about the existence of the subsidy. Jeffrey M. Perloff and Michael L. Wachter, "The New Jobs Tax Credit: An Evaluation of the 1977–78 Wage Subsidy Program," *American Economic Review,* vol. 69 (May 1979, *Papers and Proceedings, 1978*), pp. 173–79.

and randomly assign eligible firms to a treatment or control group. Comparisons between participating and nonparticipating firms in the treatment group would shed light on the reasons for participation and nonparticipation; comparisons between the participating firms in the treatment group and the potentially participating firms in the control group would shed light on the net employment impact of the subsidy. As mentioned before, however, both the experience and availability of resources for carrying out formal experiments in the social sciences are lacking in Europe.

Realistically, therefore, ex post evaluations based on comparisons between participating and nonparticipating firms appear to be the most feasible approach for future evaluations in Europe. All relevant information, however, will not be available from existing statistical records. The required data will have to be collected through sample surveys, which raises important, but manageable, technical problems about the appropriateness of sample designs, the adequacy of sample sizes, and the possibilities for bias arising from nonresponse.

A survey administered to a sample of eligible firms would generate relevant cross-sectional data. Employment growth could then be regressed against a number of independent variables, one of which would be participation or nonparticipation in the program. The survey could also include a direct question to the participating firms within the sample about their actual change in employment behavior. Provided the change in behavior was not a condition for qualifying for the subsidy, replies to this question might produce some—though rather weak—evidence corroborating the results of the regression analysis.

Longitudinal data might also be collected from participating firms and be used for modeling the firms' behavioral responses to the subsidy. The reliability of such data would be suspect, however, since firms would have to be asked *retrospectively* about their employment and other factors that prevailed before the inception of the scheme.

The net employment impact estimated from micro data of firms will present an overoptimistic picture because of likely labor market and output displacement. Some displacement effects could be captured by estimating industry-specific employment functions (intraindustry output displacement) and employment and unemployment functions for the target groups (labor market displacement within the target group). For both estimates a new and extensive data base would be needed. And the results would provide at best a partial answer, since not all displacement effects over the total national economy and over foreign economies would be captured.[22] Given these difficulties, as well as the previously mentioned problems with developing general and disaggregated equilibrium models or using existing macro models, one usually has to limit the examination of labor market and output displacement to casual evidence gauged from firm-specific micro data.

In this context it is relevant to note that the likelihood of labor force displacement will vary greatly among types of schemes. For the marginal stock subsidies discussed in this paper, as distinct from hiring subsidies, the risk will be relatively small. Under the former, if a firm were to hire two eligible workers and fire one noneligible worker, it would still receive a subsidy for only one eligible worker; therefore such firing would be discouraged. If an employed worker moves from a noneligible firm or area to an eligible firm or area, there is no reason to assume that his former job will remain vacant (provided labor supply is elastic). Moreover, most of the European schemes required that the target worker be chosen from the unemployment rolls (or, in fact, be long-term unemployed).[23] Only the French scheme provided considerable risk of labor market displacement in that workers lost through attrition could be replaced by target workers, for whom firms would receive a subsidy without a net increase in their total work force.

By far the most important and difficult task is to come to grips with possible output displacement both nationally and—since the evaluation should preferably be one for the total community of trading countries—internationally. For international displacement, some indirect but nonquantifiable evidence could be derived from knowing whether participating firms produced mainly traded or nontraded goods. Some indirect evidence about domestic output displacement could be gained from the estimation of price effects in the participating firms. In addition, questionnaires could be used to ask participating firms directly how many subsidized workers they employed on production for sale and how many on other activities (production for stock, maintenance and repair work, and

22. Although foreign output displacement may not matter or in fact be regarded as desirable from a national point of view, one must not neglect the beggar-my-neighbor aspect. Moreover, if a supranational economic entity, for instance the OECD area, is viewed as a whole, output displacement among member countries needs to be treated exactly like domestic output displacement.

23. This is not to say that even with marginal stock subsidies important redistributional effect on employment might occur. Subsidized targeted workers might be hired (or maintained) at the expense of nontargeted workers who would have been hired (or maintained) if there had been no scheme.

so forth). Firms could also be asked whether sales had been gained at the expense of domestic or foreign competition.

Both these questions were included in the enterprise survey for the U.K. temporary employment subsidy. As many as 30 percent of the firms reported that their sales were "mostly" gained at the expense of other firms. A more rigorous estimation could be carried out only by specifying demand and supply functions for individual industries or firms.

Summary and Conclusions

This paper has reviewed European evaluations of six temporary employment subsidies—four job creation subsidy schemes (Ireland, France, Germany, United Kingdom) and two redundancy-deferring schemes (Sweden, United Kingdom)—that varied considerably in design, implementation, and control. The evaluations, it was found, used a variety of approaches, lacked relevant data, and applied simplistic evaluation techniques.

Evaluation research in Europe will probably continue to be severely constrained for several reasons: the lack of relevant data for undertaking major modeling efforts to predict the general equilibrium repercussions of the subsidy programs; the lack of resources for replicating an experimental setting to examine the effects of the subsidy; and the lack of political and academic support and of interest in evaluation research. Against this background, program evaluations in Europe can at best be partial impact evaluations, so that it appears feasible to set only modest evaluation objectives.

I have proposed that future evaluations extend the base of micro data from participating and nonparticipating firms and focus on the following questions:

—What made eligible firms decide to participate, or not participate, in the program?

—To what extent have participating firms actually changed their hiring, or hoarding, decisions? (This question is identical with the assessment of windfall gains accruing to firms that would have hired or hoarded the subsidized workers anyhow.)

—What casual evidence can be obtained from micro data about labor market and output (both national and international) displacement?

Not included here are possible wage adjustments that would reduce the total net employment impact, or multiplier effects that would increase it. Short-term wage adjustments are assumed to be small because of the large-scale cyclical unemployment prevailing in Europe and above-average supply elasticities of target workers. Multiplier effects are neglected because of the small size of most of the European schemes relative to the total economy.

Evaluation objectives other than employment effects could partly be achieved by analyzing micro data on prices and output in matched samples of participating and nonparticipating firms. This, however, would result in measuring only partial effects and would not provide conclusive results on the overall impact of the subsidy on the rate of inflation and the growth of output.

Comments by Robert J. Flanagan

The paper by Peter Schwanse gives us a taste of the substantive findings of several evaluations of European wage subsidy programs and provides a critical review of the evaluation procedures used in the studies, along with suggestions for their improvement. He covers considerable ground and sensibly focuses on issues of evaluation methodology raised by the European studies. Although much of his criticism is well taken, he might have gone further in isolating issues that are missing from those studies.

The most striking feature of the evaluations reviewed by Schwanse is the gap between the questions they address and the issues raised at the conference about the microeconomic workings of a wage subsidy program. Many of the issues that have been emphasized by the theoretical papers are not addressed in either the European studies or Schwanse's critique. The following issues are particularly important.

—*Choice of target groups.* Authors of other papers and comments in this volume have recognized that the employment and price effects of a wage subsidy program on the target group will depend on the underlying labor market behavior generating the unemployment experienced by the group. Indeed, the selection of target groups ought to be based on such analyses if the effects of the program on employment and unemployment are to be maximized. Conversely, the actual employment effects, even by the measures used in some of these studies, will be related to the care with which the target groups are selected. The European studies do not appear to deal with this issue, or with the question of adverse signaling because of the breadth of targeting selected.

—*Net employment gain.* Schwanse indicates that this is the issue most frequently addressed in the European studies. The treatment is at a high level of aggregation, however, and apparently no effort is made to trace the micro adjustments underlying the macro results. In criticizing these studies, Schwanse does not give enough emphasis to the importance of estimating the impact of the program on targeted and untargeted groups.

—*Unemployment impact.* This issue requires an analysis of the combined effects of a wage subsidy program on employment and labor force participation decisions. In general, the effects of the programs on the allocation of labor between market and nonmarket activities have received scant attention in either the European evaluation studies or Schwanse's critical review. Whether the programs are structural or, as is more common in Europe, countercyclical, the labor supply responses to the program will influence measured unemployment and ought to be included in a general cost-benefit appraisal of a wage subsidy.

—*Cyclical variability of employment and unemployment effects of the program.* In their paper Burdett and Hool suggested ways in which the impact of a program could vary cyclically. Some of the variation in program impact across countries, therefore, could be related to the timing of a program with respect to general economic conditions. This factor is not mentioned by Schwanse and apparently was not considered in the evaluation studies.

—*Market structure variability of impact.* Others have pointed out the particular importance of wage subsidy programs for employment expansion in the export sector, where the world price can be taken as given. Thus market structure may influence both the incentive to participate and the size of the employment or price effects. This factor has apparently been given little consideration in the evaluations of European programs, even though the relative size of the export sector is greater in Europe than in the United States.

Finally, I have a suggestion not directly related to the issue of evaluation. There needs to be discussion of issues relating to the "political economy" of these subsidy programs. For example, why does the scale of these programs vary across countries? What are the trade-offs that must be made to pass these programs in various countries? Why do certain institutions (notably the unions) find wage subsidy programs more acceptable in some countries than in others? These questions are very different from the questions of evaluation methodology that Schwanse addressed and are perhaps the subject of another paper. But they are natural questions to consider in a study across countries.

Comments by George J. Carcagno

Peter Schwanse has provided interesting information about six employment subsidy schemes that have been tried in five European countries. As he makes abundantly clear, the evaluations of these programs were of generally poor quality, so that few firm conclusions can be drawn about their impact. The finding that only between 15 and 40 percent of the subsidized jobs represented new job creation, with the remainder of the subsidies going to support hires that would have occurred anyway, is sobering, because that finding was based on questions that directly asked employers whether or not the subsidy influenced their hiring decisions. Given that such questions are likely to yield upwardly biased responses, one can only hope that future evaluations will be better designed to determine the impact of such programs.

Schwanse correctly points out that the ideal evaluation would use an experimental setting within which firms could be randomly assigned to treatment and control groups. He goes on to suggest this is too expensive a research strategy to follow. Though it is true that the major social experiments conducted in the United States have been expensive, many relatively low cost studies have been conducted by the experimental method. Indeed, there is no reason why random assignment should use substantially more research resources than a carefully thought out comparison group approach. The real problem may lie in the process of random assignment and in its acceptability (or lack of it) as a mechanism for establishing program eligibility rather than in its cost. That is, possible political objections to randomization may make it infeasible.

Even with an experimental methodology it will be necessary to conduct surveys of firms. Survey research is a demanding field, a fact unappreciated by many researchers. The quality of the survey data reported in Schwanse's paper bears testimony to that.

The biasing nature of a direct question about whether the subsidy influenced hiring is noted by Schwanse. There were other problems as well. In the Irish evaluation, data on the number of hires in the firms surveyed were apparently not collected. As a consequence, to estimate the number of jobs created by the scheme, the researchers applied the percentage of *firms* that reported they hired more workers to the total number of subsidized *workers*. In the same study, employers were asked, "Were all the additional workers hired . . . eligible for the . . . program?" This question could result in an affirmative response only when 100 percent of hires were eligible. It thus yields only the upper limit, not an estimate of the percentage distribution of eligibility. What was surprising was not that 78 percent of the firms said no, but that 22 percent said yes.

Schwanse seems overpessimistic about the use of longitudinal data on the grounds that they would have to be acquired retrospectively. Although existing records of past hirings and terminations could be used, one could also imagine a strategy whereby a sample of firms was selected and followed over time. Current data could then be obtained on a regular basis, which would eliminate the need for gaining access to records of past employment actions.

A preferred evaluation strategy would be to use an experimental methodology in a regional setting. Employers in a given region would be randomly assigned to experimental or control groups. Data would then be obtained through periodic surveys of employers. If random assignment proves infeasible, then an approach similar to the one used in the evaluation of the U.K. small firms employment subsidy would be second best. That approach involves using a comparison group selected from a matched sample of firms in areas where the subsidy is not available. If the subsidy is national in scope, ex post selection of a comparison group is the only feasible alternative, though the selectivity bias problems noted by Schwanse must be dealt with. In any case, none of these approaches will have a substantial payoff unless care is taken in the design of the samples and in the development of the survey instruments.

Conference Participants

with their affiliations at the time of the conference

Orley C. Ashenfelter *Princeton University*

Michael C. Barth *U.S. Department of Health, Education, and Welfare*

David M. Betson *Institute for Research on Poverty*

John H. Bishop *Institute for Research on Poverty*

Kenneth Burdett *University of Wisconsin*

George J. Carcagno *Mathematica Policy Research*

Walter S. Corson *Mathematica Policy Research*

Larry Dildine *U.S. Treasury Department*

Robert Eisner *Northwestern University*

Robert J. Flanagan *Stanford University*

Robert H. Haveman *University of Wisconsin*

Ronald Hoffman *U.S. Treasury Department*

Bryce Hool *State University of New York (Stonybrook)*

George E. Johnson *University of Michigan*

Robert I. Lerman *U.S. Department of Labor*

Frank Levy *Urban Institute*

Karl-Gustaf Löfgren *University of Wisconsin*

Donald A. Nichols *University of Wisconsin*

David O'Neill *General Accounting Office*

John L. Palmer *U.S. Department of Health, Education, and Welfare*

Jeffrey M. Perloff *University of Pennsylvania*

Gosta Rehn *University of California (Berkeley)*

Isabel V. Sawhill *Urban Institute*

Peter Schwanse *Organization for Economic Cooperation and Development*

Marvin M. Smith *Brookings Institution*

Michael L. Wachter *University of Pennsylvania*

Charles A. Wilson *University of Wisconsin*

Index